Noble Nationalists

Noble Nationalists

THE TRANSFORMATION OF
THE BOHEMIAN ARISTOCRACY

Eagle Glassheim

HARVARD UNIVERSITY PRESS

Cambridge, Massachusetts

London, England   2005

Library of Congress Cataloging-in-Publication Data

Glassheim, Eagle.
 Noble nationalists : the transformation of the Bohemian aristocracy /
Eagle Glassheim.
     p.   cm.
   Includes bibliographical references and index.
   ISBN 0–674–01889–3 (alk. paper)
   1. Bohemia (Czech Republic)—Politics and government—1848–
1918.   2. Czech Republic—Politics and government—20th century.
3. Nobility—Czech Republic—History.   4. Nationalism—Czech
Republic—History.   I. Title.
DB2178.7.G59 2005
943.71'024—dc22   2005046322

Acknowledgments

A few years after I began graduate school, my adviser, István Deák, retired. Contrary to my expectations (and perhaps his own), he remained actively involved in my work, answered e-mails with his usual dispatch, and continued to dispense valuable advice on writing and academics. This was his retirement gift to me. I will always be grateful for this, and for the example he has provided of clear writing and sound scholarship. Much else I owe to my parents, Eliot Glassheim and Patricia Sanborn. In particular, I want to thank my father for encouraging an attention to style and my mother for encouraging clarity and economy of language. Both have been steady guides as I've sought to recognize truth and elegance in life and scholarship.

I am grateful to friends and colleagues both near and far for their support, challenges, and thoughtful readings of my work in progress. In particular, I would like to thank Bradley Abrams, Hugh Agnew, Chad Bryant, Chris Capozzolla, Gary Cohen, Abigail Dyer, Laura Engelstein, Michael Ermarth, David Frey, Molly Greene, Benjamin Frommer, Anthony Grafton, Pieter Judson, Padraic Kenney, Hillel Kieval, Jeremy King, Rebekah Klein, Stephen Kotkin, Katherine Lebow, Saje Mathieu, Norman Naimark, Claire Nolte, Stanislav Pejša, Alon Rachamimov, Adam Rothman, Ellen

Stroud, David Tompkins, Nancy Wingfield, and Nadia Zonis. Special thanks to the Kennebunkport Circle (Melissa Feinberg, Paul Hanebrink, and Cynthia Paces) for reading the entire manuscript and sharing several fine days by the ocean.

In Prague, my Czech and my disposition both improved greatly thanks to the self-described "holky" at SF Servis: Iva Rysková, Karin Rigerová, Markéta Slezáková, and Martina Kašparová. I'm also grateful for the friendship of Vanda Skalová, Sylva Pavlasová, Anna Šírová-Majkrzak, Ivo Šír, the Gomezovi, and Petra Doležalová. Thanks too to Kasia Stanclik and Samantha Heller, who have been wonderful friends, neighbors, and traveling companions since my first weeks of graduate school.

I received valuable advice from a number of sources at Columbia University, including Volker Berghahn, Karen Barkey, Atilla Pok, and Elizabeth Blackmar's dissertation workshop. I am also indebted to the Harriman Institute, which provided much-needed financial support.

I received generous research and writing grants from the American Council of Learned Societies (ACLS) and the International Research and Exchanges Board (IREX). Thanks also to the Woodrow Wilson Center for providing me the opportunity to participate in the rewarding Junior Scholars Seminar at the Wye Plantation. Thanks, too, to Princeton University for financial support as I revised my manuscript.

I am grateful to the numerous archivists and historians in the Czech Republic who took the time to guide an outsider to and through a bewildering array of sources. In particular, this book is much richer thanks to the help of Helena Smíšková, Otto Chmelík, and Jan Němec in Děčín; Josef Polišenský and Robert Kvaček in Prague; Zdeněk Radvanovský in Ústí nad Labem; Jarmila Dvořáková, Paní Slezáková and Eva Příhaská at the State Central Archive in Prague; Dalibor Státník of the Archive of the Ministry of the Interior; and Eva Javorská at the Archive of the Presidential Chancellery in Prague.

Finally, I dedicate this book to my beloved companions: Amy Vozel, Dingo, and Coqui/Cokie (the first American dog to visit the archives of north Bohemia). Thanks for the support, diversions, and adventures.

Contents

A Note on Names and Titles

Historians have a special burden when it comes to naming in Central Europe. Though now filled with nation-states and mostly cleansed of ethnic minorities, not long ago the region was remarkably diverse. The almost forgotten German or Hungarian or Italian names of great and small cities, mountain ranges, and provinces bespeak whole dimensions of the region's history that have been leveled by the great upheavals of the twentieth century. Part of the historian's task is to remember lost diversity, and for that we have to choose our words carefully.

Bohemia, at once a kingdom, a province, and a homeland, has long been contested linguistic terrain. Starting in the tenth century, Bohemia was a kingdom encompassing the lands of the present-day Czech Republic plus some small tracts of additional territory in what is now Poland and Germany. The current Czech Republic is a nation-state, but Bohemia historically was not. A substantial population of German and Polish speakers, as well as Jews, also lived in the kingdom for centuries. Bohemia also refers to the westernmost province of what were later known as the lands of the Bohemian crown, consisting of Bohemia, Moravia, and part of Silesia. When referring to these three provinces collectively, I usually adopt the term "Bohemia" to stand for all three.

As Czech speakers pursued linguistic control of the Bohemian lands in the late nineteenth century, the provinces' beleaguered Germans (or rather those who identified with Germanness) responded with their own autonomy movement. Seeking a collective designation to extract themselves from the equation "Bohemian equals Czech," in the early twentieth century German nationalists began using the term "Sudetenland," which originally referred to a mountainous area of northern Bohemia. By 1918, Germans used the term to refer to the entire German-inhabited borderlands of Bohemia and Moravia, and they used the label "Sudeten German" to denote all self-proclaimed Germans in Czechoslovakia. (Oldřich Krulík, "Historický a teritoriální kontext vývoje pojmu sudety," *Střední Evropa*, no. 86 [1999]: 83–106.)

Czechoslovakia itself—a conception that united the Bohemian crown lands with the Slovak-speaking area of northern Hungary—was also a latecomer, a nineteenth-century idea only realized in 1918. The Slovak region had been a part of Hungary for over a thousand years, and Slovaks did not claim a historic state analogous to the Bohemian Kingdom. Slovaks speak a west Slavic language closely related to Czech, though linguistic and historical differences have led the Slovaks to identify themselves as a distinct nation. Because of the separate history of the Slovaks and the Hungarian nobility that lived among them, Slovakia will not figure prominently in this book. I will occasionally refer to Slovakia for comparative purposes, but the history of the Hungarian nobility in Slovakia awaits future study.

Inevitably, some linguistic ambiguities have seeped into the chapters that follow. This is primarily because the Czech language does not make a distinction between Bohemians and Czechs. The province Bohemia is expressed by *Čechy* (roughly Czechia), and the crown lands by *České země* (Czech lands). In order to avoid the apparent nation-state teleology built into the term "Czech lands," I prefer the territorial designation "Bohemia" or "Bohemian lands," at least for the period before the post-1945 elimination of national minorities. The word *Čech* can refer either to a resident of Bohemia, regardless of linguistic or national affinity, or to one who identifies himself as an ethnic Czech. (The feminine noun is *Češka* and the adjective *česká*.) This poses some problems with translation, as one cannot always be sure whether the adjective *český* or the noun *Čech* means Czech or Bohemian. Some contexts are clear, such as the term *čeští Němci*, which should be translated as "Bohemian Germans," not "Czech Germans." Others are more problematic, such as *česká šlechta*, which can be rendered as either "Bohemian nobility" or "Czech nobility," depending on context (and here, tone of voice or even a raised eyebrow could determine the appropriate translation). By the late nineteenth century, German usage generally distinguished between the adjectives meaning Bohemian *(böhmisch)* and Czech *(tschechisch)*, though there were still occasional references to *die böhmische Sprache* (Czech). Each of my translations takes careful account of context. I only regret that I have not been able to preserve the ambiguities of the original Czech.

It can be equally difficult to write with clarity about the Habsburg Monarchy, though this is more a product of the monarchy's confusing structure than of linguistic ambiguity. Having acquired a conglomeration of historically distinct principalities, the Habsburg dynasty ruled each of its lands separately, while attempting to coalesce them into a cohesive whole. This led to many paradoxes, such as when in 1848, the King of Croatia went to war against the King of Hungary, while the Emperor of Austria tried to stay neutral. In fact, all three rulers were one and the same person! In 1867, the recalcitrant Hungarians finally received autonomy, as Emperor Francis Joseph agreed to divide the monarchy into Austrian and Hungarian halves. These two parts retained a joint army, foreign service, and finance ministry, but they maintained separate parliaments and internal governments. Francis Joseph remained the King of Hungary and the emperor of the collected Austrian lands, which were technically known as "the kingdoms and lands represented in the *Reichsrat* (Parliament)." To avoid this impossibly long name, contemporaries and historians sometimes adopted the terms "Cisleithania" (Austria) and "Transleithania" (Hungary), in reference to the river Leitha that divided the two halves of the monarchy. I prefer "Austria" or "the empire" to the tongue-twisting Latin formulation. I use "monarchy" to refer to either the House of Habsburg and its governing institutions or to the state of Austria-Hungary as a whole.

The spelling of noble names can be even more complicated than that of Bohemia's bilingual towns. Nobles themselves were notoriously inconsistent, sometimes using German spellings, sometimes Czech, and occasionally variations that mixed Slavic and Germanic roots (for some reflections on the spelling of noble names, see Zdeněk Pokluda, "Lobkovic a Lobkowicz," *Český časopis historický* 97, no. 4 [1999]: 896–900). Different branches of the Lobkowicz family used spellings such as Lobkovic or occasionally Lobkowitz, before settling decisively on Lobkowicz in the early twentieth century. Other variations included Wallenstein/Waldstein/Valdštejn, Sternberg/Šternberk, and Kinsky/Kinský. First names also varied according to the language of a given document. Some common pairs included Karl/Karel, Friedrich/Bedřich, Adalbert/Vojtěch, and Zdenko/Zdeněk. For both first and last names, I have chosen the spellings most commonly used by the person in question. So there are cases, like the relatives Zdeněk Kinský and Ulrich Kinsky, with different spellings of the same last name.

In the 1880s, the Bohemian high nobility was a small and clearly bounded group of landowners bearing the title count, prince, or very rarely duke. During the last four decades of the Habsburg monarchy, almost no Bohemian nobles were elevated into the high nobility from the lower ranks, which included barons, knights, and those bearing the title "von." None of the high nobility was recently ennobled.

Noble titles in order of rank

English	Czech	German
Prince (Imperial)	kníže	Fürst
Prince	princ	Prinz
Count	hrabě	Graf
Baron	svobodný pán	Freiherr
Knight	rytíř z	Ritter von
"von"	z	von

William Godsey has compiled a list of noble families considered acceptable at the Habsburg court *(hoffähig)* in the late nineteenth century, a group he describes as the "Habsburg aristocracy" ("Quarterings and Kinship: The Social Composition of the Habsburg Aristocracy in the Dualist Era," *Journal of Modern History*, no. 71 [March 1999]: 94–104). Of the 474 names in his list, 161 had their primary landholdings in the Bohemian Crownlands. If one factors in multiple branches of the families listed, as well as a few high nobles who did not make the *hoffähig* list, the number of noble families in my study reaches around three hundred. When I use the terms "nobility," "nobles," or "aristocracy," I am referring to these high noble families. Nobles of lower rank appear in the pages that follow only in the rare cases when they had close ties to the high nobility after 1918. The distinction between high and low nobility remained largely intact after 1918.

Technically, after 1918 the Bohemian nobility ceased to exist, as Czechoslovak lawmakers formally banned noble titles. I have chosen to put titles in parentheses when referring to the period of the ban. Even shorn of their titles after 1918, though, the Bohemian nobility remained a clearly defined social group.

Noble Nationalists

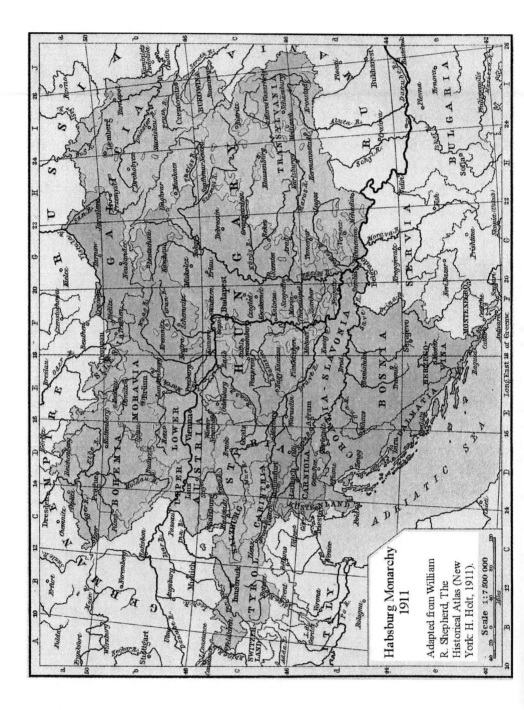

Habsburg Monarchy
1911

Adapted from William
R. Shepherd, The
Historical Atlas (New
York: H. Holt, 1911).

Scale 1:7,500,000

Introduction

$\mathcal{D}$URING THE GRAY WINTER MONTHS in Prague, smog settles over the city, shrouding its golden spires, baroque churches, and medieval fortifications in a misty haze. During these days of wintry inversion, one is most aware of the eerie absences that haunt Prague's historic streets. There is the old Jewish district, Josefov, with its synagogues and winding ghetto lanes, but there are no Jews. There is the stern but majestic castle, towering forbiddingly above the Old Town from the Hradčany hill, long emptied of king or court. There are the churches, hundreds of them, arching and jutting skyward in styles recalling centuries of Catholic devotion. But, on Sundays in Prague, most churches sit empty. The most splendid district in Prague, Malá strana, the Lesser Side, inhabits the valley bounded by the castle, Petřín hill, and the river Vltava. Its streets are a cascade of baroque palaces and gardens, still bearing the names of their former aristocratic owners: Valdštejn, Ledebur, Lobkowicz, Buquoy, and others. But Malá strana, too, is now a magnificent shell, home to embassies and government offices that have long since displaced the nobility. Perhaps Prague is quintes-

Austria, 1911. Courtesy of the University of Texas Libraries, University of Texas at Austin

sentially Central European, in that absence weighs so heavily on its historic landscape.

At the start of the twentieth century, Prague's symbolic cityscape still seemed charged with the old order's rhythms of monarchy, aristocracy, empire, and a concomitant ethnic diversity. Even so, the Habsburg Monarchy had grudgingly adapted itself to the economic and social changes of Europe's widening industrial revolution. The conservative Emperor Francis Joseph, who ruled from 1848 until 1916, had even approved the creation of a parliament and limited suffrage in Austria after 1860. By the late nineteenth century, the monarchy was a hybrid of old and new, an evolving compromise between the feudal values of its rulers and the rising aspirations of its increasingly nationalized middle classes. Most institutions of the monarchy, indeed most national, regional, and social groupings, bore the imprint of this hybridity.

The nobility, once the bedrock of feudalism, was no exception. In the 1880s, the Bohemian nobility still held a towering position in Habsburg society and government. Great magnates such as the Schwarzenbergs, Thuns, and Lobkowiczs alternated between the glittering halls of the Hofburg in Vienna and their sprawling country estates in Bohemia. In all, barely three hundred high noble families owned over a third of the land area of the Habsburgs' Bohemian crown lands, a material base that supported brilliant careers in the Foreign Office, government, and parliament. An imperial, supra-national elite, the Bohemian nobility resisted nationalism and its more virulent Czech and German advocates. But even nobles could not ignore the national and social forces that, as they saw it, were infecting public life with the germ of democracy. As suffrage expanded in the late nineteenth century, Bohemian nobles built alliances with Czech and German national political parties. Nobles hoped these steps would help contain nationalist influence while maintaining their own relevance in an increasingly democratic political system. In this way, the nobility too became a hybrid class, even as its members tried to neutralize modernizing tendencies in the empire.

Only in the wake of the First World War did the beleaguered structure of the old order most fully yield to the competing, modern political forces of popular sovereignty and nationalism. At the heart of this transformation lay the newly minted nation-state of Czechoslovakia. Between 1918 and 1948, Czechoslovakia underwent a thirty-year national and social revolution, and the once powerful Bohemian nobility became a prominent symbolic and legal target of this upheaval. When the Habsburg Monarchy collapsed, Czech revolutionaries asserted the legitimacy of their new state by repudiating the Habsburg legacy. Czech leaders portrayed nobles as a national and social enemy, a living symbol of the German-dominated monarchy that, as one legislator put it, had to be "expunged" from the history of the Czech nation.[1] In 1919, the National Assembly passed a massive land reform aiming to transfer noble estates into the hands of Czech peasants. Though the reform redistributed only half of noble land by 1938, it nonetheless began a vast reorganization of the Bohemian countryside.

The post–World War II expulsion of Czechoslovakia's 3 million Sudeten Germans, including a majority of Bohemia's nobles, broke up most of the remaining large estates in the country. Reviving interwar rhetoric conflating nobles, Germans, and the Habsburg legacy, vengeful Czechs packed many nobles into train cars with their Sudeten German neighbors and deported them to defeated Germany. Other nobles held out until the Communist takeover of Czechoslovakia a few years later. By then, the Bohemian nobility had lost everything—its political power, land, castles—and few nobles remained in Communist Czechoslovakia after 1948.

Until the Second World War, however, nobles were not passive victims of Czechoslovakia's revolution. They struggled to defend their land and define their own post-imperial identities. When the Habsburg Monarchy fell, Bohemian nobles lost a central pillar of their public-political identity. After an initial period of disorientation, many nobles embraced nationalist rhetorics. Some tried to fend off land reform by demonstrating historic Czech lineage; others emphasized their solidarity with Czechoslovakia's German minority and claimed discrimination when the government tried to confiscate their land. Czech-oriented nobles grafted their enhanced Czech loyalties onto a deep-seated Bohemian patriotism, a tendency with roots in the centuries-old historic rights ideology opposing

Habsburg centralization. German nobles too moved toward a hybrid national identification, embracing a form of German internationalism that combined an affinity with Sudeten German minority politics and a vision of pan-German and pan-European unity.

The nationally tinged internationalism of German nobles led many to support Adolf Hitler's expansionist efforts in the late 1930s, including the annexation of Austria and Czechoslovakia's Sudetenland. Many Czech nobles, on the other hand, invoked their national loyalties in opposing Nazi German territorial claims on Czechoslovakia. Hoping to weather the revolution, nobles learned to speak the new order's language of national entitlement and to negotiate a new system of national and international politics. These adaptations would not ultimately save the Bohemian nobility, but they would determine the parameters of its survival until 1948.

Nobles, Nazis, and Historians

Until recently, historians have neglected the fate of the Bohemian nobility after 1918, as nobles were prominent victims of the two episodes in Czech history that Communist rulers most sought to obscure: the expulsion of Sudeten Germans in 1945–46 and the wave of expropriations that followed the Communist seizure of power in 1948. Other holes in Czech historical memory have included Czech collaboration with the Nazis during World War II, postwar judicial retribution, and the Communist coup. Following the fall of Communism in Czechoslovakia, historians are trying to fill what Jan Křen has called the "blank spaces" of Czech history.[2] Careful studies have recently appeared on Czech fascism, the expulsions, retribution, and the transition to Communism.[3] Since 1989, there has also been growing Czech interest in the Bohemian nobility. Almanacs have appeared, bringing noble genealogy up to the present.[4] Biographies of nobles, some financed by family members with property claims in the Czech Republic, have become staples in Czech bookstores.[5] Storybooks have emerged with such alluring titles as *Blue Blood* and *Tales of the Bohemian Nobility*.[6] Little of this material is scholarly, but its volume suggests that the nobility has an important symbolic place in a developing debate over what Czech nationhood will mean in post-Communist Central Europe.[7]

Internationally, a growing literature addresses the persistence of aristocratic wealth and influence in nineteenth-century Europe, but few historians have traced the fate of nobilities after 1918.[8] In fact, nobles were still extremely wealthy and influential throughout much of Central Europe during the interwar period. In Poland and Hungary, nobles remained important members of the economic and political elite. In Czechoslovakia, noble landowners owned over a third of the country's surface area before land reform and close to a sixth afterward. Nobilities were in retreat almost everywhere, but their relative wealth, status, and influence merit far more attention than they have received.[9]

Although the economic and political history of the Bohemian nobility is important in its own right, even more striking is the group's prominent symbolic place in Czechoslovakia's thirty-year revolution. In a matter of days in late 1918, power relations reversed in the outlying provinces of the Habsburg monarchy. This dramatic structural transformation of politics drove Bohemian nobles to the margins of public life. The nobility became for a time a pariah class, a symbol of everything the new state's leaders sought to displace: Habsburg imperial institutions, social inequality, and German dominance. Though it may be hard to imagine aristocratic millionaires as victims, their marginalization within the new Czechoslovak nation-state yields considerable insight into the country's national and social transformation from 1918 to 1948.

At first stunned by their reversal of fortune and the tremendous animosity directed against them, Bohemian nobles quickly sought to adapt to the new national order. This adjustment evokes the case of Germany, where democratization transformed noble politics in the late nineteenth century, a development that accelerated with the advent of the Weimar Republic in 1919. Given the prominent role of old elites in facilitating Hitler's seizure of power in 1933, historians have long been interested in the relationship of German nobles to democracy and National Socialism. In his classic study, Hans Rosenberg argues that the Prussian Junkers adopted a pseudo-democratic stance in the late nineteenth century that predisposed

them to support a Nazi populist dictatorship in the 1930s.[10] Shelley
Baranowski writes of a Pomeranian nobility that turned to the Nazis
out of hatred for the Weimar Republic, which nobles derided as
decadent and left-wing.[11] In a remarkable, but unheralded, article
on the German Society of the Nobility *(Deutsche Adelsgenossenschaft)*,
Georg Kleine describes the group's attraction to Nazi elitism, the
language of "blood and soil," and ideals of the national community.[12] Others have written of the attempt of conservatives around
President Paul von Hindenburg to use Hitler for their own auto-
cratic ends.[13] Fascists and National Socialists often used a conservative, corporatist rhetoric of productive estates that many nobles
found appealing. The Nazi movement also had an energetic populist side that seemed to offer a mass base for the neo-corporatist
polity that these nobles envisioned.

At the same time, Nazism also had revolutionary and anticlerical
pretensions, which led some nobles to resist Hitler's regime. When
Claus von Stauffenberg unsuccessfully tried to assassinate the
Führer in 1944, he did so at the head of a military conspiracy that
included many aristocrats.[14] Others, like the Austrian von Trapp
family, immortalized in *The Sound of Music*, went into exile rather
than live under Nazi rule. Baranowski rightly stresses the small
number of nobles involved in the already minuscule German resistance.[15] Even so, both collaboration and resistance are part of the
story of the nobility in Nazi Germany.

The same holds true for nobles in Czechoslovakia, as Nazism
threatened the young state from within and without in the 1930s.
Ideological affinity and a growing nationalism led many Bohemian
nobles to support the fascist Sudeten German Party either openly
or clandestinely. Deprived of their imperial home in the former
Habsburg monarchy, these self-described "Sudeten German" nobles
turned to Nazi Germany for deliverance from what one called the
"un-state" of Czechoslovakia.[16] Some openly propagandized for the
annexation of the Sudetenland to the German *Reich*, in particular
when they hosted Lord Walter Runciman during his mission to
Czechoslovakia on behalf of Great Britain in 1938.

However, the Bohemian nobility also provided some of the
boldest opponents of the Nazi dismemberment of Czechoslovakia.

A few months after Hitler's 1939 occupation of the Czech provinces, sixty-nine Czech nobles defiantly signed a declaration of loyalty to the Czech nation. By describing how nobles moved from Habsburg supranationalism to deeply held Czech and German national loyalties, this book adds to our understanding of collaboration and resistance to Nazism among old elites.

Whereas the Polish, Hungarian, and Prusso-German nobilities were deeply enmeshed with nationalist movements in the nineteenth century, nobles in binational Bohemia were latecomers to national identification. That lateness made them particularly self-aware as they began to embrace a national rhetoric. Studying the Bohemian nobility offers a chance to observe the process of nationalization in compressed form, to document the forces that shaped noble national loyalties, and to trace the consequences of nobles' belated embrace of Czech and German nationalism. Bohemian nobles were alert political actors, frequent and articulate public speakers, and inveterate collectors of both public and private records relating to family history. They left a treasure trove of documentation, which, as far as national identity is concerned, has remained almost untouched.

Recent works on the theory of nationalism have extensively explored the relationship between national and class identities, but the focus has been primarily on bourgeois and working-class identities.[17] The few scholars who give any consideration to noble national identity almost invariably focus on the Polish and Hungarian nobilities, which were considered the standard-bearers of their respective national traditions. Because of its nineteenth-century disdain for nationalism, the Bohemian nobility does not have an obvious niche in the study of national identification. Correspondingly, theorists rarely mention it. But it is this self-conscious avoidance of nationalism in the late nineteenth century that makes the Bohemian nobility a particularly interesting case. It is a hard group to categorize, as the meanings nobles ascribed to their national identifications changed dramatically from the 1880s to the 1930s. Tinged by traditional noble cosmopolitan and internationalist tendencies, the nationalization of Bohemia's nobles did not follow the same trajectory as that of the middle or lower classes from 1848 to 1948.

In examining the evolving relationship of the Bohemian nobility to prevailing ideas of nation, this book builds on the growing critique of theories that posit ethnicity as a defining element of national identity.[18] Bohemian nobles' national identifications were primarily political and had very little cultural content. Like so many other unheralded inhabitants of the Central European borderlands, they did not have a distinct ethnicity—unless nobility itself, with its defining social and cultural rituals, counts as ethnicity. As we shall see repeatedly, noble national identifications were built from politics and not culture.

Without the anchor of ethnicity, one faces the difficulty of conveying the intensity of a given loyalty or identification. Many Czechs accused nobles of insufficient Czechness in the late Habsburg Empire. In the eyes of nationalists, it was not enough simply to claim a Czech or German identity; one had to prove one's sincerity with action. Some scholars (and most nationalists) consider war a true measure of national conviction; the ultimate test of loyalty to a group or polity is the willingness to die for it.[19] But wars are exceptional events, and warfare has its own internal logic of sacrifice. A more general measure of the depth of loyalty to a nation is the willingness to take risks or make material sacrifices in its name. As the Czech-German national struggle escalated in the late nineteenth century, Czech nationalists waged an "each to his own" (*svůj k svému*) campaign urging Czech consumers to shop only at Czech stores, drink only Czech beer, and rent only to Czech tenants.[20] Committed participants in such campaigns regularly eschewed lower priced and/or higher quality products, thereby putting "the good of the nation" ahead of their immediate material interests. In spite of their nominal identifications with Czech and German national movements in the late imperial period, nobles found the "each to his own" boycotts preposterous. Czech nationalists thus considered Czech-oriented nobles insincere in their Czechness. By the 1930s, however, nobles were willing to risk a great deal for their national loyalties. To describe this intensification of national loyalties, I have borrowed and adapted George Mosse's term "nationalization."[21]

At first it appears that noble nationalization after 1918 was opportunistic, a calculated response to the pressures of land reform. But opportunism seems inadequate to describe the intensity of noble national loyalties by the mid-1930s, when land reform had run its course. To understand this transformation, we need to look at the language and symbolism nobles used to describe their national identity. Drawing loosely on the "linguistic turn" in literary and historical studies, I argue that the nobility's national rhetoric became detached from its initial pragmatic impulses and took deep hold in noble self-understandings by the 1930s. Once rooted, national rhetoric subsequently shaped noble political behavior and perceptions of interest.[22]

The loosening of the nexus between noble interest and noble national identification by the 1930s stemmed from the broader transformation of Czechoslovakia and Central Europe after 1918. National rhetoric legitimized both the successor states to the Habsburg Monarchy and the League of Nations, with its mandate to oversee the postimperial system of nation-states and national minorities. In place of their imperial loyalties, nobles embraced the language of national entitlement, the currency of power in the interwar period. As Czechoslovakia broke down in the late 1930s, the national idiom was so thoroughly ingrained in the nobility and, indeed, in much of Europe that nationalism—either Czech or German—seemed the only response to the Nazi onslaught.

Even as nobles became increasingly national, however, they retained certain hallmarks of nobility that connected them to each other and to deeply rooted family traditions. This persistent noble hybridity proved an effective survival strategy, at least until the Second World War. The renewed revolutionary surge from 1945 to 1948 eventually leveled all in its path, however, ending Bohemia's long-standing ethnic and social diversity. By 1948, nobles too took their place in Prague's architectural index of the absent.

~ 1

Between Empire and Nation: The Bohemian Nobility, 1880–1918

> Austria is crawling out of her skin. . . . The moment is coming,
> with giant strides, when the national element alone will prevail—
> We will be crippled, because, duty bound, we feel ourselves to be
> more Imperial than the Emperor.
> ~ *Oswald Count Thun, 1898*

$\mathcal{W}$HEN OSWALD COUNT THUN (1849–1913) wrote of Austria "crawling out of her skin," he was lamenting the nationalist convulsions that seized Bohemia after the Badeni Ordinances made Czech and German equal official languages in 1897.[1] Once again, the Czech-German national conflict brought chaos to the Austrian *Reichsrat* (parliament), with inkpots flying and legislative activity at a standstill. Thun and his fellow Bohemian nobles in the parliament not only recoiled from the populist demagoguery of the Czech and German nationalists, but they also feared that nationalism would tear apart the Habsburg Monarchy. At the same time, the two leading noble political parties held fast to alliances with some of the very same national parties that were behind the turmoil in the *Reichsrat.* This irony indicates the difficult balancing act, between empire and nation, nobles maintained in the last decades of the Habsburg monarchy's existence.

On the one hand, nobles realized the need to adapt to economic, social, and political changes that altered the face of Europe and the monarchy in the nineteenth century. Their survival as a wealthy and influential class depended on it. On the other hand, too much adaptation would undermine their distinction as a caste apart in Habsburg society. Writing of the Italian nobility, Anthony Cardoza points out how modernization forced nobles "to change so as to conserve."[2] Bohemian nobles faced this same paradox as they tried to preserve their status and wealth by adapting themselves to a changing society and eventually to nationalist politics. As the primary source of wealth in the Austrian half of the monarchy moved from property to industry and finance, the Bohemian nobility diversified their investments and maintained their position as an economic elite. Socially, nobles reversed an early nineteenth-century engagement with bourgeois patriotic circles, thereby maintaining their exclusivity and status.

Nobles faced their biggest challenge, but also some hope of salvation, in the field of politics. Though Emperor Francis Joseph introduced constitutional rule and steadily expanded suffrage after 1860, the Austrian political system retained a few distinctly undemocratic features, which Bohemian nobles exploited with some success. In addition, nobles managed to maintain considerable influence at court. At the emperor's behest, they dominated top governmental posts in both Prague and Vienna. But because nobles also had to work within a parliamentary system, they could not ignore popular political forces entirely. By the 1880s, Czech and German national parties controlled enough seats in the *Reichsrat* to make them necessary partners for achieving a majority. The empire thus depended on a balance of national and supranational forces, and the nobility strove to be the "weight in the balance," the key to the precarious system's survival.[3]

The greatest threat was that the balance would tip permanently in favor of nationalism, bringing down the monarchy and the nobility both. Well aware of this danger, nobles advanced their own version of Czech and German national identities, moderated by a strong imperial loyalty. Though such a national-imperial identity had many adherents—perhaps more than historians have credited— by the late nineteenth century it was increasingly beleaguered.[4] Nationalists had little patience with so-called amphibians, and they criticized nobles for remaining aloof from national battles. As national assertiveness increased, noble dedication to the emperor rose proportionately. Unlike neighboring Germany, where the Prussian Junkers found a niche in democratic politics, most of Bohemia's nobles gravitated away from their middle-class national allies by the early twentieth century, choosing empire over nation.[5] Even so, the noble flirtation with national politics in the 1880s and 1890s left an imprint that influenced their post-imperial identifications after 1918.

Changing to Stay the Same: Nobles and Modernization in the Nineteenth Century

Traditional historiography has cast doubt on the desire or ability of nobles to come to terms with the modernization of society and politics.[6] The very word "aristocracy" has a premodern ring to it, both quaint and a little menacing to the democratic ear. To Marxists, aristocracy, and the landed property that underlay it, was the bedrock of feudalism, the dominant economic, social, and political system up to the eighteenth century. Eric Hobsbawm and countless others have written of the birth of "modernity" in the dual French and Industrial Revolutions of the late eighteenth and early nineteenth centuries, revolutions presumed to have doomed the nobility to a rapid decline relative to the "triumphant middle class."[7]

Since the 1981 publication of Arno Mayer's provocative book, *The Persistence of the Old Regime in Europe*, historians have begun to rethink the thesis of aristocratic decline in the nineteenth century.[8] David Higgs has shown that French nobles retained considerable status and class cohesiveness well into the nineteenth century.[9] For Italy, Anthony Cardoza writes of a nobility that survived economic change by both diversifying its economic interests and closing itself off to bourgeois influence.[10] Historians of the Habsburg Monarchy also have belatedly begun to examine the persistence of noble power and wealth in the last decades of the monarchy's existence. Recent Czech and German research has demonstrated that in Bohemia, as in much of Europe, the nobility thrived throughout this period of change, with much of its wealth and influence intact.

Economic Modernization

Just as Habsburg and Bohemian society was changing dramatically in the nineteenth century, so too was the Bohemian nobility.[11] Ever since its mythical origins in the thirteenth century, the Bohemian nobility regularly reinvented itself.[12] As imperial power advanced and receded, nobles sought to defend their interests or press their advantages. They also responded flexibly to economic changes. As industrialism began to spread in the eighteenth century, Bohemian nobles took advantage of new sources of profit, digging mines on their land and expanding into food processing and light industry.[13] In the nineteenth century, nobles were prominent investors in Austrian banks and railroads.[14] In the 1870s, noble-owned foundries produced 41 percent of Bohemia's iron;[15] in 1886 nobles owned 80 of the province's 120 sugar refineries.[16]

Bohemia's nobles also made the transition from seigneurialism to capitalist agriculture relatively smoothly. When Joseph II abolished serfdom in 1781, nobles turned increasingly to wage labor and successfully maintained production. During the pre-March period (1815–1848), the Bohemian nobility tended to favor the abolition of mandatory labor services *(robot)* performed by the peasantry.[17] The final elimination of seigneurialism in 1848 left nobles with an economic windfall; they promptly invested government and peasant compensation payments in stock, industry, and improvements of their remaining property.[18] As Milan Myška writes, "Estate owners transformed themselves into great agrarian capitalists."[19]

Because the Bohemian nobility possessed a large proportion of noble-managed demesne land (as opposed to rustical land with peasant tenure), the 1848 reform left nobles with millions of hectares of farm and forest.[20] Writing in 1908, Alfred Maria Mayer called Bohemia "a land of latifundists *par excellence.*" Although Bohemia's proportion of land in large holdings was close to that in East-Elbian Prussia, the number of landholders was far smaller. A mere 362 families owned 36 percent of the surface area of the province of Bohemia in the early twentieth century.[21] The largest holdings, in the hands of the 38 landowners with over 10,000 ha, covered 18 percent of the province's area.[22] A substantial portion of noble land was forest; two-thirds of the total forest in Bohemia and Moravia belonged to large landowners, primarily nobles.[23]

Percentage of Land Area in Holdings of Selected Size Ranges

	0–5 ha	5–50 ha	50–200 ha	200–1,000 ha	1,000–2,000 ha	over 2,000 ha
Bohemia	12.5	46.2	5.8	4.4	3.1	28
Moravia	16.6	45.7	5.1	4.1	2.9	25.6
Silesia	13.4	40.3	5.3	5.5	8.1	27.4

Source: Wilhelm Medinger, *Grossgrundbesitz, Fideikommiss und Agrarreform* (Vienna: Carl Gerold's Sohn, 1919), 12.

Nobles made up the overwhelming majority of owners of large estates; the top sixty-three personal landowners during the First World War were nobles or royalty. The Krumlov/Krumau Schwarzenbergs alone owned 176,000 ha, the so-called Schwarzenberg Kingdom in southern Bohemia. To put that in perspective, the Schwarzenberg estates spanned 680 square miles, or an area equaling approximately 65 percent of Rhode Island in the United States. The Colloredo family owned 58,000 ha, the Fürstenbergs 40,000 ha, the Liechtensteins 37,000 ha (not to mention scores of thousands more hectares in Moravia).[24] No non-noble holdings came anywhere close to these vast estates.

On both arable land and forests, nobles took advantage of the economy of scale. Families such as the Schwarzenbergs and the Waldsteins had been the first to mechanize farming in Bohemia, and their estate management tended to be efficient and progressive (though their pension funds and social insurance were decidedly paternalistic in tone).[25] Nobles also happened to own the best land in Bohemia and among the best in Europe. With the final emancipation of the peasantry in 1848, nobles astutely held on to much of their most productive land. The efficient practices, mechanization, and good land of noble large estates produced grain yields more than twice that of smaller holdings (under 200 ha).[26] Forests, which made up around two-thirds of large-estate total acreage in the historic provinces, were rarely profitable at anything less than

1,000 ha. Only large-estate owners could afford to hire foresters and to develop long-range harvesting plans.[27]

Social Modernization

Given the traditional association of aristocracy with feudalism, one might ask whether a noble is still noble if he becomes a successful capitalist. If "nobility" were defined solely in terms of one's relationship to production, then the answer would be no. Both in terms of law and of economic behavior, Bohemian nobles were no longer feudal after 1848.[28] But they nonetheless retained a distinct social identity as a nobility well into the twentieth century. Part of this collective identity had economic roots. Nobles still owned vast estates in Bohemia and Moravia, and contemporaries often used the term "great estate owner" (*Grossgrundbesitzer/velkostatkář*) and "noble" interchangeably in the late nineteenth century. But a constellation of other elements defined their identity as a separate and influential caste in capitalist Europe. Nobles shared actual ties of kinship (maintained through endogamy) and friendship (maintained through social exclusivity).[29] They also shared symbolic practices: preservation of a distinct honor code, veneration of family lineage, and the idealization of a manor-house lifestyle. Writing of Italian nobles in the late nineteenth century, Anthony Cardoza could just as well have been referring to the aristocracy in Bohemia: "Social resources, when accompanied by sufficient wealth, allowed a portion of the old nobility to reinvent a collective identity for themselves, an identity that helped to preserve their cohesion and exclusivity, and to legitimate their influential role in public life."[30]

Central to this exclusivity was the preservation of the "house," meaning the family and its property. The Bohemian nobility strictly protected its pedigree, rarely marrying outside of a small group of high aristocrats with the titles of count and prince. Nobles were particularly aware of family histories, often employing full-time archivists and maintaining substantial historical libraries. They also held on to the family patrimony through the practice of primogeniture, which was in many cases legally protected by entail, known in German as a *Fideikommiss*. These specially granted dispensations required imperial permission to break, thus ensuring the continuity of a family's estate. In 1900, there were still fifty-eight entails in Bohemia and twenty-four in Moravia-Silesia.[31] Even families without an officially sanctioned entail tended to practice primogeniture, a custom that maintained noble status as Bohemia's premier landholding elite.

Beyond the legal and customary enshrinement of kinship, family was a metaphor both for the structure of the household and the relationship of nobles to their peasants and the wider community. The soul of the familial model was paternalism, with the eldest male exercising dominion over other family members and peasants. With authority came responsibility, according to the model, and in fact, most latter-day Bohemian nobles took seriously their philanthropic duties to the local community. Nobles were usually the most prominent and generous patrons of churches, culture, and institutions dedicated to the poor and sick. Though feudal in conception, the familial model was not entirely incompatible with the budding nationalism of early nineteenth-century Bohemia. Seeing national education and development as part of their responsibility to the wider community, families such as the Sternbergs, Schwarzenbergs, and Thuns became patrons of the cultural efforts of the Czech national revival up to 1848. Indeed, early nationalists often used family metaphors to describe the continuity of the nation and the embeddedness of the current generation in a line connecting past and future. But ultimately, nationalism had egalitarian implications, as students of the French Revolution were well aware. Paternalism had ended up on the chopping block in Paris, and it became unpopular among Central European liberal nationalists in 1848 and after.

As the social hold of paternalism waned in the nineteenth century, nobles intensified their efforts to preserve the familial model in their own ranks. The continuity of the "house" found its concrete expression in new and renovated noble châteaux, which crowned sprawling country estates. Just as nobles had marked their ascendancy in the seventeenth century by building great baroque palaces and mansions in Bohemia, in the nineteenth century many families used architecture to reassert the historical depth of their claims to distinction and power. Turning to historicist styles, particularly neo-Gothic, they stressed the continuity of family tradition and their enduring status as a caste apart. As the Harrach family laid the foundation stone for their castle, Hradek, in 1841, they evoked this symbolic mixture of past and present. It was the master's intention, the dedication read, "to leave behind for centuries to come—for himself and his heirs—a worthy abode in the bosom of Bohemia, not only as an ornament given in [this] highly resplendent castle, but also as a proof of his devotion and heartfelt love for his ancestral homeland. . . . May our Lord give that this castle will shine for centuries as the seat of [our] glorious . . . dynasty that arose in gray antiquity."[32] Like so many other castles in Bohemia, Hradek marked the junction of past and present, noble and subject, family and country. It was to be a renewed symbol of nobility, a new seat for an old family.

The midcentury renovation of Sychrov, a baroque castle in northern Bohemia, provides a splendid example of the symbolism wrapped up in nineteenth-century aristocratic architecture.[33] In 1820 the Rohans, a recent French émigré family, purchased Sychrov from the Waldsteins (the Wallensteins of Thirty Years' War fame). Soon fully integrated into the cosmopolitan Habsburg nobility, the Rohans rebuilt the castle in the neo-Gothic style popular among Bohemian nobles at midcentury. Once completed, the old-new castle was, as one art historian put it, a *"Gesamtkunstwerk"* (complete work of art). The interior was thoroughly modern in amenities, but neo-traditional in décor, featuring "coats of arms, history paintings and ancestral portraits." The Gothic façade incorporated hints of the original baroque and early nineteenth-century classical additions. Two towers crowned the garden side of the castle: the sturdy, angular "Austrian" tower representing the family's new homeland and the round and tapering "Breton" tower, a fanciful evocation of their French heritage. As Inge Rohan's recent account of the reconstruction concludes, "With Sychrov [Camille Rohan] had built a monument for himself and his successors, a costly reliquary in which he reverently integrated the evocation of an ancient family tradition with the hopes for a future similar to the remote and glorious past."[34]

The choice of neo-Gothic historicism also reflected Bohemian

Sychrov, ca. 1900. J. V. Šimák, *Severní Čechy*

nobles' admiration for the power and wealth of the English aristocracy in the nineteenth century.[35] England was a required stop on
the noble grand tour, and Bohemian nobles sought to emulate many
of the economic and architectural innovations of their genteel English hosts. Not just indicators of a renewed claim to status in Bohemia, then, renovated châteaux were also emblems of noble internationalism and cosmopolitanism.

Beyond their imperious homes, nobles maintained their symbolic
distance from the lower classes through a range of customs and
social practices. Foremost among these was hunting for sport, to
which nobles devoted countless hours and resources. Prince Karl V
Schwarzenberg (1886–1914) shot over eleven thousand animals in
his short lifetime.[36] Nobles regularly hunted in large parties, with
guests often making extended stays at their host's manor. Horse
breeding and racing were also noble obsessions, so much so that
Alois Prince Liechtenstein reportedly spent from 3 to 5 percent of
his ample income on his stables.[37]

The most popular noble meeting place in Vienna was the exclusive Jockey Club, "the social center of gravity of the nobility."[38] In
Prague, nobles congregated at the Prague *Ressource*, another social
club with an entirely noble membership. Gary Cohen notes that
almost no nobles joined the "middle-class" German Casino in
Prague, and they rarely mingled in bourgeois society.[39] A contemporary observed in 1908 that nobles in Prague rarely attended
middle-class balls and public events unless "absolutely necessary."[40]
Further contributing to noble exclusivity, Bohemia's aristocrats were
wealthy enough that they rarely needed to marry nouveaux riches
to remain solvent. Noble endogamy helped to ensure a largely
closed social life.

Interestingly, Bohemian nobles had had closer social (though not
marital) ties with bourgeois patriots in the late eighteenth and early
nineteenth century, when nobles supported the cultural efforts of
so-called Czech national revivalists.[41] Seeking to emphasize Bohemian historic rights vis-à-vis the centralizing Habsburg state, the
Sternberg and Schwarzenberg families had supported the foundation of the Bohemian National Museum in the 1820s. Led by the
Czech historian František Palacký, the museum showcased the nat-

ural and human history of Bohemia, including the previously neglected memory of Czech/Bohemian statehood before the sixteenth
century. Noble ties with the Czech patriots receded in the wake of
the 1848 revolution, when Palacký and the Czech movement embraced a democratic and pan-Slavic rhetoric. The noble retreat
from "democratic sociability" served both to isolate and insulate the
nobility to some extent from the increasing democratization (and
nationalization) of everyday life in the late nineteenth century.

Political Modernization

Though nobles lost most of their legal privileges—such as labor
services and patrimonial courts—in 1848, in politics they retained
certain legal and customary advantages up to the end of the monarchy in 1918. Most notably, a complex curial system for elections
to the Imperial *Reichsrat* and the Bohemian Diet gave nobles a disproportionate number of representatives in both bodies. The
Reichsrat in Vienna, which until 1897 had elections in four property-
based curias, reserved for large landowners 85 seats out of a total
of 353.[42] This made nobles key players in coalition building, leverage that one or the other of the two major landowner parties
consistently used to its advantage. Though the government of Polish Count Kasimir Badeni added a universal curia in 1896, bringing
the total number of delegates to 425, landowners maintained an
influential position. Only after the abolition of the curial system
and adoption of universal suffrage in 1907 did the nobles lose their
representation in the lower house of the *Reichsrat*. Even so, they
retained control of the *Herrenhaus*, the upper house, until 1918.[43]
The noble proportion of the Bohemian Diet, or provincial assembly, was even greater than it was in the *Reichsrat*, with the landholding curia filling 70 seats out of a total of 242.[44] In Moravia, the
landowners' curia had 30 out of 100 representatives until 1905 and
30 out of 151 after that.[45] Both of the provincial assemblies retained
the curial system until the end of the monarchy, thus ensuring noble
influence. In just one example of this influence on the Imperial
level, large landowners took advantage of their domination of the

Herrenhaus to block Czech Agrarian Party legislation in 1905 that would have eliminated sugar refinery monopolies.[46]

Locally, after 1848, nobles lost the privilege (many would say burden) of providing patrimonial courts in their districts. Even so, imperial favor kept important regional bureaucratic positions in the hands of the nobility. Since their tremendous land holdings usually made nobles the largest taxpayers in rural communes, they also received special positions on communal councils.[47] As Solomon Wank writes, "The whole system of provincial and local government and administration in which the nobility held key posts and exercised great influence offered possibilities of political control and assured that noble interests would be benevolently treated in conflicts with bourgeoisie and peasants."[48] In addition, one cannot discount the persistence of deference to nobles on the local level. Through their patronage and leadership in churches, charities, and cultural and economic organizations, nobles remained in many areas the local *"Herren"* (lords).[49]

Bohemian nobles also continued to dominate top positions in the imperial cabinet, bureaucracy, and foreign service until the end of the monarchy. From the adoption of the constitution in 1867 to the end of the monarchy, twenty-three of twenty-six prime ministers in Austria were nobles, and many of these came from the ranks of the Bohemian and Moravian aristocracy.[50] Nicholas von Preradovich reports that in 1918 nobles still held 56 percent of the highest posts in diplomacy in Austria, 57 percent in administration, and 25 percent in the army.[51] William Godsey concludes that the percentage of old nobles in the Foreign Office actually increased from 44 percent to 60 percent between 1868 and the early 1900s.[52]

Above all, the high nobility retained substantial influence in the court of Emperor Francis Joseph. The high-born Grand Chamberlain controlled access to the monarch, usually limiting social contacts to those who could demonstrate at least sixteen quarterings (four generations) of nobility.[53] William Godsey has recently identified 474 families that were considered *hoffähig*, or presentable at court, during the Dualist period from 1867 to 1918. Of these, 161 (34 percent) had considerable land holdings in the historic provinces of Bohemia, Moravia, and Austrian Silesia.[54] Not only did entrée to court mark the limits of noble high society, but it also determined who would have direct access to the emperor. Given the frequent failures of Austria's parliamentary system, access to Francis Joseph could be of crucial importance in swaying government policy.

There has been spirited debate among Habsburg historians about the degree to which the Austrian half of the monarchy democratized in the late nineteenth century.[55] On the one hand, governments ruled at the behest of the emperor, not of parliament. If parliamentary life ended up deadlocked (as frequently happened), the imperially appointed government could, on the basis of Article 14 of the 1867 constitution, rule without an electoral mandate. This, combined with occasional reversions to martial law in Bohemia, has led Solomon Wank to label the empire "a constitutional monarchy which still bore strong traces of a dynastic *Obrigkeitsstaat* (authoritarian state)."[56] On the other hand, by the late nineteenth century the monarchy was remarkable for the democratic institutions it did have in place, and it was widely known as a *Rechtsstaat*, where the rule of law was supreme. Historians have recently paid particular attention to the development of local governmental institutions that had a decidedly liberal stamp.[57]

In fact, governance in the Austrian lands of the Habsburg Monarchy ran by a hybrid political system that combined elements of both bureaucratic and democratic rule. Neither elected bodies nor the emperor's representatives felt they could rule without taking the other into account. The result was a particular and sustained reliance on the nobility to play a kind of intermediary role, active both in democratic institutions (albeit with disproportionate representation) and in imperial government and administration. The nobility played this role to their advantage, professing their allegiance to the crown on the one hand and to the people on the other. This cautious and calculated balancing act would ensure the aristocracy's remarkable survival at the heights of political power into the twentieth century.

Nobles and Nationality Politics, 1880–1900

After the revival of constitutional political life in the empire in 1860, Bohemian nobles divided into two factions, one centralist and one federalist.[58] The Constitutionally Loyal Large Landowners (*Verfassungstreue Grossgrundbesitzer*) supported Viennese centralism. They remained devoted to the "Austrian state idea," a territorial notion that posited a spiritual unity of Cisleithania's manifold nations under the umbrella of the emperor. These nobles tended to favor German as the universal language of the state and Vienna-centered Germandom (*Deutschtum*) as the glue holding the empire together. Just as a faction of Bohemian nobles had benefited by supporting the emperor in the Thirty Years' War of the seventeenth century, these nobles now considered a close allegiance to the monarch to be in their best interests.

Members of the second faction, the Feudal Conservatives (*Feudale Konservativen*), favored Bohemian autonomy within a federalized empire. Basing their claims on the historic rights (*Staatsrecht*) of the Bohemian crown, the Feudals sought to increase their power by strengthening the institutions, local and provincial, in which they retained the most influence. The Feudals were the latest in a long tradition of Bohemian noble opposition to Habsburg centralism, including during the Thirty Years' War, the War of the Austrian Succession in the 1740s, and the centralizing reforms of Joseph II in the 1780s. Unlike in the first two examples, however, the Feudals did not seek the overthrow of the Habsburgs; they simply believed federalism to be the best means of securing the monarchy's (and their own) future.

Two trends pushed both noble parties in the direction of national politics in the 1860s. First, the Czech National Party adopted the historic rights program as its own in an effort to win autonomy for Bohemia and thus self-rule for the Czechs. Though the Czech national movement had worn decidedly liberal colors in the revolution of 1848, František Palacký and other Czech leaders concluded that the Habsburgs would be more receptive to a conservative appeal for historic rights than liberal demands invoking the natural right of self-determination.[59] Second, with the steadily expanding suffrage of the late nineteenth century, Bohemian Germans of all political stripes realized that, barring a division of Bohemia, centralism was their best protection against Czech dominance in the province. The two noble factions, therefore, allied themselves with respective centralist and federalist national parties, hoping to maintain their influence in an increasingly nationalized and democratized political world.

To nobles in the late nineteenth century, there appeared to be few alternatives to their ambivalent alliances with nationalist political parties. A class-based appeal would only have worked so long as the franchise were extremely limited; instead, the ever-widening curial system gave the middle classes of all nationalities substantial representation, and bourgeois parties tended to be nationalist. Given socialist hostility to the aristocracy, a cross-class "internationalist" alliance against the national parties was also unlikely. Moreover, by the late nineteenth century, Czech social democrats were almost as nationalist as the Czech bourgeois parties, finding little common cause with their Austro-German counterparts.[60]

Like many traditionally supranational actors in the late Habsburg Empire, nobles faced a narrowing of options when it came to politics. By the late nineteenth century, national rhetoric infused public discourse, becoming the coin of political contest in the monarchy.[61] National struggles made it difficult for any but the most isolated individuals to avoid identification with one of the monarchy's twelve official nationalities. Though early stirrings of national identification were manifest in Bohemia at the beginning of the nineteenth century, a combination of factors turned nation into the preeminent political loyalty it became by 1900. First, the economic success and growing middle class of the Czechs gave them fewer and fewer reasons to assimilate to Germandom as they advanced socially. By the 1860s, Bohemia hosted two discrete, socially diverse national communities. The Czechs had reached a critical juncture in their national development. They could achieve enough of their aspirations as Czechs to obviate the need to assimilate; yet not all their aspirations were met, and many blamed Habsburg favoritism toward Germans for inhibiting further progress.

Second, the monarchy ironically encouraged emerging national

divisions with a number of bureaucratic innovations in the 1880s
and 1890s. Starting with the 1880 census, Habsburg officials asked
all Austrian citizens to declare their language of daily use *(Umgangssprache)*. Though not technically a question about nationality,
it effectively became one. Jeremy King attributes Habsburg offi-
cialdom's embrace of ethnic identifications to an international tendency to enumerate and categorize linguistic usage. The premise
of the census was that all citizens could and should be counted and
categorized. As King points out, the "domestic, homogenizing zeal
of Europe's nation-states" inappropriately pressed on Austria-
Hungary a one-person, one-language approach to the census.[62]
Forced to choose a single language (in spite of widespread bilingualism in Bohemia and elsewhere), respondents increasingly were
aware they were making a political decision that would affect school
budgets, the distribution of bureaucratic posts, and other regional
funding priorities. King aptly notes that, in an age of limited suffrage, the linguistic battle in the census became the only truly democratic contest in Bohemia, but also one that pressed complex identifications into increasingly restrictive categories.[63]

Starting in the 1880s, imperial governments also encouraged
mixed localities to "solve" disputes over funding for Czech and
German schools by creating separate school boards elected by national curias. In places where this occurred, voters had to register
for one or the other curia and could only vote for a single Czech
or German school board. In a precedent-setting case in 1887, an
imperial court ruled that binationality (i.e., registration in both
curias) rendered a citizen ineligible to run for school board in either
curia.[64] Gerald Stourzh demonstrates that the school board pattern
repeated itself in hundreds of institutions in Bohemia and Moravia
by the early 1900s. Most prominently, the Moravian Compromise
of 1905 divided Czechs and Germans into separate voting rolls (ca-
dasters), which then elected a preset proportion of representatives
to the Moravian Diet in Brünn (Brno).[65] Overruling earlier prece-
dents that made the choice of nationality entirely subjective, a 1907
court ruling determined that "according to the Moravian Compromise law, the state's authorities were indeed both competent and
obliged to settle in doubtful cases, on the basis of objective indi-

cations, the national/ethnic attribution of a person."[66] The presumption of objective ethnic identity was an ominous precedent. The government had in effect institutionalized and thus hardened the previously fluid national divisions in Bohemian and Moravian society. Perversely, Habsburg public officials now undertook to enforce these divisions.

Feudal Conservatives

In 1860, with these nationalizing institutional changes still decades away, the Czech national movement remained in the noble-friendly Palacký's genteel hands. With the advent of constitutionalism, a large faction of the Bohemian nobility joined forces with Palacký's Czech National Party seeking recognition of Bohemian historic rights. These self-styled "Feudal Conservatives" were a diverse bunch, including ancient Czech families such as the Sternbergs or Lobkowiczs and seventeenth-century immigrants such as the Buquoys or Thuns. Some took Czech affinities much further than others, ostentatiously speaking Czech in public and favoring Czech employees for top positions on their estates. Many others insisted on their membership in a territorially defined "Bohemian nation" and saw the alliance with the Czechs as purely tactical. Members of the Schwarzenberg clan were known for their public speeches in superb Czech; other Conservatives did not speak Czech at all. What they all shared was a dedication to Bohemian historic rights, which, in the oft-quoted words of one Schwarzenberg, "we will defend, come what comes, as long as it is within our power, sacrificing our very lives and fortunes."[67]

Although many historians rightly see historic rights as an opportunistic rhetoric opposing monarchical centralization, it was also the legal foundation of a conservative aristocratic worldview. For many of Bohemia's great magnates, provincial autonomy promised a return to feudal hierarchy. Just as Bohemia's "rights" were rooted in history (specifically the legal continuity of the Bohemian Kingdom), so too were aristocratic privileges and status grounded in tradition and historical precedent. Correspondingly, aristocrats should occupy leading social and political positions at the local and provincial level. As the Conservative nobility insisted, Habsburg legitimacy (indeed all forms of legitimacy) depended on historical continuity.

Drawing on the historic rights tradition, Bohemian "national" identifications had a long tradition in the province, with nobles and many others asserting that Bohemian loyalty should and did trump Czech and German linguistic affiliations. "I am neither a Czech nor a German, but only a Bohemian," Count Josef Mathias Thun wrote in 1845, concluding plaintively, "Let us all be Bohemians!"[68] Linguistic nationalism was only decades old, nobles pointed out, but the historic rights of the Bohemian crown dated back centuries. Confirmed in the Renewed Land Ordinance of 1627, these traditional rights ensured a degree of provincial autonomy that had lapsed during the intervening years of increased Habsburg centralization. Drawing on historic precedent, both Czech nationalists and Conservative nobles could see the value of Bohemianism in opposing Viennese centralism. Even so, the degree of "Czechness" inherent in Bohemian identity was contested within the Czech national movement and within the ranks of the Feudal Conservatives alike.

The Schwarzenbergs were consistently among the leaders of the Feudals, and their own diversity perhaps best illustrates the diversity of opinion within the party itself—on all issues, that is, except a basic commitment to Bohemian historic rights. Divided into two powerful and distinct lines since the Napoleonic Wars, the Schwarzenberg primogeniture (Krumlov/Krumau branch) owned more land than any other family in Bohemia. The secundogeniture (Orlík/Worlik branch) also owned vast estates, but it was known even more for its political engagement. At mid-century, the family was typically divided, with Johann Prince Schwarzenberg (patriarch of the primogeniture) seeking Bohemian autonomy and his younger brother Felix Schwarzenberg leading the forces of absolutist centralism. In the decades that followed, both branches would be stalwarts of the Feudal Conservatives, with the primogeniture tending toward the binational ideal of Bohemianism (sometimes called "utraquism") and the secundogeniture toward the Czech cause.[69] Typical of the largest Bohemian magnates, both branches were relatively progressive in their estate management and markedly conservative and clerical in their politics.

Two Orlík Schwarzenbergs played a prominent role in the foundation of the Conservative Party in 1860. The outspoken Friedrich (Bedřich) Schwarzenberg (1799–1870) was a strong proponent of federalism, which he saw as the best way to strengthen the monarchy. Though he opposed both Czech and German nationalist tendencies, he believed the dynasty must rely in Bohemia on the majority Czechs, the Bohemian people. He also promoted closer ties of the Conservative nobility with Czech politicians. As he wrote to Vincenc Auersperg in 1862, the nobility needed national roots to ensure its long-term survival: "In my opinion, the nobility . . . is rooted in the people (Volk) itself: it can support the crown and tree top, but its roots lie in the soil of the people. . . . Only those nobilities rooted in the people have withstood the storms of revolution." In Schwarzenberg's view, excessive centralization had caused the French Revolution of 1789, when the nobility and monarchy had lost touch with the people.[70]

Friedrich's nephew, Karel III Prince Schwarzenberg (1824–1904), maintained the family's Czech orientation. He "supported Czech literature, dedicated several valuable gifts to the National Museum, and twice donated relatively high sums for the construction of the [Czech] National Theater."[71] In his correspondence with members of the Czech National Party, he wrote, "When the nobility is not faithful to history, when it no longer stands within the nation, when it does not have roots in the nation, then it must lose its ground, like a tree with roots undermined, with the first gust of wind."[72] Schwarzenberg offered the Conservative nobility an ideology of sorts, but one tempered by a profound distrust of popular sovereignty. "I absolutely share your view," Schwarzenberg wrote to Auersperg in 1862, "that the nobility, if it embraces an unadulterated national politics, is simply digging its own grave."[73] Some nobles were willing to put roots in the soil of the nation, but few were willing to mingle with that soil as equal to equal.

Continuing the Orlík tradition, Bedřich Schwarzenberg (1862–1936) was known as a supporter of the Czech cause since his election to the Bohemian Diet in 1893. In 1896, he gave a rousing speech in the Austrian *Reichsrat* calling for the equality of the Czech and German languages within the Bohemian bureaucracy.[74] Speaking for the Feudal Conservative caucus, he declared "complete solidarity with the Czech *(böhmisch)* people" in the name of the "historic rights idea." Given the Czech majority in Bohemia, it was only fair that the Czechs receive equal rights for their language. "The historic rights program," he added, "would advance the well-being of not only the Kingdom of Bohemia, but also the entire monarchy."[75] Speaking to a crowd of Czech supporters in České Budějovice (Budweis) in 1898, he went even further, insisting, "Everyone must be either Czech or German . . . There is no place here for amphibians."[76] The young Bedřich Schwarzenberg may have been something of an exception with his strong Czech sympathies; in 1897 he became a rare noble elected to the *Reichsrat* from outside of the landholding curia, winning the Budějovice district on a Czech slate.[77] Even so, his speech to the *Reichsrat* was representative of the Feudal Conservatives' caution in support of Czech interests. Like Schwarzenberg, party leaders couched their support of the Czechs in rhetoric emphasizing historic rights and loyalty to the monarchy.

The Czech National Party and the Feudal Conservatives had adopted the historic rights program for different reasons, the former as a palatable way to appeal to the emperor for autonomy, the latter to emphasize their traditional rights in Bohemia. But both agreed that a legalist/legitimist argument would carry far more weight in Vienna than an appeal to natural rights.[78] In 1894, Franz Thun summarized the Conservatives' somewhat watered-down program to Emperor Francis Joseph: "(1) the unity and integrity of the country (Bohemia); (2) equal rights for both languages of the country; (3) the right to elect the king in case the Habsburg family becomes extinct; and (4) the selection of representatives from Moravia and Silesia to attend any possible coronation ceremony." Thun was emphatically not seeking independence, or, at this point, even full autonomy for Bohemia.[79]

Nor did the Czechs have any illusions that Conservative nobles had suddenly become Czech patriots. Palacký's son-in-law and successor as the Czech political leader, František Rieger, was, according to Gordon Skilling, "well aware that the bulk of the feudal nobles had no real sympathy with the Czech national cause and 'were Bohemians [*Böhmen*] and nothing more,' defending state right in the interests, not of the nation, but of their class."[80] To the Czechs too, the political tie with the Conservatives was one of convenience. As Rieger put it, "The alliance with the nobility we need for the sake of the court. If the nobles did not go with us, they would suspect us there as dangerous rebels and revolutionaries."[81] For the nobles, the Czechs guarded against a slide into political irrelevance; for the Czechs, the nobles provided access to the exclusive court of Francis Joseph. From 1879 to 1891, the Czech National Party, Feudal Conservatives, German Clericals, and Poles joined in support of Prime Minister Eduard Taaffe's government, the so-called Iron Ring. Though the Czechs found themselves sharing power with the help of the nobility, they had to support the coalition's conservative and clerical program in the hopes of gaining occasional concessions for the Czechs.[82]

This was too much for a rebel faction known as the Young Czechs to bear. Eduard Grégr, the leader of the Young Czechs, wrote of the "Old Czech" leadership of the Czech National Party: "The whole delegation is hitched to the government carriage; Clam [the Feudal Conservative leader] sits on the box-seat and whips them and they pull like blind men—for they do not know why—simply on the word of Clam that all will be well!"[83] Blaming nobles for betraying the Czech cause in 1848 and after, the Young Czechs began in the late 1880s calling for an end to the alliance, "casting off the chains of foreign influences ... [inaugurating] a Czech policy, a real national policy."[84] In the elections of 1891, the Young Czechs dominated the Czech vote; in keeping with their anti-conservative, anti-noble rhetoric, they then ended the Czech alliance with the Feudal Conservatives. But five years later, the Young Czechs had lost some of their radical edge to the new mass parties on the left, and they renewed the alliance with the Conservatives.[85] In a joint manifesto of March 1897, both parties pledged their support for the historic rights program and for bilingualism in internal as well as external bureaucratic business.[86] In 1901, the much-reduced Old Czechs joined the now moderate Young Czechs in a single Czech Club, and together they reaffirmed their alliance with the Conservative nobles.[87]

Even so, many of the Feudals were uneasy with Young Czech nationalism, and the Conservatives increasingly distanced themselves from the alliance in the early 1900s. Both the raucous style and democratic implications of nationalist politics alienated the nobility. Karl III Schwarzenberg, who would later be instrumental in rebuilding the alliance with the Czechs, privately noted in 1893 that "a further agreement with the Young Czechs would lead to nothing, and only the quick and energetic suppression of the democratic scum of the *Národní listy* [the Young Czech newspaper] can bring the necessary clarification and pacification of [Bohemia]." Schwarzenberg concluded by indicating his preference for "an absolute regime in Bohemia and Vienna" that would clear up the mess that was Austrian politics.[88]

When Francis Joseph's Minister President Kasimir Badeni tried to impose a linguistic compromise on Bohemian Czechs and Germans in 1897, the political mess became an outright crisis.[89] The so-called Badeni Ordinances made Czech and German equal as official languages of Bohemia. Previously, the province's bureaucracy was required to answer supplicants in their native languages as long as their nationality made up at least 20 percent of a given region. But internal bureaucratic business had been carried out exclusively in German, to which Czechs strenuously objected. The Badeni Ordinances required all Bohemian officials to be competent in both Czech and German. This posed little difficulty for typically bilingual Czech officials, but it threatened to displace a large number of Germans who could not or would not learn Czech by the deadline of 1901. Following the promulgation of the Ordinances, German nationalists rioted in Prague and Vienna. Both the *Reichsrat* and the Bohemian Diet came to a standstill, as nationalists on both sides threw inkpots, attacked their opponents, and generally obstructed business. The Badeni government quickly fell, but the crisis continued until a new prime minister, Manfred Count Clary-Aldringen (1852–1928), rescinded the Ordinances entirely in 1899.

The Feudal Conservatives generally backed the Badeni Ordinances, though they deplored the nationalist melee that followed.

Karel IV Schwarzenberg wrote to Aehrenthal in 1899 indicating his support for the ordinances, but out of concern for the survival of the empire and not for the Czechs in particular. "For our internal peace," he elaborated, "it would perhaps be useful, if one were to consider oneself as a legal subject *(Rechtssubjekt)* more of a territory than of a language or a nation." The main goal of both foreign and domestic policy, he argued, was the preservation of the monarchy. In contrast with Aehrenthal and the Constitutionals, he believed federalism and conciliation of the non-German nationalities to be the best hope for the monarchy's survival. To counter the centrifugal forces of nationalism, it was up to the Foreign Office to nurture an Austrian patriotism.[90]

Another longtime Feudal Conservative, Rudolf Count Czernin (1855–1927), expressed in 1895 frustration that "national slogans" were preventing a compromise between Czechs and Germans in Bohemia. In a letter to prominent Constitutional Loyalist Prince Max Egon Fürstenberg (1863–1941), Czernin noted that he had considered voting for the Constitutionals out of protest against Czech tactics, but he could not bring himself to go against family tradition. Instead, he chose not to vote at all in the 1895 election.[91] Like so many of his fellow aristocrats, Czernin could not stomach either the democratic radicalism or the national chauvinism of the new generation of Czech politicians. As the Conservative mouthpiece, *Vaterland*, had asserted in 1870, the party's members were loyal, above all, to the monarchy. The Bohemian Kingdom (and its traditional estates) came next in their hierarchy of importance, followed by "the idea of nationality" and individual freedom.[92] The Young Czechs, many nobles distrustfully pointed out, had these priorities backward.

The reservations expressed by Schwarzenberg, Czernin, and other Feudal Conservatives indicated the limits of the noble alliance with the Czech National Party. Whereas the moderate nationalism of the Old Czechs proved useful in the battle against Viennese centralism, the national populism of the Young Czechs explicitly threatened noble political and social power in Bohemia. A harbinger of the mass political movements of the 1890s, the Young Czechs in the 1880s challenged both the historic rights platform and the limited franchise that kept nobles (and Old Czechs) in power. Feudal Conservatives faced a dilemma challenging old elites across Europe in the late nineteenth century: how to accommodate democratic forces without being swept away by them. The Conservative alliance with Czech nationalists helped legitimate the historic rights position in the post-1867 constitutional era. But the ultimate logic of Czech nationalism was democratic. In 1891, Czech voters made clear their preference for human rights over historic rights, and Conservative nobles had to rethink their unsteady alliance with Czech nationalism. Some Conservatives, like Bedřich Schwarzenberg, melded historic rights ideology with a populist rhetoric, whereas others proffered a genteel nationalism that would hold the line against democracy.

Constitutionally Loyal Large Landowners

Like the Feudals, the Constitutionals pledged their primary loyalty to the monarchy, but they disagreed over how best to preserve the monarchy and their own position within it. Rather than devolving power to the fractious nationalities, they favored political centralism and stressed the monarchy's German character. Aligning themselves with German liberals, who shared their German cultural orientation and commitment to centralism, Constitutionals too found themselves drawn ever deeper into nationality politics. As Ernst Rutkowski points out, they "stood on the side of Germandom, whose interest they advocated less out of purely national grounds, but because they saw in Germandom an essential bond for the survival of the empire."[93]

The Constitutionals' imperial centralism owed a great deal to Felix Schwarzenberg, the prime minister who had reasserted Austrian power in the wake of the 1848 revolution.[94] Schwarzenberg's chief goal, beyond cementing the empire's fractious lands into a unified structure, had been the construction of an Austrian-dominated Central Europe on the model of the Holy Roman Empire. With skillful diplomacy, Schwarzenberg had recaptured Austrian leadership of the revived German Confederation, a preeminence Austria would enjoy until the decisive Prussian military

victory at Königgrätz in 1866. Schwarzenberg had also tried unsuccessfully to institute an Austro-German customs union, a liberal
goal championed by Friederich List for northern Germany and
later the centerpiece (sans Austria) of Otto von Bismarck's unifying
drive.[95] An implacable opponent of democracy, Schwarzenberg's
dream of a centralized Austria within a greater-German economic
and cultural zone was an inspiration to Constitutional Loyalists in
the 1880s and beyond.

Constitutional political correspondence from 1880 to 1904 amply
illustrates the faction's Austro-German sympathies, and party members repeatedly referred to themselves as German. The party's electoral manifesto of 1895, for example, declared: "As Germans in
Bohemia we will stand by German representatives from the town
and country in the Diet in their efforts to protect their national
property *(nationaler Besitzstand)* and in their cultural efforts."[96] The
reference to "national property" intentionally evoked middle-class
nationalist rhetoric that aimed to shore up embattled German out-
posts on the language border in Bohemia.[97] In the aftermath of
Bedřich Schwarzenberg's pro-Czech speech in the Diet a year later,
party leaders reaffirmed their commitment to "the promotion of
Germandom and . . . the manifestation of a rigid German attitude
(Gesinnung)."[98]

At the same time, the Constitutionals repeatedly emphasized the
primacy of their imperial loyalties. As the head of the party, Oswald
Count Thun, noted on a number of occasions, "Our nationality has
distinct limits in our [imperial] patriotism."[99] As the party's name
implied, the Constitutionally Loyal Large Landowners supported
the constitution of 1867 and the Austro-Hungarian Compromise
(Ausgleich) that engendered it. With the Compromise, the emperor
had effectively made a deal to share power with the Hungarian and
the Austro-German elites;[100] the noble loyalists pledged themselves
to uphold this bargain, in exchange, as they saw it, for a share of
power. But even when excluded from government, they maintained
their loyalty to the monarch and the Austrian state. As the electoral
committee of the party declared in 1895, strict adherence to the
constitution was the only hope for "the reinvigoration and strengthening of our Austrian fatherland."[101]

During the unrest following the Badeni ordinances in 1897, Max Egon Fürstenberg wrote to Karl IV Schwarzenberg, a Feudal Conservative, that it was time for "all hearts loyal to the empire *(reichstreu)* to join ranks in order to save what could still be saved of our monarchy." With Francis Joseph's fiftieth jubilee approaching, "Whether we celebrate our emperor in German, Czech, Polish or Croatian, it should make no difference. . . . We all can survive, only if we rally around our emperor *viribus unitis.*"[102] At the same time, Thun and other leaders of the party expressed frustration with the emperor's occasional willingness to abandon his stalwart German loyalists in order to placate the empire's Slavs. As far as nationality questions went, Francis Joseph had no consistent strategy, sometimes yielding to national demands if he thought it would bring some domestic peace, sometimes standing fast against nationalists.

The Badeni Ordinances were a case in point. When the Constitutional Loyalists objected that the language reform had no basis in the constitution of 1867, the emperor rejected their counsel. In a letter to Alain Prince Rohan (1853–1914), Oswald Thun vented his frustration: "It is sad that no human being knows what the monarch really wants and what the government should thus do. Patriotic today means merely that one does not make a scandal. . . . We are patriots only when we are blind and dumb."[103] The Constitutional Loyalists found themselves in the sorry position of steadfastly supporting an often ignored constitution, of loyalty to a ruler who rarely returned their affection, and of devotion to an imperial idea that had little content beyond the person of the venerable Francis Joseph.

Nor could they find solace in the German national camp. As early as 1883, Aehrenthal was complaining of nationalism's ill effect on politics: "I am certainly not mistaken in attributing this unruliness *(Verwilderung)* of politics to the exaggeration of the nationality-idea to the point of absurdity."[104] Aehrenthal observed what Carl Schorske has described as a "politics in a new key" in fin de siècle Austria. It was, in Schorske's words, "a sharper key," more confrontational, with an appeal to feeling above reason. The most abrasive of its practitioners was Georg von Schönerer (1842–1921), a pan-German and radical nationalist parliamentarian with a loyal following in north Bohemia.[105] For the nobility, accustomed to deference and genteel politics, the new style was disconcerting. In 1896, Guido Count Dubsky (1835–1907) announced his withdrawal from politics, bemoaning the "sharper pitch *(Tonart)*" of politics that is "driving the imperial idea into the background" and favoring national interest groups.[106]

In the wake of German riots over the Badeni Ordinances, Alois Aehrenthal wrote to his father, "The Germans degrade themselves, when they follow the example of the Czechs and anti-Semites. The nation of Goethe is becoming more and more a nation of beer consumers with stable-boy manners!"[107] Alain Rohan echoed this sentiment in a letter to Fürstenberg a few years later, as the Badeni furor refused to go away. He wrote scornfully, "I personally will not sign a ballot on which a radical stands. I want to have nothing to do with the German national radicals of Schönerer's ilk. I consider this movement more damaging to the position of the Germans in Austria than all the national opponents."[108] Oswald Thun too rejected the nationalists' extra-parliamentary tactics, writing in his diary, "It is a disgrace for the people *(Volk)* that it recognizes a traitor like Schönerer as its leader."[109]

But given new electoral realities, the nobles could not do without their nationalist allies, at least not the moderates. In November 1897, the Constitutionals formally joined an anti-Badeni German Front with the Progressives, Liberals, and Christian Socials—all of whom had protested, sometimes violently, against the language ordinances.[110] "One simply cannot separate from a national party, once an alliance is entered," Aehrenthal wrote to Karl Count Buquoy (1854–1911), "without being thrown in among the political corpses."[111] Some nobles in the party also emphasized their Germanness in order to satisfy their more German-national colleagues within the party itself. At a party congress in mid-1897, Karl Moritz Count Zedtwitz (1830–1915) urged such an attitude, because "it makes a good impression on a part of our voters, for whom one can never be German enough."[112] Indeed, Oswald Thun commented in a letter a few months later that in closed meetings, most Constitutionals emphasized their Austrian patriotism. But "as soon as we step out before the public, patriotism gives way to nationality, because our so-called political allies these days tolerate patriotism only in homeopathic doses."[113]

For many in the party, identification with German nationalists was a painful compromise, but one that had to be made on the principle that enemies of one's enemies are one's friends. Constitutionals faced a range of no-win choices. On the one hand, an ungrateful and uncreative emperor did little to build the imperial identity they hoped for. The only other unifying force in the empire appeared to be its German-speaking bureaucracy and army, but even these were under attack by non-German nationalists. In standing firm against these attacks, the Constitutionals' only allies were German liberals, already on the ropes, and the more radical German nationalists. But the intransigence of German nationalists only further undermined efforts to find a compromise with the Czechs.

The hopelessness of the Loyalists' political position left Oswald Thun disillusioned and ill. Writing in 1898 from his winter retreat in Beaulieu on the French Riviera, Thun described how at ease he felt by the sea, knowing that the waves rolling over his feet could do him no harm. "If only I could have this feeling towards all the elements that so easily inflict upon me discomfort and nausea!" he continued.

> I am thinking about my good old Austria, and about our group, which was deluded enough to believe unshakably that ancient traditions and a certain spirit *(Geist)*, which we carefully cultivated when we were children, could not be lost. Almost in tears, I have to say that in Austria the impossible has happened—Austria is crawling out of her skin, and nothing remains to us other than to lay ourselves down to sleep on her discarded hide. . . . The moment is coming, with giant strides, when the national element alone will prevail—We will be crippled, because, duty bound, we feel ourselves to be more Imperial than the Emperor *(kaiserlicher als der Kaiser)*.[114]

Thun managed to hold on for eight more years as head of the party, but they were trouble-filled years and he was often sick. By 1906, his eyes failing him, his heart and lungs weak, he retired from politics. Though his early death in 1913 was officially caused by "paralysis of the lungs,"[115] he had also long suffered from psychosomatic illnesses. The forces tearing the empire apart tore at Thun as well; he bore in a symbolic sense the pain and unease of an entire class, unable to identify with a nationalist mindset that had conquered politics and would soon upend the empires of Europe.

Moravian *Mittelpartei*

The position of nobles in Moravia was similar in many ways to that in Bohemia in the late nineteenth century. Through their lock on the large landowner curia, they held a crucial thirty seats of the one hundred in the provincial Diet. Moravia too had its Constitutionally Loyal and Feudal Conservative noble factions, with the former tending to garner around three times as many votes as the latter.[116] As in Bohemia, Czechs and Germans were bitterly divided, with Czechs making up around 70 percent of the population and Germans 30 percent.[117] Prior to the Moravian electoral reform of 1905, a curial system slanted toward towns gave Germans disproportionate representation in the Diet. Even so, Czech migration to cities brought them into close competition with Germans in the provincial assembly in the 1880s and beyond. As in Bohemia, the noble parties were usually allied with the national parties. But uniquely, the Moravian nobility also had a small third party, the *Mittelpartei* (Party of the Middle), which often held the balance of power in the provincial Diet.

Founded in 1879 at the behest of the imperial Prime Minister Eduard Taaffe, the *Mittelpartei* began as a splinter group of Constitutional Loyalists who chose to join Taaffe's conservative/Slavic coalition. Led by Ferdinand Count Trauttmansdorf (1825–1896), the party distanced itself from both national groups, as well as from the historic rights program of the Conservatives. Its platform echoed the Constitutional opposition to the federalization of the monarchy, but it also rejected an alliance with German national parties. Robert Luft writes that "the members of the Moravian *Mittelpartei* felt that they stood above the nationalities," and they opposed any national demands that would undermine Austrian unity.[118] Like Taaffe, who was "neither a Czech nor a German, although . . . reared in a German fashion,"[119] the *Mittelpartei* maintained a strictly a-national political profile on top of their aristocratic-German cultural orientation.

This made the *Mittelpartei* uniquely suited to play the role of mediator and power broker between Czechs and Germans, as the pursuit of a political and linguistic compromise gained momentum in the wake of the Badeni crisis. Both Czechs and Germans trusted (or did not distrust) the party, and neither could control the Moravian Diet without *Mittelpartei* votes. Using this leverage, the *Mittelpartei* facilitated the Moravian Czech-German Compromise of 1905, while at the same time ensuring continued representation for the large landowners' curia in the Moravian Diet. The Compromise enlarged the Diet, adding a universal curia and dividing all three electoral curia (towns, rural communes, and universal) into Czech and German national registries (catasters). The new system guaranteed Czechs seventy-three seats and Germans forty-six, with those from each side only voting for candidates of their own nationality. The large-estate owners' curia remained unified (without Czech and German sections) and retained its 30 seats out of a new total of 151.[120] The compromise forced non-noble voters to choose a national identity; there were no options to accommodate those who might have considered themselves a-national, binational, utraquist, Austrian, or Moravian. Though the Moravian Compromise did not ultimately stop national strife in the province, Moravia became one of the few provinces in the monarchy where any sort of compromise was reached at all.[121] It was also a remarkable example of the nobility taking advantage of its position between the nationalities to hold on to its power in spite of democratic and nationalist pressure.

Nobles and the Downfall of the Habsburg Monarchy, 1900–1918

Already in 1890, with the Czech-German language dispute roiling Bohemian and imperial politics, the two main noble political parties had begun to find some common ground in pursuit of a Bohemian compromise. The resulting *punktace* (points) would have divided the province into national districts and the Diet into national curias (with the exception of a non-national landowners' curia similar to that adopted in Moravia in 1905). The *punktace* failed when the Young Czechs rejected its concessions to the Germans, and the two landowner parties would not find common cause again for a decade.[122]

In 1900, nobles tried once more to facilitate a Bohemian compromise. In a series of meetings with leaders of both Czech and German parties in Bohemia, the two noble groups served as mediators in the search for a solution to the province's linguistic impasse.[123] Though the discussions again foundered, they began a tentative cooperation between the parties that would expand when the demise of curial voting for the *Reichsrat* appeared imminent in 1906. In 1910, Conservatives and Constitutionals once more met in an effort to broker a Bohemian agreement along the lines of the Moravian Compromise of 1905. Fearing the loss of their powerful curia in the Bohemian Diet, the noble parties sought, like their Moravian counterparts, to retain a non-national landowning curia in addition to separate Czech and German electoral rolls (catasters). As their joint program concluded, "national division of the large landowners [is] not desirable." In addition, "any nationalization of the bureaucracy is to be avoided."[124] This attempt too failed, as neither Czechs nor Germans were willing to yield on their basic positions: for the Czechs, the indivisibility and fundamental Czech character of Bohemia; for the Germans, autonomy for German regions of the province.

Nor did granting universal suffrage to the *Reichsrat* make governing Austria any easier, as the emperor had hoped. Members of both noble parties began to raise the possibility of an authoritarian solution, according to which Francis Joseph would simply dissolve the *Reichsrat* permanently and appoint imperial governments. Already in 1898, Karel IV Schwarzenberg had written that "the increasing awareness that the parliamentary form of government has outlived its usefulness can cause satisfaction for us true conservatives . . . In my opinion, Austria can no longer be held together in any other way than by a modernized absolutism."[125] Many other nobles, both Feudal and Constitutional, quietly adopted this viewpoint, most prominently held by Archduke Francis Ferdinand in the years before the First World War. In 1913–14, Austria became a de facto autocracy when Count Karl Stürgkh dissolved both the Bohemian Diet and the *Reichsrat*, seemingly for good.[126] Once the war began, a noble clique would rule both Bohemia and the entire Austrian half of the monarchy until the beleaguered new Emperor Karl reconvened the *Reichsrat* in 1917.[127]

Nobles and the Great War

The war both united and divided the two leading factions of the Bohemian nobility. In the first few years of the war, both groups stressed their loyalty to the emperor and distanced themselves more than ever from nationalist politicians. Even Bedřich Schwarzenberg, who had given the impassioned pro-Czech speech in the Bohemian Diet in 1896, claimed in a 1916 letter to Otto Harrach, "I always was of the standpoint that our party should not become national."[128] The lack of Czech enthusiasm for the imperial cause during the war drove a wedge between the Czechs and most of their former Conservative allies. In a 1916 meeting in Prague, the Conservative leadership called on all provinces, parties, and nations to "stand enthusiastically behind the empire and army." Though the party remained "warm" toward the "Bohemian people" (meaning the Czechs here), the continuation of "the old friendship" required that "the Bohemian people remain loyal to the dynasty and to their ties to the empire, which alone offers a guarantee for their national existence and cultural development."[129]

The Constitutional Loyalists too remained as loyal as ever, though some members explored the possibility of an overhaul of political arrangements in Austria in order to give Germans a lasting control of government. In a report to the party leadership in June of 1915, the up-and-coming young landowner Wilhelm von Medinger (1878–1934) argued that the only way to make "order in our own house" would be to "create a parliamentary majority of state-supporting and dynastic-loyal elements." The only truly loyal citizens, Medinger argued, were German Austrians. To ensure that they held a majority in the *Reichsrat*, he proposed that the emperor grant Polish Galicia full autonomy, thus removing one-fifth of the representatives from the parliament. The Austrian half of the monarchy would then be predominantly German in character, with German as the sole parliamentary and bureaucratic language.[130]

Medinger criticized Conservatives for their earlier alliance with the Czechs, who were pan-Slavs masquerading as Austro-Slavs: "In their supposed impartiality, the (Conservatives) were against every national struggle; in this they did not understand that the battle of the Germans was a defensive struggle, while that of the non-Germans was offensive . . . Now these gentlemen themselves shudder in the face of the movement they once supported." By no means, he declared, should "our current parliament with its collection of traitors" meet again. Instead, "the most important reforms (such as electoral reform) can only be carried through by means of an *octroi.*" He urged the Constitutionals to pursue this goal with all their power and prove that they were "His Majesty the Emperor of Austria's truest officers" on the "battlefield of politics."[131]

A few Czech-loyal nobles continued to proclaim their Czech sympathies during the war. Vladimír Count Lažanský (1857–1925) came from an ancient Czech noble family, though his ancestors had sided with the Habsburgs in the Thirty Years' War and were amply rewarded afterward.[132] During the nineteenth century, the Lažanskýs were active historic rights Conservatives, and Vladimír became a dedicated Czech patriot. Though he never mastered the Czech language, he regularly contributed poetry (translated from German) to the Prague literary journal *Zlatá Praha* (Golden Prague). The writer Karel Čapek, who had been a tutor for Lažanský's son during the war, called him "one of the strongest Czech nationalists . . . right up to a passionate hatred of all things German and especially the Habsburg Dynasty." When Čapek came to apply for the job in 1916, Lažanský asked him, "Tell me, Herr Doctor, will we be victorious or the others?" Surprised, Čapek responded, "Which we, Herr Count? Do you mean Austria?" To which Lažanský replied, "But no! We Russians. We French." His opposition to the Habsburgs was an isolated case, and he remained an outsider in noble society. As Čapek later wrote, Lažanský's poems were "classical elegies of a sad and lonely man."[133]

As the war ground on, a substantial faction of the Conservative Party went the opposite direction from Lažanský and increasingly supported Medinger's vision of a German-oriented monarchy, or at least opposed Czech aspirations to a wide autonomy.[134] In May 1918, after the Conservative Foreign Minister Ottokar Count Czernin (of an old Czech family) made comments critical of the Czechs, a group of Czechophiles, led by Bedřich Schwarzenberg (of an old German family) signed a public protest against Czernin.[135] With that, the so-called utraquist wing of the Conservatives split off to form the "Imperial Party *(Reichspartei)*," which backed Czernin and the Prime Minister Heinrich Count Clam-Martinic.[136] The Conservative "Right" now openly sought autonomy for the Czechs within the empire, whereas the new Imperial Party sided momentarily with the German centralists of the Constitutionally Loyal "Left."[137] In a 1916 letter to Alfred Prince Windischgrätz (1851–1927), Ferdinand Prince Lobkovicz (1850–1926) illustrated the fundamental differences behind the split: "We are not agreed on everything, because I am an imperial-loyal Bohemian and you are a Bohemian-friendly Austrian."[138] With the monarchy itself on the verge of cracking up, nobles fragmented along national-political fault lines that deepened as the war wore on.

Amid a spate of proclamations in 1918, Clam-Martinic issued a declaration of his own on 22 October, a few days after the Czechoslovak declaration of independence. In it he asserted that "to the last breath we will remain loyal to our dynasty."[139] Clam's words became infamous among the Czechs, who cited them repeatedly as an example of noble perfidy. If this scion of the Feudal Conservatives chose the monarchy over Bohemia, they argued, did that not cast into doubt the Conservatives' motives in their earlier alliance with the Czechs? This ignored, of course, the divide in the Group of the Right; Clam-Martinic was a member of the Imperial Party faction. In any case, the Czech attacks were symbolic. With the declaration of independence, the Czechs began building their own state; nobles and Habsburgs now represented the antithesis of Czechoslovakia's middle-class and national founding ideology.

Nobles as Foreigners: The Birth of an Anti-Aristocratic Ideology among the Czechs

By the late nineteenth century, most major Czech political parties tapped into growing anti-noble sentiments among the Czech population. Czechs had not always been so hostile to the nobility, though. Before 1848, when Czech national revivalists shared and depended upon the Bohemian nobles' provincial patriotism, Palacký provided many nobles with historical evidence of their Czech roots. Though the Sternbergs, patrons of Palacký and the Bohemian museum, had a German name, Palacký wrote, "The mostly pure Slavic given names of the oldest Sternbergs suggest that they were no immigrant family, but born Bohemians [Czechs]." Accounting for the prevalence of German names among the old Bohemian nobility, Palacký explained that "[i]t was the fashion of the Bohemian nobility under Ottokar to give their fortresses and castles German names, from which they took their family name."[140] Palacký publicized these nobles' Czech roots partly out of gratitude for their support, partly out of his desire to reconstruct for the Czechs a native aristocracy on the lines of the Polish or Hungarian nobility.

Palacký retained his ties with Bohemian nobles until the end of his life, though after 1848 a growing faction in the Czech national movement considered most Bohemian nobles, no matter their origin, German and foreign. Most importantly, the Young Czech Party made a critique of the aristocracy central to its electoral strategy after 1890 as it sought to displace the more conservative Old Czechs, who had long allied themselves with the Feudal Conservatives. Writing in 1895, Tomáš Masaryk explained the rising fortunes of the Young Czechs: "The leaders of the aristocracy were unpopularly conservative, socially and philosophically backward, un-national, and consequently also un-Slavic. . . . The Old Czech party, apathetically tolerating this hereditary sin of our aristocracy, consequently degenerated and lost the support of the voting masses."[141]

Expanding on Young Czech criticisms of the aristocracy, Alfred Maria Mayer argued that the Conservative Bohemian nobility was increasingly distant from the Czech people. Mayer acknowledged

that there was once a Czech national nobility. After the Habsburgs
defeated the Protestant Bohemian nobility at the 1620 Battle of
White Mountain, however, the aristocracy was no longer Czech,
but rather "an international conglomerate of noble families."[142]
Though some of these nobles were patrons of the Czech national
movement, one could not speak of a Czech national consciousness
among them, since their language and schooling were German. Recently, a few Conservative families had adopted the Czech language,
but Mayer saw this as primarily a political calculation. "Of these
'Czech' aristocrats," he wrote, "one should note that in most cases
Czech is not their daily language *(Umgangssprache)*, and so it is no
wonder that the Czech people do not want to believe in the sincerity of the national feeling of these gentlemen."

As the most damning evidence of their half-hearted Czech-ness,
Mayer wrote, not a single "lady of aristocratic origin could be found
in all of Bohemia who speaks and writes correct Czech." These
noblewomen "have a direct aversion to all things Czech," and thus
one could scarcely call the tenor of their family life anything but
German.[143] Mayer's attack on aristocratic women reflected the assumption among Czech nationalists that the family was the primary
vessel of the nation, and that women ensured the smooth passage
of national tradition to the next generation.[144] In spite of noble
patriarchal political lineages, Mayer asserted that noblewomen undermined claims of Czech identity. "Socially," Mayer concluded,
"there exists only a single Prague nobility, and it is German—
German in language, German in tradition, and German in culture."[145]

To Mayer, the Conservatives' fickle Czech sympathies were more
a function of class interest than a deeply felt identity. But both
feudal privileges and national indifference were anachronistic. If
they persisted in their "false, unmodern, nonsensical utraquism,"
they would become a political irrelevance. And when real democracy arrives, Mayer warned, nobles beware: "The Czech nation
takes it hard that it lost its indigenous nobility. It cannot be ruled
out that once again a movement would break forth to settle accounts with the new nobility that has taken its place."[146]

During the Great War ten years later, the Agrarian publicist Josef

Holeček delivered an even more condemnatory and pessimistic critique of noble Czech sympathies. The Feudal Conservatives could hardly be called Czechs, he argued, because they had not developed their national consciousness with the rest of the nation.[147] Even historically Czech-friendly politicians, such as Franz Thun, were "politically Czech but of German nationality." Noble professions of Czech identity, Holeček argued, were opportunistic rather than deeply felt. In order to maintain their privileges, they relied on the good favor of the monarch, and therefore their primary loyalty was imperial. The Czechs, on the other hand, were by nature a democratic nation, and inherited privileges, as well as an a-national imperial identity, were foreign to them.[148]

Ultimately, Holeček wrote, the nation had its roots in the soil, the homeland *(vlast)*—or the motherland, *země mateřská*—saturated "with the blood and sweat of our ancestors."[149] In ancient times, nobility was a foreign concept to the egalitarian Czechs. Both the Czech word for nobility and the idea of a higher order of human beings came from the Germans, the root of the Czech *šlechta* (nobility) being the German *Geschlecht* (family/lineage).[150] Before the Battle of White Mountain, a Czech national nobility had emerged, but it had become increasingly distant from the people. When these "selfish and avaricious" Czech nobles faced the Habsburg armies at White Mountain, Czech peasants remained hostile to the noble cause.[151] After the defeat at White Mountain, a new nobility settled in Bohemia, but "300 years later it has still not come to feel at home on Czech soil." Holeček also noted that the Young Czech Julius Grégr had expressed doubts about the legality of the transfer of property after White Mountain. In the Bohemian Diet, Grégr had called for "the investigation of the documents by which the post–White Mountain nobility hold their estates," as there were suspicions that these nobles did not in fact have proper title to their land. "This uncertainty," Holeček continued, "has a lot to do with the fact that to us the post–White Mountain nobility is an eternal enemy."[152]

For Holeček and for many other Czech nationalists, Bohemian nobles were either foreigners or insincere Czechs. The latter were half Czechs at best. "A noble among us," he wrote, "cannot be half-hearted. . . . National half-heartedness is a sign of either insufficient consciousness or a weak character."[153] Concluding on a prophetic note, Holeček warned of the need for a "cleansing of the soil for the renewal of the social organization of the nation."[154] Capturing an increasingly dominant Czech middle-class national self-image, Holeček's book outlined the ideology that would justify a massive land reform only a few years later.

IN HIS SEMINAL BOOK, Arno Mayer advanced the thesis that the Old Regime—authoritarian monarchies, a preindustrial economic order, feudal social relations, and nobilitarian values—retained a powerful influence in Europe up until 1918 and perhaps beyond. Many historians have since criticized Mayer for understating the relative importance of bourgeois social and political forms at the end of the nineteenth century.[155] Even so, his work has sparked a much-needed reconsideration of the position of the nobility in the half-century before World War I. Without making any claim to total aristocratic dominance, historians are now presenting a more nuanced portrait of late imperial nobilities.

In order to understand the place of the nobility in nineteenth-century Europe, it is important to define the terms "Old Regime" and "New Regime." In economy, "Old Regime" refers to nonindustrial economic sectors such as agriculture and artisanal manufacturing. Socially, the Old Regime was hierarchical and patriarchal; society was organized by occupational sector rather than class. Personal relationships were supposedly more important than purely economic relationships, and religion was an ever-present influence in political and social life. The political Old Regime reflected the social; the top levels of the hierarchy held privileged voting rights and, in concert with monarchies, dominated government. In contrast, "New Regime" implied industrial capitalism, egalitarianism, secularism, and democracy. These are, of course, ideal types. Much of the drama of late nineteenth-century European history lies in the clash of Old and New Regime forces, of landed wealth and industrial capital, quality and quantity, traditional notables and tribunes of the people. Less dramatic, but equally important, was the intermingling of the two, the development of hybrid economic, social, and political forms that frustrated the expectations of sympathizers of both Old and New.

The Bohemian nobility became just such a hybrid class in the nineteenth century, an important part of the broader mix of Old and New that so marked the late Habsburg Monarchy. In many ways, the emerging New Regime forced nobles to rethink the essence of their nobility. Though few would willingly cast off their traditional privileges, most realized they could survive, even flourish, in a capitalist and meritocratic world. Nobles could, after all, boast substantial capital, education, and social resources. During the course of the nineteenth century, they diversified their income by investing in industry and finance. They modernized their estates to compete on the world commodities market. In politics, nobles took advantage of the convoluted constitutional structure of the Monarchy to survive as a powerful political class. In contrast, however, the Bohemian nobility resisted social change, successfully closing ranks against the threat of rising nouveaux riches. Nobles changed so as to conserve, but not more than they had to.

Perhaps uniquely, the Bohemian nobility allows us insight into the place of nationalism in the clash and hybridization of the Old and New Regimes. To Arno Mayer, nationalism and Social Darwinism became tools of Old Regime forces, which manipulated mass nationalist passions for their own conservative political purposes.[156] But as Geoff Eley and others have shown for Germany, and as this chapter has shown in the case of Habsburg Bohemia, the relationship of old elites to nationalism was not so simple.[157] In Bohemia, nationalism was a New Regime force, an assertion of popular sovereignty in opposition to authoritarian tendencies of the monarch and bureaucracy. Nationalists wanted power for themselves and the people they claimed to represent; they were not tools of the aristocracy or a reactionary conservative cabal.

Nationalism in fact crossed the political spectrum. Many liberals were nationalist; many conservatives were nationalist; even socialists were nationalist. Nationalism was above all a language of politics and interests. Nobles, too, tentatively employed a national vocabulary in the late nineteenth century, sensing that without it they would be doomed to political impotence. This was another noble accommodation of the New Regime. But nobles had enough of the Old Regime left in them to chafe at the stridency and coarseness of their national allies. Caught between empire and nation in the last years of the monarchy, nobles were conflicted and profoundly ambivalent about where they fit in the evolving old-new order.

～ 2

National and Social Revolution in Czechoslovakia, 1918–1920

> Today we are ridding ourselves once and for all of that aristocracy
> that played such an infamous role in the history of our nation,
> and the especially sad role from the Battle of White Mountain
> up to the present.
> ～ *František Modráček, April 1919*

$\mathcal{I}_{\text{N}}$ 1918, "redressing" White Mountain became a rallying cry among Czechoslovak state builders. The genesis of White Mountain came exactly three hundred years earlier, when a crowd of Protestant Bohemian nobles cornered two Habsburg-Catholic loyalists and heaved them out the window of the Prague Castle. The notorious Prague defenestration would be the first salvo of the Thirty Years' War. Two years later, Habsburg forces routed the Protestant rebels in the Battle at White Mountain, a bump on the landscape of suburban Prague. Though the war would rage across Europe for three decades, 1620 marked the end of the Bohemian rebellion. After White Mountain, the Habsburgs executed or exiled most of the Protestant leaders and set loose on Bohemia the Counter-Reformatory zeal of the Jesuits. Deprived of a Czech-speaking elite, the Czech language went into decline as a literary language and the historic rights of the Bohemian crown lands went unrecognized. In the nineteenth century, Czech nationalists recalled 1620 as the start of a period of *temno*, an age of cultural and political darkness for the putative Czech nation.

After the Habsburg collapse in 1918, Czechs inaugurated their new republic with a stream of symbolic, verbal, and legal attacks on the legacy of White Mountain. Many Czechs perceived the 1620 battle to be the beginning of a long and painful subjugation at the hands of the Habsburgs. One of the most popular slogans of 1918–19 declared that White Mountain must be redressed (*odčiněna*), that Czechs must reverse three hundred years of stunted historical development. A week after the Czechoslovak declaration of independence on 28 October 1918, a crowd of 250,000 Czechs met at White Mountain to commemorate the battle and to celebrate the fall of the Habsburgs.[1] From there, a smaller group marched to the Old Town Square in the center of Prague, the site of a Marian column erected in 1648 to celebrate the Habsburg defeat of the Swedes in the Thirty Years' War. Declaring the column a symbol of German Habsburg oppression, they pulled it down, reclaiming this central space for the Czech nation.[2] As Nancy Wingfield demonstrates, this was one of scores of attacks against statues with German and Habsburg themes from 1918 to 1921.[3]

On 8 November 1918, the actual anniversary of the battle, "hundreds of thousands" of Czechs again gathered to commemorate what the Agrarian journal *Venkov* called "the blackest day of Czech history."[4] The poet and nationalist politician Josef Svatopluk Machar (1864–1942) declared to the gathered crowd, "What remains of White Mountain is only this lesson: nothing without the people, everything for the people. After White Mountain, fate deprived us of our nobility." But the Czech people had remained "democrats" and proven that "dynasties fade, [whereas] nations remain." The Social Democratic author František Václav Krejčí (1867–1941) added, "The Austrian state . . . was one of the oldest remnants of feudal Europe, while our republic will be anchored on new world views, on democracy and social justice."[5] Politicians across the political spectrum called for a reversal of the historical verdict of White Mountain, the redressing of the wrongs allegedly done to the Czech nation by the Habsburgs and their noble henchmen.

Anti-Habsburg, anti-German sentiment provided Czech statebuilders with a legitimating ideology. In contrast to the feudal, authoritarian and German-dominated Habsburg Monarchy, Czech leaders declared, Czechoslovakia would be a middle-class and democratic national state of Czechs and Slovaks. In the Czechoslovak case, the high-minded principle of Wilsonian self-determination

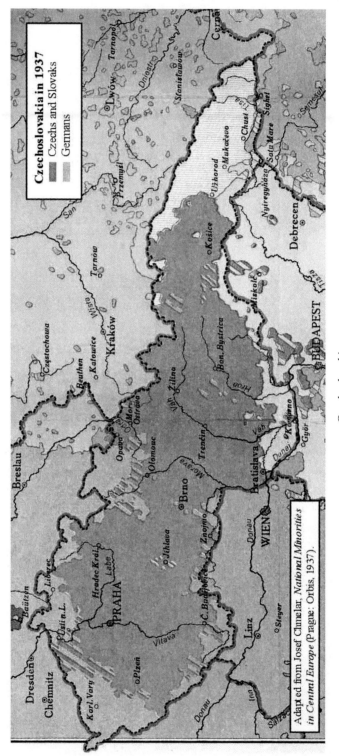

Czechoslovakia in 1937

▨ Czechs and Slovaks

▨ Germans

Adapted from Josef Chmelar, *National Minorities in Central Europe* (Prague: Orbis, 1937).

Czechoslovakia

combined with the realism of postwar alliance politics to produce what is perhaps best described as a paradoxical state. Though democratic, it was quasi-imperial in structure, with Czech Prague ruling German, Slovak, Hungarian, and Ruthenian peripheries. Though multinational, Czechoslovakia was founded and run as a nation-state, that is, in the name of a single (or here artificially double) nationality.[6] Many Czechs looked on the state's 3 million Germans as an inconvenient legacy of centuries of Habsburg rule. Since the mid-nineteenth century, mainstream Czech historical and literary narratives had also associated the Germanic spirit with feudalism. Thus in popular opinion, both Germans and the Habsburgs were seen as alien to Bohemia. When the first Czech president, Tomáš Garrigue Masaryk, let slip in late 1918 a comment about German "immigrants and colonists," he expressed a commonly held Czech view that Germans were outsiders in the new state.[7]

Czech leaders saw the Bohemian nobility as quintessentially German, Habsburg, and feudal, the antithesis of their vision of a middle-class Czech nation-state. With the imperial edifice itself gone, the Bohemian aristocracy became the most prominent living symbol of the old order. In 1919, the Revolutionary National Assembly passed a massive land reform with the goal of redistributing noble land to Czech farmers. The reform became a central pillar of the new order, both a symbolic and real reversal of the monarchy's feudal legacy and the first major step in a thirty-year upheaval that would utterly change the social and national landscape of the Bohemian lands.

The Foundation of Czechoslovakia

In a National Committee debate a day after the anniversary of White Mountain, National Democratic professor and politician Karel Engliš laid out the historical case against the nobility:

> It is well known, that after the battle at White Mountain, numerous estates of Czech nobles were given by [Emperor] Ferdinand to all sorts of adventurers in exchange for persecuting

and exterminating the Czech people. These estates remain to
this day in the hands of the descendents of these families.[8]

While introducing the land reform legislation in 1919, the Social
Democratic representative František Modráček argued typically
that "the aristocracy formed a vital pillar of the former Austro-
Hungarian Empire."[9] Drawing on the prewar rhetoric of Czech
national populists, politicians depicted the nobles as foreigners and
carpetbaggers, the rapacious beneficiaries of the Habsburg victory
over the Czechs at White Mountain.

This kind of anti-noble rhetoric had a long revolutionary pedigree in Europe. In France in 1789, Abbé Siéyès and his bourgeois
colleagues had declared the Third Estate to be the sole representative of the nation. In "What Is the Third Estate," Siéyès condemned the nobility as a "people apart, a false people which, unable
to exist by itself for lack of useful organs, latches on to a real nation
like those vegetable growths which can only live on the sap of the
plants they exhaust and suck dry." Expressing a similar contempt,
J. A. Delaure told his French countrymen: "You have been trampled
under the feet of barbarians whose ancestors massacred ours . . .
[These nobles are] all foreigners, the savages escaped from the forests of Germany."[10] Though Czechs had their own stories of noble
alienation and betrayal, they were certainly aware of the French
precedent. Unlike their French predecessors, however, the Czechs
of 1918 preferred parliamentary measures to the guillotine.

In November 1918, the Revolutionary National Assembly out-
lawed noble titles and made it clear that comprehensive land reform
was imminent.[11] The legislation against titles concisely declared that
"nobility, orders, and titles, as long as they do not stem from a
profession, are eliminated."[12] Though the law initially carried no
sanctions, in 1920 the Assembly set the punishment for use of a
noble title at one to fourteen days imprisonment or a 50 to 15,000
crown fine.[13] As far as I can determine, no one was ever arrested
for violating the law; many nobles continued to use their old visiting
cards, with their title simply crossed out.[14] Socialist and Agrarian
newspapers welcomed the legislation. As *Venkov* wrote of titles,
"Such refuse, such relics of a monarchical order . . . are unaccept-

able in a republic."[15] Taking a shot at the famous Lobkowicz wineries, the Social Democratic *Právo lidu* crowed, "Now it's only citizen Lobkowicz and wine from the cellars of citizen Lobkowicz."[16] Going beyond the symbolic, on 9 November 1918 the National Council passed a moratorium on the sale or mortgage of large landed estates, a move that would prevent landowners from dumping their property before land reform legislation could come into effect.[17]

In 1919 the National Assembly also began considering a law to eliminate entails *(Fideikommisse)*, contracts that legally prevented certain nobles from alienating parts of their estates. Until the end of the Habsburg Empire, entails carried certain political privileges, including a guaranteed seat in the upper house of the *Reichsrat* and a vote in a special section of the large landowner curia for the Bohemian Diet. Altogether, there were fifty-seven entails in Bohemia and eighteen in Moravia in 1918, covering 11.2 percent and 8.1 percent of their respective surface areas.[18] Writing just before the end of the war, the estate owner and Constitutionally Loyal politician Wilhelm von Medinger (1878–1934) defended the entail holders as pillars of the empire, "a reliable, conservative power group."[19] This is exactly what rankled Czech critics, who sought after 1918 to dismantle the Habsburg legacy. Using an argument common to all legislation aimed at the nobility, the entail bill declared that "family entail has no place in a democratic republic."[20] In spite of their conviction that the entail was a feudal leftover, the parliament did not pass the bill ending entail until 1924. It made little difference in practice, however, because the land reform would proceed regardless of the legal status of property involved.[21]

Such symbolic and legislative attacks on the nobility served a triple purpose for Czechoslovakia's state-builders. Mainstream politicians believed that the main threats to the new state were monarchism, Bolshevism, and German separatism. With legislation against the nobility, they sought to undermine the economic and social bases of noble power and thus neutralize expected efforts for a Habsburg revanche. At the same time, it was a sop to those on the left who were calling for more radical social reforms, such as the nationalization of industry and agriculture. Finally, though initially the government countered German separatism with a military occupation of separatist German regions, it also looked to land reform as a longer-term solution that would break up German territory by settling Czechs and Slovaks in the German-inhabited borderlands.

The Ministry of Interior took a particular interest in Bohemian noble ties with monarchist movements in Vienna, Budapest, and Munich. The secret services suspected, as one confidential report put it, that "[i]n Czechoslovakia certain old noble families, such as Lobkowitz, Windischgrätz, Liechtenstein, make up the core troops of the monarchist movement."[22] Interior Ministry spies infiltrated the staffs of certain Bohemian nobles, such as Adalbert (Count) Sternberg (1868–1930) and Franz (Count) Clam-Gallas (1854–1930), suspected of supporting former Emperor-King Karl's attempts to return to the throne of Hungary. In November of 1921, the correspondent for northern Bohemia reported, "During the latest attempt of ex-Emperor Karl to reach the Hungarian throne, one could observe brisk traffic among former nobles." He added that observers believed that a meeting of nobles had just taken place on the Liberec estate of Clam-Gallas.[23] Bedřich (Prince) Lobkowicz (1881–1923), the head of the family's Mělník branch, actually cooperated with the Czech government in its efforts to monitor the Karlist movement in Austria and Hungary. Even so, the Interior Ministry kept careful track of his comings and goings. Ministry spies reported, for example, that after the war he had hidden a portrait of the emperor in the house of a certain Patočka.[24]

The Ministry's informers also kept a close eye on monarchist Russian émigrés in Prague, as they believed some of the Russians to be involved in a conspiracy between the Vatican and the Habsburgs to put a Habsburg on the throne of an independent Ukraine. As part of the deal, the Ukrainian Orthodox Church was to accept the authority of the Roman Catholic papal hierarchy. Though this scenario seems far-fetched, it reflected the Czech government's belief that there existed a "mature, built up, and strongly organized European monarchist front." The Russian monarchists bore watching, moreover, as they had ties with certain Bohemian nobles such as a Deym, a Lobkowicz, and the former Austro-Hungarian foreign minister Leopold Berchtold.[25] In general, Czech authorities doubted that the monarchist movement would try to seize power in Czechoslovakia; nonetheless, they kept a close watch because they suspected monarchists of trying to destabilize Czech democracy.[26] In both the public and the official mind, the nobility was the core of the monarchist movement and was by nature antidemocratic.

In reality, many nobles had monarchist sympathies, but there was little organized "monarchism" in Czechoslovakia. Legitimism was strongest among Bohemian nobles based in Vienna, where the stalwart Organization of Catholic Nobles *(Verein katholischer Edelleute)* required from its members an oath of loyalty to the Habsburgs. But younger Bohemian nobles considered the club's monarchism old-fashioned. As Jan (Count) Hartig wrote in 1927, "The Austro-Hungarian Monarchy exists no longer. . . . The world has changed so much. . . . Any attempt of a *restitutio in integrum* must end, for the Monarch and the country, in a new debacle, because the fundamentals are lacking." For that reason, the *Grussbacher Herren*, an informal circle of nobles based in Moravia, refused to join the Catholic Nobles in their self-appointed task of rejuvenating the Central European nobility on the basis of a legitimist movement.[27] For those Bohemian nobles who would not abandon hope of a Habsburg return, there was always the "Emperor Karl Repatriation Fund," which sought after 1924 to bring the dead emperor's body back to Vienna from Madeira.[28]

Many members of the government and National Assembly sensibly feared antidemocratic movements on the left far more than those on the right. With Bolshevik regimes taking power in Russia in 1917 and Bavaria and Hungary in 1919, the threat of a Communist revolution hung over Central Europe as legislators were laying the legal foundations of Czechoslovakia. The Assembly therefore quickly passed a number of bills, including land reform and the abolition of noble titles, in order to head off more radical social reforms in 1919–1920. Those on the Czech right, in particular the Agrarians and National Democrats (the successor party of the Young Czechs), considered the Czech nation fundamentally middle class. The two parties idealized the peasant proprietor and the patriotic small-business owners respectively. In 1918, the right favored symbolic gestures against nobles and relics of Habsburg feudalism as a means of breaking left-wing momentum. In fact the majority of the Assembly, encompassing parts of both right and left, shared the sentiments of the Agrarian publicist Josef Holeček, who wrote in 1917:

> The nobility . . . forms the most radical right of society, the proletariat the most radical left. But the core of society is in the center, between them, in the middle classes: the peasantry, the bourgeoisie, and the free intelligentsia. . . . In the middle layers lies the power, hopes and future of the Czech nation.[29]

Although threats from the extreme left and right had tremendous influence on the development of the new state's institutions, the greatest and most imminent danger was German separatism. In November 1918, Bohemian Germans declared the creation of an independent republic, German-Bohemia (Deutschböhmen), which was to join the newly established state of German-Austria. Though Czech troops thwarted the attempt by occupying the German borderlands, Czechs had every reason to believe in 1919 that the Germans would again try to break away from Czechoslovakia. The country's ethnic Germans lived primarily in majority German regions bordering on Germany and Austria. These border areas also contained hundreds of thousands of acres of forest in the hands of a few prominent noble families including the Waldsteins, Buquoys, and Thuns. Czech legislators planned in the course of the land reform to convert this land to state ownership and settle Czechs on it, thereby securing the border areas against German separatism. Thus did anti-noble legislation aim to head off threats to the state on three fronts: the left, the right, and the borderlands.

Czechoslovakia's state builders found in the noble-German-Habsburg constellation both a real threat and a powerful symbolic enemy. It helped Czech parties in the National Assembly overcome divisions between left and right and find the national unity necessary to survive postwar revolutionary upheavals, as well as implement a strong, centralist constitution in 1920. Czech Socialists and Agrarians may have differed in their ideas of the nation and visions for the future, but both could at least agree on a common enemy. Like most nascent states, therefore, Czechoslovakia built its new institutions and chose its state-forming ideology in reaction both to the previous regime and to immediate threats, both perceived and real. Czechoslovakia was to be a middle-class and democratic national state, in contrast, many Czechs believed, to the authoritarian, feudal, and German-dominated Habsburg Empire. This ideology informed the basic institutional structure of the new state: it was centralized and parliamentary, with a largely Czech bureaucracy. The founders' middle-class national ideology also infiltrated secondary governing institutions in the state, most notably the State Land Office (*Státní pozemkový úřad* or SPÚ) established to carry out land reform. At first, Germans thought themselves defenseless in such an environment, but soon many placed their hopes in the League of Nations, which appeared to offer them some protection against the nationalizing Czech state.

The League of Nations and Minority Protection Treaties

Meeting at Versailles in 1919, the Big Four acknowledged the pitfalls of creating national states with large minorities. In order to discourage new wars over minority disputes, they pressured the states of Central and Eastern Europe to sign minority treaties that would, they hoped, protect minorities from the nationalizing tendencies of the new states. C. A. Macartney pointed out in 1934 that these treaties were not primarily idealistic protections of human rights. Rather they were intended to preserve the peace of Europe, which had just been ravaged for over four years in a nationalistic war. As Aristide Briand said at the League of Nations, "Peace must prevail, must come before all."[30] The peacemakers rightly saw large minority enclaves in aggressively national successor states as substantial threats to peace.

Czechoslovakia signed its minority treaty on 10 September 1919 and incorporated its provisions into the constitution of 1920. The core of the treaty was the guarantee of equal rights for minorities before the law: "Czechoslovak nationals who belong to racial, religious or linguistic minorities shall enjoy the same treatment and

security in law and in fact as other Czechoslovak nationals."[31] Moreover, anywhere that minorities made up more than 20 percent of
the local population, they were entitled to schools and public services in their own language. The League of Nations undertook the
responsibility of guarantor of the treaty's protections, setting up a
petition apparatus for grievances.[32]

The petitioning system led to the birth of scores of national and
international minority lobbying organizations in Europe, including
some very active in Czechoslovakia. Starting in 1925, these groups
met annually, often in Geneva, under an umbrella organization
known as the Congress of European Nationalities. The goal of the
Congress was to help ensure minority groups autonomous cultural
development, but on the basis of cooperation and loyalty to their
respective states. Founded by Germans in Estonia, the Congress focused primarily on issues of concern to German minorities, though
Hungarians, Ukrainians, and others also sent representatives.[33] The
International Union of League of Nations Associations (*Union Internationale des Associations pour la Societé des Nations*) was another important forum and pressure group for national minorities. Founded
in 1921, the International Union opposed the League's minority
treaties as insufficient, and it argued in particular against the premise
that minority problems were "a sovereign internal affair of individual
states."[34] Though the International Union's agenda went far beyond
minority issues, it became the organization of choice for groups
wanting to internationalize minority disputes.

One of the most active minority organizations in Czechoslovakia
was the German League of Nations Union (*Völkerbundliga*), which
was affiliated with the International Union. Founded by the large-
estate owner and senator, Wilhelm (von) Medinger in 1921, the
Völkerbundliga's stated goal was to build German support for the
League of Nations by using the League's minority protection apparatus to achieve tangible gains for Germans in Czechoslovakia.
The group had a long way to go, the first annual report noted,
given the difficulties it had even getting approval from the Czechoslovak government to incorporate. Rejected by the Czechoslovak
branch of the League of Nations Union, Medinger's German group
applied to the government for separate incorporation in the sum-

mer of 1921. They were denied twice, first on account of their application being exclusively in German, and then on the grounds that they had applied as a nonpolitical organization but had political goals. Such petty irritants, the annual report complained, were "in no way favorable for cooperation of the German and Czech nations."[35] Not expecting a fair hearing in Czechoslovakia, the *Völkerbundliga* aimed to internationalize German minority complaints in order to pressure the government for concessions to minority demands. Petitioning the League of Nations on behalf of German large landowners became one of the group's first projects.[36]

In spite of its guarantee, the League of Nations rarely took direct action on minority petitions, though neither did it ignore them. From 1920 to 1931 the League passed a total of thirteen cases to the Permanent Court of International Justice, which in all such cases provided an advisory, but not legally binding decision. Even so, hundreds of petitions came to the League's Council during the 1920s.[37] Given the later escalation of minority tension and the breakdown of the League of Nations in the 1930s, it is easy to conclude that the League's minority system was ineffective. Even so, in the 1920s, petitioners put great hopes in the League and saw it as a vehicle for internationalizing their grievances.

The minority treaties marked the intersection of the contradictory principles of the postwar settlement. In theory, the peacemakers favored self-determination, the creation of democratic national states in place of supposedly anachronistic empires. But geopolitical realism trumped democratic idealism, as the great powers backed the large multinational states of Poland, Czechoslovakia, and Romania as a counterweight to Germany in Central Europe. By the same token, Germany, rump Austria, and Hungary were to be punished for their role in the Great War by a substantial loss of territory, which included millions of ethnic Germans and Hungarians. With the Versailles treaties of 1919 and 1920, the victorious powers institutionalized the new European order of nominal national states with large minorities.

Some Germans, particularly German nobles, expressed the hope that the League could play a role similar to that of the Habsburg Empire, acting as a supranational force, a forum of ultimate appeal for national disputes. But without an army, a monarch, or any other trappings of power, there was little the League could do but offer a sympathetic ear. The League provided institutions for receiving grievances, but offered no effective means of arbitrating them. Demands of aggressive majorities were encouraged by nationalizing states; those of defensive minorities were supported by the League's protection guarantee. Thus members of a majority had an incentive to look inward, seeking favorable treatment from their national government. Minorities, on the other hand, became accustomed to looking outward, to the internationalization of their grievances. These incentives significantly shaped the strategies nobles adopted to defend their land from confiscation.

The Czechoslovak Land Reform

The Czechoslovak land reform of 1919 was, in the words of the contemporary liberal journalist Ferdinand Peroutka, one of the "three pillars" of the national revolution, the other two being the overthrow of the Habsburg state and the adoption of the constitution in 1920.[38] It was a central element of the new state's attack on the Habsburg legacy. Seeking to reverse what they saw as centuries of mistreatment at the hands of German-Habsburg feudal forces, Czech legislators, led by the Agrarian Party, created the powerful State Land Office to transfer land from large estates to small farmers and landless laborers. The reform was both national and social; though the legislation was technically free of national bias, its justification and implementation betrayed a determination to bring German and Hungarian landlords down to size and expand Czech and Slovak agrarian settlement. It was a prime example of the nationalizing state at work, of nationalism infiltrating and shaping the basic institutional structures of Czechoslovak government. It was one of many ways that the state brought the nation to the people.

Though Czech support for land reform was nearly unanimous, there was wide disagreement on its form and extent. Cast by many as "national justice," land reform became a prominent battleground over the social and political meanings ascribed to the nation. All political parties drew on national history and mythologies to justify reform, but historical interpretations varied across the political spectrum. Agrarians championed the midlevel peasant farmer as the repository of Czech tradition and language during the "dark years" *(temno)* following White Mountain. In contrast, socialists depicted the Czechs as a nation of laborers, both peasant and industrial, with deep socialist traditions dating to the Hussite wars of the fifteenth century. Correspondingly, Agrarians favored parceling noble land to small and middling farmers, whereas the socialist left supported nationalizing land into cooperatives and collective farms.

For all parties, the Battle of White Mountain served as a vivid symbol of Habsburg and German oppression and the most prominent public justification for land reform. In debate in the National Assembly in 1919, Czech politicians claimed land reform would "redress" the Battle of White Mountain.[39] Both Agrarian and Socialist supporters justified reform in national terms by arguing that German nobles had received their land at the expense of Czechs after 1620.[40] Many legislators pursued a total reversal of the historical verdict at White Mountain. František Modráček, a moderate Social Democrat in the National Assembly, spoke for the majority:

> By these several paragraphs [of the land reform bill] we are expunging the landed aristocracy from the future history of the Czech nation. Today we are ridding ourselves once and for all of that aristocracy that played such an infamous role in the history of our nation, and the especially sad role after the Battle of White Mountain up to the present.[41]

Modráček and others drew on the symbolic resonance of White Mountain, building an argument that portrayed Germans, Habsburgs, and aristocrats as a composite feudal enemy that had subjugated the Czechs after the 1620 defeat. The Bohemian nobles were, according to Modráček, primarily a Habsburg creation, foreign overlords imported after White Mountain. Other parties shared this interpretation. "In the lands of the Czech Crown," National Democratic representative Bohumil Němec argued, "there are many nationally foreign, mercenary, and rapacious noble families. Czech Catholic nobles also enriched themselves, but they soon lost their national consciousness; the Catholic restoration ended up Germanizing them." The result, he continued, was that "the overwhelming majority of large land holdings in our republic is in foreign hands." Even though three hundred years had passed since White Mountain,

> the wrong and illegality committed against the whole nation could not be swept under the rug. This case is not a question of civil law, but rather of morality, which demands the redressing of wrongs committed against the whole nation. History has its justice, and the Czech nation sees in the land reform we are carrying out just such an act of historical justice.[42]

Unlike the conservative National Democrats, who justified land reform almost exclusively in moral and national terms, Agrarians and Social Democrats additionally emphasized social reasons for land reform, most particularly the need to alleviate an increasingly radical "hunger for land" in Czechoslovakia's rural heartland. Vladimir Lenin's land reform in Russia after 1917 had raised the expectations of peasants throughout Central and Eastern Europe, and radical agitators appeared poised to use the successful example of the Russian Communists to "Bolshevize" the Czech countryside.[43] The National Assembly thus aimed to seize the initiative with land reform, thereby ensuring the loyalty of Czech and Slovak peasants to the middle-class state.

But even when making social arguments for the reform, legislators often couched them in national rhetoric. Noble land was German land; land reform would return this land to the Czechs. As Modráček concluded, "This reform is not only a social reform, but also a republican reform and in the true sense of the word, a national reform."[44] Karel Viškovský, an Agrarian and future director of the State Land Office, argued similarly, "There is no liberated nation without the liberation of the soil. . . . Land is the most solid form of national property. The removal of the latifundists means a revolution in the national side of property."[45] Viškovský's connection of national sovereignty with the control of land indicated the continuity of "national property" rhetoric from the late nineteenth-century. Formerly fought within the institutions of the Habsburg Empire, the Czech-German struggle over national property now played out in a Czech nation-state. For Czech state-builders, land reform was an excellent opportunity to press their new advantages.

The Agrarian press also stressed the national theme, calling 1919 the biggest year for Czech farmers since the peasant emancipation of 1848. "Who are the large landowners?" *Venkov* asked. "In the lands of the former Bohemian Crown," the paper continued, "they are almost entirely Germans, most of them unfriendly to our nation, hating our nation. Where they could, they repressed and germanized, exerted their influence in our villages, hindering the general progress and the education of the people. . . . They were the curse of our defeat at White Mountain." But even amid the repression, rural Czechs kept up their "national habits, morals, costume, and national individuality, while towns and industrial areas easily de-nationalized, became estranged." The countryside was the heart of the Czech nation, and it would now prosper as never before. "The National Assembly," the Agrarians triumphantly declared, "has returned to the nation that which was violently torn from it three hundred years ago!"[46]

Even the conservative National Democrats made a similar pitch. "Land," one prominent deputy wrote in *Národní listy*, is "the acknowledged foundation of the nation and the state." The land reform must therefore transfer land "into the hands of people loyal to the nation and the state." In this way, the reform "will redress the mistake made by the Przemyslides when they gave German colonists land and soil, and especially the cruel confiscation after the Battle of White Mountain, when 800 great estates were confiscated for Habsburg mercenaries."[47] National Democrats regularly demanded the Czech "resettlement" of the "Germanized borderlands" with the goal of securing the borders, redressing historical injustices, and inoculating the Czech population against revolution.[48]

Using this kind of historical symbolism, legislators made land reform a central element of Czechoslovakia's middle-class, democratic, and national founding ideology. The reform's goals, as most members of the National Assembly saw it, were: the destruction of the power of the pro-Habsburg, antidemocratic nobility; the reversal of centuries of Germanization of land in the Bohemian crown lands and of Magyarization in Slovakia; the strengthening of a Czech and Slovak agrarian middle class, which would be sympathetic to democracy and beholden to the republic; and the alleviation of a dangerous land hunger among landless rural laborers. In order both to explain and justify the reform to the Czech people in simple terms, members of the Assembly drew on a rhetoric and popular history of nobles as foreign carpetbaggers, who had received Czech land after serving the Habsburgs in the Thirty Years' War. "In the perception of most people," Ladislav Holy writes, "the land stolen from the Czech nation through confiscation three hundred years ago was now simply to be returned."[49]

The Czech Conservative Critique

Not all Czechs accepted this mythologized picture of White Mountain and the nobility that had taken hold in popular historical memory. Josef Pekař (1870–1937), a conservative historian and outspoken critic of radical land reform, wrote a series of articles for the National Democratic newspaper *Národní listy*, in which he refuted the nationalist mythology of White Mountain. The Protestant-Catholic divide in the early seventeenth century did not coincide with a Czech-German split, he argued, as old Czech noble families served on both sides of the conflict. Of three brothers in the Kinský family, for example, one was killed as a rebel, one went into exile, and one sided with the Habsburgs, who rewarded him generously.[50]

"The estates confiscated after White Mountain," Pekař continued, "were mostly bought up by the Czech nobility, the nobility descended from age-old, good Czech families." He did not deny that many foreign nobles had settled in Bohemia after White Mountain, though more than half of these had arrived or expanded their estates after the Thirty Years' War ended in 1648. Using land records from 1772, he calculated that 37 percent of noble land in Bohemia belonged to old Bohemian families, 27 percent to new families that came in the aftermath of White Mountain, and 31 percent who settled in Bohemia from 1648 to 1750.[51]

Pekař also disputed the depiction of Bohemian nobles as German enemies of the Czech nation. He pointed out the indispensable role the Bohemian nobility had played in the Czech national revival of the nineteenth century, and he argued that nobles "did not consider (no matter how strange it seems to us today) the use of the Czech language as an essential sign of Czech nationality. It was a period of Bohemian *(český)* territorial patriotism without the Czech language. . . . [These nobles were] German in language, Czech in spirit." Even more contrary to the popular stereotype, many of the most avid supporters of the revival came from the ranks of the post–White Mountain nobility (like the Thuns, for example). But although many nobles might have been national-patriotic, they refused to become nationalist. "In spite of the fact that the national idea gathered force ever more uncontrollably in public life," Pekař wrote, "it did not manage to shake the class status of the Bohemian nobility and place nobles simply into this or that national camp." This resistance to nationalism, he added, explained repeated noble attempts to facilitate a compromise between Czechs and Germans in Bohemia after the 1870s. The great service of the nobility to the Czech nation had been their persistent advocacy of Bohemian historic rights, which was, in Pekař's view, the true founding ideology of the Czech state in 1918.[52]

Pekař particularly disdained populist literature and history, such as Holeček's 1918 anti-noble tract, which distorted the past to serve a radical political agenda. Himself an empiricist in the Rankean tradition, Pekař rejected histories of the nobles that were, in Palacký's words, "very convenient, but not very just." Pekař argued instead that a historian should resist projecting his own values and prejudices into the past; one could not judge the nobility's behavior without understanding the context within which nobles acted. Given the Bohemian nobility's unique brand of patriotism that united historic rights with imperial loyalty, it was unfair to criticize nobles for supporting the monarchy during the Great War (and here he reminded his readers that most Czech political parties also had mixed records in this regard). In fact, Pekař claimed, the majority of Bohemian nobles would have rallied to the Czech cause after 1918 had it not been for the land reform. He regretted this because Czechoslovakia needed a "prudent" conservative force to counter radical tendencies.[53]

Pekař further objected on moral grounds to a nationally punitive land reform. He accepted the necessity of eliminating noble political privileges in a democratic age; however, the "punitive confiscation of inherited estates . . . would not redress the wrong [of White Mountain], but would create a new injustice" out of keeping with the "moral consciousness of our age." The general principle of private property, in his view, trumped a misplaced vision of historical justice. Czech verbal and legislative aggression against nobles and Germans reflected a lack of national self-confidence, Pekař claimed, an obsession with "smallness and weakness." But, he argued, Czechs had no reason to be insecure; they had their own state, which was economically and culturally advanced.[54]

Legislating "Historical Justice"

Members of the National Assembly believed in "historical justice," Pekař's objections notwithstanding. Even so, finding a legislative form for that justice proved harder than initially perceived. In 1918, National Democratic and Agrarian advocates had hoped to go back to land records from the 1620s and redistribute land that had changed hands after White Mountain. But an advisory group of historians and archivists disabused them of that idea, arguing that it would take years of research that would in most cases end up inconclusive. As the archivist J. Novák reported, many estates had changed owners a number of times since White Mountain. It was unclear, he wrote, what historical justice would be served by taking land from more recent owners. Pekař pointed out a year later what must have been obvious to lawmakers after reflecting on the historians' response: trying to "redress" White Mountain "would occasion a huge number of court cases, cases [so] involved and long-lasting" that they would tie up the courts for years.[55] Facing a logistical nightmare, the Assembly decided that the law should provide justice indirectly, by confiscating land on economic rather than exclusively historical criteria.

Equally problematic, Agrarians and Social Democrats could not agree on what form historical justice should take, in particular on which land to confiscate and how to redistribute it. Socialists wanted to confiscate all holdings over 100 ha, but they opposed the fragmentation of large estates. Instead, they favored either giving the land to state-controlled collective farms or leasing it to privately run cooperatives. Agrarians and parties on the right objected to the use of the term "confiscate," which they believed had Bolshevik overtones and would prejudice international opinion against Czechoslovakia. Instead, they favored language giving the government "the power to confiscate," though not the obligation. Land that was to be taken should go directly to farmers of small and medium-sized plots, as well as landless laborers.[56] "[The Socialist newspaper] *Právo lidu* wants to turn small farmers into simple hirelings on socialist latifundia," the Agrarian daily *Venkov* wrote. "The land of the latifundia must be apportioned to the little man, who yearns for ownership!"[57]

The land reform arguments reflected two very different visions of the identity of the Czech nation and thus of the fundamental structure of the new Czechoslovak nation-state. Socialists argued for a Czechness that was both old and new, rooted in the radically egalitarian Hussite tradition of the fifteenth century, yet drawing on the Czechs' more recent traditions of industrialization and urbanization. Thus Socialists wanted land reform to benefit rural laborers, not by turning them into a new agrarian middle class, but by making them the masters of collective farms or cooperatives. In their view, Czechs were (or should be) a fundamentally working-class nation, a nation that prized equality and community above all.

Agrarians, on the other hand, favored a Czech identity rooted in the countryside, the humble, but hardworking peasantry that had kept Czech traditions and language alive during the period of darkness *(temno)* after White Mountain. In this mythology, the national intelligentsia emerged from Czech villages in the early nineteenth century and began the revival that would return the Czech language and culture to its former glory. It was an essentially middle-class vision: a nation of farmers, schoolmasters, and village priests. Later in the nineteenth century, as the Bohemian lands industrialized, budding Czech capitalists made their fortunes primarily in food processing, a rural industry. Even the new Czech working class had its roots in the countryside, only a generation removed from the village and its middle-class values of family, work, and Czech patriotism. As Agrarians saw things, the land reform should strengthen this rural middle-class foundation of the nation by giving noble land directly to individual small farmers and landless peasants.

With the land reform stuck in committee in early 1919, Jan Krčmář, a professor of law at Prague University, came up with an ingenious formulation that would temporarily satisfy both sides. Thus the final legislation of April 1919 declared that all estates over 250 ha were to be *zabrány* (taken conditionally) by the state, pending their final disposition. Though the distinction is not obvious in English, in Czech *zábor* does not have the definitive connotation of confiscation *(vyvlastnění)*. It was intentionally vague, "juridically unclear," as Krčmář put it.[58] "Each person can interpret this term however he wants," Modráček declared approvingly.[59] It did not rule out confiscation, but nor did it require that all land falling under *zábor* be redistributed. In practice, an American observer wrote in 1923, under *zábor* the estate owner "remains possessor of his property. The *zábor* imposes solely on this possession a certain restriction of his rights, consisting of its being impossible for him to make on his own authority juridical dispositions concerning his property."[60] The law then created the State Land Office to oversee the land in *zábor* and determine its future status. In effect, the National Assembly left the controversies over the amount and the recipients of land unresolved, devolving them to the Land Office bureaucracy.

Ultimately, it was the Agrarian middle-class ideology that won in 1919, at least as far as the land reform was concerned. The *zábor* compromise worked to the advantage of the Agrarian Party, which took control of the State Land Office. Supplementary legislation in June of 1919 gave the Office wide-ranging powers, including complete control of redistribution of land, as well as the power to free land from *zábor* (thus returning full legal rights to owners).[61] The

Agrarians would use the Land Office to build a new cohort of small and medium-sized farmers beholden to the Agrarian Party. And because the party represented Czechs only (German farmers had a similar, but separate party), the Agrarians naturally worked to see that their own constituency—Czech farmers—received confiscated land. The Agrarian-run reform disappointed the early expectations of socialists, however, as little land went to cooperatives and large tracts remained in the hands of latifundists. Socialist discontent with the reform simmered until 1945, when the triumphant left proceeded to "complete" the reform as socialists had envisioned it in 1919.

Land Reform and the Nationalizing State

Debate over land reform made it abundantly clear that Czechoslovakia's leaders understood the country not only as a national state, but also as a nationalizing state. The more outspoken nationalists readily admitted that land reform was a useful tool for Czechifying German regions. Ostensibly a social reform, it became a national reform in practice. To Czechs, this seemed perfectly understandable: most large landowners were German, and most tenant farmers and landless laborers were Czech. Thus naturally, reform supporters argued, Czechs would receive land at the expense of "German barons." On the other hand, there is ample evidence that the State Land Office went beyond simply parceling out German land and actually followed a kind of affirmative action program for Czechs. The SPÚ did this both by settling Czech Legionaries (veterans of the Czech exile army during World War I) on German estates and by favoring Czechs in redistribution.[62]

In their final form, the land reform laws had no explicitly anti-German content. "As far as motivations for land reform are concerned," a Czech historian of the reform writes, "we find national motivation in declarations and public discussions, but not however in the statutes of laws on land reform."[63] But by adjusting the pace, order, and extent of reform, the Land Office could target Germans even without a legal mandate to do so. And there was little German landowners could do about it, because they had no representation in the government (until 1926) nor in the Land Office (ever). The tremendous discretionary power of the SPÚ allowed a Czech national agenda to infiltrate the land reform.

Contemporaries and historians have disagreed widely over the extent of national bias in the reform. There is no question that it took far more land from German landowners than from Czechs, and it gave far more to Czechs than to Germans. But this would have happened naturally under a purely social reform, because of the ownership structure of land in Bohemia and Moravia and the social structure of the German population. As defenders of the reform repeatedly pointed out, the majority of large estates had been in the hands of Germans, while small farmers and landless laborers in the provinces were overwhelmingly Czech. In an internal memorandum giving a typical defense in 1930, the Land Office wrote, "Land reform is not directed towards the persons of the owners of latifundia, but against their property. . . . The nationality, religion, etc. of the owner is a completely incidental and irrelevant circumstance." But the memo admitted to an uneven confiscation. The Land Office could not help pointing out that "the preponderance of the German-Magyar element in ownership of large estates is not a result of normal political and economic evolution, but mainly a result of political persecution by the former Habsburg Dynasty at the beginning of the seventeenth century."[64]

Among Czech historians, there is a tendency to play down the national side of land reform, or to deny it altogether. Lubomír Slezák emphasizes the social goals and achievements of the reform, and he attributes complaints about national bias to the "demogoguery and naiveté" of the large landowners' lobbies.[65] Offering some limited statistics on redistribution, Jan Rychlík claims the Land Office applied the land reform law fairly. In the Sudetenland, for example, Germans made up almost half of the recipients of confiscated property. Given that Germans were a large majority of the population there, however, this does not help Rychlík's case. Even so, he concludes from his statistics "that the Czechoslovak land reform did not have an overwhelmingly national character."[66]

German historians have been mixed in their evaluation of the national bias of the land reform. Many, such as Friedrich Prinz, simply repeat the Sudeten German propaganda against reform from the interwar period.[67] Others, when they mention the reform at all, do not make much of its national component. J. W. Brügel cautiously concludes that there was "not full ethnic justice" in the reform, but leaves it at that, citing a lack of statistics on nationality.[68] Jaromír Dittmann-Balcar, in contrast, claims that the very fact that the Land Office did not keep extensive nationality statistics speaks against an intentional policy of "Czechification." The statistics we do have on redistribution to Germans, Dittmann-Balcar writes, suggest Germans got substantially less land than their percentage of the population. But they did receive land, which argues against widespread discrimination in redistribution.[69] Dittmann-Balcar stresses that during debate over the land reform, "The main arguments in committee were of a social-political—even social-pacificatory—nature, while in public [representatives] emphasized the national-political character of the land reform." He attributes the public stand to "tactics," as national justice was far more acceptable to the bourgeois parties of the National Assembly than social justice. Even so, both Czech rhetoric and German paranoia surrounding the land reform contributed to national polarization throughout the interwar period.[70]

One of the harshest recent critics of the national bias of the land reform has been Mark Cornwall, who expands on arguments made by the Czech philosopher Emanuel Rádl in 1928. Cornwall documents the intense pressure of Czech propaganda societies (known as national unions, *Národní jednoty*) for "Czech colonization of German areas."[71] The result of national unions' influence on the State Land Office, Cornwall argues, may not have been "a systematic process of Czechification, [but] there was definite evidence in ethnically sensitive localities of discrimination against German applicants for land."[72] Cornwall concludes that neither the Czech public nor the Land Office was able to separate the national and social aspects of land reform—they saw both as two inseparable parts of the Czechoslovak revolution of 1918–19.[73]

Though a final evaluation awaits case-by-case studies of the redistribution process on individual estates, there is abundant evidence in the SPÚ archive of both petty discrimination and a programmatic anti-Germanism. This is perhaps most obvious in the minutes of the SPÚ's Oversight Board *(Správní výbor)*, which was made up of political appointees from the National Assembly.[74] Chosen before 1920 elections brought Germans into the Assembly, none of the Board's members were German, nor were German parties ever subsequently represented. The Board repeatedly put pressure on the SPÚ to speed up its work and facilitate Czech colonization in nationally mixed and German areas.[75] In some meetings, the political overseers of the SPÚ targeted individuals they disliked for national-political reasons, such as when Vladimír Drobný urged the Land Office to confiscate Wilhelm Medinger's estate "in the interest of strengthening our minorities and because the owner has consistently hindered the work of the SPÚ."[76]

The Land Office's colonization policy was perhaps the most blatant discrimination in favor of Czechs.[77] In January 1920, the Assembly passed a Law of Allotment, which gave the Land Office directions on how to redistribute confiscated land. There were a number of criteria for who should get priority in applications for land. None of the criteria were explicitly national, and the legislation did not rank them. Even so, the law gave the Land Office tremendous latitude in determining recipients of land. It also set up a Colonization Fund to help those without capital to buy land and settle on confiscated estates. In standard practice and then by explicit governmental decree in 1922, first priority for settlement went to Czechoslovak Legionaries, who had fought in Russia on the side of the Entente during and after World War I and returned to Czechoslovakia in 1920. None of the Legionaries were German or Hungarian.[78] The colonization machinery thus gave the Land Office tremendous flexibility and a powerful tool for favoring Czech interests.

Until 1924, the SPÚ focused primarily on reform in the Czech-language interior of Bohemia and Moravia, but thereafter it stepped up its redistribution of land in German and mixed districts. In 1925, the SPÚ sought from the government special funding for an increase in credit for settlers. Publicly, the Land Office attributed the request to a simple budget shortfall. But a confidential memorandum to members of the government betrayed a strictly national goal. Noting that in areas of mixed settlement, Czechs were generally in the industrial sector, they suggested that credit could be used to settle these regions with rural Czechs from elsewhere. If land reform was to fulfill its "national tasks" in mixed regions, the report argued, it would be necessary "to supplement the number of eligible local Czech and Slovak applicants with a further influx of applicants from areas purely Czech and Slovak." The SPÚ ruled out, however, the creation of German settlements.[79]

The result of this policy was predictable. In mixed regions, the SPÚ generally favored Czech recipients over Germans, though the national unions complained when Germans there received anything at all. An internal memorandum made clear the Land Office intention to break up German dominance of the borderlands by "creating independent complexes [of Czech settlement] from the Czech interior right up to the state border."[80] As Elizabeth Wiskemann reported in 1938, "Legionary and other Czech colonists were gradually settled on the available arable land all around the lignite areas where the population was most mixed, and to a lesser extent in northern Moravia, where the local Czechs demanded to have the minority strengthened."[81] In the end, according to Agriculture Ministry statistics, Germans received a total of 5.2 percent of agricultural land reallocated in Bohemia and Moravia up to 1937 (not including the automatic purchase option given to long-term leaseholders in 1919–20), though their proportion of the population exceeded 30 percent.[82]

Such national land reforms were not unusual in East Central Europe between the wars, as new nationalizing states sought to weaken minorities and strengthen members of titular nations. In Poland, government policy promoted the settlement of Poles in the eastern *kresy*, inhabited primarily by Ukrainians and Belarusians. Moreover, Polish land reform, which technically targeted estates over 300 ha in the east, exempted estates "that were devoted to highly specialized or unusually productive agricultural enterprises of national importance." This left the government the latitude to confiscate German land in the west, but to spare Polish-owned estates in the sea of Ukrainians in the *kresy* and Galicia.[83] In Romania, which redistributed the largest amount of land in interwar Europe (excluding Russia), land reform bore more similarities to the Czech reform than the Polish. As in Czechoslovakia, larger estates in Transylvania were mostly in the hands of Hungarian and German landowners, and the landless peasantry there was primarily Romanian. Like the Czechs, the Romanians merged national and social rhetoric in justifying reform.[84] In general, the most extensive land reforms in East Central Europe came in the states where ethnic minorities owned disproportionate amounts of land (Czechoslovakia, Romania, and the Baltics), while the mildest reforms occurred in those with a landowning nobility identified as native/national (Poland and Hungary).[85]

As Joseph Rothschild points out, national discrimination did not require "explicit legislative authorization . . . which was generally avoided for legal reasons or because of public relations." Rather, it could be undertaken "through silent but relentless administrative discretion."[86] This was precisely the SPÚ's tack. The Land Office and the National Assembly followed a threefold strategy: justify land reform to the right by invoking national mythologies, justify it to the left and abroad with a social argument, and implement it with a subtle discriminatory policy. In this way, Rogers Brubaker argues, "nationalism becomes an 'aspect' of politics—embracing both formal policies and informal practices, and existing both within and outside the state—rather than a discrete movement."[87] A pillar of the new Czechoslovak state, land reform both reflected and furthered the nationalization of politics and everyday life.

Bohemian Nobles and the Foundation of Czechoslovakia

Though most Bohemian nobles supported the Habsburg Monarchy to the end, they were far from united in their attitudes toward the foundation of Czechoslovakia in 1918. Given the paucity of evidence of any immediate reaction, we can conclude that most nobles, regardless of previous national/political sympathies, deemed it prudent in 1918 to withdraw from public life until the revolutionary surge had passed. The destruction of the monarchy was something few had expected or prepared for, so their silence may have been a result of confusion as much as a calculated strategy. "Beastly times!"

one noble wrote in early 1919. "Everything is so muddled and confused."[88] In spite of the confusion, a few bolder nobles took a stand on the side of either Bohemian German separatists or the newly formed Czechoslovak government.

As the Habsburg Empire was disintegrating in October 1918, Bohemian German politicians in Vienna declared the creation of an independent province of "German Bohemia" *(Deutschböhmen)* with its capital in north Bohemian Reichenburg (Liberec). Basing its claim to sovereignty on the Wilsonian principle of self-determination, the leaders of *Deutschböhmen* elected Rudolf Lodgman von Auen their president and began to set up a government. A few days later, parts of northern Moravia announced the creation of a "Sudetenland" province, which was to become a part of German-Austria. The new Prague government invited Lodgman and his followers to join the National Assembly, but Lodgman refused, preferring to maintain *Deutschböhmen*'s nominal independence until the peace conference could determine its future status. In late November, the Czechs moved to establish de facto control in the separatist German regions by sending in troops and controlling provisioning of the famished borderlands.[89]

The picture of noble activity in the borderlands during these confused days remains hazy. There is some evidence that nobles took a part in trying to maintain food supply, which seems natural given their prominence in the agricultural sector. An undated map titled "Bohemian German *(Deutschböhmisch)* Emergency Committee from the *Herrenhaus*" divided the Bohemian borderlands into eight regions, each with a prominent noble in charge of managing food.[90] It is not clear if the committee was founded to deal with wartime food shortages or those of the rebellious German provinces in October 1918.[91] Nor is it clear whether the committee actually did anything other than organize itself. For what it is worth, the Czech press later accused many of these nobles, most notably Karl (Count) Buquoy, of collaborating with the *Deutschböhmen* separatists.[92]

Rudolf (Count) Czernin-Morzin (1855–1927), who lived in the overwhelmingly German region near Hohenelbe (Vrchlabí) in northern Bohemia, complained bitterly to the government about the behavior of Czech troops in early 1919. Not only had they cut down some of his trees to heat their border post, but also they had even shot four deer on his property! Almost as bad, the "occupation" authorities in his part of the Sudetenland were using their power to "forcefully de-nationalize" the region. First, local Czech officials had refused to issue decrees in German. Then, they had sent soldiers to his chateau and demanded that he hang a Czechoslovak flag on President Masaryk's birthday. "The republic seems to want to outdo even monarchical despotism in its sharpest form," he wrote. Before the war, he had worked hard to build a Czech-German compromise in Bohemia, but compromise was now impossible due to Czech chauvinism. "This is truly not the way to establish understanding and restore order," he concluded.[93] Though Czernin-Morzin had previously been "without any national prejudice," he would write a few years later, "as a result of the political development in our state, I came to see it as my further duty to declare my solidarity with Germandom."[94]

Adalbert Sternberg, on the other hand, welcomed the Czechoslovak state, though not in its republican form. Sternberg was a junior member of an old Bohemian family; he could count among his ancestors Kašpar Sternberg, the founder of the Bohemian National Museum and a friend of Palacký's. A fiery orator and dedicated federalist, Adalbert Sternberg had been elected twice to the *Reichsrat* before the war, where he generally allied himself with Czech interests.[95] In January 1919, Sternberg published a brochure addressed to the peacemakers at Versailles. In it he argued in favor of Czechoslovakia's territorial claims on strategic grounds. A noted Anglophile, Sternberg wrote that "the Czecho-Slovak Empire [*sic*] is predestined to become England's greatest stronghold in Central Europe . . . England's arsenal."[96]

Though Sternberg considered a republic to be the ideal form of government, the situation of Czechoslovakia, with its large national minorities, made constitutional monarchy more suitable. This proposal was not as outlandish as it seems; Masaryk and Karel Kramář both had called for "a democratic kingdom on the English model" as late as 1915. Democracy of absolute majorities, Sternberg argued, was downright dangerous, given the national and social composition of the new state. He went on to defend private property, oppose large-scale confiscation of land, and rail against Socialism. The only protection for "our new homeland *(Heimat)*" against such evils was Christianity, "the largest and strongest bulwark against Bolshevism."[97]

The Lobkowiczs, another old Bohemian family, declared their allegiance to the new state on 31 October 1918. In a letter to the Czechoslovak National Committee (the predecessor to the Provisional National Assembly), Ferdinand, Max, and Jaroslav Lobkowicz acknowledged the National Committee as "our responsible government" and offered their aid in helping to secure the country's artistic and historical heritage. Claiming to speak for other "old Czech families who think similarly," they declared their willingness "to work with all our power for everything that would benefit our nation and its successful future in its independent and sovereign state." They asked only that the National Committee "find for our followers, if they are not already in the service of the nation, a place where they can take a part in the work of the nation."[98] Three weeks later, the Prague newspaper *Večer* reported that "citizen" Ferdinand Lobkowicz and a group of former Feudal Conservatives were trying to create a new Conservative Republican Party, but nothing came of this effort (if *Večer's* report was accurate in the first place).[99] Working behind the scenes, Bedřich Lobkowicz, the head of another branch of the family and the future president of the Union of Czechoslovak Large Landowners, added his own declaration of loyalty a few months later. Claiming that "the nobility in Bohemia considers me to a certain extent as their exponent," he asked to meet with President Masaryk as soon as possible.[100]

Given the wide range of noble political opinion before and during the war, the lack of a unified front regarding the emergence of Czechoslovakia is understandable. Though most nobles retreated to their estates and withheld judgment, the responses of Rudolf Czernin, the Lobkowiczs, and others suggest the poles toward which nobles would gravitate in the interwar period. There would be Czechs and Germans, republicans and monarchists, democrats and antidemocrats. Most would soon learn that the Czechoslovak government, unlike that of the Habsburgs, would show little interest in their "service" to the state. Edvard Beneš, the perennial

Minister of Foreign Affairs, would use very few nobles in the Foreign Service. Unprepared for democratic politics and unwelcome in
Czech political circles, no nobles would serve in Czechoslovak governments until after the fall of the First Republic in 1938. The few
nobles who did offer their service to the new government in 1918–
1919 were quietly rebuffed.

⟨ THE LEGITIMATING IDEOLOGY OF Czechoslovakia in-
voked a historical narrative in which nobles figured prominently. The
anti-noble, anti-German rhetoric of 1918–1920 was not mere pos-
turing; it became the foundation for a massive land reform, and it
infused the State Land Office and many other institutions with an anti-
German bias. Defining their new country as a Czechoslovak nation-
state, the largely Czech political elite used flexible or unclear laws to
favor Czech interests.

Max (Prince) Lobkowicz (1888–1967) wrote to President Masaryk
in 1924 with an example of how this could unfold in practice. Lobkowicz described how a regional Land Office director (*vrchní rada*)
pressured him to replace the manager of his estates and his head for-
ester, who were both German, with Czechs. Lobkowicz's estates happened to lie in a highly contested area, the Bilina region of northern
Bohemia, in a district that was 65 percent German and 35 percent
Czech. Citing complaints from "Czech national defense organizations," the SPÚ director urged "necessary [national] changes in leading
positions as a precondition for negotiations over an agreement on the
extent of the planned land reform in 1924." As Lobkowicz noted in
frustration, "I know that the SPÚ can confiscate my whole estate up
to the legal maximum without being required to provide any particular
reasons."[101] Thus did the Land Office use the flexibility built into the
land reform law to effect its nationalizing policy.

These pro-Czech institutional biases cast doubt on the standard narrative of Czechoslovakia's model interwar democracy.[102] Although the
constitution of 1920 guaranteed individual rights and democratic representation to all citizens, subtle discrimination against national minorities pervaded state institutions. The founding ideology of the new
state enshrined the national principle above all others, including
equality. Seeking to legitimate their state in the eyes of Czech citizens

and the world, Czechoslovakia's founders defined the country through contrasts with the defeated Habsburg Empire. In order to erase the reputedly German, feudal, and antidemocratic legacy of the monarchy, state-builders instituted an informal program of affirmative action for Czechs at the expense of Germans.

Czechoslovakia's Germans in turn defined themselves as a group apart in Czechoslovak society, adopting the collective label of "Sudeten" Germans. "To the extent that there is a strong sense that the state belongs to or exists for the sake of a particular 'core' nation or nationality," Rogers Brubaker writes, minorities "excluded from this state-owning core nation will be more likely to define themselves oppositionally and contextually in national terms."[103] Through a series of minority treaties, the League of Nations only increased the chances that both majorities and minorities would think of their interests in primarily national terms.

In the late Habsburg era, Czechs and Bohemian Germans could think of themselves as either a majority or minority, depending on context. In Bohemia, Czechs were numerically dominant, while Germans made up only a third of the population. But Germans could identify with a wider German domination of the Austro-Bohemian core of the empire. Thus most prewar German nationalists had tempered their nationalism with a degree of imperial patriotism. For nobles, this tendency had been most pronounced among the German-oriented centralists in Bohemia, but it had also marked the complex identities of Bohemia's autonomist, Czech-leaning nobility in the late Habsburg Empire. For many Germans, and even more for nobles, the transition from empire to nation-state was particularly traumatic. An essential component of nobles' national identity, as they defined it, had simply disappeared, replaced by a middle-class nation-state that treated both Germans and nobles as national antagonists.

For nobles, the land reform became the fundamental reality of their new existence; their strategies for mitigating the reforms shaped their new national self-understandings and ultimately determined their loyalty or disloyalty to the Czechoslovak state. The arbitrary nature of the law and the flexibility it gave to the SPÚ actually invigorated the nobility, as nobles formed energetic lobbying organizations seeking to save their land. The Bohemian nobility had survived great trials before, in particular the religious wars of the 1400s and the 1600s, the dynastic struggles of the 1740s, and the great social reforms of the 1780s and 1848. But the cataclysm of the twentieth century—the national and social upheavals of 1918–1948—would be more dangerous than any of those earlier crises. Hoping to weather the revolution, nobles would now dip into the arsenals of the nationalists themselves.

~ 3

Nationalization of the Nobility: Noble Lobbying Strategies in the 1920s

> In a republic, only an association with a Czech leadership can
> prosper. One with a German tint is incapable of survival.
> ~ *Bedřich (Prince) Schwarzenberg, June 1919*

*T*HE YEAR 1918 was an unprecedented turning point
in the fortunes of the Bohemian nobility. All of the goals they had
pursued under the Habsburgs—centralism or federalism, maintenance of privileges, preservation of the monarchy—had disappeared, replaced by one overriding aim: to survive the Czechoslovak
land reform. The tools at their disposal had also changed. No
longer could they rely on a protected landowners' curia or hereditary representation in an upper house of parliament. Their ultimate
protector, the Habsburg Emperor, would soon be an exile in Madeira; the government institutions they had dominated were no
more. Their identity had lost its mooring, and nobles now lived
amid nation-states that were utterly alien to them.

After an initial disorientation, Bohemia's nobles (now shorn of
titles) began to find their bearings. In 1919, they formed lobbying
organizations to fight land reform and slowly learned how to negotiate the new institutions of the Czechoslovak nation-state. Many
nobles had considered themselves more imperial than the emperor
in the 1890s, but now they began to emphasize their national credentials. Many served up histories of Czechophilia in their families,
dredging their past for Czech sympathies in the Hussite and Thirty
Years' Wars. Other nobles, primarily those inclined to a German

identity, turned to the League of Nations and the minority treaties it had pressed on reluctant Czechoslovakia. Soon after the League's minority apparatus came together, German nobles began identifying themselves more closely with Czechoslovakia's German minority, in an effort to internationalize their campaign against land reform.

Both Czech and German nobles adopted national rhetorics, but these they grafted onto deeply rooted cosmopolitan and internationalist traditions. Nobles faced a dilemma under the New Order: adaptation was necessary to their survival as a distinct social group, but too much adaptation would erase their distinction. In the 1920s, German nobles nimbly embraced a hybrid nationalist-internationalist identity, which seemed to offer a favorable alternative to what Joseph Rothschild has called the "beggar-my-neighbor" nationalism of interwar nation-states.[1] In the 1930s, though, the promise of German internationalism would yield for many to the seductive imperialism of Hitler's expansionary Third Reich.

Foundation of Lobbying Organizations

With their political power largely destroyed after 1918, nobles turned their energies to an all-out defense of their property against land reform, to save "what could be saved" in the words of Bedřich (Prince) Schwarzenberg (1862–1936).[2] As the National Assembly debated the nature of the reform in early 1919, prominent nobles met in the Schwarzenberg Palace in Prague to discuss the creation of a landowners' defense organization. Two groups emerged from these talks, each with a distinct agenda: the Union of Czechoslovak Large Landowners (*Svaz československých velkostatkářů*) and the Association of German Large Landowners (*Verband der deutschen Grossgrundbesitzer*). The *Svaz*, the larger of the two groups, favored a policy of cooperation with the Czechoslovak state in the hope that loyalty would bring lenience. The *Verband* took a more confrontational position, intending to fight reform with all means available, including international pressure.

A Czech-German divide among landowners was already apparent

in early 1919. While negotiations over the formation of the *Svaz* were beginning in March 1919, Bohemian Germans still hoped that the Paris peace treaties would grant them autonomy or independence. When Bedřich Schwarzenberg urged Adolf (Count) Waldstein to recruit German landowners for the emerging *Svaz*, Waldstein complained that the group's insistence on using the Czech language would drive away potential supporters. "Especially in North Bohemia," he wrote, "so long as the borders there are not certain, there is still the hope [among German landowners] that they will not end up attached to the Czechoslovak Republic."[3] Even if the borderlands were to be included in Czechoslovakia, Waldstein objected to the *Svaz's* Czech emphasis. Instead of minority status in a Czech organization, he hoped for a binational "utraquist"[4] union that would represent all landowners equally, with equality of both the Czech and German languages in administration. This view, in fact, mirrored the emerging position of the German minority in Czechoslovakia: the claim that Czechoslovakia should be organized as a nationalities state—with no dominant nationality—like Switzerland, and not a national state like France.[5]

In spite of Waldstein's reservations, *Svaz* founders insisted that it be a statewide interest group, include Czechoslovak in its title, and use Czech as its official language. At first, some members opposed inviting Germans and Hungarians to join the group, as it could give non-Czechs a majority in the organization. "In a republic," Bedřich Schwarzenberg told a meeting of the *Svaz's* directorate in June, "only an association with a Czech leadership can prosper. One with a German tint is incapable of survival."[6] Other members, including Bedřich (Prince) Lobkowicz and Ervín Nádherný, pressed for a more inclusive policy, accepting all those "who will stand faithfully by the Republic." In the end, the *Svaz* issued a broad invitation to all landowners, regardless of nationality and political affiliation, to join. Even so, the *Svaz's* basic Czech character and acceptance of the Czechoslovak state were non-negotiable. In a letter to Franz Wien-Claudi, a lawyer representing a number of German landowners, the *Svaz* directorate wrote: "The *Svaz* readily accepts both Czech and German large landowners. Although the official language is Czech and the character of the *Svaz* remains that of a

Czech union, German issues are to be considered in German, as was the case in the last general assembly, and German members are to receive all written communications (statutes, circulars, etc.) in German."[7]

Not satisfied with the *Svaz's* linguistic concessions, German landowners formed their own *Verband* in September of 1919.[8] The goals of the *Verband*—moderation of land reform and full compensation for confiscated land—were at first similar to those of the *Svaz*, and the two groups cooperated through a joint Central Committee.[9] But by the early 1920s, they differed substantially over strategy, with the *Svaz* stressing a corporate approach and loyalty to the Czechoslovak state and the *Verband* emphasizing its German character and the discriminatory nature of land reform against Czechoslovakia's German minority.

Loyal Czech Opponents of Land Reform

The leaders of the *Svaz* took every opportunity to stress their members' loyalty to Czechoslovakia. On the one hand, they criticized land reform on the grounds that it would be economically harmful to the state and its citizens; on the other hand, they insisted that any reform be accompanied by fair compensation. Founded "to defend the common interests of large estates and to work towards the fulfillment of economic, social, and cultural tasks" facing estate owners, the *Svaz* was both a lobbying organization and an information clearing house.[10] Though the *Svaz* itself hardly ever couched its arguments in national terms, many of its members invoked their Czechness in appeals to the Land Office and President Masaryk for lenience in the land reform.

Though dominated by noble landowners, the *Svaz* was not an exclusively noble organization. The preparatory committee initially chose a non-noble, the National Democratic politician and industrialist F. Malínský, as the group's first chairman. Given the strength of anti-noble sentiment in 1919, the *Svaz* elected another non-noble, the former professor of agriculture Otto Metal, president of the new organization. But when Metal died in 1921, the dominant noble contingent in the *Svaz* was ready to assert itself more openly.

From 1921 to 1943 three Lobkowiczs—Bedřich (1881–1923), Leopold (1888–1933), and Jan (1885–1952)—presided, and Zdeněk (Count) Kolowrat (1881–1941) became the most important functionary.[11] Though close to half of the membership was non-noble, nobles effectively controlled the *Svaz* throughout its existence.

The Lobkowicz family had deep roots in Bohemia. Divided into four prominent branches, Lobkowiczs had been political and religious leaders since the Hussite wars of the fifteenth century. After the Habsburgs gained the Bohemian crown in 1526, the family served variously in the army, at court, and in the Catholic hierarchy. Lobkowiczs appeared on both sides of the revolt of the Bohemian Estates against the Habsburgs in 1618, but in the end, most members of the family expanded their estates in the aftermath of White Mountain. In the late nineteenth century, a number of Lobkowiczs were active in the Feudal Conservative Party and often defended Czech interests.[12] Bedřich Lobkowicz, the head of the Mělník branch of the family and second president of the *Svaz*, was known for his Bohemian and Czech patriotism. After Lobkowicz's untimely death in 1923, the acting *Svaz* president, Ervín Nádherný, called a special meeting of the directorate to remember Lobkowicz's contributions to the *Svaz* and to the nation. "The Czech nation lost a loyal son," he concluded, "who . . . always took the Czech side and stood up for the rights of our homeland."[13]

The *Svaz* began with a membership of 249 in 1919. The number of members rose to 292 as the land reform hit its stride in 1922, dropping gradually thereafter to a low of 210 in 1937. Just over half of the consistent membership belonged to high noble families. The remaining members came from a variety of backgrounds, including industrial families such as the Bartoň-Dobeníns and Daněks, successful Czech farmers such as the Bergmanns, and a few Jewish financiers. Many of these wealthy families were recent recipients of patents of nobility, but their smaller holdings and petty titles set them apart from the high noble leaders of the *Svaz*.[14]

Though the *Svaz* did not keep a record of the sworn nationality of its members, in 1929 around 70 percent requested the organization's Czech-language bulletin, 15 percent requested German, and 15 percent requested both Czech and German. This statistic says little about the nationality of members, however, because bulletins often went to estate managers instead of estate owners. Moreover, it does not distinguish between high nobility and other members. Research suggests that just over one-half of high noble members of the *Svaz* identified themselves as Czech, with the others claiming German nationality. Of 246 members in 1927, only 16 (7 percent) were also members of the German *Verband*. Almost all of these joint members were German-oriented landowners with the vast majority of their land in Czech regions of Bohemia.[15]

The high number of German nobles in the *Svaz* underscores its corporate, rather than national approach to fighting land reform. The use of "Czechoslovak" in the organization's title intentionally distanced the *Svaz* from a single national identification; both Moravia and Slovakia had their own landowner organizations, affiliates of the larger *Svaz*, further emphasizing territorial over national criteria for membership. Even so, the *Svaz* carried on its business in Czech, the state language, as an indication of its loyalty to Czechoslovakia. Members of the *Svaz* paid dues based on the number of hectares they owned, and in return they received a monthly bulletin with information on land reform, tax strategy, and much else of relevance to large-estate operation. It did not discriminate against its members on the basis of nationality.

The group's lobbying focused primarily on three power centers: President Masaryk and his Chancellery, the government's Ministerial Council, and the State Land Office. Though the president technically had no jurisdiction over legal and governmental matters, Masaryk had tremendous moral influence, which he exerted on the public through occasional speeches and on individual politicians in private audiences. The *Svaz* also appealed to the government via the Ministerial Council, which had little more direct influence on land reform than did Masaryk. The most powerful of the *Svaz*'s lobbying targets was the State Land Office, but it was also the least responsive to *Svaz* appeals. Because it stood outside of the government's ministries and was instead responsible directly to the National Assembly, the SPÚ had a tremendous amount of independence. Dominated as it was by Agrarians, who headed most of Czechoslovakia's interwar governments, the most effective influence on the SPÚ came via pressure on the Agrarian Party. Perhaps realizing Masaryk's symbolic position as the embodiment of the state, perhaps seeing in him an imperial figure of old, the *Svaz* directed most of its appeals to the presidential office, hoping that he could convince leading Agrarians to moderate the reform.

An early *Svaz* memorandum to President Masaryk in December 1920 outlined the arguments the group would use against land reform for much of the next decade.[16] Land reform itself was necessary, Bedřich Lobkowicz argued in the brief, but in the revolutionary situation of 1919, "demagogic agitation radicalized reform attempts" by politicizing them. A truly economic reform would be "evolutionary" and would be fair to all involved, including estate owners. The *zábor* (expropriation) law, which at this early date Lobkowicz interpreted as effectively a confiscation, reflected "a desire for revenge" against the nobility. In contrast with his German counterparts in the *Verband*, Lobkowicz rejected arguments that Bohemian nobles were victims of national discrimination. Instead he argued that the National Assembly had targeted the nobility as an estate, and thus he offered a generalized defense of the landowners as a corporate group without regard to nationality.

Most unjust, in Lobkowicz's view, and contrary to the basic principle of private property was the Assembly's decision to set compensation at the average price of land from 1913 to 1915. With wartime and postwar inflation taken into account, the result was a substantial undervaluation of property that would, according to the *Svaz*, amount to an outright confiscation. The arbitrary setting of prices below market values and the Land Office's tremendous flexibility in carrying out the law would undermine "the whole legal order" and could threaten the rule of law in all sectors of the young state. Lobkowicz argued elsewhere that land reform had already encouraged "demagogic agitation, rancor, hatred, and vengefulness," as revenge had been "incorporated into law."[17]

The *Svaz*'s central argument in the 1920 memorandum was that radical land reform would lower agricultural productivity and damage Czechoslovakia's economy. Since 1918, Lobkowicz claimed, "agricultural production is falling precariously year after year. The main cause of this fall is the uncertainty of property rights brought on by the land reform laws." The *zábor* law, he argued, gave the Land Office a "complete dictatorship over land," and it exercised its inordinate power "capriciously." Landowners had no incentive to improve or even maintain their property, because they would soon have to give it up for inadequate compensation. Looking farther into the future, the *Svaz* claimed that large estates, which had the benefit of an economy of scale, would yield to small, inefficient farms without the capital or know-how to produce for the mass market. The whole of Czechoslovakia, and not just landowners, would thus suffer the effects of an ill-conceived reform. The *Svaz* added in another memo three months later, "We must not allow a veiled confiscation of the property of a whole class of the population, which has through its rational management ensured the public food supply and provided an inestimable service for the prosperity of the national economy in our homeland *(vlast)*."[18]

To preserve the productivity and prosperity of Czechoslovak agriculture, the *Svaz* called for major changes in the land reform law. First, the government should depoliticize the Land Office by converting it to a ministry staffed by nonparty specialists. This would prevent Agrarians and Socialists from using land redistribution to reward or win supporters. Second, the SPÚ should publish its reform agenda for a ten-year interval, thus allowing landowners to plan accordingly. Third, forests should be removed from the reform entirely. The timber industry, for which Bohemia was renowned, would suffer by the parcelization of large forests, and confiscating nonarable land would not in any case alleviate land hunger. And fourth, compensation should be close to current market value and should reflect investments and improvements. "If these conditions are met," Lobkowicz concluded, "we intend to support the government not only in the implementation of land reform, but also in the construction of the state as a whole."[19]

With the state planning to take over vast expanses of forest in 1922, the *Svaz* added new arguments to its antireform arsenal. Above all, the forest reform would deprive nobles of the income they needed to maintain the historic castles, art collections, and nature parks in their possession.[20] This approach emerged from a clause in the land allotment *(přídělový)* law of January 1920, which authorized the Land Office to leave owners enough land to preserve "monuments of natural, historical, and artistic" importance.[21] As with the earlier *zábor* law, the *Svaz* looked for openings or inconsistencies in the law and stuck in a propagandistic wedge. Moreover, the *Svaz* claimed that state management of forests would be inefficient and smacked of Bolshevism.

For the first time too, the *Svaz* sounded a national note, suggesting that the forest confiscation appeared to aim primarily at German-owned estates in the borderlands. But in making this point, the *Svaz* memorandum did not claim discrimination, arguing only that the transfer of management of forests from German to Czech hands would "widen the gulf between the state and its non-Czechoslovak population."[22] This argument typically made a careful distinction between the *Svaz*'s Czechoslovak sympathies and the interests of the German minority. It was not in Czechoslovakia's interest, the 1922 memorandum suggested, to inflame German and international opinion.

On the whole, the *Svaz* denied that land reform discriminated against Germans. When the *London Times* sent the *Svaz* a questionnaire in early 1923 concerning discrimination, the directorate pointed out that "the land reform laws are aimed against the nobility . . . the members of which were considered on the whole to be aliens—Germans in the lands of the Bohemian Crown and Magyars in Slovakia. But Czech noble families have not been spared either." The *Svaz*'s response acknowledged the anti-German rhetoric of the Assembly's debate over land reform, but it claimed (inaccurately) that the Land Office had largely abandoned its colonization program.[23] The group's caution here appears to have been calculated to avoid inflaming Czech public opinion or alienating influential politicians.

The fate of estate employees (foresters, stewards, administrators) became another potent lobbying issue for the *Svaz* after a mob of Schwarzenberg employees accosted Land Office inspectors on the Netolice estate in January of 1922.[24] Though the Czech Agrarian and Socialist press attributed the altercation to a noble conspiracy, it was in fact a sign of deep unrest among the tens of thousands of Czechs who feared the loss of their jobs as foresters, managers, and laborers on large estates. "Employees of large estates are resisting land reform tooth and nail," the *Svaz* told the *London Times* in 1923. Fearful of losing their jobs, the *Svaz* asserted, many of these employees were turning to the Communist Party, and the government was doing little to help them.[25] By expressing solidarity with Czech estate employees, the *Svaz* aimed to strengthen its Czech credentials and to demonstrate that nobles were not the only victims of land reform.

Closely allied to the Czechoslovak *Svaz*, the Moravian Union of Large Landowners *(Svaz moravských velkostatkářů)* generally endorsed the *Svaz*'s strategy and arguments against land reform.[26] Its leaders kept a regular correspondence with *Svaz* secretary Zdeněk Kolowrat in Prague, sent representatives to major *Svaz* meetings, and jointly signed most memoranda to the President and government officials. Like the *Svaz*, the Moravian Union adopted a corporatist, Czechoslovak-loyal position and used the Czech language in its official correspondence. Even so, a sizable majority of its noble members identified themselves as German.

Overall, the Moravian Union emphasized its corporatism more than its Czechoslovak loyalty. In a concept memorandum drafted in the heat of the forest reform furor in the summer of 1922, the Union declared a need to "protect the rights of [our noble] estate ... which through the centuries was the bearer of a high civilization." Although the draft did not in any way link the Union to the German cause, it did support taking "our accusations before the forum of the international world." In a formulation that does not seem to have left the confines of inter-Union communications, it concluded that the landowning estate cannot "stand on the ground of the new state, if at the same time that very ground, in the truest sense of the word, is being pulled out from under our feet." In general, though, the Moravian Union was not as confrontational as the German *Verband*, preferring to stick to arguments in favor of private property and in opposition to discrimination against landowners as a corporate group.[27] Drawing on the traditions of the *Mittelpartei* of the late nineteenth century, culturally German Moravian nobles tended in the 1920s toward an alliance with the state and neutrality in national politics.

Though nobles aligned with the *Svaz* and the Moravian Union did not themselves enter politics, some did try to influence political parties with behind-the-scenes pressure and donations. Initially, the *Svaz* focused its lobbying on a group of conservative politicians from the National Democratic and Catholic People's parties, as well as the right ("large-estate owning") wing of the Agrarian Party. The *Svaz* corresponded regularly with the Agrarians Rudolf Beran (1887–1954) and Karel Prášek (1868–1932), and the group's leaders received special invitations to Agrarian and National Democratic events, where they had access to important political figures.[28] In 1924–1925 wealthy noble landowners bankrolled Prášek's break-away Conservative Agrarian Party, which ended up a spectacular failure in the 1925 elections.[29] The *Svaz* also maintained a secret political slush fund to reward Czech politicians who voted in the interests of estate owners.[30] This was one area where the *Svaz* and the German *Verband* found full cooperation, as the *Verband* funneled money from German landowners to the *Svaz*'s political account in order to ensure that "the people in the Czech parties who stand up for the protection of property are supported."[31]

The Prášek disaster left nobles wary of efforts to found a new political party in the future. In a *Svaz* internal memo from 1927, Zdeněk Kolowrat noted that "a noble-large landowner-conservative" party would require three things: a constituency, a newspaper, and talented political candidates. In his view, all three were lacking. The public still largely distrusted the nobility, despite some sympathy on the right for Christian conservatism. A newspaper would require tremendous expense, which landowners seemed unwilling to invest at present. And Kolowrat could think of few nobles who would flourish in Czechoslovakia's rough-and-tumble democratic politics. He thus ruled out the creation of a new party, "as such an attempt would have to end sooner or later, perhaps very soon, in a complete fiasco. It would only make the situation of the nobility and large landowners more difficult." Kolowrat urged politically minded nobles to participate in politics as individuals or behind the scenes. He believed the Agrarian Party was moving to the right, and it was not unreasonable to expect that "eventually we will get people from our circles into its leadership."[32]

The Deserved Rich: Narratives of Czech Loyalty

A number of individual noble members of the *Svaz* and the Moravian Union took expressions of loyalty to the Czech nation and state much farther than the *Svaz* itself, appealing to the president or the Land Office for lenience based on their families' long service to the Czech national cause. Playing on the popular rhetoric that portrayed land reform as the reversal of the historical verdict at White Mountain, many nobles stressed that their families had supported the Czech side in the seventeenth century and thus should not suffer in the present. In a typical formulation, the old Bohemian Deym family wrote in a memorandum to the SPÚ:

> After the Battle of White Mountain, the Deym family was afflicted with an almost complete confiscation of its property. . . . As far as land reform on our present estates is concerned, we ask that the above historical facts be taken into consideration so that our family might be spared confiscation.

The Deyms added the polite request that they receive first right of purchase should the Land Office decide to redistribute their pre–White Mountain estates, some of which were now "in the hands of foreigners."[33]

Like the Deyms, the Šliks (Schliks) were of old Bohemian stock, a fact they hoped to use to save what they could of their property. In November 1923, František (Count) Šlik (1854–1925), delivered a memorandum to the Presidential Chancellery with a history of the family's service to the Czech nation since the Hussite wars of the fifteenth century. "The Šliks," the memorandum noted, "have played an honorable and outstanding role in the history of the Czech nation and state since the beginning of the 15th century." In 1415, the family had protested the execution of the Czech religious reformer Jan Hus. Again in 1620, the Šliks pointed out, their ancestors had fought on the Czech side and paid a high price: "The post–White Mountain confiscations almost completely ruined the Šlik line." As land reform now aimed to rectify post–White Mountain injustices . . . it would be fitting and just if the Šlik family were left at least their current estates, when they already sacrificed such an enormous majority of their land in the defense of freedom and in the interests of the Czech state.[34]

In this remarkable defense, the Šliks fully identified themselves with the Czech nation and pledged their support to Czechoslovakia as the inheritor of historical Czech (Bohemian) statehood.[35]

Claims of sincere Czechness appear repeatedly in Presidential Chancellery files devoted to nobles. In 1925 and 1926, Jaroslav (Prince) Lobkowicz (1877–1953) of the Křimice line of the family visited the Chancellery to complain of the low prices the Land Office was paying him, a travesty in light of the fact that "his family has always been Czech."[36] The Lobkowiczs had also long been known as good Catholics and Habsburg loyalists, of course, but typically, they formed their contemporary identity from the parts of their family history that suited them.

Ulrich Ferdinand (Prince) Kinsky (1893–1938), who would be described by a British spy in 1938 as a "fanatical" German, wrote of his great-grandfather's friendship with Palacký and ties to the Czech Revival.[37] He pointed out his own donations to the Czech gymnastics organization *Sokol* and his continued "support of Czech general public interests," concluding with the humble request that Masaryk intervene with the Land Office to head off the upcoming confiscation of forests on his north Bohemian estate.[38] Kinsky, who owned thousands of hectares in both Czech and German regions, kept a foot in both national camps, and he held memberships in both the *Svaz* and the *Verband*. His Czech strategy may have helped him preserve his 10,000 ha estate in the German district of Böhmische Kamnitz (Česká Kamenice). Perhaps preferring that this land stay in the hands of a (supposed) Czech rather than revert to local Germans, the SPÚ left Kinsky all but a few hundred hectares.[39]

Many other nobles regularly used evidence of more recent Czech loyalties in attempts to defend their land from confiscation. The Deyms, for example, included in their 1919 memorandum an excerpt from the history of the Czech National Theater, to which their ancestors had contributed. In his 1881 history, František Šubert recounted a speech by Bedřich Count Deym (1801–1853) in which he made clear his "sympathy to Czech national efforts."[40] Taking a different tack, the Schwarzenberg primogeniture, which had ruled over tens of thousands of hectares of southern Bohemia since the 1660s, emphasized the family's continual investment of resources into both the land and the people of its territory. Long before the arrival of the welfare state, the Schwarzenbergs had elaborate pension funds and social services. They were, a 1923 memorandum claimed, among the most progressive of European landowners in the nineteenth century. Without claiming an exclusive Czech identity (as the secundogeniture did), the Schwarzenberg primogeniture noted the family's contributions to the Czech *Sokol*, Czech schools, and hospitals. Neither beneficiaries of White Mountain confiscations nor oppressors of the Czech people, the brief concluded, they had run their estates responsibly and hoped to continue to do so.[41]

The director of the Harrach estate in central Bohemia (Jilemnice) wrote to the president to bring attention to the old Bohemian family's recent and sincere Czech patriotism. The dedication of Jan (Count) Harrach (1828–1896) to the Czech cause was so pronounced, the director wrote, that the emperor refused to confirm his election as mayor of his hometown in 1875 (and for the same reason denied him the Order of the Golden Fleece until he was near death in 1896). The letter also lauded Harrach's service to Czechs in Vienna, where he championed Czech-language schools for Czech immigrants. Harrach's son Otto, it went on, had continued his father's philanthropic tradition, donating over 400,000 crowns to Czech charities from 1918 to 1925.[42]

When "former Baroness" Hildprandt paid a visit to the Presidential Chancellery at the Prague Castle in 1925, she complained that the Land Office's current treatment of her family was "a disgrace" to a family that "from time immemorial was always Czech and was persecuted under Austria for its Czech radical sympathies." Her husband had "taken the severity of the land reform to heart, such that she worried about his mental state." She asked that the president intervene with the Land Office so that she and her husband might be permitted to keep what remained of their forests. She also hoped to sell the family's expensive furniture and porcelain to pay back taxes, and she wondered whether President Masaryk's recently married son Jan would be interested. Though the president's chancellor, Přemysl Šámal (1867–1941), could not speak for young Masaryk, he did offer to intervene with the SPÚ on account of Baron Hildprandt's service to the Czech cause.[43]

The chancellor was perhaps less inclined to help Leopold (Count) Berchtold (1863–1942), the Austro-Hungarian Foreign Minister in 1914. In a 1921 letter, Berchtold urged President Masaryk, in diplomatic French, to put aside the memory of Berchtold's unfortunate role in the outbreak of the Great War and take into account his family's long "solidarity with the [Czech] nation." His parents and grandparents had done the nation an inestimable service by sponsoring poor Czech students at the university and by investing the revenues from their estates locally. His son, the inheritor of the 400-year-old family estate at Buchlov in Moravia, loyally served in the Czechoslovak army after 1918. He asked Masaryk to help his son save the family estate, to intervene with the authorities to find "an equitable solution."[44]

All of these personal appeals to the president and the Land Office were premised on the assumption among nobles that good Czech credentials mattered in the land reform. Those who could, mined their family history for evidence of victimization after White Mountain, of ties to the Czech national movement, or of support for Czech social and national causes. The appeals also reflected the degree of arbitrary flexibility in the land reform law; the president's denials notwithstanding, personal intervention by either the president, his son Jan, or other influential officials could be, or was seen to be, decisive in many individual cases. Given the perceived national biases of the whole Czechoslovak state apparatus, *Svaz* members often couched their appeals in a national rhetoric.

This raises the question of the sincerity of noble national identifications in the 1920s. Some nobles, such as Ulrich Kinsky, opportunistically claimed Czech loyalties that they would later repudiate. Others, including Leopold Berchtold, professed a Czech orientation in their appeals, but they did little else to confirm that loyalty. Before the First World War, many of these nobles had a clear German cultural orientation, but they had resisted national identifications. When a French friend had asked Berchtold his nationality at Karlsbad in 1909, Berchtold had replied that he was Viennese. Pressed on how he would side in national conflicts, he responded, "The side of the Emperor." And if the empire were gone? "I would remain . . . an aristocrat."[45] Berchtold was certainly still an aristocrat, but he was also now claiming a Czech identity. Even so, he lived abroad and gave no indication in the future of Czech loyalties. Like Kinsky, we have to conclude that his appeal to Masaryk was not only opportunistic, but also disingenuous.

But opportunism did not necessarily imply deception. Most of the other petitioners would in fact remain loyal to Czechoslovakia throughout the interwar period, and many would sign declarations of loyalty to the Czech nation and state in 1938 and 1939. Without speculating on the personal meanings these nobles attached to their loyalties, it can nonetheless be concluded that their Czech identifications were sincere. As shown in chapter 4, many Czech-loyal nobles would profess an outright Czech nationalism by the 1930s.

Given the emerging Czech-German polarities among nobles in the 1920s, it is worth considering how individual families chose their national loyalties. All nobles in Bohemia spoke German fluently and most had participated in the culturally German court and high-political culture of the late monarchy. Predictably, 73 percent of Bohemian and Moravian nobles identified themselves as German in interwar Czechoslovakia.[46] Several factors pushed the other 27 percent in a Czech direction. Most significant, though not decisive, were native roots in Bohemia. Of the native families, who made up one-third of the total noble families in the Bohemian lands, 56 percent identified themselves as Czech. If we isolate the natives with prewar Feudal Conservative Party allegiance, the proportion shoots up to 83 percent Czech. Immigrant roots and Constitutionally Loyal Party membership, on the other hand, tend to predict a German identification, though a few pre-1620 immigrants, like the Conservative Schwarzenbergs, sided with the Czech camp.[47]

A final correlation of interest is that between location of estates and nationality. Of those identifying with the Czechs, 83 percent held land primarily in Czech-inhabited regions.[48] Only 15 percent of Czech nobles had estates in mixed zones, or separate estates in both Czech and German regions. Only a single Czech noble had land in German areas alone. Contrary to one recent interpretation, the majority of German nobles did not own estates in primarily German territory; indeed, 53 percent had their estates concentrated in primarily Czech districts.[49] Only 20 percent owned estates in German areas alone, whereas 27 percent had estates in both Czech and German regions or in bi-ethnic areas. These numbers suggest that Czech national identification required a connection to "Czech soil" and the "Czech people" (to use terms that nobles themselves used), whereas a German identification did not imply a similar root-edness in a German-speaking region. Although there were many cases of nobles in the Sudetenland who would invoke their connection to "German soil," the majority with land in Czech regions drew their German identification from a less localized conception of Germanness.

The Fruits and Frustrations of Loyalty

In spite of their Czech loyalties, some members of the *Svaz* became disillusioned with the *Svaz*'s efforts and with Czech good faith as the land reform rolled into a third wave of redistributions in 1924. Between 1923 and 1925, membership dropped from 280 to 233. Antonín Kubačák attributes the drop to three factors: disappointment of individual landowners over the *Svaz*'s failure to protect their land, the completion of reform on some estates, and the release of other estates from *zábor*.[50] The *Svaz* blamed its decline in membership on a failure to convince landowners released from *zábor* that the *Svaz* was still useful to them as an advisory organization. Perhaps too, many medium-sized estate owners realized that the Land Office intended to spare most estates under 1,000 ha, thus obviating the need for membership in a large landowner defense organization. Finally, the *Svaz* noted that "several German large landowners, who have until now been members of both unions of large landowners [*Svaz* and *Verband*], have decided for the purposes of decreasing overhead to remain as members only in the organization that is nationally closer to them."[51] The *Svaz's* report might also have added that the *Verband's* increasingly close identification with Czechoslovakia's German minority brought it into conflict with the *Svaz's* policy of Czechoslovak loyalty.

Beyond these technical reasons for the decline of membership, there was also a wider disappointment with the Czechoslovak government's seeming indifference toward the interests of large landowners—both Czech and German—in the mid-1920s. When an estate manager wrote urging the *Svaz* to participate in celebrations of the tenth anniversary of the Republic in 1928, the longtime general secretary of the group, Zdeněk Kolowrat, poured out his frustrations with the land reform in a bitter response. "Large estate owners, in particular the nobility, do not have the least reason to participate in ostentatious celebrations," he wrote. "[The nobility] is the single element of this state's citizenry that does not enjoy equal rights in our 'democratic' republic." Nobles were the targets of laws intended "to destroy" them as a class and were the objects of persistently hostile rhetoric and historical distortions. "The nobility as a corporate group," he added, "has no intention of celebrating the ten-year survival of the republic." Kolowrat felt he could speak the truth, because "I am not an ex post facto (*popřevratový*) Czech. I come from a Czech family whose own history has been tied to Czech history for 600 years." Like many others among the nobility, he grew up with a strong "love for the homeland (*vlast*)," a love that "was being deadened" by the circumstances of the last ten years. He concluded his "purely private manifestation" by angrily refusing to celebrate anything unless the *Svaz's* opinions received more understanding from the Czechs.[52]

The recipient of this uncharacteristically intemperate letter, Josef Sekanina, responded immediately and with some understanding. He agreed that land reform had inflicted upon nobles a series of "wrongs," aimed even against "Czech noble families tightly bound with the history of the Czech lands." Even so, he suggested, "Today, when a direct path hardly ever leads to the desired goal, an expression of loyalty" may be necessary "for tactical reasons." He then politely added that a scholarship fund for forestry students might serve the

Svaz's purposes well.[53] The exchange between Kolowrat and Sekanina is remarkable for two reasons. First, it indicates a hidden frustration many Czechoslovak-loyal nobles in the *Svaz* must have felt. In spite of all their lobbying and expressions of support for Czechoslovakia, land reform rolled on. Second, in Sekanina's response we find a reminder of the *Svaz's* general strategy of tactical Czechness— which apparently deserted Kolowrat in a moment of weakness. From its creation, the *Svaz* kept pounding away on the theme of loyalty; given the rhetoric surrounding the birth of land reform and the nature of the Land Office's petty discrimination, *Svaz* leaders considered a Czech policy to be the best way to "save what could be saved."

Many in the *Svaz* believed, with good reason, that their loyalty to the state was bearing fruit. Since the early 1920s, *Svaz* criticisms of land reform had begun creeping into President Masaryk's speeches. In his 1922 New Year's speech, Masaryk acknowledged that "large-scale production has its advantages in agriculture as in industry." He added that state ownership of land was undesirable, both because it would "undermine individual initiative" and because the state was not prepared to manage large estates. He also criticized the current uncertainty in property relations, which "was losing the state millions." Drawing almost verbatim from the *Svaz's* memoranda, Masaryk insisted that "the Land Office must be depoliticized." On the whole, Masaryk believed, land reform was necessary, but its execution had been flawed.[54] The director of the State Land Office, Viškovský, confirmed to Leopold Lobkowicz in 1923 that President Masaryk was pressing him to resolve cases "in favor of large landowners."[55]

Though never depoliticized, the Land Office did moderate both its tone and program after its initial flurry of confiscations in 1921. It paid particular attention to maintaining production, protecting natural and historical monuments, and ensuring that estate employees were not left jobless by reform.[56] Once pressure for a radical reform died down after the consolidation of Czechoslovakia by the early 1920s, the SPÚ became far more inclined to leave substantial estates, and forests in particular, in the hands of their original owners. "The reform was revolutionary in its origin," the Land

Office's Antonín Pavel wrote for an American audience in 1930, "but is soundly conservative in its results."[57] Land Office statistics largely confirm Pavel's claim. In 1934, large landowners still controlled just over half of the 4 million hectares originally under *zábor* in Czechoslovakia.[58] Landowners were also quietly pleased that the Land Office often set compensation higher than the law required. If one adds in the general recovery of the value of the Czech crown, the reform results were not nearly as dire as the *Svaz* had predicted in 1920. By the 1930s, many *Svaz* members believed their Czech loyalties had paid off, preserving more than half of their property and at least a modicum of influence in public life.

Playing the Sudeten German Card

The German *Verband* too chose a national path that led its members to a more aggressive nationalism than they had ever entertained before the war. But this outcome was not preordained, as the *Verband* began by sharing the *Svaz's* tactics and arguments, sometimes even using direct translations of *Svaz* propaganda material. The widening scope of land reform in the early 1920s, however, and the emergence of the League of Nations' minority system combined to turn the *Verband's* efforts in an increasingly national direction.

Just as in the *Svaz*, nobles dominated the *Verband's* leadership. The founding trio of Eugen (Count) Ledebur-Wicheln (1873–1945), Adolf (Count) Waldstein-Wartenberg (1868–1930), and Wilhelm (von) Medinger (1878–1934) were all nobles from north Bohemia. Of the three, Waldstein bore the most distinguished family name, shared by the great General Albrecht Wallenstein (Waldstein) of the Thirty Years' War. In spite of their illustrious ancestor's ignoble death at the hands of Habsburg assassins in 1634, the Waldsteins had managed to hold on to tens of thousands of hectares of prime agricultural and forest land in linguistically mixed north-central Bohemia. Though the family's pre–White Mountain roots gave it one of the oldest Czech lineages in Bohemia, Adolf Waldstein identified himself as German and made no pretences to having supported Czech interests during the nineteenth century. After the death of his brother Ernst in 1913, Adolf had taken over the family seat in the Austrian *Herrenhaus,* where he represented the Constitutional Loyalists.

Ledebur, who owned 2,600 ha in predominantly German Bilina, was known as an energetic politician and speechmaker and took the lead in the *Verband.* Tracing his noble roots only to the seventeenth century, Ledebur was nonetheless born a count and came from a family of Bohemian politicians. Though his grandfather had been a Constitutional Loyalist, Ledebur's father Johann (1842–1903) had made a career representing the Conservative Party in the Austrian Upper House. Johann had considered himself a German, but he had also opposed German national parties, which he thought overreacted to the perceived Czech threat. In a typical formulation, Johann announced in an 1884 speech that he was German in culture but "Czech in the political meaning of the word."[59] His son Eugen studied law at Prague's German university, and in 1920 he became a leading member of Czechoslovakia's German Christian Social People's Party.[60]

Medinger, whose industrialist father was ennobled only in 1903, owned a 1,300 ha estate in the Czech district of Železný Brod. Along with Ledebur, he became the *Verband's* chief propagandist. Before the war, Medinger had been a Constitutional representative in the Bohemian Diet, where he was known as a close ally of Josef Maria Baernreither and Ernst von Plener. He was a leading member of the *Deutschböhmen* separatists in 1918, but he later joined the German National Party and served in the Czechoslovak National Assembly. Increasingly close to the activist (state-supporting) wing of the Sudeten German political spectrum, he joined Ledebur's Christian Socials in 1925. Throughout the 1920s he was active in a number of international German cultural and political organizations.[61]

Until 1921 the *Verband's* efforts largely paralleled those of the *Svaz,* with both groups sending petitions to the State Land Office, the president, and government ministries. The *Verband,* when not simply jointly signing *Svaz* memoranda, used many of the same arguments found in *Svaz* propaganda. First and foremost, as the *Verband's* founding manifesto argued in December 1919, the land reform was a threat to the economic well-being of the state. The *zábor* law left property relations uncertain, a "Damocles sword" hanging over the head of landowners and discouraging them from investing in improvements. By breaking up large estates, the reform would surely hurt agricultural productivity, the exact opposite of the government's stated goal of lowering food imports and increasing timber exports.

Second, the land reform would have "an anti-social effect" by destroying the livelihood of thousands of estate employees.[62] Third, land hunger was a chimerical product of the war and the revolutionary mood of 1918–1919. In reality, there were not many farmers in need of land, and only the largest latifundia needed reform. Fourth, confiscation with minimal compensation was akin to stealing land from private owners, and such an approach would undermine the rule of law. Furthermore, it would discourage foreign investors by casting into doubt the security of private property. As *Verband* leader Eugen Ledebur summed up the group's arguments in early 1920, the land reform law, if carried out as planned, would "not only seriously damage this state economically, but even worse, it would make it the laughingstock of the world."[63]

Representing German large landowners, *Verband* leaders did mention the national aspect of the land reform, but before 1922 this was primarily as an afterthought. In language reminiscent of Constitutionally Loyal rhetoric a decade earlier, the group's founding memorandum expressed (on page four) sympathy for German "comrades *(Volksgenossen)*" and opposition to any program of "inner colonization" leading to a "forceful change of the national structure of the state."[64] Ledebur also complained elsewhere that Germans were not represented in either the Revolutionary National Assembly, which had passed the land reform law, or in the State Land Office.[65] But until 1922, national rhetoric remained muted in *Verband* public manifestations. In a speech on land reform in the Assembly in late 1920, Medinger, soon to be the most vocal opponent of discrimination against Germans, hardly mentioned the national question at all.[66] As late as April 1921, the *Verband* sent the Ministry of Agriculture a memorandum that simply reproduced in German a similar petition the *Svaz* had sent the ministerial council three weeks before.[67]

Differences in strategy emerged later in 1921, however, with Medinger arguing for the internationalization of the land reform issue through propaganda in England and elsewhere.[68] With a massive forest confiscation plan in the works in 1922, the *Verband* called an emergency meeting in July to discuss possible responses. Ledebur introduced the meeting by declaring that "the war of extermination *(Vernichtungskampf)* against large landowners has become acute" and that defense efforts must be intensified. Medinger outlined a two-pronged counterattack the *Verband* would use. First, the *Verband* would attempt to tie the cause of large landowners to that of Sudeten-Germandom as a whole. "The German nation has already recognized" he argued, "that the threat to German large landowners is at the same time a threat to Germans' national, *völkisch* existence." Second, the *Verband* would use its identification with Sudeten Germans to propagandize internationally. Through two German organizations, *Völkerbund* and *Völkerbundliga*, the *Verband* would "bring our just struggle before the international forum. . . . We shall not neglect any foreign political means at our disposal."[69]

The Czech *Svaz* steadfastly resisted efforts of the *Verband* to draw it into Medinger's national strategy. In response to the *Verband*'s 1922 change of direction, both Jan Lobkowicz and Zdeněk Kolowrat insisted that the *Svaz* must "rule out politics and the national approach and generate only topical and specialized propaganda."[70] In an argument in 1927 over letting Germans represent the *Svaz* at an agricultural congress in Rome, Lobkowicz repeated his reservations: "Defense against land reform in the international field is possible from two points of view, that of the violation of private ownership and that of defense of minorities." By sending Germans to international congresses, he argued, the *Svaz* would only antagonize the Czechoslovak government and give the *Svaz*'s enemies "a dangerous weapon, such that they could show that all large landowners in Czechoslovakia are Germans." He insisted that the *Svaz* not be associated with any lobbying based on nationality.[71]

Nonetheless, the *Verband* took its minority rights case to international forums without the *Svaz*'s help. Working through Medinger's *Völkerbundliga*, the *Verband* began preparing a series of petitions to the League of Nations. Medinger delivered the first official complaint on behalf of German landowners to the League in September 1922. Land reform was in direct violation of Czechoslovakia's minority treaty, the petition argued, because it treated members of a minority differently from those of the majority.[72] Though the land reform law avoided discriminatory language, its intent was clearly anti-German. In its implementation, the law was not "directed at large estate owners as such, but far more against only those large land owners who are not members of the majority nation."[73] More specifically, the land reform laws aimed at the "expulsion of Germans" from certain regions through the "redistribution of confiscated German land to Czech colonists and especially through the nationalization of German border forests." The petition urged the League to intervene to stop the State Land Office from continuing this conscious policy of "denationalization."[74]

The *Völkerbundliga*'s 1922 complaint tied the land reform to a general discrimination of the Czechoslovak government against Germans in a range of fields, including education, finance, and the bureaucracy. "A gloomy feeling of powerless despair has seized our co-nationals *(Volksgenossen)*," the petition lamented, "now that they are also to be forcefully driven off of their ancestral land."[75] The petition offered scores of quotations from Czech sources—including the National Assembly, newspapers, and public officials—betraying the national impetus of the reform. Using a vocabulary common to German nationalists in the late nineteenth century, Medinger wrote of a threat to German "national assets" *(Nationalvermögen)* and "national property" *(nationaler Besitzstand)*.[76] The petition appended a resolution from the German town of Graslitz repeating the point that land was vital to German national survival: "The attack on the German homeland *(Heimat)* will push the whole German population to unanimous resistance, because our German *Volk* is inseparably bound to its land and its forests."[77] This kind of rhetoric became typical, both in future communications to the League of Nations and in *Verband* propaganda at home and abroad.[78] With its new national strategy Medinger and the *Verband* sought to tie the fate of German nobles to that of the German minority as a whole in Czechoslovakia.

The *Völkerbundliga* thus became an important international lob-

bying organization for both noble landowners and the German minority more broadly. It counted as members prominent German
nobles such as Ledebur, Max Egon Fürstenberg, Karl Buquoy, Alain
Rohan, and Adolf Schwarzenberg.[79] Other than Medinger, the most
active Bohemian noble was Alfons (Prince) Clary-Aldringen (1887–
1978), who eventually served as president of the group after 1937.
The Clary family was originally from Tuscany and acquired its Bohemian estates through purchase in 1623, during the redistribution
of White Mountain confiscations. In the late nineteenth century,
the Clarys were active Constitutional Loyalists. Alfons Clary's uncle
Manfred (1852–1928) was Austrian Prime Minister just long
enough to nullify the Badeni Language Ordinances in 1899. Alfons
Clary inherited over 8,000 ha in the predominantly German region
around Teplitz (Teplice), and he also owned a famous spa in the
town of Teplitz itself. Clary was a noted internationalist, with a
host of contacts and friends in England. As early as 1921, German
political parties, and in particular Ledebur, looked to Clary as a
propagator of the Czechoslovak German cause in London and kept
him supplied with statistics relating to German minority complaints.[80]

Clary used this information to good effect, winning support from
a number of British aristocrats for the Sudeten Germans, including
Lord Henry Bentinck, who offered to spread the word "among the
Labour, Liberal and other centers of public opinion in England, as
well as among the League of Nations." Another contact, Sir Felix
Doubleday, arranged for Clary to meet with representatives of the
British Foreign Office.[81] Clary also managed, through the help of
Adalbert Sternberg, to win the ear of the new owner of the *New
York Herald*, Frank Munsey.

On the advice of Munsey's lawyer, Samuel Untermayer, Bohemian
German nobles formed a private committee in September 1922 to
seek support of "gentlemen in the West with big names."[82] Their
plan was to get English and American "big capital" to complain about
the Czechoslovak land reform, because, as Sternberg put it, "The
Czech politicians are aware that without English-American credit,
the economy will not function."[83] Sternberg became the group's un-
official organizer and spokesman, and prominent members included

Alfons Clary-Aldringen, n.d. (probably 1920s). SOA Litoměřice (Děčín) RA
Clary-Aldringen, k 765

Adolf Waldstein, Otto Czernin (1875–1962), the brother of the
former foreign minister of Austria-Hungary, Ulrich and Franz
Kinsky, and Clary-Aldringen.[84] Though they approached the *Svaz*
to request support, *Svaz* leaders were skeptical. "I can't tell the Czech
Svaz [our real goal]," Sternberg wrote to Karel Belcredi of the Moravian Union, "because that would evoke misgivings among the various Lobkowiczs."[85]

After 1921, Medinger, Clary, and Ledebur regularly gave speeches
at home and abroad raising complaints over land reform and treatment of the German minority in Czechoslovakia. Skillfully mar-

shalling the Wilsonian rhetoric of self-determination, Medinger's speeches portrayed the Sudeten Germans as a beleaguered minority that, denied their fatherland, only sought autonomy and linguistic rights on the Swiss model. Land reform was the most prominent of many national injustices: "The socialization practices which have penetrated into Czechoslovakia from Russia, give a lever to the Czechs for open and disguised national oppression. . . . The Czechs, abusing their political preponderance, have encroached upon German national property." Germans, Medinger declared in 1922, had faith in the League of Nations, refusing "to consider it a humbug intended only to nourish fallacious hopes among the national minorities." He urged the League to act to fulfill its mandate to protect minorities, before "radical and desperate elements on both sides are strengthened."[86]

Ledebur sounded a similar note, arguing that the land reform violated international law, as defined in the minority treaties, by discriminating against Czechoslovakia's Germans. "Nation and land are inseparable concepts," he wrote in a 1925 article titled "Land Reform and International Law." He added that confiscation of a minority's landed property *(Besitzstand)* was equivalent to an attack on its very existence. The land reform violated Czechoslovakia's minority treaty in two ways: by targeting German landowners for confiscation and by favoring Czech farmers for redistribution. As an egregious example of the former, Ledebur cited the 1923 forest reform, which had affected thirty-three minority owners and only two Czechs. The Land Office's colonization policy was, Ledebur wrote, evidence of an anti-German bias in the parcelization process. Taken together, the two policies were shrinking substantially the amount of land in German hands. "The hopeless political situation of the national minorities offers no possibility of a parliamentary defense," he complained. "Only international law, in its latest form, the minority treaty, offers the possibility of an effective remedy."[87]

Ledebur also voiced complaints of foreign landowners that the land reform law violated provisions of the Paris treaties guaranteeing their property rights in all Habsburg successor states. All told, twenty-nine Bohemian and Moravian estate owners were citizens of Germany, and at least twenty-seven were citizens of Austria.[88] Combined, German and Austrian citizens owned a total of 436,000 ha in Czechoslovakia when land reform began in 1919.[89] Ledebur argued that the land reform discriminated against foreign landowners as both members of minorities and as citizens of states other than Czechoslovakia.

The *Verband*'s international strategy did bring some rewards. First, *Verband* memoranda to the League of Nations forced the Land Office to take particular care to avoid the appearance of discrimination. Following the first wave of German petitions, the Ministry of Foreign Affairs urged the SPÚ to keep careful statistics on the nationality of both owners and recipients of confiscated land and to be prepared to present these data to the League in the future.[90] Second, leading Czech diplomats urged the SPÚ to go easy on nobles who were influential abroad. Jan Masaryk, the son of the president and ambassador to London, wrote to the president's chancellor, Přemysl Šámal, in 1928 requesting that the SPÚ give special treatment to Max Hohenlohe, Clary-Aldringen, and the Metternich family because of "their wide-ranging international connections."[91] All three did relatively well by the land reform, retaining far more of their land than did the average large landowner. Other vocal German landowners, such as Ledebur and Medinger, also received favorable settlements. In a number of cases too, the Land Office was willing to pay higher prices for land in order to get foreign landowners to retract lawsuits in international courts.[92] The Czech *Svaz* commented incredulously, "We will become witnesses of a case, hitherto unknown in history, where a state treats its own citizens worse than foreigners."[93]

Overall, though, the Land Office defended itself vigorously against accusations of bias against minorities. To refute German petitions to the League of Nations, the SPÚ provided the Ministry of Foreign Affairs with statistics showing substantial German gains in the initial phase of reform that transferred land to long-term leaseholders.[94] This was somewhat deceptive, because the Land Office had far more flexibility on subsequent redistributions and regularly favored Czech applicants over Germans. In an internal memorandum from the late 1920s, the SPÚ summarized "certain tactics from the national point of view" that it had adopted to reassure the

League of Nations while at the same time facilitating the "expansion of Czech landholdings on the whole territory of the state." The key to the strategy was to keep to the letter of the minority treaty by avoiding legal discrimination against Germans or Hungarians, but to target non-Czechs through administrative methods that fell within the law. As the Czech representatives to the League argued repeatedly, it was not their fault that the majority of large landowners in Bohemia and Moravia were Germans. Their position, the memorandum concluded, had the "full confidence of influential actors in the League of Nations," and, indeed, the League's minority council consistently ruled in favor of Czechoslovakia, when not refusing to consider German petitions outright.[95]

Even though the League did not intervene in favor of Germans on the land reform issue, or on any issue for that matter, the very existence of the minority guarantees nationalized the *Verband's* self-defense strategy. With little recourse inside Czechoslovakia, German nobles found a platform for their grievances in Geneva. And access to that platform required that they appear as German as possible. By the mid-1920s, there was a more unrestrainedly nationalist rhetoric than ever before among the German nobles of Bohemia. In the 1930s this would, for many, devolve in a *völkisch*/fascist direction, until "national property" had transformed into *Lebensraum* (living space) and borderland estates into the ancestral forests of Germania. The formerly Habsburg-loyal Bohemian nobles seemed unlikely suspects to embrace the populist demagoguery of the fascists, but the anti-German animus of the land reform and the League's institutions for minority grievances turned many of the more prominent German nobles toward nationalism.

Ideologist of German Internationalism: Karl Anton Rohan

German internationalism, the notion of German interests represented on a Europe-wide basis, was the key to the transition many nobles made from a Habsburg imperial loyalty to a strong German nationalism. One of the most prominent German internationalists was the Austrian publicist and former Bohemian noble, Karl Anton

Prince Rohan (1898–1975). He in many ways represented a new, post-Habsburg generation of the nobility, unwilling to dwell upon imperial nostalgia, but at the same time wary of majoritarian democracy. Intrigued by fascism's combination of conservative values and boundless energy, he also expressed a distaste for its love of violence and national chauvinism. Rohan's writings ranged from politics to minority rights to pacifism. He was in many senses a European, but a German European, and his pan-Europeanism reflected a desire to tear down walls that divided Germans in the new Europe of nation-states and national minorities. In this way, he shared the goals of his friends Wilhelm Medinger and Eugen Ledebur, who sought to internationalize the Czechoslovak land reform issue by internationalizing the German question. All these men hoped for some form of European unity in which German cultural, economic, and political interests could be protected.

Rohan's interest in the minority question stemmed from his early years spent at the family's north Bohemian chateau Sychrov, which lay not far from the Czech-German linguistic divide. The Rohans were an unusually cosmopolitan family, even by Bohemian standards. Before 1789, it had been one of the oldest and most powerful French noble families, with ties at court so intimate that Rohans were often called "cousins of the king."[96] For the French revolutionaries, the Rohans' relations with the monarchy were far too close, and in 1791 they fled to Austria with a wave of émigré nobles hoping to defeat the Revolution from abroad. With Napoleon firmly entrenched in France, Charles-Alain Rohan (1764–1836), now an Austrian Field Marshal, settled his family in Bohemia in 1808. Like many émigrés, the Rohans became fierce Habsburg loyalists and adopted the German language and culture as their own, albeit modified by a cosmopolitanism common among Bohemian nobles in the nineteenth century. Karl Anton Rohan's father, Prince Alain Rohan (1853–1914), was a prominent Constitutional Loyalist, member of the Austrian *Herrenhaus*, and bearer of the esteemed Golden Fleece.[97] By then, the family was thoroughly Central European—Karl Anton's grandmother was a Waldstein, and his mother was an Auersperg—such that a short biography in 1930 claimed he bore a "mix of the blood of many nations."[98]

His mixed background made him an internationalist, but a proudly German one, as he argued that true Europeanism could only rest on solidly national foundations. "The strongest ethical forces of the European nations stand behind the national ideal," he wrote in an early issue of his journal devoted to European unity, the *Europäische Revue*. For a nation to be ready to embrace Europe, it had to have a healthy national self-confidence that would preclude aggressive nationalism. "The way to Europe goes over the nation," he concluded. "Europe can only develop organically, like a dome resting on the columns of our national forces. Unity of Europe requires first a unity within nations." This new Europe would be much like the former German Empire, built of vastly different regional identities that nonetheless acknowledged a common supra-identity in Germany. And once such a Europe was established, "inter-European war will be as laughable and unimaginable as a war between Frankfurt and Darmstadt."[99]

Rohan's Europeanism had some similarities with the Pan-Europa movement, founded by Richard (Count) Coudenhove-Kalergi (1894–1972). Both were born in the 1890s, both were the sons of loyal Habsburg officials, and both grew up near the contested linguistic border in Bohemia. Born in Tokyo where his father was an Austro-Hungarian diplomat, Coudenhove was half Japanese and, like Rohan, was proud of his diverse genealogy. In 1923, Coudenhove published the manifesto *Paneuropa*, which outlined the program of the Pan-Europa Union, founded in 1922.[100] He then began a lifelong crusade to build his movement, which stressed the importance of Europe as an economic and cultural bloc with free trade and peace among its members. By the mid-1920s Coudenhove could count among his allies Aristide Briand of France, Gustav Stresemann of Germany, and Edvard Beneš of Czechoslovakia. Coudenhove had originally hoped the president of the Union would be Tomáš Masaryk, whom he described as "the personification of the genuine European spirit, rooted, but not imprisoned in loyalty to his nation."[101] Masaryk declined, claiming the post would conflict with his presidency of Czechoslovakia. Even so, Coudenhove was popular in Czech government circles, and he carried a Czechoslovak diplomatic passport until 1939.[102]

Karl Anton Rohan is the central figure in this 1931 Max Beckmann painting of Paris society. Max Beckmann, *Paris Society*, 1931. R. Guggenheim Museum. © 2003 Artists Rights Society (ARS)

Though Coudenhove based his movement in Vienna and courted German leaders such as Stresemann assiduously, he saw France as even more important to the success of his United States of Europe. Briand became his friend and hero. As foreign minister in 1929, Briand publicly proposed a plan for European unity. Stresemann and Beneš welcomed his initiative, and momentum seemed to be building for concrete steps to form a union. But soon after, the tide turned against European unification. First, Stresemann died in September 1928, and no one in the German establishment had either the prestige or conviction necessary to pursue the European project. At the same time, British support for European unity was lukewarm at best, as the country's leaders believed its colonies made it more a world power than a European one. Finally, the Great Depression and the surge of the Nazis in Germany's 1930 election dampened the ardor of pan-Europeanists all over the continent.[103] Coudenhove's Europeanism was primarily a liberal movement, and an illiberal Germany could only alienate the movement's left and centrist supporters in France and elsewhere.

In contrast to Coudenhove's liberal and ecumenical pan-European vision, Rohan stressed a unity that would favor conservative and German interests. Rohan, too, published a book on the unity of Europe, *Europa*, which made many of the same arguments that would later appear in his *Europäische Revue*.[104] And Rohan also founded his own international organization, the Union of Intellectuals, in 1924. The stated goal of both the Union and the *Revue* was to promote "the spiritual unity of Europe."[105] Though Rohan's pan-Europeanism in many ways anticipated the European Union, it was also limited by its overriding concern for Germans in the new Europe. In the end, Europe was to be a vehicle for the continent's scattered Germans to come together in an international community.[106] Correspondingly, many of Rohan's articles focused on the inadequacies of the Versailles peace treaties, in particular the war-guilt issue ("one of the strongest barriers to all-European attempts at unification")[107] and minority rights (the key to "peace in Central and Eastern Europe").[108] As one commentator pointed out, Rohan's journal aimed "to emphasize the German face of Europe and the European face of Germany."[109]

Though Rohan rejected extreme nationalism that sought to conquer other nations, he saw "national man" as the "guardian of the holiest mysteries, the deepest source of power of Europe." Without such men, who sought the essence uniting the nation as a whole, "we would quickly sink into an unstructured chaos of wild opportunism and personal battles of all against all, whose first warning signs we can already see today . . . in large cities."[110] Rohan contrasted national man, who embraced the whole community of the nation *(Volksgemeinschaft)*, with socialist or bourgeois man, whose class politics were inherently selfish. The true nationalist was conservative and maintained "an orderly family," "a patriarchal relationship to his employees," and loyalty to the state, emperor, and God. But old conservatives were an endangered species in post-imperial Europe; now the term applied primarily to those of the younger generation who opposed Communism.[111]

In describing this new generation and its mission, Rohan adopted a concept that the Austrian writer Hugo von Hofmannsthal would later describe as a "conservative revolution."[112] This paradoxical movement, in the ineffable words of Fritz Stern, "sought to destroy the despised present in order to recapture an idealized past in an imaginary future." Its supporters

> were disinherited conservatives, who had nothing to conserve, because the spiritual values of the past had largely been buried and the material remnants of conservative power did not interest them. They sought a breakthrough to the past, and they longed for a new community in which old ideas and institutions would once again command universal allegiance.[113]

Rohan was not quite as nostalgic as Stern's description of revolutionary conservatism would suggest; rather he hoped that through action and creativity his generation could forge a new conservative order that would draw from both the past and present. The new order would be backward looking in form, but modern in content. Rohan was no Luddite seeking a return to a feudal agrarian past. But like many conservatives, he sought to organize industrial society on a corporatist model.

Rohan claimed the mantel of spokesman for this new generation of conservative youth, which held unfettered liberalism and democracy suspect. Their outlook forged in the crucible of war, they favored a collectivist national identification over individual selfishness. "Our instincts are thus religious and social," he wrote. They embraced a "new sense of community . . . an organically organized society" that was capable of overcoming both class struggle and international conflict.[114] The new generation was not inherently opposed to democracy, but it rejected the French revolutionary premise that the people equaled "the sum of separate, equal individuals." Rather, "the representatives of the re-formation of democracy understand by 'the people' *(Volk)* an organically grown unity, made up of differentiated limbs and parts."[115] It was in essence a corporatist vision, with outstanding political leaders (the *aristoi*) rising to the top of corporate groups, organized by occupation or productive sector.[116] This was a transparent attempt to create a new order on the model of the old one that nobles had dominated. Some of the leaders might emerge from other social classes, but there would be plenty of room for Rohan's revitalized landowning estate. Such a corporatist regime, "the modern people's state *(Volksstaat)*," would act "not for the benefit of a single party, but in the name of the national community *(Volksgemeinschaft)*."[117]

Rohan's political vision was not so far removed from the ideals of Italian Fascism, though he could not embrace its more demagogic aspects. Already in 1923, he recognized in Fascism a revolutionary conservatism, an emphasis on traditional values combined with a youthful dynamism seeking to build "a new world order."[118] Three years later, he "affirmed the spiritual core of Fascism," while regretting its "rough edges." In particular, he embraced "the new awareness of life *(Lebensgefühl)* that Fascism has created—heroic-tragic, young-revolutionary, and traditional at the same time, un-ideological but activist noblesse in the devotion to a super-individual ideal."[119]

In keeping with the corporatist ideology of Italian Fascism and Austrofascism, Rohan promoted a collectivist but depoliticized vision of the nation. Because the triumph of capitalism made commerce increasingly a-national, the nation would become more im-

118

portant as a cultural community than as a political one. "The concept 'nation' [will be] rooted much more deeply in its original essence," he wrote in 1926, "in the spiritual-historical-cultural, in the triangle: language, history, cultural community." As Rohan put it, "There can be no true solution to the minority problem, as long as the concept of the nation is not depoliticized."[120] To pursue this goal, in 1924 Rohan founded the international Association for Cultural Cooperation, commonly known by its French name *Fédération des Unions Intellectuelles*, which worked to increase cultural contacts between nations.[121]

In his writings on the minority question, Karl Anton Rohan drew on the thought of an international community of Germans organized in groups like Medinger's *Völkerbundliga*. Eugen Ledebur, who shared many of Rohan's basic premises on nobility, politics, and minorities, was a prominent spokesman for these Germans. An occasional contributor to the *Europäische Revue*, Ledebur wrote a 1927 article on Czechoslovakia's national minorities that prefigured Rohan's 1930 proposal for a solution to the minority problem in Europe. The article began with a specific critique of Czechoslovakia's restriction of German linguistic rights, including in schools and the bureaucracy. Such discrimination, he argued, was a result of taking the "supremacy of the nation" too far. It was not in the interests of the state to identify itself solely with one nation, because this underutilized the productive powers of minority citizens. In order for the state to realize the full energies of its people, it should give minorities a fair share of resources and a right to unhindered cultural development. To achieve a balance between the needs of the state and the rights of nations, Ledebur proposed "a clear consideration of the nation as an intra-state and inter-state legal subject"—in other words, Rohan's vision of nations as corporate groups. A national community should have certain collective rights and protections, Ledebur argued, and not just the individual right to equality enshrined in the League's minority treaties. Echoing the *Verband*'s strategy of internationalizing the land reform issue, Ledebur pressed the international community to act on minority rights. "With a view to the importance of the feuding parties and their geographical location," Ledebur concluded, the conflict in Czecho-slovakia "has become a European problem."[122]

Drawing on Ledebur's critique, in 1930 Rohan convened an international group to draft a minority statute that could replace the ineffective League of Nations minority treaties.[123] The centerpiece of this proposal, which set it apart from the earlier treaties, was the treatment of minority groups as collective personalities. Each minority would be entitled to a "cultural council *(Kulturrat)*," which would represent its interests in the state government and at the League of Nations, control the group's school and cultural budget, and maintain ties with co-nationals abroad. It would have the right to bring complaints to an international tribunal, whose rulings would be binding. In many ways this was an extension of the current League arbitration system, but there was one major difference. The key, as Rohan wrote in an introduction to the proposal, was that "it not only gives the members of a national minority individual rights, but it creates the possibility for the minority as such to constitute itself as a collective personality, as a public corporate entity *(Körperschaft)*."[124] Such an approach had a number of advantages. First, Rohan believed it had a very real chance of protecting minorities against the nationalizing tendencies of interwar states. Second, it would institutionalize the collective cultural concept of nation that Rohan saw as a precondition for a European consciousness. Third, it had the potential to defuse the Greater-Lesser Germany dilemma that had troubled Germans and Europe since the mid-nineteenth century. In Rohan's projected European community, Germans would finally have the economic and cultural unity they had long sought.

Rohan also wrote on the place of the nobility in this new Europe. In a 1928 article in the *Europäische Revue*, Rohan stressed the metaphysical aspects of nobility rather than traditional legal designations. Even if nobilities were in decline, the basic noble attributes— heroism, self-sacrifice, conservatism, and moderation—were eternal. "To be noble," he wrote, "means to transcend the individual." The old noble families of Europe survived as long as they did because they placed family above the individual, seeing each generation as only a link in a chain connecting ancestors with descendents. "Tradition gives distance from the world," and the embrace of tradition made nobles particularly well suited to politics. Emperor Francis Joseph, in Rohan's view the "last great monarch of the European continent," had been "above the personal *(überpersonlich)* in the truest sense of the word." With this crucial quality in mind, Rohan stressed the need, indeed the inevitability, of a new nobility. Just as in previous revolutionary times, some old noble families would survive the storm. The key to nobility was not personnel, however; rather it was the metaphysical qualities common to all aristocracies at their best. "The nobility as a political estate is dead," he concluded. "The nobility as a moral community is still possible."[125]

Coudenhove, too, wrote a manifesto on the place of the nobility in the new Europe. In one of his earliest works, titled simply *Nobility (Adel)*, Coudenhove described a "crisis of the nobility" in the twentieth century. Not only had the old "blood nobility *(Blutadel)*," with its roots in the countryside, lost its leading edge; so too was the primarily urban and Jewish "nobility of the mind *(Geistesadel)*" yielding to selfish and spiritless capitalism. But all was not lost! The essence of both types of nobility—rural and urban, conservative and progressive, political and intellectual—would merge in the nobility of the future. The key would be a natural breeding process—Coudenhove called it "social eugenics"—where the best of both types of nobility would come together to produce a new breed of leaders, a truly modern aristocracy.[126] It is important to note that the ominous sounding "social eugenics" was used here in a progressive context. As of the 1920s, eugenics had not yet been tainted by an association with Nazis and other racists and anti-Semites. Coudenhove's bizarre formulation was an attempt to reinvent and thus justify nobility for a liberal, post-feudal order.

We could read Rohan's and Coudenhove's reflections on the nobility as a public grasping at straws; given their own class background, their search for an ideology justifying nobility seems natural. But their efforts were part of a larger mission to find a home for the Habsburg nobility in post-imperial Europe. It was this quest that led them both to pan-Europeanism, which would later be so influential in the postwar foundation of the European Community. German aristocrats from the former Habsburg Empire were among the movement's most active founders and supporters. It may come as no surprise that Otto von Habsburg, the son of the last Emperor Karl, succeeded Coudenhove as president of the Pan-Europa Union in 1973, and that both are heroes of the present-day pan-European movement.[127] The triple curse of being noble, German, and Habsburg in a new world of nation-states and minorities was an essential impetus to these men's pan-European dreams.

Rohan and Coudenhove both sought to resurrect or revitalize what they saw as the positive elements of the aristocratic German-Habsburg world of their birth. For Rohan, that essence was a German-dominated multinational empire. This was the conservative and tightly controlled pseudo-democracy of Francis Joseph, a place where people still referred to occupational estates and deferred to their superiors (nobles, Germans, and the emperor, above all). Coudenhove, on the other hand, wanted to extend the more liberal elements of the monarchy: its supranationalism and constitutionalism, its cosmopolitan mix of nationalities and religions. To reduce these positions to ideal types, Rohan advanced a conservative-national vision of the monarchy and Europe, whereas Coudenhove favored a progressive-cosmopolitan Europe.

These different ideas of Europe would lead the two men to drastically divergent responses to Hitler's Third Reich in the 1930s. For Coudenhove, the Nazi rise was a disaster for pan-Europeanism. After 1933, he turned his pan-European energies to a campaign against Hitlerism. Rohan, on the other hand, greeted Hitler's "revolutionary conservative" regime with enthusiasm. By the time Rohan realized the folly of the double paradoxes of his interwar career—revolutionary conservatism and German Europeanism—it was too late. Rohan would survive the explosive convergence of the two movements from 1938–1945, but his reputation did not. Vindicated by history, Coudenhove at least merits a footnote in histories of the idea of Europe. Rohan, however, is largely forgotten.

Even so, Rohan was the more popular "Europeanist" among Bohemian German nobles in the 1920s and 1930s. Though Rohan was not a Czechoslovak citizen—his brother Alain inherited Sychrov and Karl took over the family's Austrian estate in 1919—he gave considerable thought to the issues that troubled Czechoslovakia's German minority. He also had close ties to Bohemian nobles such as Ledebur, Medinger, and Clary-Aldringen. They shared values, politics, and interests common to the Bohemian German noble milieu.[128] Many of Bohemia's nobles also shared Rohan's sympathy for the corporatist and conservative aspects of fascism. These sympathies would lead them to support the Sudeten German Party (SdP) of Konrad Henlein in the mid-1930s, a path that made many into supporters of Nazi Germany in 1938.

Maintaining Distinctions and Distinctive Maintenance

In spite of their diverging national loyalties between the wars, nobles retained much of their social exclusivity and class solidarity. As before the war, they hunted, rode horses, and frequented noble-only clubs in Prague and Vienna. Although a handful of nobles broke with family tradition by marrying commoners, the vast majority of marriages that counted were among the high-born. In spite of increasing political loyalties to wider Czech and German national communities, nobles continued to marry and socialize among themselves. These ties consistently crossed political and national lines, at least until the decisive and divisive year of 1938. Only with the onset of the Second World War would class solidarity begin to break down, as political upheaval and economic hardship drove a wedge into genteel lifestyles.

Social life for the Bohemian nobility remained international, in spite of the manifold new borders dividing Central Europe after 1918. As before the war, Vienna was the glittering, if troubled magnet for the social set, and the Jockey Club was the core of high society, the so-called first society (*erste Gesellschaft*) of old nobility. Many Bohemian nobles had palaces in the old Habsburg capital, though most took Czechoslovak citizenship in the hopes of saving their Bohemian estates. But Vienna remained the social center. Cecilia Sternberg recalled regular visits to Vienna where her Czech husband Leopold "won and lost vast sums of money gambling in the Jockey Club." The pair joined hundreds of other nobles annually for the so-called *Jubelwoche*, "which consisted of a month of tennis tournaments, polo games, and the Vienna Derby." They also pursued polo, derbies, and gambling in Berlin, Frankfurt, Baden-Baden, and Monte Carlo. Family ties further fed the couple's *Wanderlust*, as Cecilia was related to the much-ramified German Bismarcks. There were always weddings and funerals to attend; besides, Cecilia noted, Leopold loved his fellow Czechs but got bored at home on his estate.[129]

The Viennese Jockey Club remained popular through the 1920s, though it ran into financial troubles in the early depression years. In 1931, the club's presidium sent an appeal to members for donations, without which the club could not pay its bills.[130] Whether the fund-raising letter was intentionally alarmist or the membership came through with the necessary cash, the club remained open until after the annexation of Austria to Germany seven years later. On 27 August 1938, the Jockey Club was formally dissolved, with its members incorporated into a larger Nazified organization called the *Rennverein* (Riding Club). It was to contain, according to Carl Fürstenberg, "representatives of the state, the Party, the *Wehrmacht*, as well as gentlemen from the rolls of our Jockey Club's former membership and from industrial circles."[131] The Nazis had little appreciation for the organization's traditional Anglophilia or noble exclusivity. Already undermined from within during the war, the Jockey Club would suffer a coup de grace in 1945, when allied bombers leveled the Philippshof, the club's longtime home.[132]

Prague too had its noble social club, the Prague *Ressource*, which provided a genteel refuge for a wide range of nobles who owned land in Bohemia and Moravia. Unlike the popular Jockey Club, the *Ressource* has left few traces in the archives of member families. However, there exist lists of members from 1928 and 1940, which offer some intriguing hints about Prague social life. Most importantly, the *Ressource* included the cream of both the Czech and the German nobility. The directorate, chaired by Bedřich (Prince) Schwarzenberg in 1928, was primarily Czech-loyal, though the Germans Reinhold (Count) Boos Waldeck and Johann (Count) Hartig were among the leaders in 1928. The 215 members listed for 1928 included most of the nobles that feature in this book:

multiple Schwarzenbergs, Kinskýs, Lobkowiczs and Kolowrats; Eugen Ledebur, Alfons Clary-Aldringen, and Karl Waldstein; and other Czech and German loyalists who would take opposing sides in the crises of the late 1930s.[133] Even in 1940, the directorate (elected before the 1938 Nazi annexation of the Sudetenland) was almost evenly divided between Czechs and Germans. Membership had dropped to 127, with both Czechs and Germans still represented.[134]

During the winter social season in Prague, nobles frequented balls sponsored in grand style by their wealthiest members. Zdeněk Kinský's memoirs, which read like a two-hundred-page social calendar, report annual balls at the Schwarzenberg and Clam palaces, among others. If the chronic socialite Kinský is a good indication, nobles rarely attended balls outside of their own social circle. An exception was the yearly costume ball sponsored by the American embassy, at which nobles mingled with diplomats from various countries and classes, as well as with the cream of the Czech and Slovak political establishment.[135]

After the weather cleared in the spring, noble sociability moved on to country estates, where nobles gathered for hunting, tennis, polo and preliminaries to the famous Pardubice Steeplechase. Zdeněk Kinský, an avid horseman who was married to the widowed mother of Karel and František Schwarzenberg, hosted scores of such events at his castle in Chlumec, including a 1935 masquerade depicting Napoleon's General Murat with seven of his marshals in period costume. Kinský, the president of the noble-dominated Napoleon Society since 1923, appeared as "King Murat."[136] Kinský could show off his hospitality to a wider audience in October, when international high society convened for the Pardubice Steeplechase. As president of the Prague branch of the Jockey Club, Kinský regularly presided over the event. During the 1937 Steeplechase, according to the *Wiener Salonblatt*, nearby Chlumec welcomed dozens of visitors, including a pair of nobles from Paris, "the Countess of Harrington, who came in her own airplane; Lady Rachel Howard, sister of the Duke of Norfolk, as well as members of the families Schwarzenberg, Fürstenberg, Auersperg, Kinsky, Harrach, Czernin, Paar, Aehrenthal, Dobrzensky, Deym and Thun, and naturally the

Countess Immaculata Brandis, the victor of the great steeplechase." The year was an active one for the Kinskýs, whose guestbook recorded 366 visitors in 1937.[137]

As Kinský's diverse guest list indicated, noble social life tended not to divide by nationality. Both the German Alfons Clary and the Czech Cecilia Sternberg remembered close relationships with Czech and German noble families during the interwar years. Ulrich Kinsky, whose German sympathies led him to embrace Nazism in the 1930s, was a good friend of both the Clarys and the Sternbergs. A loyal Czech and opponent of Nazism, Cecilia's husband Leopold Sternberg was disappointed with Kinsky's politics, but he never abandoned the friendship.[138] Tennis and hunting weekends remained the staples of noble sociability, and these festive gatherings did not discriminate by national loyalties. In a typical example, the German Karl Buquoy hosted a diverse group of nobles for hunting and tennis in August of 1923 at his estate in south Bohemia. The guests were mostly relatives and included two Nostitz couples (German), three Thuns (German), two Kinskýs (Czech and German), a Lobkowicz (Czech), and a Strachwitz (Czech).[139]

Though hunting and equine sports remained the most popular among nobles, many enthusiastically embraced the faster paced entertainments of flying and automobile racing. Jiří Lobkowicz (1907–1932), the young inheritor of the Mělník branch of the family, was an avid racer and died competing in an international competition in Berlin.[140] Ulrich Kinsky was an accomplished flyer and often flew his own plane to London to visit his friends. In the 1930s, he was the president of the Austrian Aeroklub.[141] Karl Waldstein was active in a regional branch of the German Flyers' Club *(Verband Deutscher Flieger)*, becoming the group's leader in 1935, a distinction that would come back to haunt him in 1945.[142]

Along with a growing interest in middle-class sports, nobles continued to move into traditionally bourgeois occupations in industry, finance, and law. We find numerous younger sons, as well as many first sons, in prominent positions at banks and insurance companies. Bedřich Schwarzenberg, for example, was president of First Czech Mutual Insurance from 1906 until his death in 1936.[143] His distant cousin Adolf Schwarzenberg of the primogeniture sat on the board of directors of the Böhmische Escomptebank; several others, including Eugen Ledebur, Ottokar Westphalen-Fürstenberg, Franz Thun-Hohenstein, and Alexander Thurn-Taxis also served as bank directors. Whereas Leopold and Jaroslav Sternberg concentrated on running their estates, their younger brother Adam was a lawyer in Prague.[144] A number of nobles, both Czech and German, worked for the landowner interest organizations. Zdeněk Kolowrat and Karel Belcredi were the business managers of the Czechoslovak *Svaz* and Moravian *Svaz*, respectively, and Friedrich Westphalen was a lawyer for the *Verband*. Scores of nobles still owned sugar refineries, breweries, and ironworks on their estates; some took an active interest in their oversight, whereas others left the task to professional managers.

Generally speaking, nobles retained a strong presence in the economic and professional elite in interwar Czechoslovakia. Although large numbers of them—non-inheriting sons in particular—worked in bourgeois occupations, it was still land that set nobles apart, both in wealth and in the public mind. Even so, few would stake their fortunes on land alone. As Oswald Waldstein wrote to his Uncle Adolph in 1924, "Industry gives completely different profits than what one can expect today (and for years out) from estates *(Herrschaft)*. And besides, industry is safe from the Land Office!" He added, "Times have changed, a fact one must consider if one intends to stay on top; land alone won't save anyone these days!"[145] Nobles had already begun to recognize this in the nineteenth century, but it was even clearer after 1918, when land reform posed a serious threat to noble landed wealth.

Nobles were far less willing to breach traditional class boundaries when it came to marriage. Class remained much more important than nationality in determining marriage patterns after 1918. In fact, Bohemian nobles were so intermarried that any two individuals had a high likelihood of being related, regardless of national loyalties. Alfons Clary's mother was a Kinský of the Czech-oriented Kostelec branch, making him "cousins" with numerous Kinskýs, Lobkowiczs, Choteks, Schwarzenbergs, and others. He also had relatives among the Polish Radziwills and Potockis and the German-international Liechtensteins.[146] Leopold Sternberg's marriage to

Cecilia Countess Reventlow-Criminil brought him into relation with the Austro-German Hoyos family as well as the famous Bismarcks of Germany. A recently published almanac of old Bohemian families indicates that Czech-loyal nobles continued to cast their marriage nets widely during the interwar period, making connections with Bohemian Germans, Czechs, Hungarians, Reich Germans, Austrian Germans, and others farther afield. In a typical example, the strongly patriotic Czechs Karel Schwarzenberg and Karel Belcredi married a German Fürstenberg and a Hungarian Kálnoky, respectively. These international and inter-national marriage patterns held for both male and female members of the family, as well as older and younger sons. National loyalties appear to have been a male prerogative, though, as there is little evidence of wives swaying the national politics of their husbands. Given the persistently patriarchal nature of noble economic, social, and political existence, the male monopoly on national identification is not surprising.[147]

It would take the territorial changes and tremendous political tension of 1938–1945 to begin to weaken the social ties of Czech and German nobles in Bohemia. With the annexation of the Sudetenland to Hitler's Reich in October 1938, a substantial number of German nobles became separated from their Czech friends and relatives by an international and psychological border. The implications of Czech and German loyalties would escalate dramatically after 1939, as Hitler's deputies used both carrot and stick to pressure Czech nobles to convert to German nationality. The war strained previously strong cross-national ties among the nobility, though it did not lead to a decisive break. In explaining why she sheltered some German noble friends in the waning days of the war, Cecilia Sternberg indicated the complexity of the Czech-German relationship: "You know how interrelated we all are," she told her cousin Eddie von Bismarck.

Even if those on the German side didn't dare go near us during the war, and we as Czechs were equally afraid to be identified with them, and both parties thought each other fools because of their convictions. You don't hate your brother or your cousin just because he's been stupid, and if he's in real trouble you help.[148]

❧ Although most in the Czech and German middle classes had nationalized during Bohemia's battles over language and municipal resources in the late 1800s, many nobles, Jews, and poorer peasants and workers had to some extent remained detached from those struggles. What all of these groups had in common was a perception that their interests were best served by loyalty to the imperial edifice, not national declarations. With the fall of the Habsburg Monarchy, neutrality lost its utility. Bohemian nobles now sought new ways to protect and advance their interests. In 1919, leading aristocrats organized landowner associations to lobby against land reform. Dominated by nobles, these organizations became the vehicles of a post-Habsburg reinvention of the nobility. Two macro-institutions, the nation-state and the League of Nations, pushed the transformation in a national direction, providing incentives for many nobles to embrace either Czech or Sudeten German nationalism.

But as in the late nineteenth century, noble national loyalties were inflected by long-standing traditions of internationalism and Bohemian historic rights. The Czech-oriented *Svaz* drew on the patrimonial traditions of historic rights ideology in recasting nobles as patriotic capitalists. Not only were noble large estates more efficient and productive than smallholdings, the argument went, but they also provided jobs, preserved natural areas for the public, and maintained hundreds of historic monuments with their forestry income. Well accustomed to preserving their own family patrimonies, Czech nobles tried to position themselves as essential custodians of the country's natural and cultural legacy.

German-oriented nobles went in two directions after 1918. A few joined the Czechoslovak *Svaz*, thereby indicating a loyalty to the Czech state, but not necessarily the Czech nation. These nobles, at least in the 1920s, were akin to the "culturally German, politically Czech" faction of the late nineteenth-century Feudal Conservatives. But a substantial portion of the German nobility took a more adversarial position toward the Czech state, preferring instead a specifically Sudeten German (as opposed to Czechoslovak German) national-political loyalty. Led by the *Verband*'s Eugen Ledebur and Wilhelm Medinger, these nobles adopted a German international strategy, emphasizing their membership in the Sudeten German minority and pleading their case before the League of Nations and other international forums. In the mid-1920s, Karl Anton Rohan became an ally and informal ideologist of Bohemia's German internationalists. Seeking better protections for German minorities throughout Europe, Rohan embraced a pan-Europeanism deeply infused with pan-Germanism. The nationalist content of Rohan's internationalism suggested a profound shift in noble identities. By the 1930s, traditional noble conservatism gave way to a "revolutionary" national conservatism, a journey that led many German nobles to National Socialism and many Czech nobles to an unwavering loyalty to the Czech state in the face of the Nazi threat.

~ 4

Czech Nobles, Nationalism, and Catholic Conservatism, 1930–1939

> We assure you that we are conscious of our inherited obligations
> to our homeland and state, a state which was the home of our
> ancestors and whose historic rights we now and have always
> desired to defend.
> ~ *"Declaration of members of the historic nobility," 1938*

$\mathcal{W}$ITH THE GREAT DEPRESSION sweeping Europe in the early 1930s, Czechoslovakia at first seemed immune to the political instability and creeping authoritarianism that plagued its neighbors. Even so, subtle shifts within Czech political parties indicated a growing conservative influence in public life, and many on the Czech right began to question the efficacy of liberal democracy in dealing with the Depression. At the same time, there were also hints of a changing attitude toward the Bohemian nobility, or at least toward those nobles who identified themselves as Czech. With land reform winding down, there were fewer public expressions of hostility toward nobles. Public figures even began quietly considering ways of making the nobility useful to the state. The conservative historian Josef Pekař reached the height of his influence in the 1930s, and he resolutely advanced a narrative of Czech history that gave nobles a prominent place in the Czech National Revival. The 1930s were not exactly a new golden age for Czech nobles—or for anyone else, for that matter—but it was a better decade than the 1920s. No longer on the defensive, many nobles could now embrace the Czech state with considerably more enthusiasm than they had in the revolutionary early years of the Republic.

The ultimate test of their loyalty would come in September 1938, when the Sudeten crisis threatened to dismember Czechoslovakia. Leading members of the Czech-loyal nobility publicly declared their support for the integrity of the state. Over the next year, as Czechoslovakia lost first the Sudetenland and then its independent statehood, these nobles reiterated their allegiance to the Czech nation and state. With the establishment of a noble-friendly conservative government in rump Czechoslovakia, nobles may have expected some political rewards from their proclamations of loyalty. But ultimately, the noble declarations were a tremendous risk in the face of encroaching German power. The willingness to take such a risk suggests a much deeper national identification than one motivated by purely material or narrowly political self-interest, the culmination of a nationalizing process that began in the late nineteenth century.

The Rising Czech Right and the Rehabilitation of the Czech Nobility

During the 1930s, the right wing of the Czech political spectrum grew slightly in size, but even more in its conservatism. Where right and center-right Czech parties had taken 32.2 percent of the state-wide vote in 1929, this increased to 34.8 percent in 1935 elections.[1] But more significantly, the Agrarians, National Democrats, and the Catholic Populists—the largest parties on the right—saw the emergence of powerful conservative wings that flirted with or even openly embraced fascist programs. This reflected a rightward shift evident throughout Europe, as many people came to doubt the ability of liberal democracy to overcome the Depression. In Czechoslovakia, the National Democrats, after a long courtship with authoritarian ideology, united in 1934 with a smattering of Czech fascist parties led by the former defense minister Jiří Stříbrný (1880–1955).[2] Agrarian conservatives under the noble-friendly Rudolf Beran (1887–1954) covertly supported the fascist agitator Radola Gajda (1892–1948) and pulled the party steadily to the right during the 1930s. The Catholic People's Party saw the rise of a strong authoritarian wing associated with the novelist Jaroslav Durych (1886–1962).[3]

As the right gained in strength, the Bohemian nobility regained a measure of its lost stature. Nobles no longer seemed threatening to the young state, as land reform was close to 80 percent complete in 1930. Though nobles still retained around half of their land, they had done so at the whim of the Land Office and its Agrarian overseers. There was no question of the Czech nobility being a significant independent political force. Nor did nobles appear any longer to be a potential ally for external forces aiming to overthrow the state. Monarchism had lost what little momentum it had with former Emperor Karl's death in 1922. After 1933, Hitler's Germany would prove a more formidable threat than monarchism to Czechoslovak stability. Czech-loyal nobles, however, evidenced a clear disdain for the upstart *Führer*, and they were traditional defenders of the integrity of the historic Bohemian crown lands.

Traditionalism seemed all the more attractive as the forces spawned by capitalist modernization seemed to turn against the people of Europe. Blaming the world economic crisis on unfettered competition, many Czechs looked nostalgically on the paternalistic aspects of feudalism. The foremost liberal writer on the Czech scene in the 1930s, Karel Čapek, wrote a glowing 1934 essay in honor of the old Czech patriot, Count Vladimír Lažanský. "He used the informal *ty* with all his subjects," Čapek recalled, "but he was also their patron, went to their funerals, and most of the time gave them their daily bread. Say what you want, but the feudal order had something familial about it."[4] In a similar vein, the right-wing daily *Polední list* commented on how much more popular noble landowners were than the "new nobility" that received so-called residual estates in the land reform. The newcomers had a reputation for exploiting their land and workers, whereas the old nobles earned the locals' praise for "their social conscientiousness and care for their employees."[5] Above all, in a time of rapid and discomforting change in the countryside, many farmers saw nobles as rooted deeply in the local soil and history. A Benešov regional journal asked, "How much truly national-economic work did those like

Prince Schwarzenberg undertake . . . [as compared to] any post-war owner of the best estates?" Answering his own question, the author clearly favored Schwarzenberg and his fellow nobles: "We independent farmers are not afraid to say publicly that the pre-war nobility, which may have been in many cases foreign to us by language, was close to us in spirit and in love for our ancestral soil."[6]

The Schwarzenbergs in particular were widely revered in the 1930s. In July 1936, shortly before the death of Bedřich Schwarzenberg (1862–1936), university and political officials gathered to honor the fiftieth anniversary of the Czech loyalist's doctorate at Charles University. Czech radio covered the event, which became something of a national celebration. When Schwarzenberg died in early October, it was an occasion for widespread mourning. Newspapers from across the center and right of the political spectrum celebrated his service to the Czech cause. A common theme in his obituaries was his true nobility, both "by descent and spirit." He was a "cavalier" and a "national noble," a "defender of Czech statehood, [who] tried to integrate the nobility into the current of national life." A number of articles made a distinction between nobility in the traditional family sense and nobility of the spirit, a personal quality. They depicted Schwarzenberg as embodying the best of both definitions of nobility: thoroughly imbued with his family's tradition of noblesse oblige, but also a convinced democrat whose heart was with the common people.[7] The implication was that nobility was a good thing, as long as it was accompanied by patriotism, generosity of spirit, and democratic credentials. These obituaries suggest that a substantial portion of the Czech political spectrum had come to accept the idea of a Czech national nobility.

As the right gained strength in the 1930s and public opinion became less hostile to nobles, the Czech nobility began to emerge from its status as a class of political pariahs. The *Svaz*'s Zdeněk Kolowrat wrote to Count Karl Podstatzky-Lichtenstein in 1934 that "various parties are striving to draw the nobility into their camp in order also to gain with their help the votes of employees dependent on noble large estates."[8] In a 1932 speech to the *Svaz* general assembly in Prague's opulent Municipal House *(Obecní dům,)* Jan Lobkowicz sounded a note of optimism. "It seems to me," he said, "almost as if the moral weight of our organization has risen some-what in our public life. They are beginning to take us seriously, and the large landowner is no longer such a *quantité negligeable* as it was in the first years after the revolution."[9]

In early 1935, two leading National Democratic deputies, An-tonín Hajn and J. Špaček, furthered this impression in an article suggesting that the previous decade's attacks on the nobility had been too extreme. "We should not have gone so far against the nobility that we repulsed them from public service," they wrote. "We should have won them over as much as possible to public and diplomatic work, as Poland and Hungary have done."[10] The left-wing press treated this proposal derisively, however, as Bohemian nobles had "negotiated on their gentlemanly hunts [the start of] the most terrible world war" in history.[11] Even so, other sources on the right would repeat the National Democratic appeal on and off through the late 1930s. *Polední list* made a similar point in early 1938, as Czechoslovakia struggled to keep British opinion on its side in the face of Hitler's efforts to pry loose the German-inhabited Sudetenland. Although Czech nobles had lost their titles, the journal noted, they had not lost their influence abroad. "Even today," the article continued, "our nobles have their own well-stocked game preserves, quaint castles and hunting pavilions, which they now intend to put at the disposition of foreign nobles. . . . Above all, this means the English nobility, which . . . will include a procession of politically engaged lords." These "noble hunts" had the potential to bring in not only "economic profit," but also "po-litical sympathy" for Czechoslovakia.[12] The Agrarian Party appar-ently agreed, contacting Jan Lobkowicz in 1935 regarding coop-eration with the nobility.[13]

Masaryk's Presidential Chancellery also considered the possibility of using nobles for diplomatic purposes, although Chancellor Šámal concluded that only the younger generation could be counted upon to support Czechoslovakia. In February 1934, Šámal received Fran-tišek Schwarzenberg (1913–1992) for a discussion on the national credentials of Bohemian nobles. Schwarzenberg noted that the cur-rent generation of noble youth tended to speak Czech as well as German and that many attended Czech schools. He concluded by asserting that a number of young nobles "exhibited an unexpected Czech nationalism."[14] Šámal asked Schwarzenberg to put together a list of noble males born after 1900 with information about their schooling. Schwarzenberg did a remarkable job, collecting 114 names from the most prominent families in the Republic. Of those, forty had attended or were attending Czech schools, and sixty-six went to German schools. Although it cannot automatically be concluded that the choice of a Czech school was a sign of Czech patriotism, it would nonetheless have been a conscious choice to be a part of Czech community life. The choice of a German school, on the other hand, was less decisive, because German was still attractive to nobles and many others as an international language. With a few exceptions, Schwarzenberg's list of school languages matches national identifications available from other sources.[15]

Not long after Antonín Hajn's 1935 article on the nobility, he stopped by the Chancellery to discuss his proposal that the government involve Czech nobles in public affairs. Šámal shared Schwarzenberg's list with Hajn, expressing the belief that at least the younger generation of nobles offered "better prospects for the future." But the current generation—meaning those born in the 1870s and 1880s who had reached adulthood under the monarchy—was unreliable. Hajn disagreed, noting the strong patriotic feelings among the Lobkowiczs, Kolowrats, Kinskýs, and Schwarzenbergs, among others.[16]

There is no record of the Presidential Chancellery following up on Hajn's proposal, though President Beneš did invite a handful of nobles to the official reception for Romanian King Carol when he visited Prague Castle in 1936, the first such invitation to nobles since 1918.[17] Even so, this was hardly evidence of a dramatically new role for the nobility in diplomacy; after the diplomatic disaster at Munich in September 1938, Czech officials would express regrets that they had not made better use of the nobility to press their case. Unlike Poland, Hungary, and the Sudeten Germans, the Czechs, and Edvard Beneš in particular, were not generally comfortable using old-boy aristocratic networks for diplomacy.[18]

Even so, nobles greatly increased their visibility in the mid-1930s, attending and even organizing major public commemorative events.

In 1935, František Schwarzenberg was a leading organizer of the statewide gathering of Catholics *(Katolický sjezd)*, and a number of nobles were active participants in the meeting.[19] Nobles also took charge of a comprehensive exhibit on the history of the baroque in Prague in 1938.[20] For the nobility, visibility was a vital component of status and distinction.[21] Where as nobles had largely avoided public activity during the height of their unpopularity in the 1920s, many seized the opportunity to reintroduce themselves as patrons and patricians in the more congenial 1930s.

The Wallenstein/Valdštejn Commemoration of 1934

Nobles also fared better in the history books, as the noble-friendly historian Josef Pekař (1870–1937) reached the height of his career and influence in the early 1930s. Editor of the *Czech Historical Journal (Český časopis historický)* since 1897, Pekař became the leader of the Czech Academy of Sciences in 1928 and rector of Charles University in 1931.[22] The most accomplished Czech historian of the interwar period, Pekař had spent much of his career opposing Tomáš Masaryk's contention that Czech history represented the unfolding of a Protestant ideal rooted in the teachings of the fifteenth-century heretic Jan Hus. To Masaryk and his followers— indeed, to many Czechs in the early years of the Republic—Catholicism was a creed alien to the Czech nation, reimposed from outside by the Counter-Reformatory Habsburgs after the Battle of White Mountain in 1620. Masaryk's philosophy of history thus underlay the myth of White Mountain that politicians used to vilify the nobility and justify land reform in 1919.

The positivist Pekař argued that Masaryk's romantic-philosophical "meaning of Czech history" was ahistorical and served political rather than scholarly goals. During his prolific career, Pekař did battle over the key points in Masaryk's narrative: the Hussite Wars and the Thirty Years' War. In several books, Pekař posited a profound Catholic influence on Czech national identity, embraced conservative and aristocratic heroes such as Albrecht von Wallenstein (Waldstein/Valdštejn), and emphasized the role nobles had played in the Czech National Revival. Though more scholarly than Masaryk, Pekař also advanced his own Czech national narrative that corresponded with his conservative Catholic political agenda.

Pekař's interpretation of Wallenstein's career and assassination is an excellent example of how he, like his opponents, mixed history and politics. The year 1934 was the three hundredth anniversary of Wallenstein's death at the hands of Habsburg assassins. Pekař and other conservative historians marked the year with a lecture series, two commemorative exhibitions, and articles in journals and newspapers. Zdeněk Kolowrat and other prominent nobles played an important role in preparing this Wallenstein commemoration.

During the Thirty Years' War, Wallenstein was a towering figure. After the Protestant Bohemian Estates revolted against Habsburg rule in 1618, the Catholic convert and Turkish war veteran Wallenstein dramatically seized the treasury of Moravia and delivered it to the Habsburgs.[23] This was a gamble that paid off, as the Habsburg victory at White Mountain in 1620 brought Wallenstein tremendous riches. Put in charge of the redistribution of confiscated Protestant property, he built himself a vast duchy in northern Bohemia. He then raised an army from among his subjects and put it at the service of the emperor. The generous general was soon the generalissimo of the Habsburg army, and he had great success against Protestant forces in northern Europe.

In 1630, though, things began to sour. Barely able to finance his huge army, Wallenstein adopted a defensive strategy that alienated Catholic leaders. The Habsburg Emperor Ferdinand soon dismissed him from the command of the army, a move that was either a betrayal or a relief to Wallenstein, depending on the historical account.[24] But two years later, with the Swedes again advancing, Ferdinand returned command of the army to Wallenstein, who restored Habsburg good fortunes and then promptly began negotiating with the enemy. In 1634, Ferdinand sent two assassins to do away with the rogue general, breaking up his vast estates and parceling his duchy to scores of Catholic Habsburg allies.

That was the traditional narrative: the enterprising and opportunistic Wallenstein got too ambitious and was eliminated by the Habsburgs. In the 1920s and 1930s, though, Pekař put a different spin on the story. In a 1934 lecture titled "Wallenstein and the

Czech Question," Pekař argued that the general was a Czech proto-
patriot, who ultimately sought to wrest Bohemia from the Habsburgs and reestablish an independent Czech kingdom (with himself
at its head, of course). Pekař reminded his listeners of the Wallenstein family's old Czech roots and their moderate Protestantism that
dated to the Hussite Revolt of the fifteenth century. The Hussites
had divided into a radical wing, the so-called Taborites, and a conciliatory wing, the Utraquists. The Wallensteins had sided with the
Utraquists, and would later oppose Lutheran influence on Czech
Protestantism in the sixteenth century. In many ways, Pekař
claimed, the Wallensteins were closer to the Catholics than the
aggressive Lutherans, and it was no surprise when Albrecht Wallenstein converted in 1606. His support of the Habsburgs in 1618,
then, was not an opportunistic betrayal of the Czech cause, but
rather a principled stand against the widening power of Luther-
anism, which was a German and foreign influence in Bohemia.[25]

Though Pekař recognized Wallenstein's eccentricities—he called
him a "mysterious hero"—he saw him as a potential savior of Bohemia in the dark years after White Mountain. Had Wallenstein
had his way, Pekař claimed, the Thirty Years' War would have
ended after only sixteen years, with a religiously tolerant Wallenstein on the Bohemian throne, the Habsburgs much reduced, and
fourteen more years of destruction and pestilence avoided. Wallenstein's assassination, Pekař declared, "was a new blow for our Czech
Lands, a blow all the more painful given the great hopes preceding
[his death] in thousands of Czech hearts."[26] Pekař's Wallenstein narrative was a Catholic nationalist mythology: like a sizable number
of Czech Catholics, Pekař preferred Catholic heroes to the proto-
Protestant Jan Hus or the Protestant rebels in the Thirty Years'
War. Wallenstein was just the figure Catholic nationalists needed
to advance their agenda of an independent, but Catholic Czech
nation-state.

In 1933, a group of conservative Czechs, including Pekař, a
number of Czech nobles, and the archivist-historian Jaroslav Prokeš
formed a committee to prepare a series of lectures and exhibitions
for 1934, the three hundredth anniversary of Wallenstein's assassination. In a letter to participants, the committee's leaders empha-

sized Wallenstein's Czech credentials: his murder by Habsburg loyalists was "one of the most important episodes of the stirring Czech struggle to reverse the defeat at White Mountain. At the end of his life, Wallenstein was preparing plans for a large, widely organized conspiracy hoping to wrest Bohemia from the power of the Habsburgs and renew its complete independence." His death, the letter added, was a great turning point in Czech history, one that ranked with White Mountain in its negative consequences for the Czech nation.[27]

The committee lined up historians to give public lectures in March and April of 1934 on different aspects of Wallenstein's life and age. Two exhibits were to follow from May to September, the first focusing on Wallenstein himself and the second on Czech history before and after the Battle of White Mountain. The committee entrusted the well-connected Czech aristocrat Zdeněk Kolowrat, the secretary of the *Svaz*, with the task of convincing current Bohemian nobles to lend artwork for the exhibition. Kolowrat approached a number of prominent noble families, including the Lobkowiczs, the Czernins, the Waldsteins, and the Buquoys. Though he managed to gather a sizable collection, he encountered some resistance from distrustful nobles who feared Czech nationalists would damage their art. Karl Buquoy, a descendent of the victorious White Mountain General Karl Buonaventura Buquoy, hesitated to lend his portraits on account of "certain worries on the basis of experiences with visitors to [his] castle, who, by excessively drastic means, expressed their antipathy to the Buquoy family."[28]

As Buquoy wrote in a letter to Kolowrat, General Buquoy was "for the Czechs the embodiment of everything atrocious ... and hateful. . . . I would even expect with some certainty that objects of General Buquoy's in the Prague exhibition would be intentionally ruined and smashed."[29] Kolowrat assured Buquoy that his contributions would be safe—not only would there be ample security, but also the exhibit was not aimed at lower-class Czechs. Kolowrat added that it would be an evenhanded presentation and would not polemicize against the nobility. Referring to Pekař and the organizers of the exhibition, Kolowrat claimed that many Czech historians had been far more "sober" in their judgment of the Bohemian nobility than the Czech populace as a whole.[30] In the end, Buquoy lent his art for the exhibit, and no harm came to any of it.

A central theme of the Wallenstein commemoration—and much of Pekař's work in general—was the importance of the continuity of Czech statehood. Whereas Masaryk and his followers emphasized the revolutionary and Czech national content of the Hussite and Thirty Years' Wars, Pekař depicted them as religious/political fights for control of the Bohemian throne and the integrity of the Bohemian crown lands. Though not ardently pro-Habsburg, Pekař saw the Habsburg defeat of the Protestant Estates in 1620 as a victory for legitimacy. His bête noire was not Catholicism, but rather revolution on the one hand and excessive centralism on the other. He saw Wallenstein, and later "feudal conservative," anti-centralist Bohemian nobles, as bulwarks against forces threatening Bohemian autonomy. Pekař argued that noble advocates of Bohemian historic rights—families such as the Sternbergs and Schwarzenbergs in the nineteenth century—had prepared the way for independent Czech statehood in 1918. Understandably, many Bohemian nobles—both Czech and German—held Pekař in high regard, seeing him as both a truth-teller and a political ally.[31]

Nobles and the Catholic Right

Pekař was also a favorite of the Catholic political right in Czechoslovakia, the group ideologically most congenial to Czech nobles. In tune with the subtle rightward shift in Czech politics in the early 1930s, the Catholic People's Party spawned a strongly conservative right wing with Fascist tendencies. The novelist and publicist Jaroslav Durych set the tone for this group in his strident journal *Rozmach* (Breakthrough) and later in the monthly *Řád* (Order). In a typical early polemic from 1925, he wrote: "Only Catholicism must rule, direct, lead, speak, and create; all the rest must be very deferential, humbly silent, if they want to be tolerated. The state must come under the protection of Catholicism."[32] In the mid-1920s, statements like this were widely viewed as clerical gibberish, but supporters viewed them as a voice crying out in the wilderness. Ten years later, Durych and his allies would have a far bigger audience and a growing legitimacy lent by authoritarian successes elsewhere in Europe.

Tainted by a pro-Habsburg policy during the First World War, the Catholic People's Party had gradually pulled itself from the brink of obscurity by embracing Czech nationalism and quietly tolerating the separation of church and state. Under the leadership of the wily and moderate priest Jan Šrámek, the Czech Populists won 7 percent of the statewide vote in 1920 elections (including the Slovak Populists, the total was 11.3 percent).[33] Their vote total would hover between 7 percent and 10 percent for the remainder of the interwar period, and like the Agrarians, the Populists became perennial members of the governing coalition. In spite of the success of political Catholicism, Durych's faction continually criticized Šrámek for abandoning traditional Catholic values by compromising with the state's secular governments. These attacks escalated in 1929, when Socialists reentered the government after a three-year hiatus. From 1930 to 1934, Šrámek appeared on the verge of losing control of his party to the hard-line wing, though he ultimately held the party together by moving to the right himself.[34]

The conservatives around Durych had three themes that animated their attacks. The first major plank of their political desiderata was the injection of Catholic morality into Czechoslovak public life. They called for increased Catholic influence in schools, marriage, and burials; a hard line against corruption; and the official recognition of Catholic symbolic heroes such as St. Wenceslas and St. John of Nepomuk. Durych's group detested the "heretic" Jan Hus and demanded the destruction of the Hus memorial on Old Town Square, a "bad monument of a bad preacher by a bad sculptor." Instead, the Catholic right wanted the toppled Marian Column rebuilt as a sign of Catholic devotion and a rejection of the anticlerical socialism and anarchism that had moved the Column's attackers in 1918.[35] On White Mountain too, Durych took a position far from the Czech mainstream. Instead of a defeat of Czech national aspirations, Durych argued, White Mountain was "a day of triumph, a day of liberation from damnation" at the hands of misguided and foreign Protestants. The hill itself, so often a rallying point for anti-Catholic forces, was actually a "holy place

... where our inheritance, our birthright, our worldly and eternal life was saved."[36]

The conservatives' second theme involved a skepticism about liberal democracy that was hardly unique to the Czech Catholic right. In addition to Durych's consistent calls for an authoritarian clerical regime, other members of the faction, such as Jan Scheinost, the editor of *Lidové listy*, praised Hitler and fascist dictatorship.[37] Liberalism, according to Durych, promoted the proliferation of political parties that undermined national unity. Catholicism, however, like fascism, opposed fragmentation and provided an alternative to the destructive factionalism of liberal democracy.

Further accentuating ideological links to fascism, the right wing's third major theme was corporatism, the organization of the economy (and politics) by productive estates rather than by class. Deeply suspicious of socialism and communism, Durych's group believed that both class struggle and unfettered capitalism undermined religion and public morality, replacing them with a primitive all-against-all individualism. This position echoed Pope Pius XI's 1931 encyclical, *Quadragesimo Anno*, which condemned "the sordid love of wealth" and called for a new order of "Industries and Professions ... in which men may have their place, not according to the position each has in the labor market but according to the respective social functions which each performs."[38]

Like their German counterparts, many Czech nobles found corporatism attractive, seeing it as a conservative alternative to both liberalism and socialism. Though data is lacking on noble party loyalties, there is evidence that a number of nobles were sympathetic to the right-wing factions of the Czech Agrarian Party and the Catholic People's Party. The Czechoslovak Catholic Congress of 1935—closely tied to the Populists—reportedly drew 270 aristocrats, by far the largest noble turnout at any public manifestation in the interwar period.[39]

At least one noble, the young Karel VI (Prince) Schwarzenberg (1911–1986), was an active publicist for the Catholic right. Writing under the pseudonym Jindřich Středa, Schwarzenberg regularly contributed to the Catholic monthly *Řád*, where he shared the stage with Durych, Scheinost, and others from the Populists' conservative wing.[40] Schwarzenberg was exceptionally prolific and engaged, and, as his leadership in 1938 demonstrated, he spoke for a wider group of Czech nobles in the mid- to late 1930s. He was a quintessential Czech Catholic-national noble, the spiritual and literal descendent of Bohemian historic rights conservatives. Schwarzenberg and many of his peers came to see Czechoslovakia as a new carrier of the tradition of Bohemian statehood, though the Czech state they envisioned was far from the left-leaning republic of Masaryk and Beneš.

Born in 1911, Karel VI Schwarzenberg inherited the family secundogeniture at Orlík at the age of three, when his father died on the Serbian front in the early months of the First World War. Karel grew up under the influence of his great uncle Bedřich, the Czech patriot so warmly remembered in the Czech press after his death in 1936. Though fascinated by history, Karel studied forestry at the Czech Polytechnic in Prague, as was fitting for the head of a family that still owned tens of thousands of hectares of forests, all located in Czech areas of Bohemia. After completing his degree in 1933, he moved on to Charles University in Prague, where he studied history under the direction of Josef Pekař.[41] His choice of mentor both reflected and reinforced his family's strong identification with conservative Czech nationalism.

A major theme of Schwarzenberg's political writing was criticism of what he called the "modern, hypertrophic state," where centralizing and secularizing governments progressively curtailed or eliminated autonomous political and social bodies.[42] He traced this centralizing tendency to the Enlightenment and the French Revolution, which led to the subordination of all autonomous bodies such as the church and corporate groups to the secular state. As the state expanded, it incorporated more and more of the social world into its purview. It created "the state school, which nationalizes (*zestátňuje*) the mind, conscription, which nationalizes the body, socialism, which nationalizes property."[43] The state became all-encompassing, a self-perpetuating behemoth with increasingly terrible technological tools of control at its disposal.

Underlying Schwarzenberg's critique was a nostalgia for the old feudal order, in which nobles had formed a powerful autonomous estate and acted as a check on royal (state) power. Supposedly un-corrupted by liberal capitalism, individualism, and secularism, no-bles had ruled their peasants according to a moral and religious vision of the good of the whole. In contrast, the new order was based on "American principles" of atomization and individualism. "A vocation is no longer an estate *(stav)*, a lasting quality inherent in a person," he wrote, "but rather a chance circumstance of the moment." He lamented a lost age of "Christian hierarchy, social order, and economic stratification," which had fallen under the weight of "capitalism, industrialization and the modern method of forced schooling." Europe had entered an age of decadence and distorted values, "a playground for upstarts, swindlers, adventurous women, and dishonorable people."[44]

The French Revolution had also spawned absolute democracy, which Schwarzenberg blamed for the French Terror and its de-scendent, Hitlerian totalitarianism. In a 1937 article in *Řád*, Schwar-zenberg outlined the path by which a tyranny of the majority could be transformed into dictatorship. Because democracy required only a simple majority to topple a government, states could expect little continuity or stability as the whims of voters changed; this served to undermine the notion of universal moral and religious values that Schwarzenberg claimed were the bedrock of the old feudal order. Concurrent with a growing particularism, the democratic state had become all powerful, and new governments often used the power of their majority to reverse laws and penalize their opponents. Once in power, modern regimes used education to indoctrinate their cit-izens, just another example of the state usurping traditionally au-tonomous functions in order to perpetuate its centralizing grip on power. Thus power itself became the justification for holding power, rather than moral or spiritual authority. Modern states therefore lacked legitimacy, Schwarzenberg wrote, which could only be found in the universalism of Christianity. The particularist na-ture of democratic government was evident when such states "made untruth into law . . . dissolved Catholic marriage, or perhaps intro-duced prohibition, sterilization, or the required wearing of nose-rings." The point was that law under democracy could be arbitrary, based only on a moody electorate (or its unprincipled representatives) and not on a higher moral order. And from there, "where the state issues all laws, the theoretical transition to a dictatorial state is very easy."[45]

Schwarzenberg considered Hitler the ultimate democrat, and this was not a compliment. Building on his electoral successes, Hitler had used the power of the state in much the same way as any modern democratic leader, namely to consolidate his own position and to destroy his opponents. Restrictive Nazi policies on education, reproduction, marriage, and labor were a direct continuation of earlier democratic regimes; Hitler simply took them to their logical conclusion, extending the state's control over the family and the nongovernmental sphere more generally. Hitler's *Gleichschaltung*, the Nazification of organizational life, was just another example of the state subordinating autonomous bodies to its ever-expanding reach. Those who saw liberalism as an antidote to Hiterlerian dictatorship were sadly mistaken, Schwarzenberg wrote. "The Hitlerites are no more than national socialists," he continued. "Like all socialists, they are the heirs and consummation of liberalism. . . . They adopted the equality of citizens; they assumed the whole apparatus of state tyranny; they escalated centralization into totality; they intensified the party system into dictatorship."[46] Although beleaguered 1930s liberals must have thought Schwarzenberg crazy to cast Hitler as the spawn of liberalism, there is a certain postmodern (not to mention premodern) logic to his argument. In the postwar period, Theodor Adorno has argued that "the logic that hides behind Enlightenment rationality is a logic of domination and oppression." Adopting a similar line of reasoning to Schwarzenberg's, this position sees the seeds of the French Terror in Rousseau's writings on democracy.[47]

In a number of articles, Schwarzenberg expressed pessimism about the possibility of salvation for the modern order; instead of salvation, he obliquely predicted an apocalypse out of which a new order might be born. Drawing on the writings of Oswald Spengler, Schwarzenberg claimed that Christianity was in decline. "Spengler wisely grasped the direction of our age," he wrote. "After a millennium of Christian culture, the world is returning to the conditions of the pre-Christian era, to zoological relations, to the battle of all against all." The growing power of states inevitably increased international competition and the likelihood of war. With modern technology, wars were increasingly dangerous. The only possible salvation was a supranational moral arbiter, the Church. But modern man had abandoned the Church. "Because humanity is no [longer] Christian," he concluded, "it will exterminate itself."[48]

Like the Church, traditional conservatism appeared to be doomed. The rise of the modern, revolutionary state had forced conservatism into a fatal contradiction. The very nature of conservatism was to defend the status quo and the state; but since the status quo was revolutionary, its defense violated conservative values. Now that "power and property" were "in the hands of the enemies of Christianity," conservatism was dead. "If revolution rules," Schwarzenberg wrote in 1936, "conservative principles demand the end of conservatism." Though Schwarzenberg did not cite Karl Anton Rohan's paradoxical "revolutionary conservatism," he shared the view that the conventional conservative embrace of stasis and the traditional order would have to give way to a more combative defense of Christian principles. "Those who are obliged to advance a Catholic order in society are no longer on the defensive, but on the attack. . . . They are rebels."[49]

Schwarzenberg's injunctions were not entirely negative. Like many of his Bohemian German counterparts, he embraced economic and social corporatism as an alternative to Socialism and capitalism.[50] The system of productive estates that had reigned under feudalism protected rather than curtailed freedom. The new corporatism would consist of intermediary bodies with certain prescribed rights and purviews, thus limiting arbitrary state power. In fact, Schwarzenberg claimed in a 1935 article in *Řád*, corporatism promised not only a just economic order, but also the foundation for a true democracy, in which all citizens could participate "in that field of life into which fate has placed them." Isolated individuals were poorly equipped to defend their rights, he continued. In spite of the implied collectivism of the corporate order, corporations would actually be better able to protect individual freedoms than individuals acting alone.[51] Preferring moral and ideological themes, Schwarzenberg himself wrote little on the details of a latter-day corporatism. But *Řád* devoted a good deal of ink to the topic, and these articles give some idea of why it so attracted Schwarzenberg and other Czech Catholic nobles.

In a 1936 article in *Řád*, Rudolf Voříšek painted corporatism as a morally and socially superior alternative to capitalism and socialism. It was the much sought-after third way, "the only possible and vital way out of [our] current social confusion." Both capitalism and socialism divided society, Voříšek argued, setting individual against individual and class against class. Corporatism, on the other hand, emphasized the organic nature of society, the interrelatedness of social and occupational groups. "Against capitalism and its atomization and individualism, [corporatism] stresses the social whole," Voříšek wrote. "Against socialism and its centralism, it stresses the autonomous function of each corporation, of each estate *(stav)*." Citing the encyclical *Quadragesimo Anno*, he added that the moral and social structure of society were intimately tied, and that the reform of both should go hand in hand. Corporatism did not mean an end to wealth or social distinctions. The foundation of corporatism, Voříšek wrote, was the family and private property. But the latter did not imply the right or the necessity of exploitation. A corporate order would represent a compromise between the individual and the community, between capitalism and socialism.[52]

Such arguments were sure to appeal to Czech noble landowners. Corporatism promised a return to a "natural" hierarchy, in which paternalistic upper classes would exist harmoniously with contented workers. Popular democracy, which had effectively disenfranchised the nobility, would revert to a democracy of estates, in which large landowners might claim special representation similar to the landowners' curia in the Habsburg Empire. Corporatism seemed an antidote to the moral and political decay nobles associated with liberal capitalism, but at the same time it would preserve private property, the traditional bedrock of noble wealth and status. Finally, it carried God's seal of approval (via the Pope) and meshed well with the nobles' conservative Catholic worldview.

A second, specifically Czech aspect of noble conservatism was a continuing defense of the historic rights of the Bohemian crown.

Karel Schwarzenberg returned to this theme repeatedly in articles on Czech conservatism, minority rights, and the true meaning of freedom and democracy. The essence of the historic rights (*státo-právní*) position, Schwarzenberg argued, was the decentralization of power. Conservative Bohemian nobles had long opposed Habsburg centralism by insisting on their traditional rights as an autonomous estate in the Kingdom of Bohemia. This further justified Schwarzenberg's support for corporatism, which in a different form had once been the legal foundation for Bohemian claims of sovereignty. Schwarzenberg, like his mentor Pekař, claimed that Czech independence also rested on the historic rights argument.[53] Under the leadership of Palacký and Rieger in the nineteenth century, Czech nationalism had been essentially conservative, seeking to devolve power to provincial and regional bodies and opposing liberal German centralism. During the war, Masaryk had hijacked the historic rights position, using it to buttress his revolutionary independence program. Like Pekař, Schwarzenberg implied that Czechs should return to their conservative roots, and oppose the secular, progressive, centralizing state that Masaryk and Beneš had built. Although he did not explicitly mention Taaffe's Iron Ring of the 1880s, one can sense Schwarzenberg's nostalgia for that alliance of Czech national forces, clerical parties, and conservative large landowners, a coalition that kept liberalism at bay and maintained a semblance of political stability for over a decade.

Although the historic rights argument led Schwarzenberg to embrace independent Czechoslovakia, he was critical of Czech nationalists who would use that independence to oppress others. In a 1937 article on national minorities, Schwarzenberg argued for a more generous policy toward Czechoslovakia's Germans, in order to win back their support for the state. Now that the Czechs had their own state, Schwarzenberg wrote, they should treat their Germans magnanimously and lay aside the "inferiority complex" that still reigned among many Czechs, particularly in the borderlands. Above all, Czechs and Germans both should emphasize their common home of Bohemia. Schwarzenberg lamented "the decline of territorial patriotism and the growth of revolutionary nationalism." Nineteenth-century nationalists had regrettably discouraged the natural loyalty of people to their homeland in favor of "a professorial concept of linguistic nationalism."

Though Schwarzenberg saw Czechoslovakia as the legitimate heir of the historic Czech state, the nationalizing tendency of the Republic was another example of centralization gone out of control. In keeping with his general political philosophy favoring the devolution of power to autonomous political bodies, he believed that Germans should have substantial room for autonomous development. Even so, Schwarzenberg maintained that the historic Bohemian crown lands were fundamentally Czech, and "any rights that the German language might have in this state, their origin in every case is the Czech nation."[54] Schwarzenberg thus advanced a moderate and tolerant Czech nationalism, one that embraced the German legacy in Bohemia but saw Germans more as honored guests than as co-owners of the state.[55]

Czech Nobles and the Radical Right

Karel Schwarzenberg and a few other Czech nobles flirted with rightist movements that took a more radical nationalist position, but there is little evidence that they embraced the extreme xenophobia and anti-Semitism that characterized these Czech Fascist groups such as *Vlajka* (Banner) and *Akce národní obrody* (Movement of National Renewal). At the height of his career as a Catholic publicist, Schwarzenberg was also a member of *Vlajka*.[56] In the mid-1930s, *Vlajka* was known for its anti-German nationalism, anti-communism, anti-Semitism, and anticapitalism. Other than an affinity for corporatism on the Italian model and a stress on values, there was little positive in its program.[57] Schwarzenberg published occasional articles in *Vlajka's* journal *Nové Československo*, the last as late as 1937, and he was also involved with the organization's youth movement and outreach to international right-wing organizations.[58] During the late 1930s, he monitored the Spanish Civil War closely and subscribed to a handful of right-wing and fascist newspapers. This was not unusual, as many on the Catholic far right also had ties to Czech Fascist organizations.[59] The *Svaz's* last director, Jan Lobkowicz, was a leading member of another Fascist-leaning group,

Akce národní obrody, which espoused a program of national and moral regeneration and the rule of a conservative elite.[60] Though it is not clear how many other nobles were members of these groups, Tomáš Pasák presents evidence that at least the Schwarzenbergs, Lobkowiczs, and Lažanskýs provided financial support to fascist organizations.[61]

In spite of these indications of some support for the Czech nationalist right, it is difficult to generalize about the strength of national sympathies among Czech-leaning nobles in the 1930s. We have Karel Schwarzenberg's brother František's 1934 report of "an unexpected Czech nationalism" among the younger generation, and the Schwarzenberg brothers certainly fit this description.[62] A 1937 article in *Polední list* reported that many younger Czech nobles were loyal to the Czech state and had "applied themselves to active public work."[63] Even so, noble archives neither confirm nor disprove František Schwarzenberg's assertion of noble nationalism; the majority of Czech nobles kept a low public profile in the early 1930s. Ultimately, it would take national crises in 1938 and 1939 to test the depth of noble loyalty to the Czech nation and state; during these crises, Karel Schwarzenberg became a prominent spokesman for the Czech nobility.

The Declaration of 1938

When Hitler and the Sudeten German Party provoked a showdown with the Czechoslovak government over the Sudetenland in the summer of 1938, Czech nobles emerged as strong supporters of the integrity of Czechoslovakia. In a public display of patriotism, members of the Schwarzenberg clan donated hundreds of thousands of Czech crowns to an effort to improve border fortifications against a German attack.[64] The Czech *Svaz* also tried to arrange for loyal Czech nobles to meet with Lord Walter Runciman during his visit in August and early September. In their strongest expression of Czech loyalty, at the height of the Sudeten crisis in September 1938, a group of nobles delivered to President Beneš a public declaration of support for the integrity of the Czech state.

Drafted by Karel Schwarzenberg and signed by representatives

from twelve prominent noble families, the declaration was ostensibly a call for national unity in the face of the Nazi threat.[65] But
it was also a renewed assertion of noble relevance after two decades
of marginality in Czech public life. The declaration began by expressing the desire of "all estates and classes of our nation . . . to
prevent the violation of the historic borders of our state." Speaking
for "a number of historic families of our homeland *(vlast)*," the
proclamation tied the Czech nobility to the Bohemian historic
rights tradition and indirectly to the nationalism of Palacký and
Rieger. "Loyalty to the Czech/Bohemian *(český)* state, which our
ancestors helped to build and to maintain for a thousand years, is
for us so obvious an obligation that we hesitate to even express it
explicitly."[66] The unity of the Bohemian crown lands was anchored
deeply in history, a history shared by both the nobility and the
Czech nation. Curiously, the declaration made no mention of Slovakia. The emphasis on the Bohemian Kingdom seems to imply
that these nobles cared only about the integrity of Bohemia and
Moravia, though they may, like many others at the time, have identified the whole of Czechoslovakia with the historic Czech state.

Just as nobles in the late nineteenth century had tried to act as
conciliators, the declaration called for Czechs and Germans to join
together in a common Bohemian patriotism. "Our ancestors always
pursued friendly relations between the two nations of Bohemia,"
the nobles wrote, "and we too desire that our German-speaking
compatriots might share our love for an undivided homeland."
Moreover, the declaration made a point of expressing loyalty to the
Czech state without an explicit identification with Czech nationalism. With the exception of a single reference to "our nation *(naš
národ)*" in the first line, the text stuck to a territorial vocabulary
(state, homeland, historic borders, Bohemian crown lands). This
seems calculated to offer Bohemian Germans an alternative to
Hitler's pan-Germanism.[67] Though Schwarzenberg hoped that nobles could serve as intermediaries between the Czechs and the Germans, the declaration had little practical effect other than to raise
noble stock with the Czech public.

Though it is not surprising that Czech nobles employed a historic
rights argument when declaring their allegiance to Czechoslovakia,

it is remarkable that they made any sort of statement at all during the grim month of September 1938. They may have been gambling that Czechoslovakia would survive the Sudeten crisis intact and reward noble loyalty, but by mid-September the odds of that were poor. In fact, had pure opportunism ruled, nobles should more sensibly have remained silent until the Sudeten crisis had taken its course. Historic rights ideology was malleable and could just as well have justified the destruction of Czechoslovakia—which included, after all, the very unhistorical provinces of Slovakia and Ruthenia. Had Czech nobles been acting out of purely material interest, they would not have taken the risk of declaring so publicly their loyalty to the teetering Czechoslovak state.[68] Under the German occupation that began a year later, the signatories of the declaration would in fact pay dearly for their loyalty.

Czech Nobles and the Aftermath of Munich

After the humiliating diktat at Munich, Czechoslovak democracy went into a tailspin. President Beneš resigned and went into exile in October 1938. Before leaving, he appointed a new government under the leadership of the General Jan Syrový. As a figurehead president of Czecho-Slovakia, Syrový's caretaker government chose the aging Catholic-conservative Supreme Court justice, Emil Hácha. The Germanophile František Chvalkovský, who had previously served as ambassador to Fascist Italy, became the new foreign minister. Syrový's government, and that under his Agrarian right-wing successor Rudolf Beran, worked to coordinate Czech domestic and foreign policy with that of Nazi Germany. First, they simplified the party system by eliminating all but two parties, the ruling conservative Party of National Unity *(Strana národní jednoty)* and the listless opposition National Labor Party *(Národní strana práce)*. Next, Chvalkovský undertook regular trips to Berlin to gauge Hitler's desires and assure him that Czechoslovakia would follow a pro-German line internationally.[69]

With the once-powerful left demoralized and democracy discredited, right-wing political and cultural forces surged to fill the gap. If there was one thing Hitler would abide in rump Czecho-

Slovakia, it was an inwardly focused nationalism marked by xeno-phobia and anti-Semitism. As Jan Rataj writes, the sour Czech mood after Munich produced a "strong crisis of national self-confidence" and inspired a repressed "desire for revenge," which found alternate targets to the untouchable Germans.[70] Radical right-wing groups, such as the fascist *Vlajka* movement, took to the streets, denouncing "Jewish scum" and calling for the cleansing of Czech vocabulary and signs of foreign words.[71] The noble Jindřich Thun-Hohenstein spoke prominently at several gatherings during this time, calling for the revocation of Jewish citizenship in Czecho-Slovakia.[72]

The "new order" was an opening for conservative and Catholic forces, which favored authoritarian government, limits on civil lib-erties, and religious education. These forces took every opportunity to discredit the democratic First Republic. As one Catholic publicist put it, the last twenty years marked "the saddest chapter of Czech history—a period of planned and systematic destruction of all moral values among Czechs."[73] Munich, another wrote, was punishment for twenty years of sin; the Second Republic, therefore, must effect the moral and spiritual regeneration of Czech society.[74] Christian conservative groups, such as those surrounding the Catholic jour-nals *Řád* and *Tak*, embraced fascist programs. "The hierarchical na-ture of Catholicism," one of *Tak*'s leaders had written in 1928, "its authoritarian character and un-democratic structure, all this links fascism to Catholicism more than we think." In 1939, *Tak* advanced a detailed version of fascist corporatism, calling for a return to a society of estates, echoing what *Řád* had advocated since the mid-1930s.[75]

Though the Catholic right gained in influence after Munich, it was the former Agrarian Party under Beran that dominated the rump Second Republic until its demise in March 1939. Beran had led the Agrarians since 1935, when he had consolidated the right wing's growing control of the party. Under his leadership, the Agrarians had made peace with large-estate owners, reached out to the conservatives in the Catholic People's Party, and begun refer-ring to themselves as the largest Catholic force in the Republic.[76] Beran had also covertly supported various Czech fascist organiza-

tions in the mid-1930s. Under Beran, the Agrarians had opposed
Beneš's pro-French foreign policy, working instead toward improved relations with Nazi Germany and cooperation with the Sudeten German Party.

In November 1938, Beran became the leader of the new Party
of National Unity. He chose deputies primarily from the now, de-
funct Agrarians, Populists, and National Democrats, but the leadership also included the fascists Stříbrný and Gajda.[77] The government that emerged from this political grouping called itself an
"authoritarian democracy." Its relatively vague program stressed
order, national unity, and Christian values. Though not avowedly
fascist or particularly repressive, it nonetheless marginalized the opposition and remained largely immune from parliamentary control.
Jan Rataj sees the National Unity government as a hybrid regime:
"Authoritarian democracy in Czecho-Slovakia at the end of 1938
was an incomplete and transitional form of a totalitarian system; it
maintained the formal aspects of a democracy, but it aimed towards
their removal."[78]

The new conservative order proved attractive to members of the
Czech Catholic-nationalist nobility, and they in turn found a warm
reception in the ruling circles around Hácha and Beran. Sensing
opportunities for an increased role for the Czech nobility in public
affairs, Zdeněk Kinský visited the Presidential Chancellery on 25
October 1938 with the proposal that a loyal Czech noble become
the next president of Czechoslovakia. Because Karel Schwarzenberg
was still too young at twenty-eight, Kinský suggested Jan Lobkowicz, the current president of the Czech *Svaz* and a prominent
patron of the Czech Philharmonic.[79] Though nothing came of this
idea, it marked the beginning of a more active noble role in public
affairs.

In January 1939, a delegation of Czech nobles came to Prague
Castle to offer their services to President Hácha and the rump
Czech state. Led by František Kinský, the group included Karel
Schwarzenberg, Jan Lobkowicz, Karel Belcredi, and eight other
representatives of prominent noble families, many of whom had
signed the noble declaration in September 1938.[80] In a short speech
later released to the press, Kinský began by reminding Hácha of
the Czech nobles' 1938 pledge to "devote all their powers to serving

their homeland *(vlast)*." Invoking the "ancient castle of Czech kings" in which they spoke, Kinský emphasized historic Czech statehood and the nobility's long tradition of service to the state. In these trying times, he continued, "the unity of the nation in all its constituent parts . . . turns to you to lead the state well and justly." Czech nobles, he declared, were prepared "to serve the state to the best of our powers and abilities." Whatever comes, he concluded, "we will hold fast to the loyalty that binds us to the homeland of our ancestors."[81]

Hácha warmly thanked his noble visitors and assured them of the importance of their loyalty. He expressed his "longtime conviction that the participation of our old Czech families in the public life of our country is of tremendous value to the state." Their activity was not simply opportunistic, he added, but had deep roots in their historic ties to the nation. Agreeing with Kinský's association of the nobility with historic Czech statehood, Hácha claimed that "the old families, those that emerged from our nation and remained loyal to it, were and are living evidence that our nation already centuries ago reached a high level of civilization."[82] Like Pekař and other conservatives in the mid-1930s, Hácha acknowledged, even celebrated, a Czech national nobility. A lot had changed since 1918, when the entire political spectrum had depicted the nobility as foreign and inimical to Czech national interests.

Only days later, the Party of National Unity began considering a proposal to restore the right of nobles to use their ancestral titles (count, prince, etc.). In reporting the debate, the Catholic newspaper *Lidové listy* argued that the law against titles and the whole anti-noble campaign had been a mistake. "Among the old Bohemian nobility," the paper claimed, "the majority of families is truly Czech, not just because they emerged from our own history and our own soil, but because they correctly and sincerely cleaved to the Czech language and nation." Not only were Czech nobles loyal patriots, but they were also a diplomatic resource totally ignored by Czechoslovakia: "This was a social stratum that was preeminently capable of propagating the good name of the nation and trust in our revived state among influential Western aristocrats, not to speak of the fact that we could have drawn from them many capable individuals especially for diplomatic and administrative service." *Lidové listy* welcomed the government's plan to restore noble titles and believed it would engender little opposition. "The people will accept it sympathetically," the paper claimed, "because today it is no longer true that they would take an unfriendly or malicious attitude towards the old Czech nobility."[83]

In a sign of the degree of ideological shift that had taken place since the founding years of the First Republic, the nominally oppositional newspaper *Národní práce* only hazarded a timid disagreement with *Lidové listy*. Though the journal was "inclined to trust the loyalty of certain members of old Czech families," it doubted the loyalty of others. If the restoration of noble titles meant the restoration of the noble estate as it existed under the Habsburgs, the population would not in fact welcome the change.[84] A few days later, *Lidové listy* dispensed with this weak rejoinder, pointing out that a restoration of titles would not mean a restoration of privileges.[85]

There were a number of reasons for the rising currency of the Czech nobility under the Second Republic. Above all, Munich effectively destroyed the left, leaving the political field open to Catholic-conservative forces on the right that had previously been more sympathetic to the nobility. Moreover, after the truncation of Bohemia and Moravia, Czechs looked to nobles as traditional supporters of the unity of the historic Bohemian crown lands. The noble declaration of September 1938, with its historic rights rhetoric, confirmed Czech nobles' dedication to the Czech state, making a strong impression in a time of troubles. Ladislav Feierabend (1891–1969), the Czech minister of agriculture in the Beran government, would later praise Czech nobles for their "uncompromising attitude towards Czechness and their loyalty to the state . . . in these times of shifting values and political vacillation."[86] "State" was the key word; though Czechs could not openly advocate a return of the Sudetenland, the Czech nobility was an important symbol of the continuity of Czech statehood within Bohemia's traditional borders.[87]

❧ LIKE SO MANY OTHERS in Europe of the 1930s, Bohemia's nobles lamented the perceived crisis of capitalism and democracy and sought a workable social and political order. Seeking to reconcile the stability of the feudal world with the dynamism and realities of modern industrial society, Karel Schwarzenberg developed a hybrid Catholic-nationalist-corporatist ideology that drew on both historic rights precedent and contemporary fascist ideology. Though his thought had much in common with that of Karl Anton Rohan, Schwarzenberg's commitment to historic rights and Czech national politics turned him against Rohan's vision of a greater Germany. Ironically, for Czech national nobles, fascist inclinations inspired anti-Nazi behavior in the late 1930s, most notably in the risky declarations of loyalty to the Czech state in 1938 and 1939.

A dual process led Czech nobles to these declarations. On the one hand, the tide of anti-noble sentiment had begun to turn in the 1930s, as Czech public life moved in a more conservative direction and the resonance of symbolic anti-noble rhetoric faded. By the mid-1930s many nobles came to believe that public activity was once again viable. "The regime's unwillingness to allow members of the nobility entry to public life steadily declined," František Schwarzenberg later recalled, "and the willingness of the nobility to participate steadily increased."[88] Many conservative nobles, like the Schwarzenberg brothers, found a home on the Czech political right. Although declarations of noble national loyalty had begun as a defense strategy against land reform in the 1920s, by the mid-1930s these claims of Czechness transcended material interests. This was part of a broader European trend in the 1930s, as the disorienting influence of the Depression and subsequent political chaos ideologized political life to an extent unheard of since the rise of mass politics. This is not to say that class was no longer operative in shaping political choices, but class did not have the strong hold it once had.[89]

In 1918 nobles had largely remained silent when Czechs declared their independence from the Habsburg Empire, preferring to wait to see what the new order would bring. Noble class interests trumped whatever national sympathies most nobles may have held. Over the next decade, noble expressions of national loyalty were also closely tied to their material interests. The difference in 1938 was that noble national loyalties had gained in strength, to the point that many nobles appeared willing to sacrifice their material interests to what they perceived as the national interest. Their historic rights tradition, the sanctity of the Crown of Saint Wenceslas, had been nationalized in the two decades since the foundation of Czechoslovakia. In 1938, Czech nobles cast their lot with the Czech nation. During the ensuing German occupation and war, these nobles would share the fate of their fellow Czechs, suffering confiscations and arbitrary arrests like so many other Czechs. The Nazi challenge to Czechoslovakia tested the national loyalties of Czech and German nobles alike, and both factions responded with an unforeseen fervor. During World War II and its aftermath, the two groups would pay a great price for their nationalism.

~ 5

German Internationalism and National Socialism: German Nobles in the 1930s

Year after year approach was made to the League of Nations, charged by the terms of the Covenant with seeing that minorities got fair play. Year after year we were sent about our business. . . . The eyes of the whole population turned to Germany as their only hope of deliverance from despair.
~ *Alfons Clary-Aldringen, October 1938*

$\mathcal{B}$Y THE EARLY 1930s, Bohemia's German nobles were deeply disillusioned with the League of Nations and its minority protections. Karl Anton Rohan, Alfons Clary-Aldringen, and other leading German internationalists had hoped that the League would replace the supranational Habsburg state, providing an umbrella unity for German minorities and majorities in far-flung lands of Central and Eastern Europe. But the League's impotence was increasingly evident to all, both friend and foe. Bohemia's German internationalists now sought alternative means of securing German rights and interests in an increasingly German-dominated Central Europe. By the late 1930s, this would lead many of them to embrace fascism and ultimately National Socialism.

In crucial respects, the noble path to Nazism mirrored that of Konrad Henlein (1898–1945) and those who flocked to his Sudeten German Party (SdP) after 1933. Like so many others in the crisis-ridden 1930s, German nobles were looking for a "third way" in politics, economics, and social relations. Politically, many already skeptical nobles joined the growing chorus of criticism of democracy, favoring instead authoritarian government run by a conservative elite. In the economic realm, they embraced various forms of a German-dominated *Mitteleuropa*, which would put an end to the destructive autarkic policies of the region's nation-states. Socially, they sought national unity, a "national community" *(Volksgemeinschaft)* that would bury socialism and class struggle in favor of a narrowly defined conservative nation.

Though both the SdP and its noble supporters employed a fascist rhetoric and program as they pursued their third way, their relationship to Hitler and National Socialism was ambivalent in the mid-1930s. The SdP's politics initially tended more toward Catholic-conservative Austrofascism than the more radical social revolutionary vision ascribed to Hitler. But the events of 1938 put an end to any ambiguities in the relationship with Nazi Germany. After the annexation of the Sudetenland by Germany in October 1938, the SdP dissolved into the Nazi Party, and many Bohemian German nobles openly expressed their allegiance to the Nazi regime. By way of the Sudeten German identity they had begun to embrace in the 1920s, Bohemia's German nobles now found a new empire to replace the great German cultural and economic community they had lost in 1918.

The Rise of Sudeten German Fascism

If the 1890s heralded a "politics in a new key," the mobilization of the masses, then the 1930s were shriller yet, with left- and right-wing paramilitaries taking to the streets throughout much of Central Europe. In 1933, Nazi Brown Shirts transformed themselves from a public nuisance into the long arm of the law, as Adolf Hitler took power in Germany and the Austrofascist regime of Engelbert Dollfuss eliminated parliamentary life in Austria. These developments, along with the lingering economic crisis triggered by the Great Depression, had a profound effect on Sudeten Germans in Czechoslovakia, and by extension on the Bohemian German nobility. By late 1933, a popular fascist, though not necessarily Nazi, movement emerged in German Bohemia. Publicly stressing moderation, the new Sudeten German Party (SdP) at first embraced the very German internationalism earlier championed by Wilhelm Medinger, Eugen Ledebur, and Karl Anton Rohan. For that reason, as well as for reasons of ideological affinity, a number of prominent Bohemian German nobles supported the SdP and its genial leader Konrad Henlein. Like Henlein, many German nobles were subsequently drawn into the expanding Nazi orbit in the late 1930s.

Nobles disenchanted with democracy had a wide variety of fascisms to choose from in the 1930s.[1] Most versions of fascism stopped well short of the racial and genocidal tendencies of Hitler's National Socialism.[2] The typical fascist movement espoused some form of authoritarian dictatorship (the leadership principle), economic and social corporatism, strong anti-Bolshevism, and vigorous nationalism. Fascists tended toward a romantic and vague "organic" view of the nation, stressing the national community over individual interests. Where fascist movements most differed was in the degree of hate they evinced, their attitude toward violence, and their relationship to religion and old conservative elites. Hitler's paganism was widely noted, though he began his rule in 1933 in a relatively cautious alliance with Germany's conservative right. The dominant versions of Austrian and Sudeten German fascism in the 1930s had a strong religious component. Engelbert Dollfuss, for example, was the standard bearer of the Christian Socialist Party when he created an authoritarian government in Austria in 1933. To distinguish the Dollfuss regime from more radical fascist movements, many historians have labeled it "Austrofascist" or "clerico-fascist."[3]

Sudeten Germans did not start the decade in a radical mood. The Depression only hit Czechoslovakia full force in the early 1930s, and Sudeten Germans could still look across the border in 1930 and be glad they did not live in the free-falling Weimar Republic. Since the mid-1920s, most Sudeten Germans had taken an "activist" approach to the Czechoslovak state, and German bourgeois parties were regular members of Czech coalition governments after 1926. But when the Depression arrived, it struck the Sudeten regions particularly hard. Burdened by an overreliance on traditional export-oriented light industry (textiles) and luxury goods (glassware), the Sudeten Germans were ill equipped to deal with the contraction of the world market. When Weimar banks collapsed in 1931, Czechoslovak Germans also lost much of their reserve capital; Sudeten banks lost millions of crowns and could no longer offer credit to industry.[4] The economic crisis fed a rising dissatisfaction among Czechoslovakia's Germans, who blamed their difficulties on perceived Czech discrimination, as well as on Jews and global capitalism.

Capitalizing on the rising disaffection among Sudetenlanders, Konrad Henlein, the leader of the Sudeten German gymnastics movement, began building a "nonpartisan" all-German political organization in 1933.[5] Using propaganda methods perfected by the Nazis in Germany, Henlein managed to attract a wide following by emphasizing what his party was against (socialism, Czech discrimination, Jews, and rampant capitalism) and keeping its positive program to a bare minimum (a vague corporatism, the mystical *Volksgemeinschaft*, and national autonomy). As Elizabeth Wiskemann observed in 1938, Henlein's platform was "down with the Jews, down with the Reds, and unite in the spirit of the front-line soldiers like the leader Konrad Henlein who fought in the Great War."[6] Drawing votes from the moderate bourgeois activist parties, as well as from the banned Sudeten German Nazi Party, Henlein's Sudeten German Party won over 60 percent of the German vote in Czechoslovakia's 1935 elections.

Though most historians rightly label the SdP Fascist, it was not simply a Nazi wolf in sheep's clothing. For the first four years after its founding in 1933, Henlein's movement had more in common with the Austrofascism of Christian Socialists like Dollfuss, and it bore the distinct imprint of the charismatic Viennese professor Othmar Spann (1878–1950). In the 1920s, a number of disenchanted young Sudeten German intellectuals had gone to study at the university in Vienna. Formerly a professor in Moravia, Spann had been deported to Austria after 1918.[7] Now a popular lecturer in Vienna, Spann held forth on the evils of capitalism and individualism and called for the regeneration of the German spirit. He also sharply criticized popular democracy, arguing that "the true state was to be a *Ständestaat* [made up of estates] ruled by the best rather than by the many."[8] This combination of Nietzschean elitism and Habsburg conservatism proved attractive to Spann's Sudeten pupils, who returned home and founded a Spann circle in northern Bohemia in 1923. Under the leadership of Walter Heinrich and Heinrich Rutha, the group became known in the late 1920s as the *Kameradschaftsbund* (Society of Friends—KB) and founded a journal, *Die Junge Front* (The Young Front), in 1930. The gifted young organizer and publicist Walter Brand became a key figure in the group after 1931, when he completed an intellectual apprenticeship with Spann in Vienna.[9]

The KB considered itself the kind of new elite Spann had envisioned. Its members, including Konrad Henlein, began gradually to work themselves into high-level positions in prominent Sudeten German organizations, including the Gymnastics Association and Wilhelm Medinger's *Völkerbundliga* in the late 1920s and early 1930s. With a ban of the Sudeten German Nazi and Nationalist parties imminent in 1933, the KB saw its chance to enter politics. From the SdP's foundation until at least 1936, Brand and Rutha were Henlein's closest advisers and KB members largely controlled the party. Even so, the SdP had a substantial Nazi wing, which took over *Die Junge Front* in 1934. In his careful study of the SdP, Ronald Smelser documents a bitter rift between the KB "traditionalists" and Nazis in the party.[10] Ironically, Hitler backed the KB group, seeing in the relatively moderate Henlein a more useful tool for his expansionist foreign policy. Hitler rightly feared that Czechoslovakia would move quickly to ban a fully Nazified SdP, and he preferred that the party stay intact and available for future manipulation. In many ways this matched Hitler's domestic policy of reining in Nazi radicals in 1934 in order to placate his conservative allies in the army. In any case, Hitler's moral and financial support for Henlein was covert, and the SdP would maintain its nominal independence from the Nazi Party until the fateful summer months of 1938.

From German Internationalism to National Socialism

There was much about Henlein and the SdP that Czechoslovakia's German nobles found attractive. Even in the 1920s, many had shared Rohan's skepticism of democracy and Ledebur's condemnations of socialism and espousal of a corporate/collective "national community." Though there is no evidence of noble membership in the secretive KB, many German nobles shared its anticapitalism and conspiratorial elitism. A group of nobles around Rohan even had their own circle of intellectuals, the *Grusbacher Herren*, named after the Moravian estate of Karl (Count) Khuen-Lützow (1879–1963). German internationalist nobles around Rohan, Medinger, and Ledebur shared many of the ideological premises of the KB, an affinity that brought them into alliance with the SdP in the mid-1930s. Like a large number of conservative nobles in Germany who saw Hitler as a palatable alternative to the hated Weimar democracy, the SdP attracted many Sudeten German nobles who resented land reform, despised Czechoslovakia, and sought closer ties to international Germandom.

As economic despair and political impotence spread through Central Europe in 1930, Rohan and his colleagues struggled for an explanation of the growing crisis and sought, in largely abstract terms, a way out. Early in 1930, Rohan returned to the subject of fascism in an article titled "Leadership" *(Führertum)*. Much of Europe was now looking for strong leadership, he wrote. Since the French Revolution of 1789, hierarchy and personal leadership had declined in the face of liberal notions of equality and brotherhood. Monarchy (patriarchal rule) had given way to parliamentary government and democracy (fraternal rule). Since 1918, the materialism of the left was associated with democracy, which counted individuals as equal units. The right, by contrast, favored quality over quantity, the personal and spiritual over the material. Rohan saw materialism and its principle of fraternalism as a revolt "against the father myth, against the paternal symbol." But a reaction was now underway, as the wartime generation was coming of age politically. Idealizing the front experience of strong leadership, the new generation sought a synthesis of "the personal and the material principle in politics." Though Rohan did not yet outline the content of this synthesis, the implications were clear. It would be a populist dictatorship, a regime run by a paternalist elite in the interests of the national community.[11]

When Hitler seemed to usher in just such a regime in 1933, Rohan saw it as a world historical breakthrough. In ecstatic prose,

Karl Anton Rohan, 1937. Karl Anton Rohan, *Schicksalsstunde Europas*

Rohan welcomed the triumph of the heroic and spiritual over the hedonistic and materialist trend of the past century. He saw the victory of National Socialism as a double revolution: the triumph of the leadership principle and the unification of the body of the *Volk*. The Nazis rejected equality, which had no basis in nature, favoring instead the rule of a "new type of human being" who emerges as leader from the crucible of struggle. "Thus have all aristocracies begun," Rohan wrote. "This revolution seeks to create a new elite, perhaps a new nobility."[12] The leader and his chosen elite embodied the national community, which united the national and social principles. Liberal and socialist materialism had driven the national and the social apart, setting the individual versus the community and class versus class. National Socialism and fascism put the community first by encompassing social identity within national identity. One was not simply a worker, but rather a German worker. Community, Rohan believed, was central to the European tradition, and National Socialism appeared poised to lead Europe back to its future. In Hitler's rise, Rohan sensed the growing momentum of a "conservative revolution."[13]

In a separate article reprinted in 1933 from the Berlin-based *Deutsches Adelsblatt*, Rohan brought his 1928 reflections on nobility up to date with the revolutionary changes taking place in Germany.[14] The meaning of nobility was threefold, he argued. It was an attitude toward life; "a complex biological result of breeding" involving "spirit, power, and blood"; and a social group. Only those who met the criteria of all three categories were truly noble.[15] Rohan repeated many of his points from 1928 regarding the importance of family, soil, and tradition to noble identity. But his stress on "breeding" *(Züchtung)* and blood set his 1933 reflections apart from his initial ideas on nobility. Attracted to Nazi elitism, Rohan also adopted Hitler's racial-biological conception of genetic superiority. The greatest pull of the revolution, Rohan wrote, was "the yearning for morally certain leadership *(Führertum)*, for the organization of society, for a renewed realization of the natural law of the inequality of mankind, for the affirmation of the noble and the rejection of lesser beings *(Untermenschentums)*." To Rohan, the nobility was a ready-made genetic elite, the very Aryan "superior beings *(Übermenschen)*" whom Hitler claimed to favor.[16]

Inclined to action as well as reflection, Rohan had long been involved in noble circles that sought to rejuvenate the Central European nobility and place aristocrats at the head of a conservative revolution. Having abandoned the conservative Catholic group *Ös-*

terreichische Edelleute in 1926 because of its unyielding monarchism, Rohan preferred to associate himself with a circle of nobles in Czechoslovakia known as the *Grusbacher Herren*. Though it is unclear how many members the group had, its most active participants were prominent Bohemian German nobles such as Alfons Clary-Aldringen, Karl Buquoy, Ulrich Kinsky and Adolf Dubsky.[17] Others such as Eugen Ledebur, if not members themselves, received occasional circulars from the *Grusbacher* leadership.[18]

The group took its name from the estate of Karl Khuen-Lützow in south-Moravian Grusbach (Hrušovany nad Jevišovkou) near the Austrian border.[19] Khuen was a descendent of an ancient Tyrolian family that had settled in Moravia in the 1630s. The Khuens were known as strong Habsburg loyalists, and Karl Khuen had been a highly decorated officer in the First World War.[20] He was also well-connected internationally thanks to his 1923 marriage to Nora (Countess) Lützow, whose family had strong English ties and whose father Heinrich (1852–1935) had been a longtime Austrian diplomat. Khuen added the Lützow name to his own when it became clear in the 1920s that the line would have no male heir. The marriage also made Khuen the brother-in-law of Adolf Dubsky, a fellow Moravian and active *Grusbacher.*[21]

The initial agenda of the *Grusbacher Herren* in the mid-1920s was to work toward the regeneration of the nobility of Central Europe. In a 1926 memorandum aimed at winning supporters in Austria, Karl Rohan outlined what would become the group's early program. First, he argued, the old aristocracy had to abandon feudal thinking for good. After the revolutions of 1918, there would be no return to the political prominence of the Habsburg years or the social dominance of the late Middle Ages. "However," he wrote, "the essence and true tradition of the nobility is rooted much deeper than its political engagement." Rather, it was metaphysical, a set of values. The goal of the *Grusbacher Herren* was to preserve noble values and to convince an increasingly soulless Europe that those values offered salvation. As Rohan wrote, "European humanity . . . seeks old values that can be incorporated in the new forms, the new context" of postimperial Europe. Practically speaking, the noble movement needed to organize lectures on the meaning of nobility,

social outlets to encourage noble endogamy and networks, and programs to imbue noble youth with a sense of political and ideological
mission. The ultimate goal was "to train a young class of leaders."[22]

Though the group did not start as a political organization per se,
the eventual political engagement of its members on behalf of the
SdP and Hitler requires a closer look at the politics of individual
participants in the early 1930s. Karl Rohan, as illustrated, was an
early admirer of fascism, a stance shared by Khuen, Adolf Dubsky,
and other *Grusbachers*. But not all of his colleagues were as enthusiastic about Hitler as Rohan was in 1933. Dubsky thought him
"vain and a big talker" and hoped he would just disappear.[23] A friend
of the ex-chancellor Franz von Papen, Dubsky seemed to share the
German conservatives' view that Hitler was a necessary evil. He
was particularly incensed at the lack of tact Hitler showed toward
the Jews. "I consider Jewry to be a plague," he wrote in his diary
in 1933, "but not one that can be healed by inadequate methods."
Hitler's anti-Jewish measures were alienating England, a most important ally in Dubsky's opinion.[24] Though many Bohemian nobles
likely shared Dubsky's qualified anti-Semitism, almost none of them
expressed anti-Jewish racism publicly.

In spite of his reservations, Dubsky was not opposed to National
Socialism in principle. "Above all," he wrote to the German Count
Hermann Keyserling in 1932, "I see in the National Socialist movement the expression of a passionate protest against the peace im-
posed in 1918 and against the constitution of Weimar." After 1918,
Germans suffered from a loss of face and a loss of confidence.
"Hitler understood masterfully the need to accent the restoration
of German honor." This alone, Dubsky wrote, explained why conservatives were moving toward Hitler's camp in spite of the "demagogic points" in the National Socialist program. So far, he added,
the Nazis had only a vaguely defined program, which would need
working out. But the movement's popularity was understandable:
"The essence of National Socialism is only comprehensible when
one sees it as a kind of convulsive struggle for inner cleansing, a
reflex of the German national body *(Volkskörper)*, so to speak." Its
task would be to remove the stain of revolution from Germany, to
bring order to the chaotic and ungovernable Republic.[25]

Like Rohan, Dubsky also sought to formulate a new European order that would eliminate "soulless" states like Czechoslovakia and Austria. Though he spent much of his time in Vienna, Dubsky was in fact a Czechoslovak citizen. His family was of old Bohemian lineage and had sided with the Protestants against the Habsburgs in the Thirty Years' War. But the Dubskys had soon returned to the Habsburgs' good graces and had gone on to distinguished service in the army and bureaucracy. Adolf Dubsky's uncle Adolf (1833–1911) had been a Constitutionally Loyal representative in the Bohemian Diet and the *Reichsrat*, where he also had ties with the Moravian *Mittelpartei*.[26] Young Adolf carried on this tradition, serving in the Austrian embassy in London starting in 1913.[27]

Dubsky identified himself as an "imperial old Austrian," but also as a German in the national sense.[28] He believed that the Austrian spirit had been universalist, as the Habsburgs were traditionally the "pathfinders and culture carriers of the West towards the East." But the Austrian mission had little meaning without Germany and a great empire, he said in a 1927 speech at the Theresianum, an elite school in Vienna founded by Maria Theresa in the eighteenth century. The time had come, Dubsky declared, for a new "West-East Reich," one in which Austrians should take a prominent part. Though Germany was to be the brawn of this new empire, Austria was to provide its universal mission. "Germany without Austria must remain spiritually impoverished," he concluded.[29]

Dubsky considered a Habsburg revival as highly unlikely, but neither could the current proliferation of "soulless" mini-states persist. "The political independence of Czechoslovakia in its present form is an absurdity," he wrote in 1927. It had inherited all of the weaknesses of the old Austria-Hungary without any of its strengths. Six million Czechs surrounded by 80 million Germans would inevitably have to submit to German rule. Indeed, Bohemia was the spiritual heart of Austria, the source of many of its greatest leaders, writers, and generals. An *Anschluss* of Austria and the Bohemian lands to Germany would reunite the creative forces of the Holy Roman Empire and reignite the German mission of spreading culture to the East and defending against Eastern barbarism, which now took the form of Soviet Communism. "I have no desire," he concluded, "either for myself or my children, to be displayed as some strange specimen of a dying race in a wax museum!" Austria still had hope, but only as part of Germany.[30]

Members of the *Grusbach* circle followed a trajectory common among Sudeten Germans in the years from 1918 to 1938. Beginning the period as Habsburg loyalists, they soon left their monarchism behind in the face of political reality. In the 1920s, they put their faith in the League of Nations and in other attempts at international understanding that would serve as a kind of ersatz Habsburg Empire. But by 1934, after the League's impotence had become obvious to all, Dubsky would express the commonly held view that "the League of Nations is the most monumental humbug that was ever concocted by victorious states."[31] With the League failing and a new German empire on the rise after 1933, many nobles came to embrace the concept of a Greater Germany under the leadership of Hitler, even if they had doubts about Hitler's personal fitness for such an exalted position.

Rohan and Dubsky were relative newcomers to a *Mitteleuropa* concept with a long lineage. As early as the 1830s, Friedrich List had promoted the idea of a large German economic union in Central Europe, an idea that had also proven attractive to Austrian statesmen such as the post-1848 Prime Minister Felix Schwarzenberg. During the First World War, Friedrich Naumann revived List's originally liberal idea in his 1915 book *Mitteleuropa*, and German war aims came to include large-scale annexations to create a so-called German *Wirtschaftsraum* (economic space).[32] Rohan was an admirer of both List and Felix Schwarzenberg. As Rohan wrote in 1936, "Friedrich List's prophetic vision of a technocratically defined middle European union remains a relevant theory up to today."[33] Echoing Naumann, Rohan too called for a *Wirtschaftsgrossraum* (greater economic space) in Central Europe.[34]

Rohan shared many of the views of Wilhelm Medinger, who wrote an article on *Mitteleuropa* for *Deutsche Rundschau* in early 1933. Medinger lamented Czechoslovakia's economic and political orientation toward France and the Little Entente, claiming that its natural trading partners were Germany and Austria. In "childlike joy at [its] new self-rule," Czechoslovakia had passed up the opportunity of integrating its economy with that of its neighbors. He blamed this policy for the severity of the economic crisis in Czechoslovakia, and he too called for a "a great economic region" that would encompass Germany and the former Habsburg Empire.[35] A variety of *Mitteleuropa* ideas circulated during the interwar period, with some more liberal than others. But by the mid-1930s, Peter Stirk points out, "The growth of Nazi power and ambition closed off options." *Mitteleuropa* was increasingly associated with Hitler's policy of *Lebensraum* (living space) and Germany's hegemonic aspirations.[36]

Rohan's vision of a Greater Germany was no exception, though he initially stuck to a formula that stressed the spiritual-cultural unity of Germandom more than political unity. Like Dubsky, Rohan sought a return to the universalist goals associated with the Holy Roman Empire. Consistent with his pan-Europeanism of the 1920s, Rohan opposed the national state, particularly in the German case where so many Germans lived outside of Germany. The division of Germans among Germany, Austria, Czechoslovakia, and other countries contradicted the spiritual unity of the German nation. By 1937, Rohan turned to Nazism to provide a new ideology for his pan-German vision. Rather than a subjective (and thus changeable) German cultural identity, National Socialism posited an objective German racial identity. The repository of this identity was German blood, "the carrier of not only biological, but also the highest spiritual and intellectual forces" of the nation.[37] This curiously echoed Rohan's earlier musings on the blood-borne essence of aristocracy.

In spite of his adoption of Nazi racist ideology, Rohan did not in 1937 see a pressing need for Germany to annex the parts of East Central Europe that contained large German populations. Credulously taking Hitler at his word, Rohan believed that the Nazis sought only to unite Germans in the spirit of "national citizenship" *(Volksbürgerschaft)* rather than "state citizenship" *(Staatsbürgerschaft)*. In other words, Rohan believed in the spiritual unity of the German people above all. Though no pacifist, he did not support a German war of expansion.[38] Rohan thought Konrad Henlein a model practitioner of the spiritual unity–political independence dichotomy. As of 1937, Henlein was still publicly pursuing autonomy for Germans within Czechoslovakia and strong cultural ties of the Sudetenland with Germany. By recognizing that Germans could be proud and active members both of a national community (Germandom) and of a non-German state (Czechoslovakia), Rohan wrote, Henlein "had made a grand contribution of fundamental importance for a just solution of the nationality problem."[39] Indeed, Henlein's goals were similar to the minority protection reforms Rohan had advocated in 1930.

Henlein and the Sudeten German *Kameradschaftsbund* were also influenced by the *Mitteleuropa* ideas of Friedrich Naumann and Othmar Spann in particular. In his lectures, Spann taught that Germandom was the carrier of the highest ideals of mankind, and that Marxism, liberalism, and revolution were only temporary setbacks on the way to a universal German spiritual (and by extension political) empire.[40] Though not himself a racial nationalist, Spann's idea of a pervasive "spirit" animating German culture was not far removed from Rohan's concept of a spiritual identity born by German blood. Both were metaphors of connectedness and both implied the need for a larger German unity, be it political or primarily cultural.

The obsession of Rohan and many of his Bohemian-German noble colleagues with the animating spirit of Germandom reflected their struggle to define a place for themselves in a post-Habsburg Europe. Strong imperial patriots before the war, they could summon little loyalty for rump-Austria or the other successor states after 1918. Rohan, Ledebur, and many others first turned to the League of Nations as a possible vehicle for their German-flavored Europeanism. As Rohan wrote in 1937, the League in the 1920s had the potential to become an imperial super-state that could implement a system of international laws to ensure cultural autonomy for Germans (and other minorities) all over Europe.[41] But circumstances rendered the League impotent, the "monumental humbug" dismissed by Dubsky in 1934.

At the same time that the League was losing its luster, fascism, in its various guises, offered disaffected Germans in Central Europe an alternative internationalism, a German-internationalist "national community." Ledebur, Rohan, and other nobles had already grasped the post-imperial advantages of an international German *Volksge-meinschaft* in the 1920s. Hitler and Henlein gave the idea further political force, and their anti-socialism, Nietzschean elitism, and "revolutionary conservatism" were particularly attractive to German nobles searching for a new old order in the 1930s. Karl Rohan liked to think of himself as a composite Austrian-German-European. His was a post-Habsburg imperial identity in search of an empire in the 1920s and 1930s. Hitler's promise of a new German thousand-year Reich proved hard to resist.[42]

Internationalization of the Sudeten German Question

In spite of all their efforts to internationalize the Sudeten German question in the 1920s, Medinger and Ledebur had achieved little more than occasional admonitions from abroad over land reform. Even so, the *Völkerbundliga* had built a strong following in Czecho-slovakia and secured powerful connections in Geneva and Britain. In 1935, Henlein and the SdP leadership saw in Medinger's orga-nization a useful tool for developing its own foreign policy, inde-pendent of that of Czechoslovakia's Foreign Minister Edvard Beneš. Using preexisting *Kameradschaftsbund* networks in the minority lob-bying community, the SdP effectively took control of the *Völker-bundliga* and used it and its noble members' connections in England to promote the Sudeten German cause. In effect, the SdP became the flag bearer of the German internationalism espoused by Rohan and Ledebur in the 1920s. In return, the well-connected *Grusbachers* Alfons Clary-Aldringen, Adolf Dubsky, and Karl Khuen would be among the SdP's most valued propagandists abroad.

The key early link between Bohemian German nobles and the SdP was through Medinger's *Völkerbundliga*, which retained strong noble support up to 1938.[43] Heinrich Rutha, a KB traditionalist and the foreign policy chief of the SdP, worked closely with minority organizations after 1933 and was a vice president of the *Völkerbun-dliga* at the time of his death in 1937.[44] In addition to Rutha, the SdP had a number of representatives in the executive committee of the group, including one of Henlein's leading propagandists, Wil-helm Sebekowsky, and Artur Vogt of the SdP's "Office for Nationalities and League of Nations Questions."[45] Above all, though, it was Alfons Clary-Aldringen who turned the *Völkerbundliga* into a willing tool of the SdP. Clary was vice president of the organization for much of the 1930s, and in 1937 he became president, officially joining the SdP soon after.[46]

Trying to build on SdP momentum in 1935, the KB moderates Heinrich Rutha and Walter Brand sought to bring the Sudeten German cause to prominent ears in Britain. "We recognized with complete clarity," Brand would recall later, "that the key to aid from abroad lay in England. For that reason we cultivated relations there carefully."[47] A number of factors combined to make Britain the most important target of SdP lobbying. Above all, much of Britain's political elite believed the Treaties of Versailles had been flawed, and they were sympathetic to German desires for revision. Both for that reason and because of the Czechoslovak-Soviet mutual assistance pact of 1935, the Chamberlain government was hostile toward Czechoslovakia. At the same time, the United States, which had championed self-determination in 1918, was taking one of its customary breaks from European affairs in the 1930s. France was still strongly anti-German in the 1930s and was an ally of Czechoslovakia and the Soviet Union. In the post–World War I cordon enveloping Central Europe's Germans, Great Britain appeared to be the weak link.

The Bohemian German nobility proved a valuable asset to the SdP as it worked to win influential Englishmen for the Sudeten German cause. Karl Khuen, who was well connected in London, introduced Henlein to Colonel Graham Christie, the former Royal Air Force attaché to Berlin, and Sir Robert Vansittart, the permanent under-secretary of state at the Foreign Office. Vansittart opened the door for Henlein's first visit to London, which took place in December 1935. Henlein's speeches and meetings in London over the next few years focused on Czech "Bolshevism," discrimination against Sudeten Germans, and the SdP's desire for a peaceful solution to the minority question in Czechoslovakia. Vansittart proved a particularly sympathetic listener, and Christie helped Henlein get access to a wide array of high officials and influential academics.[48] Moreover, Christie himself came to have great respect for Henlein, an attitude expressed in letters and visits to friends such as R. W. Seton-Watson and Arnold Toynbee. "I am convinced of the sincerity of this man," Christie wrote to Seton-Watson in late 1935. He urged Seton-Watson to use his influence in Czechoslovakia to win "a concession to such a policy as Henlein propounds."[49] Vansittart, too, began advocating on Henlein's behalf, asking Foreign Secretary Anthony Eden to press Edvard Beneš for concessions to the Sudeten Germans.[50]

Bohemian nobles also used their connections in England to lobby on their own for the Sudeten German cause. As head of the Vienna branch of the *Deutsch-englische Gesellschaft* (known in Britain as the Anglo-German Fellowship), Adolf Dubsky visited London several times during the late 1930s. While there, he met with the British ambassador to Germany, Neville Henderson, and prominent aristocrats such as Lord Londonderry and Lord Arnold. Among the members of the English branch of the Fellowship was also Leslie Runciman, son of the respected shipping tycoon Walter Runciman. Dubsky's central mission was to build sympathy in England for Germans and Germany, and he was unstinting in his criticism of the "un-state" Czechoslovakia.[51] He also wrote anti-Czech and pro-German articles for the *Deutsch-englische Hefte*, a journal based in Berlin.[52]

Ulrich Kinsky, who had made much of his "Czech roots" when land reform threatened his estates in 1926, was even more active than Dubsky in pressing the Sudeten German cause in England. Using his own airplane to fly to London on several occasions, he lobbied to create pressure on Czechoslovakia to give in to Henlein's demands for autonomy in 1937 and 1938.[53] Jan Masaryk, the Czech ambassador to Britain, wrote to the Czech Foreign Ministry in 1938 warning of a steady stream of visitors propagandizing for the SdP. He singled out Dubsky, Khuen, and Ulrich Kinsky as lobbyists for Hitler. "Kinsky is behaving particularly incorrigibly," Masaryk reported. "He is asserting that Czechoslovakia is a Bolshevik monster and must be destroyed."[54] As the British government was mooting the possibility of a mission by Lord Runciman in 1938, Kinsky sought him out personally in July to urge him to make the trip to Czechoslovakia.[55]

Bohemian German nobles also proved useful to the SdP on the home front. Using contacts in the British embassy in Prague, Rutha and Brand managed to steer visiting dignitaries in the direction of gracious noble hosts. As Ronald Smelser writes, "Conservative Britons were wined and dined; trout fishing expeditions to the estates of Bohemian nobles lent an air of respectability to the SdP, while trips through the depressed Sudeten German industrial areas generated the desired degree of sympathy."[56] Arnold Toynbee was just such an important and potentially sympathetic visitor in 1937; during a fact-finding trip in late May, he stayed with Khuen at Grusbach, probably at the suggestion of their mutual friend Christie. There is no record of their conversations during Toynbee's stay, but it is known that Khuen considered himself a friend of Henlein and was working actively for the SdP in 1937. When Toynbee published an article on "Czechoslovakia's German Problem" a few months later in the *Economist*, Khuen's wife proudly pasted it into the Grusbach guest book, claiming in the margin that the Khuens had been the "inspiration" for the article.[57]

This could not have been entirely true, however, because Toynbee did not share the Khuens' unequivocal support for Nazi Germany. Even so, Toynbee's depiction of the Czechs was far from flattering. "In Czechoslovakia today," he wrote, "the methods by which the Czechs are keeping the upper hand over the Südeten-deutsch [*sic*] are not democratic." In pursuing a "policy of Czechization," Toynbee added, the Czechs "antagonize the Germans on both sides of the frontier." He believed that Henlein genuinely sought only "to secure tolerable conditions of existence for his own people within the framework of the Czechoslovak Republic, without changing the existing frontiers or setting up a state within the state." The Sudeten question was in fact part of the larger problem of the future of Central Europe. The persistent misery in the region, he asserted, "must mean that there is some radical defect in the peace settlement." Any new settlement in Central Europe could not ignore German power and influence, though Toynbee opposed a *Naumannsche Lösung* (solution à la Naumann) that would include political hegemony. "The European statesmen have to find a solution," he concluded, "which will give Germany as large an economic scope in Central Europe as may be compatible with the maintenance of the political independence and integrity of Germany's eastern neighbors."[58] This was similar to the ideas of a greater-German economic and cultural zone that so appealed to Rohan and many of his Sudeten German noble colleagues. Understandably, the *Grusbacher Herren* were pleased with Toynbee's article.[59]

The *Grusbachers* were far less pleased with Elizabeth Wiskemann's book, *Czechs and Germans*, which appeared in early 1938. A fellow of Toynbee's Royal Institute, Wiskemann too visited the Khuens, in July of 1937. But Wiskemann's book was much fairer in its depiction of the Czech-German conflict. Without minimizing the extent of Czech nationalism, she gave ample documentation of the more pernicious aspects of the SdP. She concluded that the ultimate blame for the Sudeten problem lay with the concept of "racial nationalism" on both sides. Only "the humanism of Thomas Masaryk" offered any hope for peace among Central Europe's nationalities. But given the feverish nationalism of 1938, she was not optimistic. The Khuens stuck an advertisement for Wiskemann's book next to her entry in their guest book. Someone had scribbled on the ad: "terrific sleeping medicine."[60]

In spite of the dedicated efforts of Bohemian German nobles on behalf of the SdP, their importance to the German lobbying effort should not be overestimated. Heinrich Rutha and Walter Brand were the leading propagandists for the SdP, and their work was perhaps most influential in winning sympathy for the SdP in England and elsewhere. As vice president of the *Völkerbundliga*, Rutha regularly attended international minority conferences on behalf of the SdP. He used these trips to lobby fellow delegates on behalf of the Sudeten Germans, to meet with influential politicians, and to deliver propaganda materials to press outlets.[61] With pressure for a solution to the Sudeten question picking up in 1937, the SdP set up a full-time press bureau in London headed by Brand.[62] The SdP's propaganda efforts, then, were a highly organized and orchestrated affair. The lobbying of Sudeten German nobles was a small, though influential, part of the larger project.

The Runciman Mission and Munich

A confidant of Neville Chamberlain, Lord Walter Runciman arrived in Czechoslovakia in August 1938 with the intention of pressing the Czech President Edvard Beneš to meet Sudeten German demands for autonomy. Like Chamberlain, Runciman believed that any solution was preferable to a war with Germany. So when Henlein's demands escalated in early September 1938, Runciman came to the conclusion that the only peaceful solution to the Sudeten problem would be the annexation of the Sudetenland to Hitler's Reich. This was exactly Chamberlain's view, and it is unlikely that Runciman's report of 21 September did anything more than confirm the British prime minister's intention to grant Hitler's demands at Munich. Even so, the Runciman mission is interesting precisely because of its symptomatic qualities. It offers insight into the mentalities that kept British leaders from comprehending Hitler's aggressive designs.[63] The mission also marks the culmination of the Bohemian-German nobility's nationalization and accommodation with the SdP.

Runciman and his entourage did not want to think badly of Henlein or Hitler, and Runciman's friends among the now solidly "Sudeten German" nobility genteelly reassured him that both were decent men. The SdP smartly returned to its habit of using nobles to butter up the party's English sympathizers. During Runciman's six-week stay in Czechoslovakia, he spent all but one weekend as a guest of Bohemian nobles. He ate lavish dinners with them, hunted partridges on their estates, and toured the countryside in their motorcars. This is not to say that Lord Runciman was trying to escape from the primary duties of his mission: finding facts and mediating between the Czech and Sudeten German leadership. Runciman and his team actually collected a huge amount of information and met numerous times with representatives of both sides. But if his primary goal was to take the tenor of the dispute, to judge the merits of Sudeten German claims of discrimination, Runciman's social visits with the Grusbach crowd surely had an influence.

It was no accident that Runciman spent his weekends with nobles. The SdP had prepared well, as usual, forming in advance a "political staff" under Karl Hermann Frank and a "social staff" organized by

Runciman's acquaintance Ulrich Kinsky.[64] Runciman's social program included stays with Kinsky, his distant cousin Zdeněk Radislav Kinský (1896–1975), (Prince) Max Hohenlohe (1897–1968), and Alfons Clary-Aldringen. Runciman and other members of his entourage also lunched and toured the countryside with the Kinskys, Karl Khuen, Adolf Schwarzenberg and the *Verband* stalwarts (Counts) Josef and Friedrich Westphalen. With the exception of Schwarzenberg, whose national politics remain obscure, and Zdeněk Kinský, who would later declare his allegiance to Czechoslovakia, all of Runciman's noble hosts sympathized with the SdP.

Throughout Runciman's visit to Czechoslovakia, Hohenlohe served as an intermediary between Henlein and members of the mission. Hohenlohe was one of the few Bohemian members of an ancient and powerful Reich German family. The Hohenlohes had drifted in and out of Bohemian history, serving as generals on the Protestant side in the Thirty Years' War and in the Habsburg army in the nineteenth century.[65] Max Hohenlohe inherited the 11,000 ha estate at Rothenhaus (Červený Hrádek) in the largely German district near Komotau (Chomutov). He shared many of Clary and Khuen's ties in London, including Vansittart, Runciman, and Frank Ashton-Gwatkin, Runciman's aide from the Foreign Office.

During the first few weeks of Runciman's visit, Henlein had avoided a direct meeting with the British representative. Hohenlohe attributed this to the pernicious influence of Karl Frank, who, as Hohenlohe related to Ashton-Gwatkin on 14 August, had urged Henlein "to ignore the Runciman Mission; to allow it four weeks in which to waste time and to show that it could accomplish nothing; and then to have come out with the demand for a plebiscite, which means in fact demand for *Anschluss* with Germany." Hohenlohe met with Henlein in Zurich, Switzerland, around 9 August, and he managed to convince Henlein to meet Runciman on 18 August at Rothenhaus.[66]

In the meantime, Hohenlohe and Ulrich Kinsky hosted Runciman at Kinsky's shooting lodge Balzhütte in north Bohemia on 13–15 August. On Sunday August 14, Kinsky took Runciman on a tour of the area around his estate in Kamnitz (Česká Kamenice). In Ober-Kamnitz, a delegation of local SdP leaders met the group and took Runciman to see an idle factory, a bunch of dilapidated houses, and a run-down center for sick children. In a secret report to the British Foreign Office, a German informer noted that Kinsky's tour utterly misrepresented conditions in the Sudetenland, taking Runciman to visit "the dirtiest smelters" and "the worst house" in the area.[67]

On the evening of 14 August, the Runcimans and Ashton-Gwatkin took dinner at Kinsky's lodge with the Khuens, the Clarys, one of the Westphalen brothers, and Hohenlohe. Ashton-Gwatkin's Foreign Office report on the dinner depicts these nobles as thoroughly enamored with Henlein and the SdP. All of the nobles present were "of the same political trend of thought," Ashton-Gwatkin reported. He summarized this as follows:

1. They are strong supporters of the S.D.P.
2. They are personally very fond of 'the Chicken' [Henlein].
3. They are pro-German, and (with reservations) pro-Hitler.
4. But they prefer on the whole that the Sudeten land should not be absorbed.
5. But they approve, on the whole, of the Anschluss with Austria. Count Khuen, who has a 'farm' in Austria, says that farm-prices are much better; and that to all the farming and working population the change has brought nothing but benefit.
6. They think poorly and contemptuously of the Czechs. 'A Czech can be a good fellow—yes; I had many in my regiment in the War; but a gentleman—never!' (Count Khuen).
7. They have a horror of Russia and 'Bolshevism', which they believe is a real danger to them, to what is left of their possessions, and to the tradition for which they still stand.
8. They admire England and the English; and believe that friendship between England and Germany (not excluding France, but keeping France in her place!) can save the world.[68]

This summary also more or less describes the sympathies of many other nobles from the Grusbach circle and beyond. In fact, there is little in Ashton-Gwatkin's description that could not be said of a sizable proportion of the Sudeten German population as a whole. Not just enthusiastically German, the assembled counts and princes at Kinsky's dinner were now also Sudeten Germans. Having tied their fate to Sudeten Germandom in the 1920s, Bohemia's German nobles seemed on the brink of reaping their reward. As it turned out, though, their latter-day German nationalism would send them hurtling toward a far less inviting precipice in 1945.

Lord Runciman's first meeting with Henlein came, as planned, on 18 August at Hohenlohe's estate. For two hours they traded arguments, with Ashton-Gwatkin and Hohenlohe himself translating. Henlein declared that the only possible solution to the Sudeten German problem would be complete autonomy or a plebiscite, which would almost certainly result in *Anschluss* to the Reich. He accused the Czechs of lying and bad faith and demanded that Czech police leave the Sudetenland at once. Runciman responded almost pleadingly that the Czech government was trying hard to meet the SdP's demands and that Henlein should show some forbearance. As a gesture of good will, Runciman announced a promise from Prime Minister Milan Hodža (1878–1944) to increase the number of German postal officials in the Sudetenland. Henlein scoffed at Hodža's offer, arguing that it would take much more than that to reverse twenty years of Czech discrimination. The Sudeten German temperature was rising, Henlein declared, and it would soon become difficult to prevent dangerous unrest. Runciman then asked for a follow-up meeting with Henlein, and Ashton-Gwatkin concluded by delivering a greeting from Vansittart in London.[69]

Hohenlohe remained the go-between for Runciman and Henlein for the duration of the mission, and nobles continued to be Runciman's preferred hosts. Runciman spent the weekend after his first tense meeting with Henlein relaxing in the luxury of Adolf Schwarzenberg's sprawling south Bohemian estate.[70] Insisting that the visit was private and nonpolitical, Schwarzenberg refused to allow SdP supporters access to Runciman during his stay. Czech intelligence sources noted that Runciman and Schwarzenberg spent their time together fishing for trout.[71]

The following weekend Runciman moved on to Clary-Aldringen's chateau in Teplitz for some partridge hunting.[72] But there was also plenty of political discussion, as Runciman's wife Hilda's journal indicates. A prominent politician in her own right, Hilda Runciman was her husband's trusted confidante, an important assistant in his mission. Among her impressions of the visit with Clary, Hilda reported that Clary's sister, Elisabeth de Baillet Latour, produced an autographed photo of Hitler, with whom she had visited several times and considered misunderstood by the British. Indeed, Baillet Latour claimed that Hitler admired the British and did not want to start a war with them. As Runciman credulously concluded in her journal, "All this doesn't sound like a man who is eager to take over all of Europe, which so many people persistently believe."[73]

Alfons Clary-Aldringen is second from left, followed by his sister Elisabeth de Baillet Latour and his wife Ludwina. Date unknown (probably late 1920s or early 1930s). SOA Litoměřice (Děčín) RA Clary-Aldringen, k 765

On the final weekend of his stay, Runciman had the opportunity to meet with nobles supposedly less sympathetic to SdP demands. On 9–11 September, the Runcimans visited with Eugen Czernin at Petersburg, an estate located in a German region of western Bohemia, but near the language border. Arranged by Basil Newton, the British minister to Prague, this meeting was supposed to have been an antidote to the steady stream of SdP propaganda Runciman had faced.[74] Czernin, though German, was reportedly pro-Czechoslovakia. In spite of Czernin's professed neutrality, on Sunday morning he allowed an SdP group to meet with Runciman at Petersburg.[75] The Czech noble Jan Lobkowicz arrived to join them for lunch, but, disgusted by a large pro-SdP demonstration outside, he promptly left.[76]

The Czech Interior Ministry later claimed that Czernin had orchestrated the demonstration and was in fact an SdP supporter.[77] Czernin's diary entry for 9 September indicated that he had met with SdP representatives that morning, agreeing only to pass a request for a meeting to Runciman. In an entry for 11 September, however, Czernin expressed "surprise" that his SdP visitors declared to Runciman that "the Sudeten Germans want to go home to Germany *(Heim ins Reich)*." He also wrote of his disappointment that SdP demonstrators shouted "Sieg Heil" and "Heil Hitler" in what he hoped would be a "neutral" visit for Runciman. But he also concluded that it was "good that Lord Runicman for once got to see the real opinion of the people *(Volk)*."[78] Though Czernin's relationship to the SdP remains unclear, his hospitality to Runciman undoubtedly served the SdP's interests.

Pro-Czech aristocrats from the Czech *Svaz* were not entirely absent from the battle for British sympathies. In early July of 1938, a Beneš ally wrote to R. W. Seton-Watson noting the creation of a group to reach out to "our friends in France and in England." Among the first visitors of the group to London were to be the "Czech aristocrats" Jindřich Kolowrat and Karel Schwarzenberg.[79] With the Runciman mission about to begin, the *Svaz* tried to round up a team of Czech nobles to offer hospitality to the visiting dignitaries. "There is a fear," the *Svaz* secretary wrote, "that the opposing side will apply every lever in order to sway Lord [Runciman]." The memo suggested that Czech nobles, too, should be ready to take Runciman hunting or fishing and to meet him at lunches and receptions. In urging nobles to take part, the *Svaz* concluded that "it is a service to the state that we cannot refuse."[80]

In spite of its good intentions, however, the *Svaz* failed to arrange more than a few meetings with Runciman, and even these did not have the desired effect. Consistent with the *Svaz*'s long-standing domestic strategy, Czech nobles were less accustomed to lobbying foreign officials, and their lack of organization in 1938 showed this inexperience. The *Svaz* had hoped to get Jan Masaryk to make the necessary connections with the British visitors, but Masaryk was out of Prague during the crucial days leading up to the mission.[81] It did not help that the *Svaz*'s initiative started only days before Runciman was to arrive. Neither were Czechoslovak officials as deft at manipulating British opinion as were their SdP counterparts. The Czechoslovak government appears to have been outmaneuvered by the SdP in efforts to win Runciman's ear. Not accustomed to turning to nobles for anything, the government let slip the opportunity to fill Runciman's social time with visits to pro-Czech nobles. Finally, we can safely assume that Runciman favored the company of his old Sudeten German noble acquaintances to that of the Czechs. Personal ties did, after all, remain important, even in the new Europe of ideologies.

Ultimately, events outpaced the Runciman mission, with Hitler's demands escalating in mid-September. When Chamberlain told Runciman on 14 September of his plans to meet Hitler the next day at Berchtesgaden, Runciman considered his mission at a close. On 16 September, he returned to London, and he issued a report five days later.[82] Given that appeasement was already Chamberlain's policy, Runciman's report is interesting more for its reflection of Runciman's mindset than for its influence. Though Runciman blamed the breakdown of talks on the SdP, the report was otherwise highly favorable to Henlein's demands and critical of Czech behavior toward Sudeten Germans.

"I have been left with the impression," he wrote in his public letter to both Chamberlain and Beneš, "that Czechoslovak rule in the Sudeten areas for the last twenty years, though not actively

oppressive and certainly not 'terroristic', has been marked by tact-
lessness, lack of understanding, petty intolerance and discrimination, to a point where the resentment of the German population
was inevitably moving in the direction of revolt."[83] He pointed to
the land reform as just such a case of discrimination, no doubt
reflecting the view of his noble hosts, as well as of a tendentious
brief on the land reform provided to the mission by one of the
Westphalen brothers.[84] The desire of Sudeten Germans to join the
Reich was "a natural development in the circumstances." He urged
that the international community give them the "full right of self-
determination at once." Given the likelihood that Sudeten Germans
would vote for *Anschluss* to Germany, preparations should be made
immediately to facilitate the peaceful transfer of the Czechoslovak
borderlands. Indeed, this was exactly Chamberlain's position at Munich, and there is evidence that Ashton-Gwatkin drafted Runciman's memorandum according to Chamberlain's diplomatic
needs.[85] Runciman concluded by thanking his hosts—both Czech
and Sudeten German alike—for their "personal courtesy, hospitality
and assistance" during his stay.[86]

After a careful consideration of the Runciman papers, Vaughan
Baker has concluded that Runciman's report drew largely on SdP
propaganda and ignored much of the conflicting evidence collected
by his own mission. Runciman had been known for his fairness and
judiciousness, making it all the more difficult to comprehend his
final conclusions. Baker suggests that "Runciman's selective inattention to the evidence collected by his own assistants . . . shows in a
glaring light the extent to which he and the members of the Chamberlain government were unable to face the implications of Nazi
theory and policy."[87] Many Bohemian German nobles shared this
selective reading of the Czechoslovak and international situation.
Appeasers and nobles alike took the statements of Hitler and Henlein at face value, believing they negotiated in good faith. What
they failed to understand was that these leaders were not gentlemen,
that power and force mattered more to them than fair play or their
word of honor. Men such as Clary-Aldringen, Khuen, and Ulrich
Kinsky admired precisely these British gentlemanly qualities. Runciman found in his noble hosts men of like mind, and they no doubt

reinforced each other's inability or unwillingness to see the deeper meaning of the Nazi threat.

Annexation of the Sudetenland: Hitler's "Act of Liberation"

Within a week of Runciman's final report, Chamberlain was on his way to Munich to arrange a transfer of the Sudetenland to the Reich. With negotiations still under way at Munich on 29 September, Ulrich Kinsky shot off an urgent telegram to Ashton-Gwatkin, in which he called for "an immediate occupation of the Sudetendeutsch territory by the German Army as the only way for an immediate stop of all cruelty, further devastation and incendiary by Czech troops and red mob mostly already led by Russian Bolshiviks [sic]."[88] The British and French obliged, and Hitler's troops began occupying the Sudetenland on 1 October. Clary-Aldringen's archive contains a cruel memorial to the Munich decision: an obituary for Czechoslovakia. "After a long and painful illness," it announced, Czechoslovakia had finally passed away. A celebratory mass would take place on 28 October, the twentieth anniversary of Czechoslovak independence. It was signed "the League of Nations, parents" and "Litwinow-Finkelstein, Stalin, uncle."[89] There was indeed great celebration in the Sudetenland with the arrival of the German *Wehrmacht*. Few Germans regretted the death of Czechoslovakia.

Many German nobles too greeted the destruction of Czechoslovakia at Munich with considerable public enthusiasm. The *Grusbacher* Karl Buquoy warmly welcomed the arrival of the German army in October. "I received the honorable task," he said in a speech to assembled dignitaries in Rosenberg (Rožmberk), "both for me and for our whole homeland *(Heimat)*, to personally greet *Generaloberst* von Brauchitsch of the *Wehrmacht* in the name of our south Bohemian homeland and especially in the name of the entire estate of large landowners." He went on to describe the history of the region, which his ancestor Carl Bonaventura Buquoy had liberated from the Protestants 319 years before during the Thirty Years' War. "Since that time," he continued, "South Bohemia has become our homeland. . . . We stand together after three centuries, the common soil is our common homeland, in true German *Volk* unity." In a rousing finish, Buquoy rejoiced at the arrival of the German army: "Comrades! The German *Wehrmacht* is here! The German *Wehrmacht*, our joy, our pride, the German *Wehrmacht*, our longtime desire . . . the German *Wehrmacht* in which our sons will once again serve, to the joy and pride of their fathers and to the honor of the great German *Reich*."[90]

Speaking a few months later, Karl Waldstein told an enthusiastic crowd of German foresters in north Bohemia that with Adolf Hitler's rise, "a fresh wind of new life swept through our Sudeten German region." The current representative of the old Bohemian family of Wallenstein (Valdštejn), this mustachioed aristocrat peppered his speech with the mystical *völkisch* idiom so common in the 1930s: "The German *Volk*'s essence . . . serious and hard-blooded . . . was formed in the forests of Germania." He went on to praise the *Führer* for bringing the Sudetenland home into the Great German Reich.[91] In a short letter to *Verband* members, Franz Anton (Prince) Thun-Hohenstein (1890–1973) expressed similar sentiments. "Our *Führer*'s act of liberation has brought us Sudeten Germans home into the Reich," he wrote. "We add to our thanks an assurance that we will devote ourselves to the service of our nation *(Volk)* and our homeland *(Heimat)*."[92]

Not all German nobles welcomed Hitler's annexation of the Sudetenland with such enthusiasm, however. Though sympathetic to Sudeten German complaints of discrimination, Eugen Czernin did not support the SdP's separatist leanings. From an old Bohemian family, Czernin still held out hope in 1938 that Czechs and Germans could live in peace in Czechoslovakia. As Lady Runciman reported in her diary, he professed "Bohemian" rather than Czech or German sympathies, though he found it next to impossible to maintain neutrality in the current environment, when one side or the other pounced on every decision as discriminatory.[93] "Shaken" by the news that Czechoslovakia was to be partitioned, Czernin complained that it was "the fruit of twenty years of bad and obstinate policy against the nationalities and above all, a dreadful foreign policy, which alienated all our neighbors and had us as friends of

France and Soviet Russia."[94] Though Czernin's diary expressed on several occasions misgivings about Hitler, his greatest fear was the threat of Communism and civil war. Although not happy about the destruction of Czechoslovakia, his relief at the avoidance of war in 1938 was palpable.

Many other German nobles, however, saw the breakup of Czechoslovakia as the just reward for two decades of discrimination against Germans and against nobles in particular. In an early October letter to the *Times* of London, Clary-Aldringen explained the failure of coexistence:

> Property has been confiscated under the pretext of land reform. . . . Public office was the monopoly of the Czechs and the result was a regime of petty persecution based on racial hatred and only too often applied with sadistic satisfaction. . . . Year after year approach was made to the League of Nations, charged by the terms of the Covenant with seeing that minorities got fair play. Year after year we were sent about our business, while the action we sought was taken on behalf of more favoured minorities. . . . The eyes of the whole population turned to Germany as their only hope of deliverance from despair.[95]

In the more intimate setting of a local gymnastics event, Clary was less restrained. He chastised the Czechs, and in particular President Beneš, for discriminating against Germans and for pursuing socialist policies such as the land reform. With the onset of depression, Sudeten Germans had become demoralized. But the great leader Konrad Henlein had emerged to unify Czechoslovakia's Germans and to renew their hopes for national justice and prosperity. Ultimately, Clary declared, Henlein's greatest achievement was to bring Sudeten Germans into Hitler's Reich. "The German *Volk* thanks Adolf Hitler for all he has done," Clary concluded. "Thanks to him the German Reich stands proud and strong as never before, and thanks to this strength we too finally have our long-awaited liberation. . . . We will never forget the jubilation and our deep, heartfelt joy when the first soldiers of the German *Wehrmacht* arrived as liberators; nor will we forget above all the overflowing feeling of thanks for our great *Führer.*"[96]

〜 By THE MID-1930s, Karl Rohan's "conservative revolution" had arrived in much of Central Europe. In Germany and Austria authoritarian regimes eliminated Socialist opposition in the name of the national community and adopted, at least in theory, a corporatist economic and social model to replace the supposedly soulless and fissiparous capitalist and liberal-democratic *Gesellschaft* (society). These ideals had a tremendous attraction for Czechoslovakia's Sudeten Germans, who blamed capitalism and Czech discrimination for their economic woes in the early 1930s. Sudeten German nobles shared this critique and found much else about fascist ideology to their liking. The Nietzschean elitism of the leadership principle resonated with a nobility that had long considered itself a class of born leaders. Nobles were also drawn to corporatism, which hearkened back to a noble-dominated society of estates, and to the national community, which favored national unity over class struggle. "Changing to stay the same" found its new form in the "conservative revolution" of the 1930s; attracted by Hitler's conservative rhetoric and vigorous nationalism, few nobles could sense that the Nazi revolution would soon burn its bridges to their idealized past.[97]

For many of Bohemia's German nobles, however, the biggest draw of National Socialism was its potential for bringing together the scattered Germans of Central Europe into a greater German economic and cultural community. Nobles such as Adolf Dubsky and Ulrich Kinsky lamented the inward-looking cultural and economic autarky of nation-states such as Czechoslovakia, and they yearned for a return to the cosmopolitan German-dominated culture and common market of the Habsburg Empire. As the League of Nations seemed ever less capable of protecting minorities or diminishing the cult of borders in Europe, many German nobles turned to National Socialism as a vessel for their German internationalist aspirations.

Not all Bohemian German nobles embraced Hitler in 1938. A few would oppose Nazism in emigration. Richard Coudenhove, the cosmopolitan pan-Europeanist, fled Czechoslovakia in 1939 and took a professorship in European studies at New York University in 1942.[98]

Some German nobles chose inner emigration, simply withdrawing to their estates, or more rarely, covertly resisted Nazi rule in the Sudetenland. But no Bohemian German nobles other than Coudenhove spoke publicly against Hitler or protested the breakup of Czechoslovakia. The welcoming speeches of Buquoy, Thun, and Waldstein were all too common in 1938.

The trajectory of Alfons Clary-Aldringen illustrates the evolution of German internationalism in a nationalist and fascist direction. Looking back four decades after Munich, Clary wrote that "nationalism was the scourge of our century."[99] Loyal to imperial Austria, Clary had mourned the foundation of national successor states and had turned to the League of Nations as a possible antidote to the nationalism he claimed to despise. But his internationalism bore a strong German tint, such that it is hard to avoid pinning the nationalist label on Clary himself. A German national loyalty was the basic engine of his political engagement, both in the *Völkerbundliga* and in Sudeten German public life. The *Verband*'s German international strategy of the 1920s accelerated the nationalization of nobles like Clary, and the economic and political conjuncture of the 1930s radicalized the content of their nationalism in a fascist and greater-German direction. An admirer of Henlein and a supporter of the SdP in the late 1930s, Clary was no longer the "old Austrian" he would later claim as his fundamental identity. In 1938, he was little different politically from other Sudeten German nationalists who valued national unity above all and welcomed the annexation of the Sudetenland with enthusiasm.

∼ 6

War and Revolution:
The End of the Old Regime,
1939–1948

> We can today make the proud claim that finally, all these years
> after the White Mountain disaster, the cleansing process will be
> brought to a conclusion once and for all.
> ∼ *Rudé právo, June 1945*

$\mathcal{T}$HE GERMAN ANNEXATION of the Sudetenland
upset the 1918 territorial settlement, but along with the *Anschluss*
of Austria it was only the beginning of Hitler's reorganization of
Central and Eastern Europe. In March 1939, Hitler seized on
Slovak demands for independence to destroy rump Czecho-
Slovakia, replacing it with an independent Slovak state and the Protectorate of Bohemia and Moravia. From 1939 to 1945, the Protectorate would have nominal autonomy, though it was in fact ruled
by the German *Reichsprotektor* under orders from Berlin. Fortu-
nately for the Czechs, and in particular for nobles, the first *Reichsprotektor* was the conservative aristocrat, Konstantin von Neurath
(1873–1956). During his two-year reign, von Neurath ran a
relatively lenient regime. Though he closed Czech universities and
repressed manifestations of Czech nationalism, Czechs also enjoyed
generous ration levels and a degree of economic normality.[1] Under
the new circumstances, many Czech nobles entered politics once
again, if only temporarily. But in 1941, the new acting *Reichsprotektor* Reinhard Heydrich severely curtailed Czech public activity.
Sharing with Hitler a particular disdain for Czech nobles, Heydrich

sequestered the estates of several prominent families, including most of the signatories of the 1938 declaration of loyalty.

During the occupation, there were collaborators and resisters in both the Czech and German noble camps, though far more collaborators were German and more resisters Czech. Many German nobles hoped that the German regime would return property they had lost in the Czechoslovak land reform, but the Nazis proved little more sympathetic to the nobility than the Czechs had been. Nevertheless, most nobles—both Czech and German—would emerge from the war with their landholdings intact. A few Czech nobles played a role in the wartime resistance, though more would wait until 1945 to unearth hidden hunting rifles and join Czech attacks on the retreating Germans. On the whole, noble collaboration and resistance were modest in scope and had little effect on the fortunes of the nobility either during the war or after. The decade from 1938 to 1948 saw the height of ethnic collectivism in Central Europe, and one's ultimate fate depended more on membership in collectivities than on individual behavior.

Upon liberation, Czechs expelled hundreds of thousands of Sudeten Germans from their homes, sending most across the border to occupied Germany and interning others in makeshift concentration camps. The Potsdam agreement sealed the fate of those remaining, preparing the way for another 2 million Germans to leave in the "organized transfer" of 1946. All Germans lost their property without compensation unless they could demonstrate active resistance to the Nazi occupation. Borrowing rhetoric from the 1918 revolution, Czech leaders—Communist and non-Communist alike —once again made nobles a central symbolic target of their self-proclaimed "national and social revolution." The Czech press regularly referred to a "cleansing" of the borderlands of foreign elements.[2] Almost all German nobles lost their land and citizenship in 1945. Czech nobles would hold out until 1948, when the victorious Communists seized their remaining land and drove most into exile. Thus in Bohemia, it was not the wartime occupation, but rather the liberation that finally destroyed the last vestiges of the Old Regime.

Czech Nobles and the German Occupation

Just hours after Hitler arrived in Prague on 15 March 1939 to survey his new possession, the Czech fascist organizations *Vlajka* and *Akce národní obrody* (ANO) formed a national committee to approach the German occupiers with an offer of collaboration. Two nobles in particular were prominent in *Vlajka* and ANO during these days: Jindřich Thun-Hohenstein (1913–?) and Jan Lobkowicz (1885–1952), the president of the *Svaz* and a signatory of the 1938 declaration of loyalty.[3] German intelligence reports also indicate that František Schwarzenberg, the younger brother of the Catholic publicist (and former *Vlajka* member) Karel Schwarzenberg, was in close touch with *Vlajka* during this time.[4] In the end, the Czech fascist national committee only lasted a few days, as Hitler preferred a more malleable Czech government to the vigorously ideological fascists. Even so, the Czech right, and with it a number of nobles, would hold prominent positions in the Protectorate government for the next few years.

Czech nobles thrived during the first two years of the Protectorate, as they established close ties with von Neurath and finally entered the top levels of Czech politics—or rather the authoritarian political movement that filled the void left by banned democratic parties. The so-called National Partnership (*Národní souručenství*—NS) became the only legal party after March 1939, and by summer it could claim the membership of 98 percent of adult Czech males in the Protectorate.[5] A number of nobles were active in the leadership of the Partnership, including Jan Lobkowicz and František Schwarzenberg in Bohemia and Karel Belcredi and Hugo Strachwitz (1900–1978) from Moravia.[6] Czech nobles and German officials alike considered these four men representatives of the Czech nobility, not only for their leadership of the *Svaz* in Bohemia and Moravia, but also for their prominent support for the noble declaration of loyalty to Czechoslovakia in 1938. Beyond the four noble political leaders, the interwar Catholic publicist Karel VI Schwarzenberg, an avid student of heraldry, sat on a commission appointed by President Hácha to design a new state flag for the Protectorate.[7]

Predictably, Lobkowicz served on the Partnership's agriculture and forestry committees, in addition to committees addressing culture and anti-Communism. František Schwarzenberg, who was born in 1913, was active on the youth committee and headed the Partnership's United Youth organization, while also sitting with Lobkowicz on the Partnership's central committee.[8] Both men, but particularly Schwarzenberg, were active public speakers during the first two years of the German occupation. In his speeches, Schwarzenberg stressed the importance of a Czech nationalism based not in democratic ideology, but rather in "blood and soil," which were the true guarantees of national continuity.[9]

The Czech government in the Protectorate, appointed by President Hácha and subject to Hitler and von Neurath's approval, was not formally responsible to the National Partnership. Even so, the government and Hácha tried to cooperate with the Partnership, while also taking into account constraints put on them by both Germany and the London-based Czechoslovak government in exile. One noble, Count Mikuláš Bubna-Litic (1897–1954) served as minister of agriculture from 1940 to 1942, though the nobility as a whole does not appear to have drawn any particular benefit from his position.[10] Given the dominance of German organs in the Protectorate, the Czech government had little room for independent action.[11]

Even so, Czech nobles secured some influence in von Neurath's Protectorate administration by cultivating ties with the *Reichsprotektor* and his aristocratic deputies. Walter Jacobi, the Prague chief of the Nazi Security Service (*Sicherheitsdienst*—SD), later testified that the SD kept a close eye on noble activity and political tendencies during von Neurath's reign from 1939 to 1941. As Jacobi put it, the von Neurath regime demonstrated "visible signs of friendship towards the nobility."[12] Reich German nobles were well represented in the Protectorate administration, and they were frequent social guests of Bohemian nobles.[13] Likewise using social connections for political access, František Schwarzenberg struck up a friendship with President Hácha's daughter, allowing him contact with Hácha even after Schwarzenberg's retreat from public political life in 1941.[14] When the Krumlov branch of the Schwarzenberg family faced sequestration of its vast holdings in 1941, both von Neurath and Hácha intervened with Reich officials in an effort to stop it. In spite of von Neurath's efforts, the powerful Sudeten German Nazi Karl Hermann Frank convinced Hitler to carry out the confiscation. This was, Jacobi reported, the beginning of the end for von Neurath, "a humiliation that led several months later to his recall from Prague."[15] With the arrival of von Neurath's replacement, the brutal and humorless SS General Reinhard Heydrich, German officials would cut their ties with the Czech nobility.

German Nobles in the Protectorate, 1939–1941

Many Bohemian German nobles expected material benefits from the Nazi occupation, though these hopes went almost entirely unrealized. Soon after the annexation of the Sudetenland, the *Verband* made contact with Reich German officials seeking the return of German land lost during the Czechoslovak land reform.[16] These negotiations dragged on with little result.[17] A decree of 12 November 1938 technically allowed the authorities in Sudeten German districts to take control of Czech and Jewish property. Some of the subsequently confiscated land (around 50,000 ha total) then became available to the Reich-based German Settlement Organization, though there would be few actual settlers. Czechs who became Reich citizens generally could keep their land.[18] The German government took direct title of borderland forests that had been confiscated earlier by the Czechoslovak state, but none of the former owners received any of this land. Though Konrad Henlein continued to seek the restitution of arable land given to Czechs during the interwar reform, Heinrich Himmler vetoed the effort because of worries about Czech morale in the Protectorate. During the war, Czech military-industrial production took precedence over local German goals in the Sudeten provinces, including the reversal of land reform.[19]

The Czech Protectorate government generally succeeded in fending off land grabs by individual German nobles. In one example, Max Egon Fürstenberg, the former owner of Masaryk's presidential estate at Lány, approached the Czech Agriculture Minister

Ladislav Feierabend and demanded the return of the property taken from him in the interwar reform. Though Fürstenberg was a prominent and well-connected Nazi, Feierabend managed to resist his claims.[20] Overall, restitution was a low priority compared to the necessities of a war economy and the goal of resettling German

Max Egon Furstenberg on his seventieth birthday, 1933. SOA Litoměřice (Děčín) RA Clary-Aldringen, k 765

refugees. Though Hitler had effectively used conservative (including noble) support to consolidate his power in Germany, his regime was not particularly noble-friendly during the war.

Nobles in the Protectorate did gain a symbolic victory when the Czech government in September 1939 finally overturned the 1918 ban on noble titles. This was a mixed blessing, though, as titles now acquired the taint of appearing to be a gift from the Nazis. Oswald Kostrba-Skalicky suggests that most nobles who sympathized with the Czechs continued to abjure their formal titles.[21] Even so, an official list of noble members of the Prague Ressource in 1940 provides titles, in both Czech and German. Ironically, nobles in the Protectorate who had taken Reich German citizenship were not technically eligible to use their titles under Protectorate law. The reasoning of German officials was that the affected former nobles had no titles when they had become citizens of the Reich in March 1939. They were no longer subject to Protectorate law when the restoration of titles was promulgated in September, so their titles were a question for Reich German law. On the other hand, the German *Verband*'s representative in Prague suggested that the use of titles could not be punished, since such punishment had been taken off the books by the September decree and since no such law existed in Germany. The *Verband* believed a formal resolution of this legal conundrum would have to wait until the end of the war.[22]

Though there are no statistics on how many nobles in the Protectorate took Reich German citizenship (which also required a declaration of German nationality), at least a handful did take this step. For many, there was tremendous pressure from German authorities to choose German nationality. In central Moravian Prostějov (Prossnitz), for instance, German officials threatened Countess Kálnoky with confiscation of her land if she did not assume German nationality.[23] Petr Němec suggests that the Germans targeted central Moravian landowners in particular, as the Nazis hoped to build a so-called nationality bridge of German estates to cut the Czech parts of Moravia in two.[24]

Another Moravian, Hugo Prince Salm-Reifferscheidt, faced the loss of his property when he declared himself Czech and joined the National Partnership in early 1939. Salm had actually indicated

German nationality in the 1930 census, "out of opposition to the current Czech regime," as he put it. But his estates were in an overwhelmingly Czech region, his wife was from the Czech family of Mensdorff-Pouilly, and his children went to Czech schools. Above all, he wrote, he now felt Czech and should not be forced to declare a nationality he did not want.[25] When the German pressure increased in late 1939, local Czechs urged Salm to accept German nationality so that his land did not fall under the control of the SS. He finally took German nationality in December 1939, only to have his land sequestered anyway in 1942. Czech officials capped this sad story in 1945 when the local national committee confiscated Salm's property on the basis of his "German" nationality.[26] Though Salm's was an unusual case, it demonstrates the tremendous difficulty of maintaining a "culturally German, politically Czech" identity after 1938. Neither the Nazis nor the postwar Czech government would abide "amphibians."

Partly in response to the Nazi attempts to "convert" Czech nobles, sixty-nine Czech nobles delivered a second declaration of Czech national loyalty to President Hácha in September 1939. Seeking to clear up "substantial confusion" on the subject of noble nationality, the petitioners embraced a subjective definition of national identity. In Bohemia's long history of independence, "The nobility's political obligations were always tied to service to the Bohemian state and king." Originally Czech "by blood and language," the nobility was traditionally "a state institution, and as a self-contained community was spared from nationality conflicts." Even under the Habsburg Empire nobles remained the "governing or political layer of the Bohemian state."[27]

Since the seventeenth century, foreign nobles had also made their home in Bohemia. "Through perpetual administrative contact with the people," the declaration continued, "the new families living in Czech-speaking regions merged with the Czech nation in such a way that their various origins could in no way change their undeniable affiliation with the Czech national community." Similarly, many originally Czech families took on a German identity after living for centuries in German-inhabited regions. Echoing Ernest Renan's classic subjective definition of the nation, the petitioners wrote that "inherited identification with a national community is not . . . determined by the circumstances of the day, but is created by the reality of social life, of political, cultural, and economic co-operation, and also by a shared history, fate, and responsibility for future generations of the nation."[28]

The declaration also noted that the most recent Reich-German census had determined nationality subjectively (this in spite of Nazi biological/racial rhetoric, which was not conducive to legal codification). Czech nobles asked only that they be allowed the same choice as Reich citizens, the right "to embrace the nation among whom they live, the nation which they have chosen as their own and whose members accept them . . . even if [they] were not always of Czech origin." The petitioners concluded with a rousing declaration of loyalty: "With the conviction of the unity of all parts of our nation, and above all the conviction that descendents of the joint creators and upholders of the Bohemian state idea can still serve their nation and their homeland no matter the conditions, we want always and under all circumstances to identify ourselves with the Czech nation."[29]

Unlike the earlier declaration of 1938, in which Czech nobles emphasized the historic unity of the Bohemian lands, this time they stressed their loyalty to the "Czech nation" and their "responsibilities to the national community." On the one hand, this reflected the drastically changed political circumstances since the historic rights declaration of a year before. Not only had the Nazis dismembered the historic Czech state; now they were trying to denationalize it. Nazi pressure on nobles and other Czechs to adopt German nationality appeared to be part of a policy of fragmenting Czech national settlement in preparation for absorbing the Protectorate into the Reich. Even without the Sudetenland, the Protectorate at least offered a semblance of continuity with earlier Bohemian state-forms. Indirectly drawing on the Nazi concept of "racial" statehood, nobles defended their Czech nationality in an effort to bolster the (rump) Czech state.[30]

But there are also other possible explanations for nobles' decisions to sign the 1939 declaration. Some may have wanted an incontrovertible record of their Czech loyalty, in case the Nazis tried to force them to take German nationality. Others may have desired to avoid *Wehrmacht* service, from which Czechs were exempt.[31] But the tremendous risks involved with signing the declaration suggest that something beyond opportunism or material interest was at work. Noble national loyalties had been politically motivated in the late Habsburg Empire and materially motivated in the early years of the Czechoslovak Republic. By the 1930s, though, these loyalties had become profound convictions for many, such that they endured in spite of their lack of immediate material or political utility.

As many signatories of the declaration would soon find out (and as they must have expected), they would pay for their defiance of Nazi Germanization efforts. The ultimate test of nobles' Czech convictions was persistence in the face of material consequences. By signing the 1939 petition, therefore, the sixty-nine nobles indicated a profound Czech loyalty. The National Partnership certainly saw the noble declaration as a brave act, and its leaders praised nobles for their continued loyalty to the Czech nation. The importance of the declaration could not be overestimated, the Partnership's executive committee wrote to President Hácha, given that it came "during a period of [the people's] greatest national distress."[32]

Heydrich's 1941 Crackdown

Czech distress would soon be even greater, and Czech nobles too would feel the Nazi vice tighten. In September 1941, Hitler replaced the "mild" *Reichsprotektor* von Neurath with the hard-line SS official Reinhard Heydrich, who promptly declared martial law in major Czech cities. Heydrich's appointment marked the victory of Nazi radicals in the Protectorate, just as the SS approached the height of its power and influence in wartime Germany. Like many of his colleagues in the SS leadership, Heydrich opposed neo-corporatism, disliked the nobility and Catholic Church, and distrusted Henlein and the former "traditionalist" wing of the SdP. Heydrich expressed particular animosity toward Othmar Spann, the neo-corporatist Austrian who had been such a strong inspiration to Henlein and Bohemian nobles.[33]

After his appointment, Heydrich proceeded to arrest or sack much of the Czech government, dissolve the executive committee of the National Partnership, and rule the Protectorate almost exclusively through the office of the *Reichsprotektor*.[34] Thereafter, Heydrich and his successors followed a carrot-and-stick policy. Czech workers received Reich-level rations and free vacations in return for maintaining production. Acts of sabotage, however, were severely punished, often with collective reprisals.

With Czech nobles still resisting efforts at Germanization in 1941, Heydrich applied the stick, sequestering ten estates owned by signatories of the 1938 declaration of loyalty to Czechoslovakia.[35] Fifty-five more estates followed by November 1942.[36] The *Svaz* and individual nobles complained to Hácha of the illegality of the confiscations, but to no avail.[37] Most of the sequestered property came under the control of the Protectorate's Land Office until the end of the war. Reconstituted by German authorities in 1939, the Land Office was controlled by officials of the SS Race and Settlement Office *(Rasse-und Siedlungshauptamt)*.[38] Though Heydrich and the Land Office planned to use the land for future "German infiltration and settlement," little of it actually went to German settlers.[39] Instead, Germans appointed by the Land Office administered sequestered properties until the end of the war, when Czech nobles regained control of their estates. After 1941, most Czech nobles could only wait quietly for what they hoped would be the total defeat of Nazi Germany.

Collaboration and Resistance

Among Czech nobles, there were some noteworthy attempts at accommodation with the German occupiers, though most Czech nobles either signed the 1939 declaration of loyalty to the Czech nation or kept as low a profile as possible. A few Czech nobles joined the resistance during the war, and some of those were captured and died in concentration camps. Most noble "resisters" only became active in the waning days of the war, when Czechs turned out en masse to harass the retreating German army. German nobles were more likely to collaborate, or at least cooperate, with Nazi rule, though they too had a few notable resisters. Among both groups of nobles, the range of collaboration, accommodation, and resistance reflected that of the Czech and German national groups as a whole.

There were only a few cases of formal collaboration among Czech nobles, and even these rather deserve the label "coopera-tion." Two prominent Moravian nobles, Karel Belcredi and Hugo Strachwitz, played a leading role in the so-called Czech Union for Cooperation with the Germans (*Český svaz pro spolupráci s Němci—ČSSN*). Belcredi, the longtime secretary of the Moravian Union of Large Landowners, led the Moravian branch of the ČSSN and also served as a vice chair of the Bohemian Union. Strachwitz was a member of the National Partnership leadership and sat on the Part-nership's "Commission for Cooperation with Germans," which overlapped with the ostensibly nonpolitical ČSSN. It is not clear how many more nobles joined the ČSSN. Jindřich Šlik was the chairman of the regional branch of the organization in Jičín, but so far no similar examples of noble local participation have emerged.[40] Šlik himself was a tepid booster of the organization, at best. A postwar investigation by the local national committee revealed that Šlik had convened few meetings. Upon arriving at one gathering, Šlik determined that no Germans were present. He then declared that no cooperation was possible without Germans in attendance and dismissed the meeting.[41]

Founded in mid-1939, the Union had two stated goals: to en-courage good relations between Czechs and Germans and "to spread knowledge of today's National Socialist Reich and the world-views on which its empire is built." In explaining the foundations for Czech-German cooperation, the Union's Jan Mertl advanced a narrative of historical Czech-German symbiosis. Czech nationalism had its roots in the ideas of Herder and Hegel, he explained. During a long history of coexistence, Czechs and Germans had developed similar national traits: "The Czech nation, like the German nation, is industrious, loves order, and has a sense of discipline.... The social composition of both nations is also very similar." He asserted that previous Czech distrust of Nazi Germany had been based on misinformation. The Union's goal, therefore, was to educate the public about National Socialism's main tenets, above all the principle that "the good of the whole [must come] before the good of the individual."[42] To fulfill its primary mission, the Union sponsored lectures and concerts with German music; it also wrote letters to von Neurath and Hitler pledging cooperation with the Reich.[43]

On the whole, though, the Union did very little, and it ceased activity entirely in mid-1941, as German policy towards the Czechs became increasingly repressive.[44] Nor did German officials trust the Union. Suspicious SD spies reported an ironic tone and underlying hostility to Germans among many members, concluding that the group was opportunistic and insincere.[45] Finding little resonance among either Czechs or Germans, the Union was formally dissolved in 1942.[46] Technically, postwar retribution law considered the ČSSN a "fascist organization," though only "functionaries and leading members" were subject to prosecution.[47] Neither Belcredi nor Strachwitz faced trial for participation in the Union.

Nobles with Reich German citizenship were more likely to be active in Nazi Party and state activities. On the model of the 1933 *Gleichschaltung* (coordination) of German organizational life along Nazi lines, most Sudeten German organizations Nazified in 1938, thereby turning large numbers of Sudeten Germans into instant collaborators, legally speaking at least. The Sudeten German Party (SdP) dissolved in late 1938, with members required to apply for Nazi Party membership. Close to half of the SdP membership (including Karl Waldstein, Eugen Ledebur, Karl Buquoy, and many other noble members of the SdP) did so, with most receiving provisional party cards in 1939.[48] In another example, the Union of German Flyers *(Verband deutscher Flieger)* became the National Socialist Flyers' Corps *(Nationalsozialistisches Fliegerkorps—NSFK)*. The Union's pre-1938 president, Karl Waldstein, was later sentenced to a year in prison for his wartime membership in the Flyers' Corps.

As a latecomer to the SdP, Alfons Clary-Aldringen learned to his disappointment that his application for Nazi Party membership was rejected in 1938. He reapplied in mid-1939, only to be turned down again. In November 1939 he took his case directly to Hitler's chancellery in Berlin, offering several compelling excuses for his official nonpartisanship up to 1938. As head of the *Völkerbundliga* and other regional organizations, he argued, one needed to maintain an appearance of impartiality. Even so, Clary claimed, he had been a strong supporter of the SdP and had worked directly with Konrad Henlein to promote *völkisch* dominance within his organizations, as well as the exclusion of Jews and Social Democrats from leadership roles. He had joined the SdP in May 1938 when he no longer considered nonpartisanship necessary.[49] Clary received a temporary NSDAP membership in November 1940, but his case dragged on into 1941. A Foreign Office memorandum reporting interwar ties with Jews and President Edvard Beneš appears to have sunk his candidacy.[50]

Some nobles hoped that the Nazi regime would accord them honors denied during Czech rule. Karl Khuen sought permission from the German army to use his former Habsburg military title *Rittmeister*, which the Czechs had removed after 1918. Permission was granted in December 1938, and Khuen was overjoyed, writing in thanks that Hitler had arrived as a "protective angel" to wake Sudeten Germans from a twenty-year Czech nightmare.[51]

A new nightmare took its place, however, when Khuen's protective angel plunged Germany and its recent acquisitions into a prolonged and, ultimately, self-destructive war. Many Sudeten German noble sons went off to war, and several would die on the Eastern front. Adolf Dubsky's sons Oswald and Eugen, enthusiastic Nazis in their own right, fell in the East in 1942 and 1944 respectively.[52] Gerolf Count Schönborn (1915–?), whose cousins Erwein and Franz had signed the 1939 Czech declaration of loyalty, began pestering German officials with requests to join the *Luftwaffe* even before the annexation of the Sudetenland. After some strategically placed hunting invitations and donations to Nazi organizations, he at least won membership in the Nazi Flyers' Corps in late 1940.[53] Franz Anton Thun's son Ferdinand was captured in the Soviet Union in 1943 and miraculously survived the next five years in captivity. Alfons Clary-Aldringen proudly saw his two sons join the *Wehrmacht* in 1939. The older, Hieronymus, won an Iron Cross for bravery in 1940 and died a year later in a tank battle in Ukraine. Clary's younger son, Karl Georg, fell in Croatia in 1944.[54]

Reflecting a widespread sense of disappointment among Sudeten

German nobles, Clary faced the last year of the war with considerable bitterness. Surprisingly, though, his anger was not aimed at Hitler and the Nazi regime. In a letter to his son Karl in October 1944, Clary lamented the outbreak of war, caused by a "great alliance of Israelites . . . [and] Freemasons." He blamed the Jews not only for Communism, but also for dragging America into the war.[55] Neither here, nor in his published memoirs, did Clary acknowledge any responsibility for his 1938 part in encouraging Hitler's expansionist frenzy.

At least one German noble, Joachim Count Zedtwitz (1910–?), actively resisted Nazi rule in the Protectorate. The Zedtwitz family had settled in far western Bohemia in the fourteenth century, where they were known for their Protestantism and stubborn resistance to Habsburg rule. The family went into decline in the nineteenth century, when financial difficulties forced the sale of a number of estates. Some branches, apparently including Joachim's, ended up landless.[56] Before the occupation, Zedtwitz had studied in Prague, where he befriended the internationalist Czech writer (and friend of Franz Kafka), Milena Jesenská.[57] Zedtwitz considered himself nationally German, but politically Czech, and in 1938 he founded a small group called *Tat* (Action) that united anti-Nazi and pro-Czech Germans. From March until September 1939, Zedtwitz helped to smuggle Socialists, Jews, and anti-Nazi journalists to Poland. Arrested in March 1940, Zedtwitz spent over a year in German prisons; feigning insanity, he was eventually released and spent the rest of the war working in German hospitals. Ironically, when he returned to Czechoslovakia after the war, the new government tried to expel him on the basis of his German background. His anti-Nazi record won a reversal of the decision in court. It would be a Pyrrhic victory, however, as the Communist takeover in 1948 drove him into exile for good.[58]

The most prominent Czech resisters were the Counts Bořek-Dohalský, three brothers from an old Czech noble family that no longer owned land in Bohemia. The Nazis arrested the oldest brother, Antonín, in the wake of Reinhard Heydrich's assassination in 1942, and he died soon afterward in Auschwitz. The journalist Zdeněk Bořek-Dohalský worked for the Czech underground, where he was known as the Scarlet Pimpernel *(Červený Bedrník)*. Until his arrest in November 1941, he served as an important link between Hácha and the Beneš government in exile. Heinrich Himmler personally ordered his execution in Theresienstadt (Terezín) in 1945.[59] The youngest brother, František, was a signatory of the 1939 noble declaration and spent much of the war in Theresienstadt and Dachau. He survived and became the Czechoslovak ambassador to Austria from 1945 to 1949.[60] Like Joachim Zedtwitz, the Bořek-Dohalský brothers may have been more likely to resist actively because of their lack of landed property.

A few other nobles were known for more modest contributions to the Czech resistance. Karel Schwarzenberg was "active in the preparation of national resistance" and appeared "weapon in hand" during the Czech uprising on 5 May 1945.[61] Soon after the war ended, Schwarzenberg also joined the Czech Anti-fascist Society and the Union of Friends of the Soviet Union in Czechoslovakia.[62] Karel's brother František claimed to have had ties to the Czech underground throughout the war. He was active in the Prague uprising of 5–9 May and broadcast multilingual appeals for outside help from the recaptured Czech radio studios.[63] In 1945, František Schwarzenberg would take up the post of Czechoslovak legate to the Vatican, a post he held until the Communist putsch of 1948.[64] František Kinský and his two sons were reportedly involved with the resistance as well.[65] Jindřich Kolowrat (1897–1996) was in the resistance and served as postwar Czech ambassador to Turkey until 1948, when he refused to take an oath of loyalty to the Communist regime.[66] Leopold Count Deym noted after the war that his pregnant wife had been briefly jailed by the Gestapo for sabotage in 1944. When the baby was born, the couple defiantly named her Světlana after Stalin's daughter.[67]

Alois Count Podstatzký-Lichtenstein became a kind of national double agent, taking German nationality in order to provide secret support for Czech partisans. When his wife Josefa's father, Franz Harrach, gave her the estate Velké Meziříčí early in the war, the couple found themselves living in the middle of the strip of Moravia that the Nazi occupation authorities wanted to settle with Germans. Both Podstatzkýs had claimed Czech nationality in the 1930 census, and they were strong enough Czech patriots to maintain dangerous ties with the Czech underground. German officials insisted in 1940 that they take German nationality, backing this with a threat to confiscate their estate and to send the couple to a concentration camp in Lublin. After consulting with the leader of the local Czech underground, the Podstatzkýs accepted German nationality. They then used their position to provide supplies and intelligence to the Czech underground, to intervene on behalf of imprisoned Czechs, and to distribute hidden weapons to Czech partisans in May 1945. Like the Schwarzenbergs, they too took part in the May uprising, "weapon in hand." Threatened with loss of Czechoslovak citizenship after the war, the couple would receive a certificate of "national reliability" from the Velké Meziříčí District National Committee in August 1945.[68]

Other than these cases, there is little evidence of widespread noble participation in organized resistance. A few Czech nobles, such as František Kinský, spent the late war years in Gestapo prisons for relatively minor offenses.[69] Most Czech nobles waited until the Reich was collapsing before they dug their hunting rifles out of closets and joined Czech uprisings in early May 1945.

Unlike in Poland, where both Nazis and Soviets targeted the old elites for liquidation, most Bohemian nobles survived the war with their lives and much of their land intact. On the whole, the German occupation did not substantially change the profile of noble land ownership. The Nazis tended to ignore the German nobility entirely, treating nobles like other landholders whose production was seen as essential to the Reich. Though some Czech nobles temporarily lost their land to punitive Nazi sequestrations, their estates were not broken up. Most of these reverted to their original owners at the end of the war (with the exception of the "utraquist" Adolf Schwarzenberg's property, which was confiscated permanently by special legislation in 1947). The war itself did not prove fatal to the Bohemian nobility; rather its aftermath, a new wave of national and social revolution from 1945 to 1948, finally destroyed the aristocratic latifundia.

White Mountain Revisited

In the late Habsburg Monarchy, nobles still had the ability to shape their own fate and, to some extent, that of other classes and institutions around them, including the empire itself. The rising tide of nationalism and the growing power of the middle classes in the late nineteenth century began to erode noble influence, though only with the revolutions of 1918 would nobles become more acted upon than actors in the political-historical sense. Even so, nobles had substantial room to maneuver in the interwar period, and they managed to play the game of nationality politics well enough to survive as a landholding elite until 1945.

In the wake of the Second World War, Bohemian nobles lost all control over their own fate. Vengeful Czechs expelled 3 million Sudeten Germans in 1945 and 1946; like their compatriots, most Bohemian German nobles lost their land and citizenship, taking refuge in Germany, Austria, or beyond. Czech nobles survived the immediate postwar retribution, but they too would lose their property in Communist-inspired land reforms in 1947 and 1948. For the most part, then, the story of the nobility after 1945 is no longer about nobles themselves; rather, by necessity, it focuses on Czechs, who again made nobles into the symbolic targets of a renewed national and social revolution. Unlike in the interwar revolution, this time nobles lost everything. The story of the Bohemian nobility as a discrete social group would come to an end in 1948.

National and Social Revolution

Following the Soviet army on its way west, the new Czechoslovak government announced the general outline of its postwar program in Košice on 5 April 1945. The government and National Assembly effectively consisted of five parties united in a so-called National Front.[70] The Košice Program banned the Agrarian Party and the National Democrats because of alleged collaboration, a move that diluted the already weakened political right. German collaborators (later extended to all Germans, save proven anti-fascists) were to lose their citizenship and faced expulsion. The program directed

locally elected national committees to choose "national administrators" to oversee German property.[71]

Once the government arrived in Prague in May, the Ministry of
Agriculture sent a directive to national committees clarifying policy
with regard to German land. Local and regional committees were
to act at once to secure German land, "without waiting for the
appropriate laws to be enacted." They were to select members of
agrarian commissions "for the preparation of parcelization of confiscated land." Finally, the directive declared, "the property of the
foreign Germano-Hungarian nobility will be confiscated without
compensation."[72]

The returning Czechoslovak government enacted the Košice
Program in a series of presidential decrees, later known as the Beneš
Decrees. These laws covered a wide range of issues relating to property, citizenship, and retribution. The most important, Decree 33
of 2 August 1945, formally codified the government's determination
to revoke the citizenship of all Germans and Hungarians, with the
exception of those who suffered under or resisted Nazism.

Defining a German in multilingual Bohemia proved an often difficult task. The Interior Ministry ruled that national committees
should look first to the Czechoslovak census of 1930 and the Nazi
census of 1939 to determine a person's nationality. When that failed
to yield a definitive result, the Ministry suggested officials take into
account other "objective markers," such as German party or club
membership, language of schooling, and even language used in private life. Curiously, "Germans and Hungarians, who during the period of heightened threat to the republic made official declarations
of Czech or Slovak nationality, should not be considered Germans
or Hungarians who should lose their Czechoslovak state citizenship."[73] Decree 33 thus defined German nationality in both ethnic
and political terms. Ethnic criteria, especially language, determined
membership in the German nation; those who could prove their
"Czech" (i.e., anti-fascist) political credentials, however, were exempted from this group's collective fate.

On 21 June 1945, President Beneš issued Decree 12, mandating
"the confiscation and rapid distribution of agricultural property of
Germans, Hungarians, traitors and enemies of the Czech and

Slovak nation."[74] The decree formally confiscated all German landed property without compensation, placing it temporarily in a National Land Fund. The Fund was to take applications from Czechs and Slovaks for up to 12 ha of land. Priority in redistribution fell to "those who served in the fight for national liberation, particularly soldiers, partisans, former political prisoners and deportees." In overwhelmingly German areas, the Fund would hold the land for eventual (post-expulsion) colonization. Local national committees, often dominated by Communists, were to elect delegations of farmer-applicants to suggest and oversee plans for redistribution. Final decisions over parcelization rested with the Communist-led Ministry of Agriculture, which was also given a "technical" advisory role locally.[75]

As returning politicians sought to justify expulsions and confiscations in 1945, they revived historical arguments about redressing White Mountain. Once again, Czech leaders claimed to be carrying out a national and social revolution, though this time the revolution went much farther than the partial land reform of the interwar years. Invoking White Mountain, Czechs now sought a far more radical solution to their German question: the wholesale dispossession and removal of over 3 million Bohemian and Moravian Germans. Though all Czech political parties called for expulsions, the Communist newspaper *Rudé právo* typically made the point the most vividly (and distorted history most effectively):

> The historical roots of the de-nationalization of Czech soil lead 300 years back, all the way to the catastrophe at White Mountain, where the majority of our soil came into the hands of a foreign nobility. . . . We can today make the proud claim that finally, all these years after the White Mountain disaster, the cleansing process will be brought to a conclusion once and for all.[76]

On 1 July 1945, thousands of farmers and workers gathered at White Mountain to hear politicians invoke the 325th anniversary of the battle. Social Democratic Prime Minister Zdeněk Fierlinger compared the results of White Mountain with the German occupation from 1939 to 1945:

> With today's celebration we want to emphasize that the wrong inflicted upon us after White Mountain, which was again to have been repeated under the Nazi regime, will be completely rectified; that Czechs and Slovaks will again be the masters of their own land.[77]

Fierlinger's speech typically connected Czechs and Slovaks, as well as their putative national enemies, the Germans and Hungarians. Curiously, many Slovak politicians (especially Communists) also used the White Mountain formula for denouncing Hungarians in Slovakia, in spite of the lack of a significant Hungarian or Slovak connection to the 1620 battle.[78]

Other Communist and Social Democratic speakers from the National Front reiterated Fierlinger's theme. The minister of agriculture, Slovak Communist Július, Duriš declared, "White Mountain is undone! German aggression is historically liquidated."[79] Social Democratic Minister of Food Supply Václav Majer invoked White Mountain to justify expulsions and a new land reform: "We are free once again. We have our own state. Therefore it is only just that the agricultural property of Germans be confiscated without compensation . . . an act finally undoing the unfortunate legacy of White Mountain."[80] The implications were clear: confiscation and expulsion were acts of historical justice.

How did the White Mountain rhetoric's implications change so dramatically by the end of World War II? As in 1918–1919, White Mountain proved to be a powerful symbol for uniting national and social revolution. But this time, Czechs were prepared to go much further in carrying out their revolution. All over Europe, depression, heightened national tension, and Nazi brutality had radicalized the sense of the possible since the 1920s. Begun in the mid-1920s in the Balkans, massive population exchanges enjoyed increasing legitimacy. In contrast, transfer or expulsion had not been raised as a serious possibility in 1919, when social-political

threats seemed more pressing: the influence of feudal and monarchist elements on the one hand, Bolshevism on the other.

In 1945 Czechs considered the main enemy and threat to be
national; after six years of a humiliating and often brutal occupation,
expulsion seemed to Czechs the best available way to secure their
future as a national state. The White Mountain rhetoric was already
familiar and popular, and Communist and non-Communist politicians alike adapted it successfully. Indeed, the most extreme anti-
German, anti-noble discourses of 1918 rose to dominance in Czech
society during World War II and its aftermath. It is ironic that this
swing to the extreme left followed a sharp turn right in the late
1930s, when many Czech and Slovak parties had flirted with fascism
and nobles had regained a measure of their prewar prestige. At the
same time, it is not surprising that war and occupation promoted a
kind of reverse radicalization. Extreme conservatism and compro-
mises with Nazi Germany had failed to save rump Czecho-Slovakia
in 1939. After six years of occupation (and to some degree, collaboration), social revolution and alliance with the Soviet Union
seemed more promising. For nobles, this national mood swing had
ominous implications.

Retribution against the German Nobility

The worst violence against Germans took place from mid-May to
late July of 1945, as Czech civilians, soldiers, and paramilitaries
indiscriminately drove Sudeten Germans across the border, interned them in concentration camps, and passed revolutionary justice on suspected collaborators. In all, around 700,000 Germans
were expelled, 300,000 fled, and perhaps 30,000 were killed or died
in concentration camps in 1945.[81] At the Potsdam Conference at
the end of July, the Allied powers demanded that the Czechs put a
stop to the "wild" expulsions of the summer, though at the same
time they approved an "organized transfer" of the remaining 2 million Sudeten Germans to take place in 1946.

Though German nobles held a special symbolic position in the
rhetoric of retribution, their experience of the expulsions was similar to that of most other Sudeten Germans. Some fled or were

forced across the borders soon after liberation. The Czechs arrested others and put them on trial for collaboration. Eugen Ledebur ended up in Terezín, the former Nazi camp, where he died in November 1945 while waiting to be expelled.[82] Many German nobles hunkered down on their estates and were shipped out in the regularized transfers of 1946. The Thun family was typical in this regard. Franz Anton Thun, who had welcomed the Nazi arrival in the Sudetenland on behalf of the *Verband* in 1938, awaited his fate with his two daughters in the north Bohemian town of Děčín/ Tetschen. On 16 April 1946, Czech soldiers herded the Thuns into a packed railroad car, which would take them across the border into Germany. The Děčín regional archive contains files stuffed with identification cards of tens of thousands of expellees like the Thuns. Now fully tied to the Sudeten German cause and fate, Franz Thun's card looked just like any other, with one exception. Under occupation, a dutiful official had typed simply, "Count."[83]

A few German nobles were arrested and put on trial for collaboration. Karl Waldstein was interned on 14 May 1945 and accused of membership in the National Socialist Flyers' Corps (NSFK) and propagation of Nazism by giving "material and moral" support to the SdP and NSDAP. Though Waldstein's membership in the NSFK was not in doubt, he claimed it was purely formal. Waldstein had been the pre-1938 head of the German Flyers' Club *(Verband der deutschen Flieger)*, which was incorporated into the NSFK after the annexation of the Sudetenland.[84] Waldstein vigorously denied the charge that he had in any way "propagated" Nazism. He admitted to attending a number of SdP rallies and having ties with "leading functionaries of the Nazi Party," but he claimed that he had gone to the rallies out of curiosity and that social connections with fellow Germans, regardless of their own criminal status, did not amount to collaboration. The court ruled Waldstein guilty of membership in the Flyers' Corps, but concluded that there was insufficient evidence to convict him of propagating Nazism. His sentence, passed on 30 April 1946, was forfeiture of property and one year in prison.[85] Having already been in prison for a year, he was released two weeks later. Waldstein and his family soon left for Austria, where they took up residence with relatives.[86]

In a similar case, the Extraordinary People's Court in Ostrava convicted Johann Count Larisch (1917–?) in absentia for membership in the NSFK, though he was suspected of much wider collaboration with the Gestapo. An old Silesian family, the Larisches owned a large estate near the Polish border as well as a sprawling mining concern. Though Larisch had fled to Austria in May before the arrival of the Red Army, he protested his innocence from abroad and appealed for the return of his Czechoslovak citizenship. He was sentenced in absentia to five years in prison, and the court issued a warrant for his arrest with a fifty-year expiration date.[87] On the whole, though, relatively few Germans were tried under the Czechoslovak retribution decrees, as Czech authorities preferred expulsion to trial for all but the most serious offenses.[88] This made the Larisch and Waldstein cases exceptional, both for nobles and for the larger German population in the Sudetenland.

More typically, German nobles simply lost their citizenship, and national administrators took over control of their property.[89] In one of many examples of such confiscations, Hugo Salm-Reifferscheidt watched his land slip away before dying in early 1946. Already in June 1945, the Red Army set up a prison camp for German and Hungarian POWs in the gardens of Salm's chateau in Rájec. Though declared German and subject to confiscation, Salm continued to insist on his Czech patriotism and cheerfully hosted Soviet officers in his house. His forests—reaching perhaps 10,000 ha— reverted to the government in June 1945 and were quickly parcelled out to area farmers. A factory and a power plant were nationalized. Salm's personal belongings were inventoried in 1945 and again in September 1946, at which time they were due to be sold. Half the proceeds went to the Fund for National Renewal, half to to the local national committee, though reports also suggest that some of the property went home directly with national committee members.[90]

The Beneš Decrees also led to the dispersal of Karl Buquoy's vast estate. Buquoy, who spent over a year in prison after the war awaiting trial for collaboration, was widely hated by Czechs, and officials moved quickly to confiscate his property. The Buquoy forests and fish ponds officially reverted to state control in late 1945.

National administrators took over control of the family's remaining arable land. The government set aside Buquoy's main castle at Nové Hrady to become a museum, and another was rented to Prague's Central Council of Unions for the benefit of workers. Finally, the National Land Fund took possession of Buquoy's palace in Prague, renting it out to the French embassy.[91]

In all, the National Land Fund took control of 510 noble castles and chateaux.[92] Several became depositories for valuable art collections and period furniture, eventually opening as museums. Others reverted to local and regional institutions, including schools, orphanages, and factory councils. And dozens would serve as archives, providing atmospheric (if often under-heated) surroundings for research on the nobility. The fate of Buquoy's holdings was typical for German landowners, as various government agencies divvied up German property (much of it immediately confiscated upon liberation) in the latter half of 1945.

Some confiscations were not quite so clear-cut. In a bitterly contested case, Franz Josef Prince of Liechtenstein lost almost 70,000 ha in Moravia to a national administrator in late June 1945. Not only was Liechtenstein German in nationality *(národnost)*, according to the Ministry of Agriculture's explanatory note, but he was also a beneficiary of the "White Mountain catastrophe" of 1620 and a notorious Germanizer. Though Liechtenstein himself had spent the war abroad (in his eponymous statelet abutting Switzerland), his "leading German officials and German personnel were mostly organized Nazis."[93] Liechtenstein denied these charges, but to no avail. Offering a challenge to reigning Czech ethnic conceptions of nationality, he claimed that he was a citizen of Liechtenstein and considered himself of Liechtensteinian nationality. In the Czech census of 1930, he had listed his mother tongue as German, though he did not consider this a decisive marker of nationality. In a biting criticism, he added, "Certainly it is not the intention of the Czech government to proceed according to a racial criterion."[94] But by making a putative ethnic identity the determining factor for confiscation and expulsion, that is exactly what the Czech government intended. Liechtenstein lost his appeal, and Czech relations with the principality remain strained to this day.

There were several more cases of ambiguous nationality that required legal consideration after the war. Leopold Deym, the enthusiastic Czech who named his new baby Světlana after Stalin's daughter in 1944, fought the Brno Regional National Committee's decision to confiscate his mother Marie's Hajany estate. His mother had declared herself German in 1930, however, and she had no record of anti-fascist activity to protect her from confiscation. Deym's appeal claimed that his mother had been mentally ill in 1930, and thus that her declaration of German nationality was invalid. The national committee rejected the appeal on the grounds that Marie Deym had not been ruled legally incompetent until 1934. The committee's judgment also noted that a German court had declared her competent again in 1940 and that an investigation had uncovered the "German orientation of Marie Deym and members of her family" before the war.[95] To Czech officials, insanity was no excuse for German national sentiments.

The Deym and Liechtenstein cases illustrate the convergence of national and social revolution in 1945. By depriving Germans of their citizenship and then expelling them, the Czech government set in motion a new land reform that would eventually dwarf the interwar reform. As the Ministry of Agriculture's Communist propagandist, Jiří Koťátko, wrote: "The wholesale transfer of the German population from Czechoslovakia [means] the liquidation of German land ownership on Czechoslovak soil, the national purge of Czech land, the national revolutionary period of the new land reform."[96] Haste was vitally important, Koťátko argued, in order to prepare the borderlands for immediate colonization with Czech and Slovak settlers. "Don't hesitate, confiscate, allocate!" was the "basic line," Koťátko's sound bite for local Communist functionaries, who should act "without scruples for various legal formalities."[97] Millions of hectares changed hands in a matter of months. The dispossession and expulsion of Czechoslovakia's Germans became the first stage in a vast reorganization of the Czechoslovak countryside from 1945 to 1949.

The National Land Reform

The "national land reform" occasioned by the expulsion of Czechoslovakia's Germans involved a total of 1.65 million ha of arable land and 1.3 million ha of forestland, almost 25 percent of the country's surface area.[98] By the end of the resettlement action, around 1.1 million ha of arable land had been distributed to private individuals (a total of 122,000 families). Of the remaining arable land, 100,000 ha went to cooperatives, and 75,000 ha remained unallotted as of 1948.[99] Forestland went primarily to the state, which transferred 840,000 ha to the National Forestry Administration.[100] Of the total confiscations of around 3 million ha, only 546,000 ha fell in Slovakia. Because of Czechoslovakia's failure to expel its Hungarians, most Hungarian land was not redistributed under the national land reform. The overall picture is of a substantial increase in the number of Czech small farmers working their own plots of around 10 hectares.

Because the land reform in the German borderlands was seen as primarily national, statistics on its impact on individual Bohemian nobles are scarce. But it is likely that German nobles lost between 500,000 and 700,000 ha to the confiscations of 1945.[101] The Liechtenstein family, for example, stood to lose around 70,000 ha, the Buquoys 20,000 ha, the Waldsteins 20,000 ha, the Clam-Gallases 18,000 ha, the Clary-Aldringens 7,000 ha, and the Thun-Hohensteins 10,000 ha. After the interwar land reform, the majority of remaining noble land was forest. In effect, then, the state took over the role of the German latifundists as the administrator of vast forested estates in the borderlands.

For arable land, the government tapped into a wide-ranging resettlement apparatus coordinated by the Ministry of the Interior.[102] The first stage, set up by Decree 5 of 19 May 1945, called for applications for positions as national administrators, who were sent to the borderlands to oversee German property. The key paragraph in the decree was typically vague, empowering national committees to send national administrators "to all properties that require uninterrupted operation of production and of economic life, especially ... those that are held, administered, rented or leased by people

considered unreliable with regard to the state."[103] Though it was
intended to apply to German firms and property that would be
vacated in 1945 or 1946, the Communist government used the same
law to deprive *kulaks* (or *"zbohatlici*—the rich ones" as the Czechoslovak Communists preferred) of their farms after the 1948 takeover.[104] Overall, by 1946 there were eighty-two thousand national
administrators of agricultural land, of whom seventy thousand
would gain full title to their fiefdoms after the Germans were expelled.[105]

Parcelization and resettlement continued feverishly in the first
half of 1946. Local farmers' commissions and national committees
worked through a total of 157,000 applications for land, approving
a total of 122,000. Successful applicants tended to come from the
ranks of landless laborers, small farmers, and occasionally nonagri-
cultural workers. Agricultural resettlement formed part of a vast
colonization of the whole Sudeten region, or approximately 20 percent of postwar Czechoslovakia. Altogether, 1.8 million Czechs (and
some Slovaks, Hungarians, and Gypsies) moved into towns and
cities in the borderlands, occupying former German houses, taking
over German land, and receiving title to German businesses.

Overall, the Communists reaped a huge political and administrative bounty through the land reform-expulsion-resettlement process. The Ministry of Agriculture, under the relentless Slovak Communist Julius Ďuriš, was seen as the primary mover behind
redistribution as well as the champion of small farmers. In areas
where the population was overwhelmingly German, the Communist
Ministry of Interior appointed regional administrative commissions
as a substitute for elected national committees. Thus Communists
directly controlled redistribution in areas that had the most land
subject to confiscation. Many, and perhaps most, national committees also ended up under Communist control. As Kot'átko suc-
cinctly noted, "The decisive factor in the first [interwar] land reform was the bureaucratic machinery of government, controlled by
the reactionary Agrarian Party. The new land reform is being carried out by Farmers' Committees, democratically elected, and fully
supported . . . by the Ministry of Agriculture."[106] With the Agrarian
Party banned because of alleged wartime collaboration, the Com-

munist Party mopped up both Agrarian supporters and government posts.

Communists dominated the whole process of confiscation and redistribution, expulsion and resettlement. In the May 1946 elections, in which the Communist Party won a decisive 40 percent plurality in the Czech lands, settlers voted overwhelmingly for the Communists.[107] There is some disagreement over whether the settlers were more likely to vote Communist out of gratitude for receiving German property or because they came primarily from social groups inclined to vote for the Communists anyway (landless rural laborers and dissatisfied urban workers). Though the current state of research on the question does not permit a definitive answer, it seems likely that the Communist patronage machine increased the party's support substantially.[108] In Slovakia, however, where resettlement was minimal and socialist parties were historically weaker, the Communists did poorly. Nevertheless, seen as the guarantors of the tremendously popular expulsions and land reform, the Communists built a vast reservoir of support that would help to ensure a smooth seizure of power in 1948.

With the expulsions largely complete and resettlement well underway in late 1946, the National Assembly began planning to extend the land reform to non-German landowners in the interior of the country. In early 1948, Kot'átko summarized the results of land reform to date. "We can safely say," he wrote, "that the problem of German ownership of land has been solved completely in Bohemia and Moravia-Silesia . . . The first stage of the new Land Reform is thus at an end, having achieved its aims; it only remains to deal with the problem of large estates in the hands of Czech and Slovak landlords."[109] In late 1946, the National Front began what became a rancorous debate over Kot'átko's stage two, the parcelization of non-German large estates. The subsequent bill, known as the Revision of the First Czechoslovak Land Reform, passed in July 1947. Combined with legislation creating a United Association of Czech Farmers, the revision further consolidated the Communist hold on the countryside during the crucial months leading up to the February crisis in 1948.

All Czech parties of the National Front agreed that interwar land reform had been incomplete. Though 4 million hectares had fallen under *zábor* in 1919, only around half had been redistributed to small farmers or taken over by the state. Close to 2 million hectares had been released to large landowners, most of them members of the former nobility. With resettlement of the Sudeten borderlands almost complete in late 1946, the National Front began work on a bill that would return remaining large estates to *zábor* and then redistribute them to small farmers or the state. It is important to note that much of the 2 million ha released from *zábor* in the interwar period had belonged to German nobles, and thus had already been confiscated in the course of the national land reform in 1945–1946. Overall, the National Assembly estimated that 450,000 ha would fall under the new legislation in 1947.[110] The Communists also insisted that the bill contain a revision of so-called residual estates, owned primarily by former Agrarian Party backers. The Communist slogan was "land to those who work it," and they saw residual estates as a bastion of absentee land ownership.

The new land reform law set up a revision commission to reconsider the interwar release from *zábor* of any holdings over 250 ha. In addition, the commission was to re-expropriate all residual estates in excess of 50 ha. The fact that the term "large estate" now meant any property over 50 ha bore witness to a remarkable revalorization of interwar rhetoric.[111] Like the "foreign aristocrat" that had come to symbolize all Germans in Czechoslovakia, now the concept of aristocratic landowner had begun to apply to *kulaks*, land speculators, and anyone with over 50 ha. Like the German population, this group would have to be "liquidated."

The Communist-dominated Ministry of Agriculture was responsible for naming commissioners and setting the commission's agenda, though both required the approval of the government as a whole.[112] The process of revision proceeded slowly, only beginning in early 1948.[113] A little over 1 million ha came under review, including 627,000 ha of large estates and 400,000 ha of residual estates. Around three-quarters of the total was forestland, and therefore went to the state. Most of the rest was divided among small farmers.[114] Because the national confiscations of 1945–1946 had not been consistently carried out in Slovakia, just over 50 percent of the total revision now took place there. It is difficult to determine how much of the revision land was redistributed before the Communist putsch of 20 February 1948, as well as the eventual amount of compensation received by the owners. Kot'átko claimed that the revision commission settled "more than half of all revision cases" before the February crisis.[115] Vlastislav Lacina suggests that very few cases were resolved before the government crisis, but that "after February, the tempo of the commission sped up markedly."[116] In any case, the commission was decisively pro-Communist and worked closely with the Ministry of Agriculture; its revisions served further to cement small-farmer support for the Communist Party.

The National Assembly also passed a special law in July 1947 confiscating the 55,000 remaining hectares of Adolf Prince Schwarzenberg's south Bohemian estates.[117] The head of the family's primogeniture, Schwarzenberg (1890–1950) had spent the war years abroad, where he received a doctorate in political science at Columbia University in 1945.[118] Schwarzenberg was one of the few nobles who remained of ambiguous nationality in the 1930s. His estates were so vast that he employed large numbers of both Czechs and Germans, with whom he was widely popular, and he also supported both Czech and German charitable causes. In 1940, the Gestapo sequestered his property, giving him the reputation of a persecuted opponent of National Socialism. Even so, the postwar Czechoslovak regime considered him a German, as he had declared German nationality in the 1930 census.[119] In May 1945, the Schwarzenberg estates reverted to the control of a team of national administrators, but there was no consensus about the land's ultimate fate. Schwarzenberg, who never returned to Czechoslovakia, tried in vain to regain control of his property. Gradually, regional national committees began chipping away at the Schwarzenberg holdings in late 1945, taking forests for municipal uses or giving arable land to local farmers. The property's status remained in doubt until the 1947 legislation, which transferred it definitively to the state, without compensation.[120]

By the end of 1948, the fragmentation of the Czechoslovak countryside was complete. Few farmers owned more than 50 ha, and the majority held under 10 ha. The once strong large- and medium-estate lobby no longer existed; the Agrarian Party too was gone. Communists now dominated both the political and administrative organs of the countryside, leaving little democratic space for farmers to resist the transition to collectivization that would begin in 1948–1949.[121]

Jiří Koťátko admitted in 1945 the role land reform would play in the socialization of agriculture. His model was the Soviet Union. In spite of the Bolsheviks' collectivist convictions, he wrote, they had handed out land to 5 million peasants, thus creating a deep well of support for the fight against counterrevolution. "And it was this very redistribution of land that brought the Soviet power, after a blink of the eye in the cycle of dialectical evolution, to the socialization of land, to the victory of the *Kolchoz* system! Without the redistribution of land in October 1917, there would have been no collectivization in 1929." Czech Communists were also following a pragmatic course, Koťátko wrote, because farmers were unlikely to settle the depopulated borderlands without the promise of their own land. Though breaking up large estates might be a temporary setback on the road to collectivization, it was only "the first step" in the agricultural revolution. "We know where we're going," he assured his Communist readers, "and we see our goal clearly!"[122] By 1960 over 90 percent of Czechoslovak land would be collectivized.[123] Exiled nobles must surely have seen the irony of this return to large estate agriculture, the workers' latifundia.

The End of the Bohemian Nobility

Only a few nobles remained in Czechoslovakia after 1948 to see the changes firsthand. Hugo Strachwitz, a signatory of the 1938 declaration, ended up "a cattle feeder on his former estate."[124] Of the Schwarzenbergs, only Karel's Uncle Arnošt (d. 1979) remained in Czechoslovakia, "to care for the family crypt," as he said. He spent four years in prison, from 1953 to 1957, including two years at forced labor in the uranium mines in Jáchymov. Denied a regular job because of his class origins, Arnošt lived on the edge of poverty, sometimes working on a chamomile farm to supplement a meager pension.[125] František Kinský, who had a hand in both noble declarations of loyalty in 1938 and 1939, retired to a parsonage near his former castle in Kostelec after the Communist government evicted him from his home in 1951.[126] A handful of Czech nobles were allowed to stay and work on their socialized estates. Jindřich Šlik was first a secretary and then a driver on his former estate.[127] Max Wratislav drove a tractor, dragging logs out of his former forest near Tábor; in an rare case of upward mobility among former aristocrats under Communism, his son eventually drove a combine on a nearby collective farm. Asked why he hadn't emigrated, Max Wratislav responded that he would "rather be a worker at home than a lord abroad."[128] At least in some cases, then, the nationalization of the nobility reached its ultimate conclusion, with nationhood decisively trumping class identification.

The vast majority of nobles left Czechoslovakia between 1945 and 1949, though few became lords abroad. Karel Schwarzenberg escaped to Vienna in 1948, where he worked as a historian and oversaw the Slavic manuscript collection of the National Library. His brother František emigrated to the United States and taught political science at Loyola University in Chicago. After stays in New York and Florida, Leopold and Cecilia Sternberg settled in Jamaica, where they ran a guest house overlooking the sea.[129] Karel Belcredi, who stubbornly fought the passage of a new land reform in 1947, finally fled with his brothers to Austria two months after the Communist takeover of February 1948.[130]

German nobles too dispersed throughout Europe and beyond. With Soviet forces threatening to overrun Bohemia in early 1945, Konrad Henlein's interpreter Max Hohenlohe fled to Spain, where Francisco Franco protected him from extradition to postwar Czechoslovakia.[131] Alfons Clary-Aldringen tried to escape Czechoslovakia with family valuables in May 1945, but was apprehended and spent some months confined in a hospital ward at the Terezin concentration camp.[132] Before his expulsion from Czechoslovakia in September, he was sent to forced labor on a farm in western Bohemia, where he remembered "deriving downright pleasure from harvesting, rather like Levin in Tolstoy's *Anna Karenina*." He would eventually retire in Venice in an old family townhouse and became a favored guest at the art critic Bernard Berenson's Villa I Tatti, where he was admired for his great knowledge of Habsburg history.[133]

After five years as a prisoner of war in the Soviet Union, Ferdinand Thun managed to find a new home in Communist East Germany in 1948. Upon his return, he completed a brief de-Nazification course and then began working his way up the ranks in the Communist Foreign Ministry. He eventually served as the East German ambassador to Iran and Afghanistan from 1973 to 1975.[134] All told, Bohemian nobles scattered after 1945, settling around the world into diverse careers and lifestyles. With noble social ties now dissolved, the Bohemian nobility ceased its collective existence.

⁓ IN AN INFLUENTIAL ARTICLE, Jan Gross argues that the Second World War revolutionized East Central European societies by destroying or discrediting old elites, eliminating autonomous local bodies, increasing state control of the economy, and displacing millions of people. All these trends, he suggests, facilitated Communist seizures of power in the immediate postwar period. Gross's analysis indicates significant continuities between the periods of Nazi occupation and the consolidation of Communist control of the region. The Nazis in effect provided an example of violence, expulsion, and arbitrary state power that inured Czechs, Poles, and other East Central Europeans to Communist methods of eliminating their enemies. With this in mind, Gross recommends the re-periodization of the postwar revolutions to include the Nazi occupation beginning in 1939 (for Czechs and Poles) and extending to Communist takeovers in 1947 and 1948.[135]

In many respects, evidence from the Czech case bears out this reinterpretation of the transition to Communist rule. The expulsions of the Sudeten Germans were accompanied by Nazi-style violence and a rhetoric to match. By eliminating autonomous political bodies and discrediting the Czech right, the Nazi occupation also began the shrinking of civil society that would accelerate under Communist pressure in 1946 and 1947. Rule by presidential decree indicated the persistence of a wartime mentality in Czechoslovakia after May 1945. Throughout 1945, local and national Czech officials warned continuously of German "werewolf" terrorist bands that threatened violence against Czechs and their restored state.[136] After most Germans were expelled in 1946, the Communists urged continuing vigilance, only now against internal enemies. As the flexible Communist use of the word "cleansing" showed, it was not very far from cleansing of Germans to cleansing of class enemies.

Reflecting in the 1970s on this continuity from the Nazi occupation to the expulsions to the Communist seizure of power, Czech *samizdat* historians began to consider the moral implications of the expulsions, arguing that the removal of Czechoslovak Germans had undermined respect for property, the rule of law, and democracy.[137] Certainly the expulsions and land reforms helped prepare the way institutionally for the Communist seizure of power in February 1948. Along with control of security forces and national committees, the Communists used the apparatus of confiscation and resettlement to dominate local politics and limit the democratic space available for opposition. By 1948, very few truly democratic institutions remained through which citizens could oppose Communist power.

If we view the postwar revolution from the vantage point of the Bohemian nobility, we see even longer-term continuities than Gross suggests. Czech politicians referred to the expulsions and postwar confiscations as a continuation of a process that had begun with land reform in 1919: a national and social revolution that was to reverse the effects of the Battle of White Mountain and the subsequent Germanization of the Bohemian elite. Noble landholdings remained largely intact during the war, and the postwar land reform rhetoric in fact drew more from the 1919 reform than from the Nazi example.[138] Moreover, with the important exception of the murdered Jews, Czech economic and social structure changed little during the years of occupation. In that sense, the Czech experience differed markedly from that of the Poles, whose elites were decimated by punitive Nazi and Soviet occupations from 1939 to 1945. In Czechoslovakia, the postwar revolution had both prewar and wartime antecedents, but it far surpassed both earlier revolutionary waves in intensity and extent.

The revolution from 1945 to 1948 finally destroyed the Bohemian nobility as a class. Though the Communist new order was not fully in place until a few years later, the elimination of the latifundia prepared the way for the eventual collectivization of agriculture. Most Bohemian

German nobles fled or were expelled by the end of 1946. Czech nobles held on for a few more years, though they too lost their remaining land after the Communists consolidated power in February 1948. Though a handful of broken nobles remained in Czechoslovakia, the Communist revolution effectively liquidated the last vestiges of the Old Regime.

Conclusion

$\mathcal{I}$N THE CENTURY FOLLOWING the revolutions of 1848, Habsburg Central Europe modernized, nationalized, and ultimately fragmented into a bevy of egalitarian, mostly homogeneous nation states. In one sense, the region went from unity to diversity, as the Habsburg Monarchy progressively lost control of its periphery, yielding power to new regional political actors and eventually to independent nation-states. But this political fragmentation stemmed from a social and national transformation in the opposite direction, from diversity to unity. In the nineteenth century, cities like Prague, Lemberg, and Vienna were home to a cascade of languages and cultures. By the mid-twentieth century, nationalism, separatism, and ethnic cleansing had undermined and then destroyed this diversity. Socially, a feudal society of orders, dominated by nobility and the monarch, shaded into an increasingly democratic new order, with the middle and lower classes asserting their rights to economic and political power. After 1918, new regimes eliminated the monarchy entirely, and nobles became ordinary citizens. Postwar communist regimes simplified the picture even more, undertaking a project of social leveling unprecedented in its scale. By the late 1940s, East Central European societies were largely egalitarian in social structure, a remarkable transformation of what were once the most socially stratified parts of Europe.

In the mid-nineteenth century, Bohemian nobles occupied the pinnacle of the economic, social, and political order, making them an excellent barometer of the subsequent transformation of Habsburg Central Europe. As the monarchy's economy and society modernized, nobles transformed their feudal estates into successful capitalist agricultural enterprises and struck alliances with surging nationalist political parties. But even as nobles changed to accommodate the burgeoning new order, they also maintained customs and traditions that embodied their nobility. Not only did the nobility remain a closed social group, but nobles also followed patterns of political engagement that reflected a deep attachment to the feudal concept of Bohemian historic rights, as well as a strong imperial loyalty. Though nobles divided over the precedence they gave to Bohemian rights and in their choice of Czech or German national allies, their class solidarity persisted well after the fall of the monarchy in 1918. Like the monarchy itself, nobles responded to social and political modernization by becoming a hybrid of old and new. For both nobles and the emperor, this meant an intricate calibration of democratic and feudal tendencies, national and supranational forces.

The monarchy's delicate balance could not survive the First World War, however, and the birth of Czechoslovakia in 1918 seemed to herald the end of the Old Regime. Most of the country's founders viewed Czechoslovakia as a democratic, middle-class, Czech national state. State-builders discovered in the nobility an effective negative symbol, associating nobles with German, Habsburg, and feudal dominance. But Czechs themselves divided over the meaning of their nationhood, and their views of the nobility reflected those divisions. Again nobles served as a barometer, now of the Czech national mood. For many integral nationalists, Germans and nobles were a reactionary force that threatened to undermine the Czech nation and state. Although some radical voices favored full dispossession and possibly expulsion of nobles and Germans, the prevailing view sought to use land reform and administrative methods to "de-Austrianize" Czechoslovakia. At first, only a few Czechs defended the nobility as a stabilizing economic and political force, though this position gained supporters in the more conservative 1930s.

Once Bohemian nobles found their bearings in 1919, they tried to weather the postimperial revolution by reviving the old formula: "change so as to conserve." With the advent of the nation-state, change meant finally coming to terms with nationalism. During the 1920s, many nobles expressed increasingly vigorous national loyalties in the hopes of mitigating the nationally inspired land reform. Both Czech and German nobles grafted elements of Christian nationalism (bordering on fascism) onto earlier imperial and historic rights traditions. And in spite of national divisions, nobles retained their class solidarity, socializing and marrying across national lines, but rarely outside of their own circles. By the late 1930s, however, Hitler's expansionist intentions forced nobles decisively into opposing camps. The Bohemian nobility divided into Czech and Sudeten German factions, loyalties that led some to a bold defiance of Hitler and others to various degrees of collaboration.

With the defeat of Nazi Germany in 1945 and the liberation of Czechoslovakia, the most radical anti-German and anti-noble rhetoric from 1918 came to dominate public discourse. The Beneš Decrees dispossessed the two-thirds of nobles identified as German, and most either fled or faced expulsion with the rest of the Sudeten German population. A renewed land reform targeted remaining nobles for confiscation, a process that began in earnest in 1948 after the Communist seizure of power. With the expulsion of Bohemian Germans and the subsequent destruction of the residual landowning and capitalist elite, Czechoslovakia in effect cut its ties to Western Europe. Indeed, Germans, nobles, and Jews had long been important vehicles for Western influence in Bohemia and throughout East Central Europe. After 1948, the loss of those ties suited Czechoslovakia's paranoid Stalinists well, though the country's subsequent isolation from Europe would have a devastating effect on culture and public morale. Indeed, Czechoslovakia's thirty-year transformation from 1918 to 1948 leveled and homogenized what had once been an extremely diverse and stratified society. Even today, the Czech Republic and Central Europe still struggle with the troubling memories of their lost diversity.

Return to Bohemia, Return to Europe

Since the 1880s, the Bohemian nobility has been a bellwether of Czech attitudes about nationhood, politics, and Bohemia's place in Europe. After communism's fall in 1989, scores of nobles returned to Bohemia, and once again they have taken on an important, though ambivalent, symbolic role in Czech efforts at self-definition. As the Czechs have sought to gain and then consolidate membership in the European Union, many have seen nobles as avatars of internationalism.[1] Once pariahs and emblems of the vanquished Old Order, nobles are now popular symbols of Bohemia's "return to Europe." Conversely, a sizable minority of Czechs has bristled at the prospect of wealthy nobles, still seen as foreigners, returning to claim forests and chateaux that now count as part of the national patrimony.

Karel VII Prince Schwarzenberg (1937–) has been the most prominent noble returnee and a focus of tremendous public interest. Widely respected for his support of Czech underground literature and work for human rights during the Communist period, Schwarzenberg triumphantly returned from Vienna in 1990 and served as the head of Václav Havel's Presidential Chancellery until 1992. Many saw Schwarzenberg's cosmopolitanism and global financial reach as both an asset and an inspiration as Czechs worked to undo the international isolation and economic stagnation inherited from the Communist regime.[2] Schwarzenberg and other nobles also, ironically, became the darlings of the freewheeling free-marketeers who populated Václav Klaus's center-right government from 1992 to 1997. In the rush to privatize state-owned assets, former noble landowners offered an easy way to get state-owned land into private hands quickly. Restitution legislation in 1991 allowed for the return of all property confiscated by the Communist regime after 25 February 1948.[3]

By choosing this date, however, the Czechoslovak Parliament intentionally excluded former Sudeten Germans from the right to restitution, a decision that has rankled many in Germany and Austria.[4] It also places the Bohemian nobility near the center of debates over restitution and the expulsion of Sudeten Germans, as Czech noble families are eligible to receive property, while German nobles are not. The line drawn in 1991 was clearly national, not social, testifying to the persistence of the idea of "national justice" in the Czech public mind. Indeed, a survey of Czech newspapers in the 1990s concludes that stereotypes of nobles as foreigners and exploiters persist, particularly in left-wing and tabloid newspapers.[5] "Czech" nobles such as Schwarzenberg and the Lobkowiczs have largely escaped this resentment.

Two high-profile restitution cases illustrate the very different receptions Czech and German nobles have received since 1989. After the Communist putsch in 1948, Max Lobkowicz, the war-time Czechoslovak ambassador to London, fled to Boston, where his family had already taken refuge during the war. Both Lobkowicz's son Martin and grandson William went to Harvard, after which they settled into careers in Massachusetts finance and real estate. In 1991, Martin returned to Czechoslovakia to reclaim the family patrimony: several grand, but leaky castles, vast forest complexes, and a trove of artwork by European masters. William Lobkowicz has since become the popular manager of the family's revived empire, now known as the Lobkowicz Foundation. Indeed, Lobkowicz depicts himself as an administrator of a sizable piece of Czech cultural heritage.[6] A few years ago, the family opened a museum at its Nelahozeves castle to exhibit restituted artwork. It also runs a travel agency, brewery, and winery, all bearing the highly recognizable Lobkowicz name. The goal, William Lobkowicz says, is to make the Lobkowicz Foundation self-supporting. "We're custodians," he adds, just trying to keep "the places open for the public."[7] Lobkowicz's claim of public service echoes an argument used by the *Svaz* to oppose land reform in the 1920s: nobles are not only a part of the Bohemian historical landscape, but they also have an important role in preserving Bohemia's natural and historical monuments. The success and popularity of the Lobkowiczs suggest that nobles have begun to find a niche in the growing Czech heritage industry.

Carl Albrecht Waldstein, the grandson of Karl Waldstein, has not been received as warmly as the Lobkowiczs, at least not by the general public. The Czechoslovak Interior Ministry granted Waldstein citizenship in 1992, though he was not technically eligible.[8] A Ministry official explained the exception, also given to eight other former German nobles, as an attempt to gain both sympathy abroad and possible investment.[9] Soon after receiving Czech citizenship, Waldstein filed a claim for the restitution of his family's property in north Bohemia. The state had confiscated 20,000 ha and six castles from his grandfather Karl in 1945. At the time, Karl Waldstein had been in prison awaiting trial for collaboration. Though acquitted of "propagation of Nazism" in 1946, Waldstein was convicted of membership in the Nazi Flyers' Corps, a supposedly paramilitary organization.[10] Following his release from prison in May 1946, Waldstein and his family immigrated to Austria.

His grandson claims Karl was neither a German (in the national/political sense) nor a Nazi, and that his membership in the Nazi Flyers' Corps was purely formal. According to the family's restitution claim, Waldstein lost his property due to his indictment and not because of his German nationality. If the conviction were overturned, Carl Waldstein concludes, so too should the confiscation.[11] Thus far, Czech courts have not proven sympathetic to either case, and in 1996 the Czech Social Democratic Party warned that returning property to the Waldsteins would set a precedent that could lead to hundreds of thousands of Sudeten German claims.[12] For many Czechs, if not a majority, the nobility still triggers fears of German financial and political dominance, not to mention the possibility of vast transfers of property.

The return of the Rohan family to Bohemia has been less controversial and suggests avenues for coexistence between Czechs and Germans in the new Europe. Seeking neither citizenship nor restitution, the Rohans have built a close relationship with the Czech administrators of their former chateau Sychrov. Confiscated from Alain Rohan in 1945, Sychrov later became a museum, which included an exhibition on the history of the working class. Since 1989, Rohan family members from all over Europe have cooperated with efforts to restore the chateau to its nineteenth-century grandeur.[13]

Now a conference center and popular tourist destination, Sychrov has become a monument of reconciliation between Czechs and the former German nobility. But the troubles of the 1930s and 1940s have not been entirely forgotten. A tour of the main house leads visitors through the well-appointed library. There a copy of Adolf Hitler's *Mein Kampf* rests conspicuously on a shelf near the entrance, seemingly the last book touched before the previous inhabitants fled.[14]

As former nobles have trickled back into the Czech Republic and sought restitution of their property and a renewed role in public life, the popular response has ranged from nostalgic welcome to angry claims of carpetbagging. This ambivalence is in part a legacy of the noble record of wartime collaboration and resistance. But it is also complicated by the fact that nobles were prominent victims of both the postwar expulsion of Sudeten Germans and the Communist takeover in 1948. Czechs are still trying to come to terms with intermingled senses of guilt and victimization that were a product of the immediate postwar years. Victims both of and with the Czechs, nobles have again become potent symbols in Czech attempts to come to terms with their past and to fashion a postimperial identity for their small state in the heart of Europe.

Abbreviations

AKPR	Archiv kanceláře prezidenta republiky (Archive of the Chancellery of the President of the Republic)
AMV	Archiv Ministerstva vnitra (Archive of the Ministry of Interior)
ANM	Archiv Národního musea (Archive of the National Museum)
AÚTGM	Archiv Ústavu Tomáše Garrigue Masaryka (Archive of the Tomáš Garrigue Masaryk Institute)
c	čislo (number)
ČSSN	Český svaz pro spolupraci s Němci (Czech Union for Cooperation with the Germans)
ic	inventární čislo (inventory number)
k	karton (carton)
KB	Kameradschaftsbund (Society of Friends)
KPR	Kancelář prezidenta republiky (Chancellery of the President of the Republic)
MA	Městký archiv (City Archive)
MV	Ministerstvo vnitra (Ministry of Interior)
MZ-S	Ministrstvo zemědělství-sekretariát (Ministry of Agriculture-Secretariat)

MZA   Moravský zemský archiv (Moravian Provincial Archive)

MZV   Ministerstvo zahraničních věcí (Ministry of Foreign Affairs)

n.d.   no date

NSDAP   Nationalsozialistische Deutsche Arbeiterpartei (German National Socialist Workers' Party)

NSFK   Nationalsozialistische Fliegerkorps (National Socialist Flyer Corps)

NV   Národní výbor (National Committee)

PO MV   Propagační odbor Ministerstva vnitra (Propaganda Department of the Ministry of Interior)

PRO FO   Public Records Office, Foreign Office

RA   rodinný archiv (family archive)

SČV   Svaz Československých velkostatkářů (Union of Czechoslovak large landowners)

SdP   Sudetendeutsche Partei (Sudeten German Party)

sig   signatura (signature)

SOA   Státní oblastní archiv (State Regional Archive)

SOkA   Státní okresní archiv (State District Archive)

SPÚ   Státní pozemkový úřad (State Land Office)

SÚA   Státní ústřední archiv (State Central Archive)

sv   svazek (sheaf)

VdG   Verband der deutschen Grossgrundbesitzer (Association of German Large Landowners)

ZA   Zemský archiv (Provincial Archive)

~ APPENDIX

Declarations of the Czech Nobility, 1938 and 1939

Declaration of members of the historic nobility, delivered 17 September 1938 to President Edvard Beneš

Mr. President,

In these difficult days all estates and classes of our nation *(národ)* unanimously express their will to prevent the violation of the historic borders of our state. In the same spirit, a number of historic families of our homeland *(vlast)* would like to present to you similar sentiments. Loyalty to the Czech/Bohemian *(český)* state, which our ancestors helped to build and to maintain for a thousand years, is for us so obvious an obligation that we hesitate to even express it explicitly. We consider it our duty to preserve the legacy of our fathers. The Lands of the Bohemian Crown have been unified for so long, have survived so many storms, that we trust they will make it through the present period of unrest and violence.

Our desire, that the historic borders of the Bohemian Crown remain unviolated, stems too from concern over the future of our descendants as well as from a sense of responsibility for the freedom and well-being of Bohemian Germans. Our ancestors always pursued friendly relations between the two nations of Bohemia, and we too desire that our German-speaking compatriots might share our love for an undivided homeland. We trust that they will. Above all, we hope that Christian fundamentals will preserve order and culture in our land.

Expressing faith in a better future, we assure you that we are conscious of our inherited obligations to our homeland and state, a state which was the home of our ancestors and whose historic rights we now and have always desired to defend.

Signed by Karel Schwarzenberg, Jan Lobkowicz, Zdeněk Radislav Kinský, František Kinský, Zdeněk Kolowrat, Rudolf Czernin, Leopold Sternberg, W. Colloredo-Mannsfeld, Karel Parish, Jindřich Dobrzenský, Hugo Strachwitz, and Karel Belcredi.

Text and signatures in AKPR D 3038/40. Text also in František Schwarzenberg, *Český šlechtic František Schwarzenberg* (Prague: Rozmluvy, 1990), 253.

Declaration of members of the historic nobility, presented to President Emil Hácha in September 1939

Honorable Mr. President,

There has recently been talk about the position of the nobility in the Czech nation, and there has emerged in this regard substantial confusion. We therefore consider it appropriate to offer some explanatory notes on the subject.

The nobility was, like everywhere, a state institution, and as a self-contained community was spared from nationality conflicts. The nobility's political obligations were always tied to service to the Bohemian state and king. The core of the noble estate always belonged to the Czech nation, of course, not so much culturally, but by blood and language. In the early days of the Bohemian Kingdom, when the whole countryside was linguistically Czech, nobles also moved in a Czech environment. This nobility, by origin and by language Czech, made up the governing or political layer of the Bohemian state, both before the emergence of the Monarchy of the House of Habsburg, as well as long after. These nobles left behind a memorial of their culture in Czech knightly songs, in the annals of Historic Rights legal theory, in military terminology, in their castles and chateaux, and in the construction of cultural institutions.

The noble families that have shared for centuries the fate of the Czech nation and have never become estranged from their roots—these families must even today be ascribed to the nation whose blood circulates in their veins.

Other than this indigenous nobility, several families of foreign origin—and not at all just German—were uprooted by the course of history and settled on the territory of the Czech state. These families received representation in the Diet, took part in public affairs in Prague, Brno, and Olomouc, and were entrusted with the provinces' highest administrative authority. Through this perpetual administrative contact with the people, the new families living in Czech-speaking regions merged with the Czech nation in such a way that their various origins could in no way change their undeniable affiliation with the Czech national community.

Similarly, several descendents of Czech families—boasting clearly Czech names and coming from the oldest of Czech blood—live in German surroundings and have taken on a German national identity. In light of these families' German convictions, the German nation willingly has recognized them as their sons and sees no barrier in their Czech origin.

We are convinced that just as we acknowledge the right of these individuals to embrace the nation among whom they live, the nation which they have chosen as their own and whose members accept them, so too on the other hand will no one deny the right of members of noble families inhabiting the Protectorate to identify themselves with the Czech nation—with whom their ancestors have lived for generations, sharing rights and responsibilities, good and bad times—even if those families were not always of Czech origin.

Inherited identification with a national community is not therefore determined by the circumstances of the day, but are created by the reality of social life, of political, cultural, and economic cooperation, and also by a shared history, fate, and responsibility for future generations of the nation.

With great fanfare, the Czech nation has had its national independence guaranteed by the Führer and Reich Chancellor of the German nation. Certainly our nation can consider it a right and responsibility to declare emphatically—if any doubt about it should emerge—the reality that the nation contains as one of its elements the Czech nobility, which never abandoned the Czech nation and, if given a choice, never will.

During the last census in the German Reich, national identity was set on the basis of voluntary confession. The relevant administrative decrees use the principle that each person is a member of the nation to which they feel themselves intimately tied and which they acknowledge as their own. Undoubtedly the organs of the German Reich will adopt this principle on the territory of the Protectorate as well. Just as the German nation asks its members to carry out all their responsibilities to the national community, so too are the Czech people and the Czech nobility convinced of their solidarity. With the conviction of the unity of all parts of our nation, and above all the conviction that descendents of the joint creators and upholders of the Bohemian state idea can still serve their nation and their homeland no matter the conditions, we want to always and under all circumstances identify ourselves with the Czech nation.

Sixty-nine Signatures:

Guido Battaglia, Mikuláš Bubna-Litic and for his father Michal, Dr. Josef Colloredo-Mansfeld, Weikhard Colloredo-Mansfeld, Jeroným Colloredo-Mansfeld Jr., Jeroným Colloredo-Mansfeld Sr., Rudolf Czernin, Edmund Czernin, Huprecht Czernin, Jan D. Czernin, Karel Dlauhoweský for himself and his sons Jan and Karel, Jan Dobržerský, Jan Jr. Dobržerský, Jindřich Dobržerský, František Dobržerský, Mikuláš Daczický z Heslowa for himself and his brother Bedřich, Dr. Hugo Daczický z Heslowa, Fr. Bořek-Dohalský for himself and his son Jiří, Bedřich Hildprandt, Josef Hrubý-Gelenj, Artur Kerssenbrock for himself and his brother Kl. Kerssenbrock, Zd. R. Kinský, František Kinský, Bedřich Karel Kinský, Alfons Kinský, Josef Kinský, František Antonín Kinský, Hanuš Kolowrat-Krakowský for himself and brother Otomar, Zdeněk Kolowrat-Krakowský, Egon Kolowrat-Krakowský, Jaroslav Lobkowicz for himself and for Kl. Kerssenbrock Sr., Moric Lobkowicz, Bedřich František Lobkowicz, Josef Lobkowicz, Jaroslav Lobkowicz, JUDr. Jan Lobkowicz, Fr. Mensdorff-Pouilly, Dr. Ervín Nádherný for himself, his son and brother Ing. Ervín Nádherný and Dr. Oskar Nádherný, Alfons Paar, Karel Parish, Jan Pálffy in his own name and for Dr. František Josef Czernin, Dr. Ing. Karel Pálffy, Dr. Bohuš Rieger, Dr. Fr. Schoenborn and for his brother Ervín, Karel Schwarzenberg, Dr. František Schwarzenberg and for Otakar Dobrženský, Arnošt Schwarzenberg, Leopold Sternberg, Emanuel Mensdorff-Pouilly, Schlik, František Schlik, Zikmund Schlik, Jindřich Schlik, Ondřej Schlik, Max Wratislaw, Jan Mladota, Jiří Sternberg, Arnošt Thun-Hohenstein, Theodor Podstatzký, Hugo Strachwitz, Karel Belcredi, Alfons Karel Mensdorff-Pouilly, Dr. Gustav Kálnoky, Richard Belcredi, Jindřich Belcredi, Alois Serényi, Jos. Osw. Wratislaw, Maximiliá Wratislaw, René Baillet-Latour

Text and signatures in AKPR D 3038/40. Text also in František Schwarzenberg, *Česky šlechtic František Schwarzenberg* (Prague: Rozmluvy, 1990), 254–255.

Archives Consulted

Archiv Kanceláře prezidenta republiky (AKPR) [Archive of the Chancellery of the President of the Republic] Prague

Archiv Ministerstva vnitra (AMV) (Archive of the Ministry of Interior) Prague

Archiv Národního musea (ANM) (Archive of the National Museum) Prague

- Fond Josef Pekař
- Fond Vojtěch Mastný

Archiv Ústavu Tomáše Garrigue Masaryka (AÚTGM) (Archive of the Tomáš Garrigue Masaryk Institute) Prague

- Fond EB (Edvard Beneš)
- Fond TGM (Tomáš Garrigue Masaryk)

Městký archiv (MA) (City Archive) Brno

- RA Belcredi (Velkostatek Líšeň)

Moravský zemský archiv (MZA) (Moravian Provincial Archive) Brno

- RA Althann/Khuen-Lützow
- RA Berchtold
- RA Seilern (Milotice)
- RA Trautmansdorff (Hostinec)

Moravský zemský archiv (MZA) (Moravian Provincial Archive) Opava (Janovice)

- RA Dubský (velkostatek Žadlovice)

Public Records Office, Foreign Office (PRO FO) London

- Runciman Mission (#800)

RA Kolowrat, Rychnov nad Kněžnou

Státní oblastní archiv (SOA) (State Regional Archive) Litoměřice

- Mimořádný lidový soud (Extraordinary people's court)

Státní oblastní archiv (SOA) (State Regional Archive) Litoměřice (Děčín)

- RA Clam-Gallas
- RA Clary-Aldringen
- RA Ledebur-Wicheln
- RA Rohan
- RA Thun-Hohenstein

Státní oblastní archiv (SOA) (State Regional Archive) Plzeň (Klatovy)

- RA Schönborn
- RA Windischgrätz

Státní oblastní archiv (SOA) (State Regional Archive) Prague

- RA Chotek
- RA Valdštejn

Státní oblastní archiv (SOA) (State Regional Archive) Třeboň

- RA Buquoy
- RA Schwarzenberg Sekundogenitura

Státní oblastní archiv (SOA) (State Regional Archive) Třeboň (Jinřichův Hradec)

- RA Czernin
- RA Paar

Státní oblastní archiv (SOA) (State Regional Archive) Zámrsk

- RA Kinský-Kostelec
- RA Schlick
- RA Sternberg (Častolovice)
- RA Thun-Choltice

Státní okresní archiv (SOkA) (State District Archive) Děčín

Státní ústřední archiv (SÚA) (State Central Archive), Prague

- Ministrstvo zemědělství-sekretariát (MZ-S) (Ministry of Agriculture-Secretariat)
- Svaz Československých velkostatkářů (SČV) (Union of Czechoslovak large landowners)
- Ministerstvo zahraničních věcí-vystřizkový archiv (MZV-VA) [Ministry of Foreign Affairs]
- Státní pozemkový úřad (SPÚ) (State Land Office)
- SdP (Sudetendeutsche Partei) (Sudeten German Party)
- Narodní výbor 1918 (NV) (National Committee)

Notes

Introduction

1. František Modráček in the National Assembly on 16 April 1919 (session 46). Text at Elektronická knihovna—Český parlament: dokumenty českého parlamentu [Electronic Library—Czech Parliament: documents of the Czech Parliament], *www.psp.cz/cgi-bin/win/eknih/* (accessed 13 September 2004).

2. See Jan Křen, *Bílá místa v našich dějinách* (Prague: Lidové noviny, 1992).

3. See Tomáš Pasák, *Pod ochranou Říše* (Prague: Práh, 1998); Tomáš Pasák, *Český fašismus 1922–1945* (Prague: Práh, 1999); Tomáš Staněk, *Odsun Němců z Československa 1945–1947* (Prague: Naše vojsko, 1991); Mečislav Borák, *Spravedlnost podle dekretu* (Ostrava: Tilia, 1998); Karel Kaplan, *Pět kapitol o únoru* (Brno: Doplněk, 1997); and Benjamin Frommer, *National Cleansing: Retribution against Nazi Collaborators in Post-War Czechoslovakia* (New York: Cambridge University Press, 2004).

4. See Vladimír Pouzar, ed., *Almanach českých šlechtických rodů* (Prague: Martin, 1996, 1999, 2001, 2003), and Jan Halada, *Lexikon české šlechty* (Prague, 1993).

5. See, for example, Karel Albrecht Waldstein-Wartenberg, *Tisíc let Valdštejnů v Čechách* (Bratislava: IRIS, 1998), and Vladimír Škutina, *Česky šlechtic František Schwarzenberg* (Prague: Rozmluvy, 1990).

6. See Petr Mašek, *Modrá krev* (Prague: Mladá fronta, 1994), and Vladimir Votypka, *Příběhy české šlechty* (Prague: Mladá fronta, 1995).

7. One scholarly exception is the brief consideration of the nobility in the 1920s and 1930s that appears in Zdeněk Kárník's interwar survey, *České země v éře První republiky, díl třetí, O přežití a o život (1936–1938)* (Prague: Nakladatelství Libri, 2003), 577–585.

8. On pre-1918 nobilities, see Arno Mayer, *The Persistence of the Old Regime in Europe* (London: Croom Helm, 1981); David Higgs, *Nobles in Nineteenth-Century France: The Practice of Inegalitarianism* (Baltimore, Md.: Johns Hopkins University Press, 1987); and Anthony Cardoza, *Aristocrats in Bourgeois Italy: The Piedmontese Nobility, 1861–1930* (Cambridge: Cambridge University Press, 1997).

9. The British aristocracy, however, has received substantial coverage. See in particular David Cannadine's magisterial synthesis, which systematically traces the economic, social, and political decline of the British nobility from the 1880s to the 1980s: *The Decline and Fall of the British Aristocracy* (New Haven, Conn.: Yale University Press, 1990).

10. Hans Rosenberg, "The Pseudo-Democratisation of the Junker Class," in *The Social History of Politics: Critical Perspectives in West German Historical Writing since 1945*, ed. Georg G. Iggers (Dover, N.H.: Berg, 1985), 81–112. This article was originally published in German in 1958.

11. Shelley Baranowski, *The Sanctity of Rural Life: Nobility, Protestantism, and Nazism in Weimar Prussia* (New York: Oxford University Press, 1995).

12. Georg Kleine, "Adelsgenossenschaft und Nationalsozialismus," *Vierteljahrshefte fuer Zeitgeschichte* 26 (1978): 100–143.

13. Among many works dealing with the subject of the conservative relationship to Hitler, see the essays on Germany in Martin Blinkhorn, ed., *Fascists and Conservatives: The Radical Right and the Establishment in Twentieth-Century Europe* (London: Unwin Hyman, 1990).

14. See Peter Hoffman, *German Resistance to Hitler* (Cambridge, Mass.: Harvard University Press, 1988).

15. Baranowski, *Sanctity*, 186.

16. "Un-state" comes from Adolf Dubsky, letter to Doctor Grosse, 10 April 1939. ZA Opava (Janovice), RA Dubský, k 19.

17. See, for example, John Breuilly, *Nationalism and the State* (Chicago: University of Chicago Press, 1993), and Prasenjit Duara, introduction to *Rescuing History from the Nation* (Chicago: University of Chicago Press, 1995).

18. See among others, Rogers Brubaker, *Nationalism Reframed: Nationhood and the National Question in the New Europe* (Cambridge: Cambridge University Press, 1996), and Jeremy King, *Budweisers into Czechs and Germans: A Local History of Bohemian Politics, 1848–1948* (Princeton, N.J.: Princeton University Press, 2002).

19. If war were the criteria, Czech nationalists would have been right about Bohemian nobles. During the First World War, hundreds of Bohemian nobles were willing to die for the monarchy, and many of them did. We do not, however, find any nobles risking their lives in the Czech Legions in Russia during the war. But neither did very many Czechs, who also fought and died for the Habsburg monarchy. War is in fact a problematic test of national loyalty, because wars are usually made by states and not nations. During World War I, for example, a deeply loyal Czech could also have been enough of a Habsburg patriot to go to war for the monarchy.

20. On the "each to his own" campaigns, see Catherine Albrecht, "The Rhetoric of Economic Nationalism in the Bohemian Boycott Campaigns of the Late Habsburg Monarchy," *Austrian History Yearbook* 32 (2001): 47–67.

21. George Mosse, *Nationalization of the Masses: Political Symbols and Mass Movements in Germany* (Ithaca, N.Y.: Cornell University Press, 1996 [1975]).

22. My conclusions here have an affinity to those found in Gareth Stedman Jones, *Languages of Class: Studies in English Working Class History 1832–1982* (Cambridge: Cambridge University Press, 1983). He writes on page 22: "We cannot therefore decode political language to reach a primal and material expression of interest since it is the discursive structure of political language which conceives and defines interest in the first place."

1. Between Empire and Nation: The Bohemian Nobility, 1880–1918

1. Oswald Thun to Max Egon Fürstenberg, 28 December 1898, in Ernst Rutkowski, ed., *Briefe und Dokumente zur Geschichte der österreichisch-ungarischen Monarchie unter besonderer Berücksichtigung des böhmisch-märischen Raumes, vol. 1, Der Verfassungstreue Grossgrundbesitz 1880–1899* (Munich: Oldenbourg Verlag, 1983), 580.

2. Anthony Cardoza, *Aristocrats in Bourgeois Italy: The Piedmontese Nobility, 1861–1930* (Cambridge: Cambridge University Press, 1997), 10, 219. Cardoza credits Pierre Bourdieu with this formulation, but it also brings to mind the young aristocrat Tancredi's comment to his uncle in di Lampedusa's novel *The Leopard*: "If we want things to stay as they are, things will have to change." Giuseppe Tomasi di Lampedusa, *The Leopard*, trans. Archibald Colquhoun (New York: Knopf, 1991), 41.

3. "Zünglein an der Waage" comes from Alfred Mayer, who used it in reference to the noble position in the Bohemian Diet around 1900. See Alfred Maria Mayer, "Die nationalen und sozialen Verhältnisse im böhmischen Adel und Grossgrundbesitz," *Čechische Revue* 2 (1908): 518. See also Lothar Höbelt, " 'Verfassungstreue' und 'feudale': Die beiden österreichischen Adelsparteien 1861–1918," *Etudes Danubiennes*, 7, no. 2 (1991): 104.

4. On national-imperial identity, see Jeremy King, *Budweisers into Czechs and Germans: A Local History of Bohemian Politics, 1848–1948* (Princeton, N.J.: Princeton University Press, 2002).

5. On the Junkers and democratization, see Hans Rosenberg, "The Pseudo-Democratisation of the Junker Class," in *The Social History of Politics: Critical Perspectives in West German Historical Writing Since 1945*, ed. Georg G. Iggers (Dover, N.H.: Berg, 1985), 81–112.

6. By modernization, I mean the processes of industrialization, urbanization, expansion of political awareness and participation to middle and lower classes, and the emergence of mass-based national consciousness.

7. See Eric Hobsbawm, *The Age of Revolution, 1789–1848* (New York: Vintage Books, 1996).

8. Arno Mayer, *The Persistence of the Old Regime in Europe* (London: Croom Helm, 1981).

9. David Higgs, *Nobles in Nineteenth-Century France: The Practice of Inegalitarianism* (Baltimore, Md.: Johns Hopkins University Press, 1987).

10. Cardoza, *Aristocrats*.

11. There is a plethora of recent work on economic modernization in the late Habsburg Empire. See in particular the fine synthetic work of David

Good, *The Economic Rise of the Habsburg Empire* (Berkeley: University of California Press, 1984).

12. See Josef Macek, in *Česká středověká šlechta* (Prague: Argo, 1997), chapter 1.

13. Hannes Stekl, "Zwischen Machtverlust und Selbstbehauptung: Österreichs Hocharistokratie vom 18. bis ins 20. Jahrhundert," in *Europaeischer Adel 1750–1950*, ed. Hans-Ulrich Wehler (Goettingen: Vandenhoeck & Ruprecht, 1990), 151.

14. Nobles financed one-third of the Kreditanstalt in 1857. Stekl, "Zwischen Machtverlust," 157. Herman Freudenberger points out that nobles also put up two-thirds of the capital for the Chartered Bank of Vienna (also known as the Schwarzenberg Bank) in 1788. It collapsed after the Habsburg state bankruptcy of 1811. Herman Freudenberger, "The Schwarzenberg Bank: A Forgotten Contributor to Austrian Economic Development, 1788–1830," *Austrian History Yearbook* 27 (1996): 41–64.

15. Milan Myška, "Der Adel der böhmischen Länder," in *Der Adel an der Schwelle des bürgerlichen Zeitalters 1780–1860*, ed. Armgard von Reden-Dohna and Ralph Melville (Stuttgart: Franz Steiner Verlag, 1988), 182.

16. C. A. Macartney, *The Habsburg Empire, 1790–1918* (New York: Macmillan, 1969), 622.

17. Jerome Blum, *Noble Landowners and Agriculture in Austria, 1815–1848* (Baltimore, Md.: Johns Hopkins University Press, 1948).

18. Landowners received 70 million gulden as compensation. See Mayer, "Die nationalen," 352. See also Alois Brusatti, ed., *Die wirtschaftliche Entwicklung*, vol. 1, *Die Habsburgermonarchie 1848–1918* (Vienna: Der Oesterreichischen Akademie der Wissenschaften, 1973), 410–415.

19. Myška, "Der Adel," 180. See also Solomon Wank, "Aristocrats and Politics in Austria, 1867–1914: A Case of Historiographical Neglect," *East European Quarterly* 26, no. 2 (June 1992): 136.

20. Milan Myška, "Šlechta v Čechách, na Moravě a ve Slezsku na prahu buržoazní éry" *Časopis Slezského muzea* series B, no. 36 (1987): 46–65.

21. Mayer, "Die nationalen," 349–351.

22. Wilhelm Medinger, *Grossgrundbesitz, Fideikommiss und Agrarreform* (Vienna: Carl Gerolds Sohn, 1919), 32. In Moravia, fourteen landholders owned 13 percent of the province, in Silesia, four owned 25 percent. Note that Mayer's statistics are from 1908 or before, whereas Medinger's are from 1917 or before. Both sets of statistics are similar, as there was little change in large-estate ownership from 1900 to 1918.

23. Of 2.4 million ha of forest in Bohemia, Moravia, and Silesia, 1.54 million ha belonged to estates of over 200 ha (and most of these were over 1,000 ha). Ibid., 13.

24. Statistics from ibid., 34.

25. Ibid., 48–49.

26. Ibid., 16–17.

27. Ibid., 13, 20–21.

28. The only exception was noble political privileges, which are considered later.

29. Citing Benedict Anderson, Anthony Cardoza notes that nobilities had "concrete, rather than imagined solidarities . . . the products of kinship, friendship, and personal acquaintance." Cardoza, *Aristocrats,* 8.

30. Ibid., 127. David Higgs notes a similar phenomenon among the French nobility in the nineteenth century. See Higgs, *Nobles.*

31. Medinger, *Grossgrundbesitz,* 13.

32. Hradek foundation document, 1841. Quoted in Inge Rohan, *Sychrov Castle: Monument of the Rohan Family* (Turnov, Czech Republic: Friends of Sychrov Castle, 1996), 19.

33. For a detailed look at nineteenth-century chateaux renovations, see Jiří Kuthan, *Aristokratická sídla období romantismu a historismu* (Prague: Akropolis, 2001).

34. Rohan, *Sychrov,* 26–27.

35. Kuthan, *Aristokratická sídla,* 6.

36. Zdeněk Bezecný, "Karel V. ze Schwarzenberku," *Opera Historica* 4 (1995): 286. Schwarzenberg's take was nothing compared to Emperor Francis Joseph's, whose lists numbered over eight hundred thousand beasts shot over his long lifetime.

37. Dominic Lieven, *The Aristocracy in Europe, 1815–1914* (New York: Columbia University Press, 1992), 157.

38. Ibid.

39. Gary B. Cohen, *The Politics of Ethnic Survival: Germans in Prague, 1861–1914* (Princeton, N.J.: Princeton University Press, 1981), 75–76.

40. Mayer, "Die nationalen," 584.

41. Rita Krueger documents this democratic sociability in "From Empire to Nation: The Aristocracy and the Formation of Modern Society in Bohemia, 1770–1848" (Ph.D. diss., Harvard University, 1997).

42. On curial voting, see table 18 in Bruce Garver, *The Young Czech Party and the Emergence of a Multi-Party System, 1874–1901* (New Haven, Conn.: Yale University Press, 1978), 349. The curias were 1) large landowners, 2) chambers of commerce, 3) municipalities, 4) rural communes, and, after 1896, 5) universal.

43. Wank, "Aristocrats and Politics in Austria, 1867–1914," 137. See also Gerald Stourzh, "Die Mitgliedschaft auf Lebensdauer im österreichischen Herrenhaus 1861–1918," *Mitteilungen des Instituts für österreichische Geschichtsforschung,* no. 73 (1965): 63–117.

44. Garver, *Young Czech Party,* 346. In 1908, 17 percent of Bohemian Diet representatives were high nobles. See Robert Luft, "Die Mittelpartei des Mährischen Grossgrundbesitzes 1879–1918," in *Die Chance der Verständigung: Absichten und Ansätze zu übernationaler Zusammenarbeit in den böhmischen Ländern 1848–1918,* ed. Ferdinand Seibt (Munich: R. Oldenbourg, 1987), 191.

45. For more on the Moravian Diet and the particular importance of the nobility there as powerbroker, see Luft, "Die Mittelpartei," 187–243.

46. Daniel Miller, *Forging Political Compromise: Antonín Švehla and the Czechoslovak Republican Party, 1918–1933* (Pittsburgh, Pa.: University of Pittsburgh Press, 1999), 25.

47. Adam Wandruszka and Peter Urbanitsch, eds., *Die Habsburgermonarchie*

1848–1918: Verwaltung und Rechtswesen, vol. 2 (Vienna: Verlag der oesterreichischen Akademie der Wissenschaften, 1975), 281. On 1848 and its legacy, see
also Ralph Melville, *Adel und Revolution in Böhmen : Strukturwandel von Herrschaft und Gesellschaft in Österreich um die Mitte des 19. Jahrhunderts* (Mainz:
Verlag Philipp von Zabern, 1998).

48. Wank, "Aristocrats and Politics in Austria, 1867–1914," 139.

49. Stekl, *Zwischen Machtverlust,* 163–164. See also Medinger, *Grossgrundbesitz,* 51–53.

50. Wank, "Aristocrats and Politics in Austria, 1867–1914," 138. Wank
does not distinguish between high and low (mostly service) nobles. Of the
twenty-six prime ministers, fourteen came from the high nobility. More tell-
ingly, high nobles held the prime ministerial post for thirty-nine of the empire's
last fifty-one years. For a list of prime ministers, see Miroslav Buchvaldek et
al., eds., *Československé dějiny v datech* (Prague: Nakladatelství Svoboda, 1986),
586–593.

51. N. von Preradovich, *Die Führungsschichten in Österreich und Preussen
1804–1918* (Wiesbaden, 1955). Cited in Hannes Stekl, "Zwischen Machtver-
lust und Selbstbehauptung. Oesterreichs Hocharistokratie vom 18. bis ins 20.
Jahrhundert," in *Europaeischer Adel, 1750–1950,* ed. Hans-Ulrich Wehler
(Goettingen, Germany: Vandenhoeck & Ruprecht, 1990), 161. On nobles in
the Habsburg officer corps, see István Deák, *Beyond Nationalism: A Social and
Political History of the Habsburg Officer Corps 1848–1918* (New York: Oxford
University Press, 1990), 156–164.

52. William Godsey, *Aristocratic Redoubt: The Austro-Hungarian Foreign Office on the Eve of the First World War* (West Lafayette, Ind.: Purdue University
Press, 1999), 31.

53. William Godsey, "Quarterings and Kinship: The Social Composition
of the Habsburg Aristocracy in the Dualist Era," *Journal of Modern History,* no.
71 (March 1999): 64.

54. Ibid., 62, 94–104.

55. For a good summary of the debate over democracy in the empire, see
Gary Cohen, "Neither Absolutism nor Anarchy: New Narratives on Society
and Government in Late Imperial Austria," *Austrian History Yearbook* 29 (1998):
37–61.

56. Wank, "Aristocrats and Politics in Austria, 1867–1914," 139. Macartney shares this view. See Macartney, *Habsburg Empire,* 604.

57. On liberalism in Austria, see Pieter Judson, *Exclusive Revolutionaries:
Liberal Politics, Social Experience, and National Identity in the Austrian Empire,
1848–1914* (Ann Arbor: University of Michigan Press, 1996).

58. The two noble factions were parties in the sense of *Honoratiorenpar-
teien,* (parties of notables), which they remained until 1918. Given their very
small constituencies, they had a minimal administrative apparatus and did not
run campaigns in the normal sense.

59. Garver, *Young Czech Party,* 51.

60. Technically, Czech Social Democrats shared a party structure with
their German-Austrian counterparts until 1911. But national interests divided

Czech and German socialists long before then. See Macartney, *Habsburg Empire*, 683–685, 803–804.

61. In another context, Rogers Brubaker writes of "the nationalization of narrative and interpretative frames, of perception and evaluation, of thinking and feeling. It has involved the silencing or marginalization of alternative, non-nationalist political language. It has involved the nullification of complex identities by the terrible categorical simplicity of ascribed nationality." Rogers Brubaker, *Nationalism Reframed: Nationhood and the National Question in the New Europe* (Cambridge: Cambridge University Press, 1996), 20.

62. This is akin to the recently abandoned (and similarly inadequate) requirement in the United States census that respondents choose a single "race." On the census, see King, *Budweisers*, 58–59.

63. Ibid., 132–139.

64. Gerald Stourzh, "Ethnic Attribution in Late Imperial Austria: Good Intentions, Evil Consequences," in *The Habsburg Legacy: National Identity in Historical Perspective*, ed. Ritchie Robertson and Edward Timms (Edinburgh: Edinburgh University Press, 1994), 71.

65. On the Moravian Compromise, see Luft, "Die Mittelpartei."

66. Stourzh, "Ethnic Attribution," 74. King documents a similar compromise, brokered by the crown (but not implemented), in Budweis in 1913. See King, *Budweisers*, 137–147.

67. Karl III Prince Schwarzenberg, 1871 speech in the Reichsrat. Quoted in Milan M. Buben, "Česká zemská šlechta: Schwarzenberkové sekundogenitura," *Střední Evropa* 12, no. 56 (1996): 106.

68. Count Josef Mathias Thun, *Der Slawismus in Böhmen* (Prague: J. G. Calvesche Buchhandlung, 1845), 17, 23.

69. "Utraquism" had a long history in Bohemia. It originally referred to the practice introduced by Jan Hus in the early fifteenth century of delivering the Eucharist *sub utra specie*, that is, both bread and wine. This set him apart from the traditional practice of offering wine only to the clergy. During the Hussite Wars, the ultimately victorious moderate faction of Hussites adopted the name Utraquists. They rejected the radical egalitarianism of the Taborites and were more conciliatory toward the Catholic Church. Among nobles in the nineteenth century, utraquism signified a moderate federalism that acknowledged the Czech and German duality of Bohemia.

70. Friedrich Schwarzenberg to Vincenc Auersperg, 8 September 1862. Reproduced in Antonín Okáč, *Rakouský problém a list Vaterland 1860–1871* vol. 2 (Brno, Czechoslovakia: Musejní spolek, 1970), 129–134.

71. Robert Sak, "Der Platz der Schwarzenberger in der tschechischen Politik der zweiten Hälfte des neunzehnten Jahrhunderts," *Opera Historica Editio Universitatis Bohemiae Meridionalis* 2 (1992): 108.

72. Karl III Schwarzenberg to František Rieger, 23 April 1862. Quoted in Okáč, *Rakouský problém*, vol. 1, 77.

73. Karl III Schwarzenberg to Vincenc Auersperg, August or September 1862. Reproduced in Okáč, *Rakouský problém*, vol. 2, 125–128.

74. This issue dominated Bohemian and imperial politics for much of the

last decade of the nineteenth century. Germans opposed the change because official bilingualism would have effectively removed scores of German monolingual civil servants. Both sides rioted in the Diet and *Reichsrat* over the language question, and it brought down two imperial governments.

75. Bedřich Schwarzenberg speech in Reichsrat, quoted in *Fremden-Blatt*, Vienna, 7 November 1896, 3.

76. 6 Jan 1898, quoted in King, *Budweisers*, 98. Bedřich was the younger brother of Karl IV of the secundogeniture.

77. Buben, "Schwarzenberkové sekundogenitura," 107. See also Zdeněk Bezecný, "Němci nebojí se nikoho mimo Boha a prince Schwarzenberga (Bedřich ze Schwarzenberku a volby do říšské rady v roce 1897)," *Jihočeský sborník historický*, 72 (2003): 70–80.

78. On the historic rights program, see Garver, *Young Czech Party*, 49–53.

79. Franz Thun quoted in Jan Havránek, "The Development of Czech Nationalism," *Austrian History Yearbook*, 1967: 236.

80. Gordon Skilling, "The Politics of the Czech Eighties," in *The Czech Renascence of the Nineteenth Century*, ed. Peter Brock and Gordon Skilling (Toronto: University of Toronto Press, 1970), 265–266. Rieger's quote came from a letter on 23 February 1883.

81. Rieger, letter of 10 December 1889, quoted in ibid., 206.

82. Concessions included the advent of official bilingualism for the public business of the Bohemian bureaucracy (1880), the split of Prague University into Czech and German parts (1882), and an expansion of the franchise (1882). The classic work on the Iron Ring is William Jenks, *Austria under the Iron Ring, 1879–1893* (Charlottesville: University Press of Virginia, 1965).

83. Quoted in Skilling, "Czech Eighties," 266.

84. Quoted in ibid., 268.

85. Garver, *Young Czech Party*, 228.

86. Ibid., 240.

87. Ibid., 309.

88. Alois Aehrenthal to his father, 5 June 1893, in Rutkowski, *Briefe*, vol. 1, 185. Schwarzenberg repeated this call for absolutism in an 1898 letter to Aehrenthal: "In my opinion, Austria can no longer be held together in any other way than by a modernized absolutism." Quoted in Wank, "Aristocrats and Politics in Austria 1898–1899: Some Letters of Count Alois Lexa von Aehrenthal and Prince Karl Schwarzenberg," *Austrian History Yearbook* 19–20, pt. 1 (1983–1984), 170.

89. On the Badeni crisis, see Garver, *Young Czech Party*, 245–76 and the comprehensive volumes by Berthold Sutter, *Die Badenischen Sprachenverordnungen von 1897*, Kommission für Neuere Geschichte Österreichs, *Veröffentlichungen: 46 and 47* (Graz, Austria: H. Böhlaus Nachf., 1960, 1965).

90. Karl Schwarzenberg to Alois Aehrenthal, 4 May 1899, in Rutkowski, *Briefe und Dokument* vol. 1, 684–685.

91. Rudolf Czernin to Max Egon Fürstenberg, 20 November 1895, in Rutkowski, *Briefe und Dokumente*, vol.1, 240

92. "Der entscheidende Punct," *Vaterland*, 9 January 1870. Cited in Okáč, *Rakouský problém*, vol. 1, 226.

93. Rutkowski, *Briefe und Dokumente*, vol. 1, 17.

94. On Felix Schwarzenberg, see the nostalgic political biography by his great-grandnephew: Adolph Schwarzenberg, *Prince Felix zu Schwarzenberg, Prime Minister of Austria 1848–1852* (New York: Columbia University Press, 1946).

95. On Friedrich List's pursuit of a German customs union, see Roman Szporluk, *Communism and Nationalism: Karl Marx versus Friedrich List* (New York: Oxford University Press, 1988).

96. "Wahlaufruf," Prague, 6 November 1895, in Rutkowski, *Briefe und Dokumente*, vol. 1, 235.

97. See Pieter Judson, " 'Not Another Square Foot!' German Liberalism and the Rhetoric of National Ownership in Nineteenth-Century Austria," *Austrian History Yearbook* 26 (1995): 83–97.

98. "Bericht über die Wahlkomiteesitzung vom 16. November 1896," in Rutkowski, *Briefe und Dokumente*, vol. 1, 285–286.

99. Oswald Thun to Alain Rohan, 15 March 1898, in Paul Molisch, ed., *Briefe zur Deutschen Politik in Österreich von 1848 bis 1918* (Vienna: Wilhelm Braumüller, 1934), 364. See also Oswald Thun to Franz Thun, 9 March 1898, in Rutkowski, *Briefe und Dokumente*, vol. 1, 462. Oswald Thun was a descendent of Joseph Mathias Thun of the Klösterle branch of the family. He served as head of the Constitutionals from 1890 to 1906.

100. On the *Ausgleich*, see Solomon Wank, "The Habsburg Empire," in *After Empire: Multiethnic Societies and Nation-Building, The Soviet Union and the Russian, Ottoman, and Habsburg Empires*, ed. Karen Barkey and Mark Von Hagen (Boulder, Colo.: Westview Press, 1997), 51.

101. "Wahlaufruf," 6 November 1895, in Rutkowski, *Briefe und Dokumente*, vol. 1, 234.

102. Max Egon Fürstenberg to Karl Schwarzenberg, 30 December 1897, in Rutkowski, *Briefe und Dokumente*, vol. 1, 422.

103. Oswald Thun to Alain Rohan, 22 December 1897, in Rutkowski, *Briefe and Dokumente*, vol. 1, 417.

104. Alois Aehrenthal to his father, 23 August 1883, in Rutkowski, *Briefe und Documente*, vol. 1, 113.

105. Carl Schorske, *Fin-de-Siecle Vienna: Politics and Culture* (New York: Vintage Books, 1981), 119. It was particularly galling to nobles that von Schönerer was himself noble, albeit of low rank. His father had been granted a title of nobility in 1860 in honor of his work constructing railway lines. See Schorske, 121–122.

106. Guido Dubsky to Joseph Maria Baernreither 3 August 1896, in Rutkowski, *Briefe und Dokumente*, vol. 1, 261–263.

107. Alois Aehrenthal to his father, 12 May 1897, in Rutkowski, *Briefe und Dokumente*, vol. 1, 328–329.

108. Alain Rohan to Max Ego Fürstenberg, 10 April 1899, in Rutkowski, *Briefe und Dokumente*, vol. 1, 679.

109. Oswald Thun, diary entry 16 September 1897, in Rutkowski, *Briefe und Dokumente*, vol. 1, 90.

110. Macartney, *Habsburg Empire*, 681.

111. Alois Aehrenthal to Karl Buquoy, 13 December 1889, in Rutkowski, *Briefe und Dokumente*, vol. 1, 152.

112. Karl Moritz Zedtwitz to Baernreither, 2 July 1897, in Rutkowski, *Briefe und Dokumente*, vol. 1, 355.

113. Oswald Thun to Alain Rohan, 15 March 1898, in Molisch, *Briefe zur Deutschen Politik*, 364.

114. Oswald Thun to Max Ego Fürstenberg, 28 December 1898, in Rutkowski, *Briefe und Dokumente*, vol. 1, 580.

115. Rutkowski, *Briefe und Dokumente*, vol. 1, 24.

116. Robert Luft, "Die Mittelpartei des Mährischen Grossgrundbesitzes 1879–1918," in *Die Chance der Verständigung: Absichten und Ansätze zu übernationaler Zusammenarbeit in den böhmischen Ländern 1848–1918*, ed. Ferdinand Seibt (Munich: R. Oldenbourg, 1987), 205. On noble politics in Moravia, see also Jiří Malíř, "K vývoji velkostatkářských stran na Moravě," *Časopis matice moravské* 115 (1996): 35–57.

117. Garver, *Young Czech Party*, 324.

118. Luft, "Die Mittelpartei," 209.

119. Gustav Eim, quoted in King, *Budweisers*, 55.

120. See Luft, "Die Mittelpartei," 205, 217–219, 229–230; and Garver, *Young Czechs Party*, 360.

121. The other was Bukowina in 1910. See Macartney, *Habsburg Empire*, 798.

122. On the *punktace*, see Jan Křen, *Konfliktní společenství: Češi a Němci 1780–1918* (Prague: Academia, 1990), 230–238. See also Jenks, *Iron Ring*, 239–74, and Jiří Kořalka, *Češi v Habsburské Říši a v Evropě 1815–1914* (Prague: Argo, 1996), 164–166.

123. On the *Verständigungskonferenzen* of 1900 see Ernst Rutkowski, ed., *Briefe und Dokumente zur Geschichte der österreichisch-ungarischen Monarchie unter besonderer Berücksichtigung des böhmisch-märischen Raumes. Teil II: Der Verfassungstreue Grossgrundbesitz 1900–1904* (Munich: Oldenbourg Verlag, 1991), 613–634.

124. "Schlussprotokol über die in Prag und in Wien von den Vertretern der beider Gruppen des Grossgrundbesitzes in Böhmen abgehalten Besprechungen über eine Reihe von den deutsch-böhmischen Streit bildenden Fragen," 1910. SOA Litoměřice (Děčín), RA Clam-Gallas, k 618, ic 2319.

125. Karl Schwarzenberg to Alois Lexa von Aehrenthal, 3 February 1898. Quoted in Wank, "Aristocrats and Politics in Austria, 1867–1914," 141–142. Similar thoughts seemed to be on Oswald Thun's mind when he wrote in June 1897: "The further words from the Emperor: 'We have laws with which one can not govern' give occasion to very deep reflection." Oswald Thun to Alain Rohan, 14 June 1897, in Molisch, *Briefe zur Deutschen Politik*, 355.

126. Wank, "Aristocrats and Politics in Austria, 1867–1914," 142.

127. Robert Kann, *A History of the Habsburg Empire, 1526–1918* (Berkeley: University of California Press, 1974), 489.

128. Quoted in Höbelt, " 'Verfassungstreue' und 'feudale,' " 111f.

129. Friedrich Schwarzenberg, report of meeting of members of the Conservative Large Landowners, 16 January 1916. SOA Plzeň (Klatovy), RA Windischgrätz, k 656, ic 4113.

130. Wilhelm Medinger, "Referat in der Versammlung des Verfassungstreuen Grossgrundbesitzes," Prague, 13 June 1915, pp. 11–13. SOA Litoměřice (Děčín), RA Clam-Gallas, k 618 ic 2319.

131. Ibid., 20–21, 24.

132. On the Battle of White Mountain, see chapter 2, "National and Social Revolution in Czechoslovakia, 1918–1920."

133. Karel Čapek, *Ratolest a vavřín* (Prague: F. R. Borový, 1947), 97–98, 100, 297. See also Petr Mašek, *Modrá krev* (Prague: Mladá Fronta, 1994), 110–115.

134. The party was also now known as the "Right," with the Constitutionals dubbed the "Left." The Conservative Clam-Martinic, who became prime minister in December 1916, favored a pro-German government dictated by an imperial *octroi*. See Todd Wayne Huebner, "The Multinational 'Nation-State': The Origins and the Paradox of Czechoslovakia, 1914–1920" (Ph.D. diss., Columbia University, 1993), 40, 105.

135. Oswald Kostrba-Skalicky, "Die 'Burg' und der Adel," in *Die Burg*, ed. Karl Bosl (Vienna: R. Oldenbourg, 1974), 165. In addition to Schwarzenberg, signers of the protest included Friedrich Prince Lobkowicz, Count Bohuslav Kolowrat, and Adalbert Count Sternberg. See also Lothar Höbelt, "Adel und Politik seit 1848," in *Die Fuerstenberger*, ed. Erwein Eltz and Arno Strohmeyer (Schloß Weitra, Austria: Niederösterreichische Landesausstellung, 1994), 374–375.

136. Oskar von Parish-Senftenberg to Prince Alfred Windischgrätz, 29 May 1918. Excerpt in Molisch, *Briefe zur Deutschen Politik*, 393.

137. On the split, see Lothar Höbelt, "Die Konservativen Alt-Österreichs 1848 bis 1918: Parteien und Politik," in *Konservatismus in Österreich: Strömungen, Ideen, Personen und Vereinigungen von den Anfängen bis heute*, ed. Robert Rill and Ulrich Zellenberg (Graz, Austria: Leopold Stocker Verlag, 1999), 143.

138. Ferdinand Lobkovicz to Alfred Windischgrätz, 7 June 1916. SOA Plzeň (Klatovy), RA Windischgrätz, k 656, ic 4113.

139. Antonín Kubačák, "Činnost Svazu československých velkostatkářů' v letech 1919–1943," *Sborník archivních prací* 37 (1987): 339. In addition to Clam-Martinic, signers of the declaration included Zdeněk Lobkowicz, Jaroslav Chotek, Adalbert Schönborn, Josef Nostitz, F. Lichtenstein Jr., and Eugen Czernin.

140. Palacký quoted in Krueger, "From Empire to Nation," 50.

141. George Kovtun, ed., *The Spirit of Thomas G. Masaryk* (London: Macmillan, 1990), 75.

142. Mayer, "Die nationalen," 340, 342.

143. Ibid., 582.

144. On gender and Czech nationalism, see Cynthia Paces, "Religious Images and National Symbols in the Creation of Czech Identity, 1890–1938" (Ph.D. diss., Columbia University, 1998).

145. Mayer, "Die nationalen," 584.

146. Ibid., 593.
147. Josef Holeček, *Česká šlechta: Výklady časové i historické* (Prague: Česko-moravské podniky tiskařské a vydavatelské, 1918), 13–14.
148. Ibid., 58–60, 149.
149. Ibid., 68.
150. Ibid., 77.
151. Ibid., 120.
152. Ibid., 56–57.
153. Ibid., 160. This quote was a sign of the times. Only a year later, Teddy Roosevelt said similarly: "There can be no fifty-fifty Americanism in this country. There is room here for only 100% Americanism, only for those who are Americans and nothing else." Speech, 19 July 1918, to the State Republican Party Convention, Saratoga, New York. Quoted in Microsoft Bookshelf 2000.
154. Holeček, *Česká šlechta*, 164, 168.
155. Among others, see Lieven, *Aristocracy*, and David Blackbourn and Geoff Eley, *The Peculiarities of German History* (New York: Oxford University Press, 1984).
156. Mayer, *Persistence*, 300.
157. See Geoff Eley, *Reshaping the German Right: Radical Nationalism and Political Change after Bismarck* (New Haven, Conn.: Yale University Press, 1980).

2. National and Social Revolution in Czechoslovakia, 1918–1920

1. Nancy Meriwether Wingfield, "Conflicting Constructions of Memory: Attacks on Statues of Joseph II in the Bohemian Lands after the Great War," *Austrian History Yearbook*, vol. 28 (1997): 149. The gathering at White Mountain and destruction of the Marian Column took place on 3 November, five days before the anniversary of the battle. Other celebrations followed, including a large manifestation on the actual day of the battle, 8 November.
2. See Cynthia Paces, "Religious Images and National Symbols in the Creation of Czech Identity, 1890–1938" (Ph.D. diss., Columbia University, 1998), 157–158. Paces also notes an anti-Catholic agenda of the vandals, though they later emphasized the social and political content of their protest.
3. In the early years following Czechoslovak independence, crowds and local governments attacked or removed numerous statues of Joseph II, who was "generally considered the personification of Germandom." Zdeněk Hojda and Jiří Pokorný, *Pomníky a zapomníky* (Prague: Paseka, 1997), 133, 142. Hojda and Pokorný also document a wave of attacks on Marian columns in the Czech countryside (p. 30). See also Wingfield, "Conflicting Constructions."
4. "Bílá Hora," *Venkov*, 8 November 1918, 1.
5. "O Bílé Hoře k mládeži, *Venkov*, 8 November 1918, 4.
6. Czechoslovakia was officially a state of the Czechs and Slovaks, referred to collectively as Czechoslovaks. Though a small minority of interwar citizens accepted this amalgam as their national identity, the vast majority identified as either Czech or Slovak. The two languages are closely related and mutually intelligible, but they are clearly not two dialects of one language.

7. Joseph Rothschild, *East Central Europe Between the Two World Wars* (Seattle: University of Washington Press, 1992), 80. Masaryk was otherwise sympathetic to the Germans and a voice of reconciliation. Even so, Germans and Czechs alike seized on his comments to press their national agendas. See Fred Hahn, "Masaryk and the Germans," in *T. G. Masaryk: Statesman and Cultural Force*, ed. Harry Hanak (London: Macmillan, 1989), 99–124.

8. Stenographic Protocol of the Meeting of the National Committee (Národní Výbor), 9 November 1918, 106. Copy in SÚA, NV 1918, k 1, sv 4–5, ic 156.

9. Národní shromáždění, Meeting 46: 16 April 1919. Text at *www.psp .cz/cgi-bin/win/eknih/* (accessed 13 September 2004). Technically Modráček was a member of a splinter social democratic party in 1919. He rejoined the Social Democrats in 1924. See Josef Tomeš, *Slovník k politickým dějinám Československa 1918–1992* (Prague: Budka, 1994), 124.

10. Sieyes and Delaure are both quoted in Liah Greenfeld, *Nationalism: Five Roads to Modernity* (Cambridge, Mass.: Harvard University Press, 1992), 172.

11. The Revolutionary National Assembly based its representation on the elections of 1911, which gave the following membership: fifty-four Agrarians, fifty Social Democrats, thirty-six National Democrats, twenty-eight National Socials, twenty-four Catholic Populists, plus ten co-opted Czechs and forty Slovaks. Bohemian and Moravian Germans received no representation in the Assembly until after new elections in 1920. See Lucy Elizabeth Textor, *Land Reform in Czechoslovakia* (London: George Allen & Unwin, 1923), 27.

12. Zasedání Národního shromáždění československého roku 1918, Tisk 4. See also the article, marred by orthodox Marxism, by Ladislav Soukup, "Zrušení šlechtictví v ČSR," *Pravně historické studium* 17, no. 83 (1973): 101–110. Czechoslovakia was the first successor state to outlaw noble titles. Austria followed with legislation in April, 1919. In August of 1919, Germany eliminated all noble privileges, but allowed nobles to keep their titles as a part of their name. Oswald Kostrba-Skalicky, "Die 'Burg' und der Adel," in *Die Burg*, ed. Karl Bosl (Vienna: R. Oldenbourg, 1974), 167. Henceforth titles will appear in parentheses, because technically they no longer existed.

13. Jiří Doležal, "Úvahy o české šlechtě v case První republiky," *Svědectví* 20, no. 77 (1986): 60, note 3. Law #243:1920 in *Sbirka zakonů* 1920: 533.

14. See for example the calling card of Dr. Bedřich Lobkowicz, AKPR T453/21.

15. "Bez šlechty,"*Venkov*, 16 November 1918, 1.

16. *Večerník Práva lidu*, 15 November 1918: 1. Quoted in Soukup, "Zrušení šlechtictví," 108.

17. Ferdinand Peroutka, *Budování státu*, vol. 1 (Prague: Fr. Borový, 1933), 244.

18. Wilhelm Medinger, *Grossgrundbesitz, Fideikommiss und Agrarreform* (Vienna: Carl Gerold's Sohn, 1919), 65–69.

19. Ibid., 103. Medinger did not, however, support the Fideikommiss unconditionally. See *Grossgrundbesitz*, 122–127 for his reform proposals.

20. Legislation summarized in "Vyjádřtení držitelů čekatelů svěřenství o

ósnově zákona o zrušení svěřenství," 25 August 1920, 1. SOA Litoměřice
(Děčín), RA Clam-Gallas, k 155, c 468. Entail holders, led by Jan Schwarzenberg, countered that "Even a modern democratic state . . . cannot lack conservative actors, who are capable of defending the people against the alternative
of a demogogic or Ceasarist monstrosity." "Vyjádření," 3.
    21. E. Vondruška, "K chystanému zrušení fideikomisů," Pozemková reforma,
4, no. 6–7 (June–July 1923): 109–112.
    22. "Mitteilungen über die Taetigkeit der österr. Monarchistenpartei," 20
April 1921. The author of this report is not specified, but it appears to have
come to the Propaganda Division (Propagační odbor) of the Interior Ministry
via Austrian intelligence. Copy in AKPR PO MV k 17 c 276.
    23. "Zpráva důvěrníka ze severních Čech," 15 November 1921, Propagační
odbor of the Interior Ministry. Copy in AKPR PO MV k 17 c 276.
    24. See Propagační odbor report of 15 October 1921 and Lobkowicz let-
ters to KPR from 1920–21. Copy in AKPR T453/21 Dr. Bedřich Lobkowicz.
    25. "Ruští monarchisté v Praze," undated (around 1920), Propagační odbor
of the Interior Ministry, 3–4. Copy in AKPR PO MV k 17 c 276.
    26. See in particular "Ruští monarchisté," 6, and "Zpráva důvěrníka," 3
November, 1921. Copy in AKPR PO MV k 17 c 276.
    27. Franz Hartig to Heinrich Clam-Martinic, 6 January 1927. Copy in
SOA Litoměřice (Děčín), RA Ledebur, k 24 ic 193.
    28. See Verein krieger Heimbringung (Kaiser Karl Heimbringungsfond)
to Leopold Berchtold, 23 June 1932. MZA Brno, RA Berchtold, k 131 ic 430.
    29. Josef Holeček, Česká šlechta. Výklady časové i historické (Prague: Česko
moravské podniky tiskařské a vydavatelské, 1918), 168.
    30. Quoted in C. A. Macartney, National States and National Minorities
(London: Oxford University Press, 1934), 279.
    31. See ibid., 505 and Gyula Popély, "Mezinárodní ochrana menšin, Čes-
koslovensko a Společnost národů," Střední Evropa, 19 (1991): 61.
    32. "The League of Nations and Minorities" (Geneva: League of Nations
Secretariat, 1923).
    33. József Galántai, Trianon and the Protection of Minorities (Highland Lakes,
N.J.: Atlantic Research and Publications, 1992), 119–129.
    34. Popély, "Mezinárodní ochrana," 69–70.
    35. "Bericht der deutschen Völkerbundliga in der Tschechoslowakischen
Republik über ihre Tätigkeit im Jahre 1922," January 1923, 1–2. SOA Lito-
měřice (Děčín), RA Ledebur, k 14 c 201. The executive committee of the
Völkerbundliga contained three former nobles in 1922: Medinger (president),
Alfons Clary-Aldringen (who would become president in the late 1930s), and
Erwein Nostitz-Rieneck. As of December 1922, the group had 511 members.
See "Bericht," 10–11.
    36. See chapter 3, "Nationalization of the Nobility: Noble Lobbying Strat-
egies in the 1920s," for documentation of the Völkerbundliga's close ties to
German large landowners.
    37. Galántai, Trianon, 116–118.
    38. Ferdinand Peroutka, Budování státu, vol. 2 (Prague: Fr. Borový, 1934),
877.

39. Peroutka reports that a "majority" of the Assembly took this view. See *Budování státu*, vol. 2: 867.

40. See the debate on land reform in the National Assembly on 16 April 1919 (session 46). Text at Elektronická knihovna—Český parlament: dokumenty českého parlamentu, *www.psp.cz/cgi-bin/win/eknih/* (accessed 9 September 2004).

41. Modráček, National Assembly, Meeting 46 (16 April 1919).

42. Němec, National Assembly, Meeting 46 (16 April 1919).

43. Vlastislav Lacina, "Boj o uzákonění pozemkové reformy v letech 1918 a 1919," *Sborník k dějinám 19. a 20. století* 5 (1978): 123. See also Jaromir Dittmann-Balcar, "Die Bodenreform in der Anfangsphase der Ersten Tschechoslowakischen Republik: Instrument im Volkstumkampf oder sozialpolitische Massnahme" (master's thesis, Ludwig-Maximilian University, Munich, 1995), 59.

44. Modráček, National Assembly, Meeting 46 (16 April 1919). Peroutka and numerous historians then and since share this verdict, though some Czech historians still deny a national bias in the reform. Peroutka writes, "The goals of land reform were not economic, but rather social and national, the strengthening of democracy and the state." *Budování státu*, vol. 2: 871.

45. Karel Viškovský, speech to the Czech Agrarian party, quoted in *Venkov*, 1 May 1919: 1–2. Cited in "Beschwerde der deutschen Grossgrundbesitzer der Tschechoslowakischen Republik, die die Ankündigung der Konfiskation ihres Eigentumes für den 1. Jänner 1923 erhalten haben, gerichtet an den Völkerbund" (Prague: die Deutsche Völkerbundliga in der Tschechoslowakischen Republik, September 1922), 45.

46. "Velikonoce 1919 ve znamení veliké reformy pozemkové," *Venkov*, 20 April 1919: 11.

47. B. Kral, "Pozemková reforma," *Národní listy*, 28 March 1922. Quoted in "Beschwerde," 46.

48. See examples in "Beschwerde," 46–48.

49. Ladislav Holy, *The Little Czech and the Great Czech Nation* (Cambridge: Cambridge University Press, 1996), 121.

50. Josef Pekař, *Omyly a nebezpečí pozemkové reformy*, (Prague: Vesmír, 1923), 10. The articles in this collection originally appeared in *Národní listy* from 24 December 1922 to 11 March 1923. Incidentally, Eugen (Count) Czernin translated Pekař's book into German.

51. Pekař, *Omyly*, 6, 10–12.

52. Ibid., 12–18.

53. Ibid., 20–23.

54. Ibid., 25, 58–59. The Czech philosopher Emanuel Rádl (1873–1942) agreed with Pekař's general critique, arguing that a discriminatory national confiscation would have to be based on "power and not justice." Such actions "dull the people's sense of justice; the people learn to believe in power in place of truth." Ultimately, arbitrary confiscations on a national basis would, Rádl believed, undermine the rule of law. See Emanuel Rádl, *Valka Čechů s Němci*, (Prague: Melantrich, 1993), 202–207.

55. See Peroutka, *Budování*, vol. 2: 869 and expert opinion of Dr. J. Novák,

Director of the Provincial Archive of the Kingdom of Bohemia, 27 November 1919. SÚA, SPÚ sig. G I/2/I, k 300. Also see Pekař's expert opinions reproduced in *Omyly*, 68–80. Pekař's quote from page 77 of *Omyly*. Restitution legislation in 1991 trying to redress Communist confiscations from only forty years earlier demonstrate the legal complications such legislation can produce.

56. Lacina, "Boj," 124–130.

57. "Sociální demokraté proti rozdělení latifundií drobným zemědělcům, domkářům a zemědělským dělníkům," *Venkov*, 30 November 1918:6.

58. Krčmář quoted in Lacina, "Boj," 130.

59. Modráček, National Assembly, Meeting 46 (16 April 1919).

60. Textor, *Land Reform*, 29.

61. Lacina, "Boj," 135.

62. For evidence of the intent to favor Czechs and Slovaks, see the records of the Administrative Committee (Správní výbor), SÚA, SPÚ, k 132. See, for example, meetings on 30 September 1920, 31 January 1921, and 4 June 1921.

63. Vlastislav Lacina, "Představy o pozemkové reformě v ČSR před jejím uzákoněním," in *Československá pozemková reforma 1919–1935* (Uherské Hradiště, 1994), 37.

64. "Pozemková reforma s hlediska ochrany menšin," SPÚ internal memorandum, 1930. SÚA SPÚ GVII/IC.8, k 355.

65. Lubomír Slezák, "Tvůrci, kritikové a odpůrci pozemkové reformy," *Moderní dějiny* 1 (1993): 214.

66. Jan Rychlík, "Sociální a národnostní dimenze československé pozemkové reformy v mezinárodním kontextu," in *Československá pozemková reforma 1919–1935* (Uherské Hradiště: Slovácké museum, 1994): 49.

67. Prinz cited in Dittmann-Balcar, "Bodenreform," 142. See chapter 3, "Nationalization of the Nobility," for a summary of Sudeten German arguments against the land reform.

68. J. W. Bruegel, *Tschechen und Deutsche* (Munich: Nymphenburger Verlagshandlung, 1967), 537–539. Cited in Mark Cornwall, " 'National Reparation'?: The Czech Land Reform and the Sudeten Germans 1918–38," *Slavic and East European Review* 75, no. 2 (April 1997): 261.

69. Dittmann-Balcar, "Bodenreform," 143–144. Dittmann-Balcar cites a memorandum of the Sudeten German Party from 1938 that reported that of the total of 55,206 ha of land redistributed in the German "Sprachgebiet," 31,172 ha went to German farmers.

70. Dittmann-Balcar, "Bodenreform," 145–147. See also Jaromir Balcar, "Die Anfänge der Bodenreform in der Tschechoslowakei 1919/20," *Vierteljahrshefte für Zeitgeschichte* 46, no. 3 (1998): 391–428.

71. Cornwall, "National Reparation," 270. Rádl went so far as to claim that many national union leaders became SPÚ functionaries, including the director of the Olomouc office of the SPÚ. Rádl, *Valka*, 204.

72. Cornwall, "National Reparation," 276. Rádl claimed that through 1925 Germans had received only a negligible portion of redistributed land. Rádl, *Valka*, 204–205.

73. Cornwall, "National Reparation," 280.

74. Cornwall also discusses Administrative Committee records in ibid., 269–271.

75. See, for example, Zápis schůze správního výboru, 30 September 1920, 31 January 1921. SÚA SPÚ, k 132.

76. Zápis schůze správního výboru, 4 June 1921. SÚA SPÚ, k 132. See also Cornwall, "National Reparation," 270. For reasons discussed in chapter 3, "Nationalization of the Nobility," Medinger managed to save most of his land.

77. For a brief survey of the colonization program, see Daniel Miller, "Colonizing the Hungarian and German Border Areas during the Czechoslovak Land Reform, 1918–1938," *Austrian History Yearbook* 34 (2003): 303–317.

78. Textor, *Land Reform*, 70–74.

79. "Doplněk k důvodové zprávě o vládním návrhu zákona o úvěrových opatřeních pro Státní pozemkový úřad," Víškovský to Ministerial Council, 9 July 1925. AÚTGM Fond EB, Pozemková reforma, k 187/1.

80. "Území kolonisační," undated State Land Office memorandum. SÚA SPÚ GV11/1c.8, k 355.

81. Elizabeth Wiskemann, *Czechs and Germans* (London: Oxford University Press, 1938), 156.

82. Ibid., 152. A 1932 internal Land Office estimate put the amount of land received by Germans in Bohemia and Moravia at 50,303 ha, or 7.2 percent of the total redistributed arable land in the two provinces. Statistics were up to 31 December 1931. See SÚA SPÚ, k 118 c 57.2.

83. Joseph Rothschild, *East Central Europe Between the Two World Wars* (Seattle: University of Washington Press, 1992), 67. See also Rogers Brubaker, *Nationalism Reframed: Nationhood and the National Question in the New Europe* (Cambridge: Cambridge University Press, 1996), 91–92, 101.

84. Rothschild, *East Central Europe*, 290.

85. See Wojciech Roszkowski, *Land Reforms in East Central Europe after World War One* (Warsaw: Polish Academy of Sciences, 1995).

86. Ibid., 13.

87. Brubaker, *Nationalism Reframed*, 84.

88. Franz Czernin to Franz Clam-Gallas, 14 February 1919. SOA Litoměřice (Děčín), RA Clam-Gallas, k 156 ic 468.

89. Peroutka, *Budování státu*, vol. 1, 159–162, 185–202, 359–371.

90. "Deutschböhmisches Notstandskomitee aus dem Herrenhause," n.d. District leaders were Erwein Nostitz (Karlsbad), Karl Georg Buquoy (Joachimstal and Gratzen), Ottokar Westfalen Fürstenberg (Teplitz), Karl Kinský (Tetschen), Franz Clam-Gallas (Reichenberg), Rudolf Czernin (Hohenelbe) and Johann and Adolf Schwarzenberg (Krumau). SOA Litoměřice (Děčín), RA Clam-Gallas, k 618 ic 2319.

91. Because the Habsburg Empire was not officially dissolved until 12 November 1918, the Herrenhaus technically still existed when Sudeten Germans created Deutschböhmen on October 30. See Peroutka, *Budování státu*, vol. 1, 264 and 359.

92. On Czech accusations against Buquoy, see 25 June 1920 KPR notes in

AKPR D7653/20. The Šumava National Union accused Buquoy of financing the Sudeten German "Volkswehr" in 1918. Narodní Jednota Pošumavská to V. Johannis (Minister of Supply), 16 June 1920. Copy in SOA Třeboň, RA Buquoy, k 275 ic 1351. Buquoy claimed he was falsely accused. In a letter to the KPR from 25 August 1920, he wrote, "I am a German . . . but even under the Monarchy I always felt every nation should pursue its own aspirations. I have never since the breakup of the Monarchy agitated against the Republic." AKPR D7653/20.

93. Rudolf Czernin-Morzin to the Ministerial Council of the Czechoslovak state, letters dated 26 February and 11 March 1919. AKPR D7653/20.

94. Rudolf Czernin-Morzin to unspecified minister, 15 January 1923. Copy sent to President Masaryk. AKPR T2170/22.

95. Petr Mašek, *Modrá krev* (Prague: Mladá Fronta, 1994), 169.

96. Adalbert Count Sternberg, *Vor dem Frieden von Versailles* (Vienna: Hermann Goldschmiedt, 1919), 20.

97. Ibid., 20–25, 37. On Masaryk's monarchism, see Kostrba-Skalicky, "Burg," 164.

98. Copy of letter from Ferdinand Prince, Max Prince, and Jaroslav Prince z Lobkovicz (*sic*) to the National Committee, 31 October 1918. SOA Zámrsk, RA Kinský-Kostelec, k 4 ic 97.

99. "Tvoří se konservativní strana republikánská," *Večer*, 20 November 1918.

100. Bedřich Lobkowicz to KPR, 3 September 1919. AKPR T453/21.

101. Arnošt Barbořík (Max Lobkowicz's lawyer) to Presidential Chancellery 31 July 1924 and Max Lobkowicz "První pokračování memoranda," 14 August 1924. AKPR D10429/47. Statistics on Bilina from *Statistický lexikon obcí v Čechách* (Prague: Státní úřad statistický, 1923).

102. On recent critiques of Czechoslovak interwar democracy, see T. Mills Kelly, "A Reputation Tarnished: New Perspectives on Interwar Czechoslovakia," Woodrow Wilson International Center for Scholars, Meeting Report #278. Available at www.wilsoncenter.org (accessed 2 June 2004).

103. Brubaker, *Nationalism Reframed*, 49.

3. Nationalization of the Nobility: Noble Lobbying Strategies in the 1920s

1. Joseph Rothschild, *East Central Europe Between the Two World Wars* (Seattle: University of Washington Press, 1992), 22.

2. Bedřich Schwarzenberg to Adolf Waldstein, 29 March 1919. SOA Prague, RA Valdštejn, VI-59, k 170.

3. Adolf Waldstein to Bedřich Schwarzenberg, 5 April 1919. SOA Prague, RA Valdštejn, VI-59, k 170.

4. On the historical significance of the term "utraquist," see chapter 1, "Between Empire and Nation: The Bohemian Nobility, 1880–1918."

5. For a succinct statement of this argument, see Wilhelm Medinger's article "The Situation of the Germans in the Czecho-Slovak State" in *Reconstruction*, 1 June 1922. My copy of the article is from an unpaginated reprint.

Ironically, Edvard Beneš would promise to create a Swiss-style nationalities state in a memorandum to the Paris Peace Conference in May 1919. It was to prove an empty promise. See Elizabeth Wiskemann, *Czechs and Germans* (London: Oxford University Press, 1938), 92–93.

6. Protokoly o schůzích představenstva SČV, 3 June 1919. SOA Třeboň, RA Schwarzenberg Sekundogeniture, k 332 ic 1571.

7. Svaz československých velkostatkářů (SČV) to Franz Wien-Claudi, 26 August 1919, SÚA, SČV, k 46 ic 390.

8. Verband der deutschen Grossgrundbesitzer (VdG) to SČV, 6 September 1919. SÚA, SČV, k 46 ic 390.

9. On the Verband's early goals, see "Denkschrift des Verbandes der deutschen Grossgrundbesitzer Böhmens," 12 December 1919, SOA Prague, RA Valdštejn, signature V-1/VI#2/ c 4.

10. The *Svaz*'s founding statute of 1919 quoted in Antonín Kubačák, "Činnost Svazu československých velkostatkářů v letech 1919–1943," *Sborník archivních prací* 37 (1987): 328.

11. Kubačák, "Činnost," 330–331.

12. See *Ottův slovník naučný* (OSN), vol. 16 (Prague: J. Otto, 1900), 221–229.

13. "Protokol mimořádné valné hromady," SČV, 23 October 1923. SÚA SČV, k 3 ic 86.

14. Membership numbers from Kubačák, "Činnost," 329. Estimate of one-half derived from list of 193 members appended to Kubačák, "Činnost," 367–37. In that list, 102 are high nobles, 22 low nobles, and 69 commoners. The proportion of high noble members dropped to around one-third by 1929, though the absolute number (88) was close to that in Kubačák's list. See membership lists in SÚA SČV k 1 and 3 ic 60 and 71.

15. Svaz 1927 and 1929 membership lists in SÚA SČV, k 1 and 3 ic 60 and 71. Verband 1927 list in SÚA SČV, k 46 ic 397. Location of estates and nationality statistics for those estates derived from Jan Voženílek, *Předběžné výsledky československé pozemkové reformy* (Prague: Státní pozemkový úřad, 1930) and *Statistický lexikon obcí v Čechách* (Prague: Státní úřad Statisticuý, 1923).

16. The following paragraphs summarize "Opis petice panu presidentu republiky," signed by Bedřich Lobkowicz for SČV. SÚA SPÚ k 109.

17. "Pamětní spis," SČV to Presidium minsterské rady, 22 March 1921, signed by Bedřich Lobkowicz and Karel Belcredi. SÚA, SPÚ, k 109.

18. "Ohražení Svazu československých velkostatkářů proti osnově zákona náhradového," Svaz brief, 26 February 1921. SÚA SČV, k 101 ic 851. Elsewhere Lobkowicz wrote, "The large estate, just as in the past, will remain in the present and the future the bearer of economic progress" in the countryside. He cites as reasons the availability of capital, the development of experimental fields, and the employment of educated estate managers. "Pamětní spis," SČV to Presidium minsterské rady, 22 March 1921, signed by Bedřich Lobkowicz and Karel Belcredi. SÚA, SPÚ, k 109. *Svaz* claims that land reform threatened productivity would later prove to be unfounded.

19. SČV, "Opis podání panu presidentu republiky," 20 December 1920. SÚA SČV, k 109.

20. See, for example, "Pamětní spis předložený dne 5. dubna 1923 panu presidentu republiky," in *Věstník*, vol. 3 (31 March 1923): 2. SÚA SČV, k 8 ic 125.

21. Law #81§20 (Zákon přídělový), 30 January 1920, Sbírka zákonů a nařízení, 16 (1920), 139.

22. SČV and SMV memorandum to President Masaryk, 21 July 1922. SÚA SČV, k 7 ic 117.

23. "Quéstionnaire týkající se Pozemkové reformy a příbuzných otázek," prepared by SČV in response to *London Times*, 16 January 1923. SÚA SČV, k 8 ic 133. For more on colonization, see chapter 2, "National and Social Revolution in Czechoslovakia, 1918–1920."

24. As SPÚ officials were visiting the Netolice estate to survey it for the next wave of land reform, the estate director called together a crowd that threw sand on them and shouted, "We'll parcel you out with our bare hands! Leave Schwarzenberg in peace!" Quoted in Josef Vraný "Vzpoura 'jihočeského krále' r. 1922," *Venkov*, 20 January 1922. See also *Večer*, 20 January 1922, and *Právo lidu*, 21 January 1922.

25. "Quéstionnaire týkající se Pozemkové reformy."

26. The Moravian Union had 145 members in 1930, the vast majority of whom were noble. "Seznam členů mor. velkostatkařů v Brně," 1930. SÚA SČV, k 50 ic 413.

27. SMV concept memo, summer of 1922. MA Brno, RA Belcredi, k 58 c 446.

28. See the *Svaz* correspondence with political parties in SÚA SČV, k 104. Examples include a letter from the National Democratic senatorial club inviting the *Svaz* to send a representative to their private conference in 1928 (ic 884) and notes regarding an upcoming secret meeting of the Agrarians in 1930 (k 191 ic 1609).

29. See Dušan Uhlíř, "Dva směry v československém agrárním hnutí a rozchod Karla Práška s republikánskou stránou," *Sborník historický* 18 (1971): 113–146; also see the Prášek file in SOA Litoměřice (Děčín) RA Thun-Hohenstein, A3XXIX#82.

30. Antonín Kubacák, "Činnost Svazu československých velkostatkářů v letech 1919–1943," *Sborník archivních prací* 37 (1987): 335–336.

31. Report of Eugen Ledebur in VdG, "Aufzeichnung über die am 30. Oktober 1925 stattgefundene Besprechung." SOA Litoměřice (Děčín) RA Thun-Hohenstein, A-3XXIX #94.40. The Moravian Union played this game in reverse. Though ostensibly following a pro-Czech policy, Karel Belcredi, the Union's chief administrator, directed money to the German Christian People's Party. See letters from Robert Mayr-Harting to Karel Belcredi, 19 January, 22 October, and 1 December 1925. MA Brno, RA Belcredi, k 58 ic 447.

32. Untitled memorandum, ZdenRk Kolowrat, 1927. SÚA SČV, k 190 ic 1597.

33. Bedřich and František Deym, Memorandum to State Land Office, 15 December 1919. AKPR T 24/25. Note that Bedřich Deym wrote a follow-up note to the SPÚ on 20 February 1925 complaining that he was being treated

unfairly in the land reform in spite of his solid Czech credentials. AKPR D 8078/32.

34. František Schlik, "Memorandum" presented to the Office of the President, 20 November 1923. AKPR T 24/25. Note that the memorandum spells the family name Czech style, "Šlik" throughout, but it is signed "Schlik." Statistics from the SPÚ in 1930 indicate that 1,848 ha of the family's 4,269 ha were redistributed, with the remainder released from zábor. *Předběžné výsledky,* 1930.

35. František Schlik also published a pamphlet defending the nobility from accusations of disloyalty to the republic. See Schlik, *Jak to nazvati?* (Jičinoves, Czechoslovakia, 1921).

36. Reports of meetings from 6 April 1925 and 23 December 1926. AKPR T886/21. Jaroslav was only distantly related to the three Lobkowiczs who presided over the Svaz from 1921 to 1943.

37. "Abschrift eines Briefes einer Arbeiterin. Zum Weekend Lord Runcimans bei Ulrich Kinsky," August 1938. PRO FO 800/307 #29–32. Because of this German loyalty, I use the German "Ulrich Kinsky" rather than the Czech "Oldřich Kinský."

38. Oldřich Ferdinand Kinský, memorandum to Chancellery of the President, 4 January 1926. AKPR D8078/32/A (k D88/26). The Czech spelling of Kinsky's name is used in the memorandum.

39. *Předběznévýsledky,* 1930.

40. Frant. Ad. Šubert, *Národní divadlo v Praze* (Prague: J. Otto, 1881), 23. Excerpt in Deym memorandum to State Land Office, 15 December 1919. Copy in AKPR T 24/25.

41. "Zábor statků J. Schwarzenberga," brief to KPR, July, 1923. AKPR T 24/25.

42. "Výňatek z činnosti hraběte Jana Harracha a celého Harrachovského rodu," 16 June 1926. AKPR T 153/25.

43. Záznam KPR 23 January 1925, AKPR, T136/25. Šámal was an old friend of Masaryk from the Realist Party, and he was a leader of the underground Czech "Mafia" in Prague during World War I. The Hildprandts were one of the few baronial families from Bohemia to have been accepted in Habsburg Court circles in the late nineteenth century. See William Godsey, "Quarterings and Kinship: The Social Composition of the Habsburg Aristocracy in the Dualist Era," *Journal of Modern History,* no. 71 (March 1999): 98.

44. Leopold Berchtold to President Masaryk, 1 March 1921. AKPR T 24/25.

45. Michael Karolyi, *Memoirs of Michael Karolyi: Faith Without Illusion,* trans. Catherine Karolyi (London: Jonathan Cape, 1956), 15.

46. Statistics on nationality come from a database of 194 noble landowners I compiled in the course of my research. For database methodology and details, see Eagle Glassheim, "Crafting a Post-Imperial Identity: Nobles and Nationality Politics in Czechoslovakia, 1918–1948" (Ph.D. diss., Columbia University, 2000), chapter 4.

47. Constitutional Loyalists, regardless of family origin, were most likely to be German (92 percent). Around 15 percent of immigrant families indicated

Czech nationality between the wars. Almost all of these came from a Feudal Conservative background.

48. A "primarily" Czech or German region, in my analysis, was one with over 80 percent of the given nationality. The official cutoff for minority language rights was 20 percent in a given jurisdiction. "Mixed regions" refer to those where a minority makes up more than 20 percent of the population.

49. The supposition that location of estates determined noble nationality came from František Schwarzenberg, letter to the editor, *Svědectví*, 20, no. 79 (1986): 704.

50. Kubačák, "Činnost," 329.

51. SČV report from annual meeting, 11 May 1925. SÚA SČV, k 3 ic 86.

52. Zdeněk Kolowrat to Josef Sekanina, 7 May 1928. SÚA SČV, k 190 ic 1590.

53. Josef Sekanina to Zdeněk Kolowrat, 9 May 1928. SÚA SČV, k 190 ic 1590.

54. Masaryk 1922 New Year's speech quoted in the Land Office's journal *Pozemková reforma*, 3, no. 1 (January 1922): 2.

55. Porada mezisvazové komise, 13 November 1923. SÚA SČV, k 4 ic 88.

56. See Karel Viškovský, "Přípravy pro nové pracovní období Státního pozemkového úřadu," *Pozemková reforma*, 4, no. 1 (January 1923): 1–3.

57. Antonín Pavel, "Public Guidance in Land Utilization in Czechoslovakia," offprint from *The Annals of the American Academy of Political and Social Science* (July 1930): 11. Copy in SÚA SPÚ, k 85 ic 25.

58. For tables of land reform results see: Jan Voženílek, *Předběžné výsledky československé pozemkové reformy* (Prague, 1930), 28*; and "Výsledky pozemkové reformy do konce r. 1934," in SÚA SPÚ, k 118 ic 57#2. In all, 12.6 percent of the country's 14 million hectares changed hands by 1936. Of the original *zábor* of 4.1 million hectares, 43.4 percent came under new ownership (including that of the state) and 43.4 percent was released fully to the original owners. For 1936 statistics, see "Pozemková reforma," in *Ottův slovník nové doby, dodatek*, vol. 4, no. 2 (Prague: Novina, 1937): 1360–1371.

59. OSN, vol. 15 (Prague: J. Otto, 1900), 768.

60. Petr Mašek, *Modrá krev* (Prague: Mladá Fronta, 1999), 156.

61. *Ottův slovník nové doby, dodatky*, vol. 4, no. 1 (Prague: Novina, 1936), 156. For a sympathetic evaluation of Medinger's career and goals, see Peter Krueger, "Wilhelm von Medinger, die internationale Ordnung nach 1918 und der Schatten des Mannes aus der Mancha," *Bohemia* 26 (1985): 257–276.

62. "Denkschrift des Verbandes der deutschen Grossgrundbesitzer Böhmens," 1 December 1919. SOA Prague, RA Valdštejn, V-1/VI#2, item 4.

63. "Rede des Obmannes des Verbandes der deutschen Grossgrundbesitzer Böhmens, Grafen Dr. Eugen Ledebur-Krzemusch," *Deutsches Agrarblatt*, 21 January 1920, 1–2. Copy in SÚA SČV, k 46 ic 392.

64. "Denkschrift," 1 December 1919.

65. "Rede des Obmannes," 21 January 1920.

66. Medinger speech of 1 December 1920, cited in Mark Cornwall, "National Reparation'? The Czech Land Reform and the Sudeten Germans, 1918–38," *Slavic and East European Review* 75, no. 2 (April 1997): 266.

67. VdG to Minister für Landwirtschaft, 9 April 1921. SÚA SPÚ, k 109. Compare SČV "Pamětní spis" to Presidium of the Ministerial Council on 22 March 1921. SÚA SPÚ, k 109.

68. Protokol schůze Ústředního výboru Svazů, 30 June 1921. SÚA, SČV, k 4 ic 88.

69. "Bericht über die am 11. Juli 1922 stattgefundene Sitzung der Grossgrundbesitzerverbände zur Abwehr gegen die Kündigung." SÚA, SČV, k 7 ic 117.

70. Zdeněk Kolowrat at Porada mezisvazové komise, 16 October 1922. SÚA SČV, k 4 ic 88.

71. Protokol schůze Ústředního výboru Svazů, 23 March 1927. SÚA, SČV, k 4 ic 88. See also Protokol of 16 October 1922 for the *Svaz* leadership's opposition to using nationality arguements in international courts.

72. This refers to Article 8:1 of the treaty of St. Germain en Laye, 10 September 1919. See "Beschwerde der deutschen Grossgrundbesitzer der Tschechoslowakischen Republik, die die Ankündigung der Konfiskation ihres Eigentumes für den 1. Jänner 1923 erhalten haben, gerichtet an den Völkerbund" (Prague: die Deutsche Völkerbundliga in der Tschechoslowakischen Republik, September 1922), 6.

73. Ibid., 9–10.

74. Ibid., 27.

75. Ibid., 4

76. Ibid., 20–21.

77. "Kundgebung der Stadtgemeinde Graslitz vom 18. Juli 1922," in ibid., 61.

78. See, among many examples, Wilhelm Medinger, "Landwirschaft: Die Waldverstaatlichungs-Pläne," *Prager Tagblatt*, 3 March 1922. Copy in SÚA MZV-VA #1379 k 2701. It is clear in other German newspapers, such as *Bohemia*, that much of their information on the forest confiscations came from Medinger and/or the *Verband*. New petitions and memoranda to the League of Nations followed in 1924, 1925, and 1926.

79. Membership and donation lists in SOA Litoměřice (Děčín) RA Clary-Aldringen, k 447. Franz Clam-Gallas also made substantial donations. He was listed as a "founding" donor in 1922. See SOA Litoměřice (Děčín) RA Clam-Gallas, "Vereine," k 156 ic 468.

80. See Deutschpolitische Arbeitstelle to Alfons Clary-Aldringen, 28 July 1921 and Eugen Ledebur to Alfons Clary-Aldringen, 11 August 1921. SOA Litoměřice (Děčín) RA Clary-Aldringen, k 446.

81. Lord Henry Bentinck to Alfons Clary-Aldringen, 12 September 1921, and copy of letter from Felix Doubleday to Sir William Timell, 4 August 1921. SOA Litoměřice (Děčín) RA Clary-Aldringen, k 448.

82. "Die Genesis und die Ziele des Komitees," author unknown, 25 September 1922. MA Brno, RA Belcredi, k 58 ic 446. The Czechoslovak Interior Ministry reported that Clary had met with the British ambassador G. F. Clerk on 19 July 1922 to present evidence of the national bias of land reform. The same report also noted Untermayer's ties with Bohemian nobles. It described him as "representative of an American consortium that is buying Archduke

Friedrich Habsburg's large estates in Czechoslovakia." Propaganda Division report, 20 July 1922. AKPR PO MV, k 18 ic 276.

83. Adalbert Sternberg to Karl Belcredi, 27 September 1922. MA Brno, RA Belcredi (Velkostatek Líšeň), k 58 ic 446.

84. See Adalbert Sternberg to Zdenko Kolowrat, 10 August 1922. SÚA SČV, k 190 ic 1606. See also the long quote from the Paris edition of the *New York Herald* in "Kampaň šlechtické reakce proti pozemkové reformě," *Pravo lidu,* 13 September 1922. Copy in SÚA SČV, k 12 ic 166.

85. Adalbert Sternberg to Karl Belcredi, 27 September 1922. MA Brno, RA Belcredi (Velkostatek Líšeň), k 58 ic 446.

86. Wilhelm Medinger, "The Situation of the Germans in the Czecho-Slovak State," speech delivered at the Conference of the Committee for the Protection of National Minorities of the League of Nations Unions, reprinted in *Reconstruction: International Economic Monthly* (Vienna), 1 June 1922.

87. Eugen Ledebur-Wicheln, "Bodenreform und Völkerrecht," *Wochenschrift für Kultur, Politik, und Volkswirtschaft,* vol. 7, no. 20–21 (14 and 21 February 1925): 483. Copy of article in SOA Litoměřice (Děčín) RA Ledebur, k 14 ic 190.

88. See 1919 SČV list of landowners living outside of Czechoslovakia in SÚA SČV, k 7 ic 111; and SPÚ 1928 list of Reich German citizens with estates in Czechoslovakia in SÚA SPÚ GVII/ic 8 k 355. Antonín Kubačák gives the number of Austrian citizens as twenty-seven. See "Provádění pozemkové reformy na majetku cizích státních příslušníků v období první republiky," *Vědecké práce Národního zemědělského muzea* 29 (1991–1992): 37.

89. Ibid., 44.

90. See MZV to SPÚ, 12 January 1924. SÚA SPÚ, k 85 c 25. In spite of the Foreign Ministry request, I have not found evidence of systematic Land Office record-keeping on nationality.

91. Kubačák, "Provádění," 38. Metternich had over 16,000 of his 20,000 ha as of 1930; Clary still had over 7,000 ha out of 8,000; Hohenlohe retained over 9,000 out of 11,000 ha. The average for all large landowners was close to 50 percent, so these nobles did remarkably well.

92. See, for example, the plan for an agreement with Max Egon Fürstenberg in 1922: Jan Voženílek, "Návrh výkupu majetku Fürstenbergského" [1922]. AKPR T470/22. See also Kubačák, "Provádění."

93. Report of SČV annual meeting, 11 May 1925. SÚA SČV, k 3 ic 86.

94. See correspondence between MZV and SPÚ from 1925, for example. SÚA SPÚ k 354 sig G VII/IC.

95. Quotations from undated (late 1920s) internal SPÚ memorandum, "Pozemková reforma a národní menšiny. Stížnosti u minoritní sekce Společnosti Národů," SÚA SPÚ G VII/IC.8 k 355. On the League's rulings, see Cornwall, "National Reparation," 275–279.

96. Karl Anton Prince Rohan, *Umbruch der Zeit* (Berlin: Georg Stilke, 1930), 15. Cardinal Louis de Rohan was infamous for his part in Marie-Antionette's diamond necklace affair.

97. His complete title was Alain Duke Rohan, Twelfth Duc de Montbazon

et de Bouillon, Prince de Guémenée, de Rochefort et de Montauban! See Ernst Rutkowski, ed., *Briefe und Dokumente zur Geschichte der österreichisch-ungarischen Monarchie unter besonderer Berücksichtigung des böhmisch-märischen Raumes. Teil I: Der Verfassungstreue Grossgrundbesitz 1880–1899*, vol. 1 (Munich: Oldenbourg Verlag, 1983), 26–27.

98. Rohan, *Umbruch*, 15.

99. Rohan, "Die Utopie des Pazifismus," *Europäische Revue*, vol. 1 (1925): 131–132.

100. The English version appeared as Richard Coudenhove-Kalergi, *Pan-Europa* (New York: 1926).

101. Richard Coudenhove-Kalergi, *Crusade for Pan-Europe* (New York: G. P. Putnam's Sons, 1943), 72.

102. Ibid., 90. Coudenhove did not, however, speak Czech.

103. Ibid., 127–137.

104. Karl Anton Rohan, *Europa* (Leipzig: Neuer Geist Verlag, 1923).

105. Karl Anton Rohan, "Vorwort des Herausgebers," *Europäische Revue*, vol. 1 (1925): 1.

106. Interestingly, a conservative Austrian historian told me that he, and many other Austrians, see the current European Union as a kind of Grossdeutsch unification of the Germans in contemporary Europe.

107. Rohan, "Das Problem der Kriegsschuld," *Europäische Revue*, vol. 1 (1925): 132.

108. Rohan, "Das Problem der nationalen Minderheiten (1930)," *Umbruch*, 126.

109. Rochus Freiherr von Rheinbaben, "Einleitung," in Rohan, *Umbruch*, 12.

110. Rohan, "Inventar der politischen Grundhaltungen im heutigen Europa (1929)," in *Umbruch*, 41. Individual articles in this collection originally appeared in Rohan's journal *Europäische Revue*. Dates of original publication are in parentheses.

111. Rohan, "Inventar," 42.

112. Hofmannsthal first used the phrase "conservative revolution" in a speech to students in Munich in 1927. See Jeremy Noakes, "German Conservatives and the Third Reich: An Ambiguous Relationship," in *Fascists and Conservatives: The Radical Right and the Establishment in Twentieth-Century Europe*, ed. Martin Blinkhorn (London: Unwin Hyman, 1990), 80. Note that Hofmannsthal was an occasional contributor to Rohan's *Europäische Revue*.

113. Fritz Stern, *The Politics of Cultural Despair* (New York: Doubleday, 1965), 6–7.

114. Rohan, "Inventar," 56.

115. Rohan, "Krise der Demokratie (1930)," *Umbruch*, 173.

116. Rohan, "Krise," 174.

117. Rohan, "Der moderne Rechtsstaat (1930)," *Umbruch*, 179.

118. Rohan, "Fascismus (1923)," *Umbruch*, 21. Rohan called Fascism "revolutionary" and "conservative," but Hofsmannthal would be the first to publicly put the two words together in 1927. Following Robert Paxton, I capitalize

Fascism when referring to the Italian variant and use lowercase for the more general phenomenon. See Paxton, "The Five Stages of Fascism," *The Journal of Modern History* 70 (March 1998): 1.

119. Rohan, "Fascismus und Europa (1926)," *Umbruch*, 31.

120. Rohan, "Nation," *Europäische Revue*, vol. 2 (1926): 321, 323.

121. Rheinbaben, "Einleitung," 11.

122. Eugen Ledebur, "Die nationalen Minderheiten in der Tschechoslowakei," *Europäische Revue*, vol. 2 (1927): 168–175.

123. See "Entwurf eines Minderheitenstatuts," *Europäische Revue*, vol. 6 (1930): 455–466.

124. Rohan, "Das Problem der nationalen Minderheiten," *Europäische Revue*, vol. 6 (1930): 398.

125. Karl Anton Rohan, "Adel," *Europäische Revue*, vol. 4, no. 1 (1928): 13–20. The prolific and popular writer Hermann Count Keyserling shared many of Rohan and Coudenhove's views on the future of the nobility. In a 1926 letter to a noble organization in Germany, Keyserling cited the two young men as perfect examples of noble "leaders of the grand style." Keyserling to Dr. von Stegmann, 23 October 1926. Copy in Eugen Ledebur's papers, SOA Litoměřice (Děčín), RA Ledebur, k 24 ic 193.

126. Richard Coudenhove-Kalergi, *Adel* (Leipzig: Neuer Geist Verlag, 1923). Eugenics quote appears on p. 44.

127. See Paneuropa Austria *www.paneuropa.or.at/paneuropa/* (accessed 13 September 2004).

128. For more on Rohan's close ties to Bohemian nobles, see the section in chapter 5, "German Internationalism and National Socialism: german Nobles in the 1930s," on the *Grusbacher Herren.*

129. Cecilia Sternberg, *The Journey* (London: Collins, 1977), 18, 71.

130. Das Präsidium des Jockey Club für Österreich to Alfons Clary-Aldringen 30 October 1931. SOA Litoměřice (Děčín) RA Clary-Aldringen, k 434.

131. Carl Egon Fürstenberg to Alfons Clary-Aldringen, 14 September 1938. SOA Litoměřice (Děčín) RA Clary-Aldringen, k 424.

132. Lothar Höbelt, "Adel und Politik seit 1848," in *Die Fuerstenberger,* ed. Erwein Eltz and Arno Strohmeyer (Schloß Weitra, Austria: Niederösterreichische Landesausstellung, 1994), 377.

133. Seznam členů Pražské Ressource/Verzeichnis der Mitglieder der Prager Ressource, 1 January 1928. SOA Prague RA Chotek, k 335 ic 2783. The membership list is entirely bilingual, including both Czech and German versions of most first names (this regardless of national loyalty). In keeping with the law, no titles are listed.

134. Seznam členů Pražské Ressource/Verzeichnis der Mitglieder der Prager Ressource, 1 January 1940. SOA Třeboň RA Schwarzenberg-Secundogeniture, přírůstek, k. 3 ic 27. The 1940 membership list was still entirely bilingual, including both Czech and German versions of most first names (regardless of national loyalty). Due to the change in law of 1939 (see chapter 6, "War and Revolution: The End of the Old Regime, 1939–1948"), titles were now listed.

135. On the American ball, see Zdenko Radslav Kinsky, *Zu Pferd und zu Fuss, 70 Jahre aus Erinnerungen* (Vienna: 1974), 96. On the mixing of nobles among the diplomatic and political elite in Prague, see František Schwarzenberg, "Tribuna Svědectví," *Svědectví* 20, no. 79 (1986): 705–706.

136. Ibid., 122–123.

137. *Wiener Salonblatt* of 31 October 1937, quoted in Kinsky, *Zu Pferd*, 137. For the number of visitors in 1937, see Kinsky, *Zu Pferd*, 138.

138. Sternberg, *Journey*, 134. Ulrich Kinsky died in 1938, so the friendship of Sternberg and Kinsky was not tested by occupation and war. Clary was also distantly related to Kinsky. See Alfons Clary-Aldringen, *A European Past*, trans. Ewald Osers (London: Weidenfeld and Nicolson, 1978), 45.

139. Karl Buquoy to Staatsanwaltschaft in B. Budweis, 30 August 1923. AKPR T594/23. For seemingly endless accounts of hunting, tennis, and polo, see Kinsky, *Zu Pferd*.

140. Ibid., 187.

141. "Alte Geschlechter in neuer Zeit," *Montagsblatt*, 27 December 1937.

142. Protokoll über die am 14. März 1935 in Böhm.-Leipa im Hotel "Knobloch" abgehaltene Hauptversammlung der Ortsgruppe Böhm.-Leipa des Verbandes Deutscher Flieger. SOA Prague, RA Valdštejn, k 170 sig VI-59.

143. *Tradice*, no. 3–4 (July–December, 1936): 316.

144. "Alte Geschlechter in neuer Zeit," Montagsblatt, 27 December 1937. On Ledebur's connections to the German Agrarian-Industrial Bank, see SOA Prague RA Valdštejn, k 163 sig VI-51/1.

145. Oswald Waldstein to Adolf Waldstein, 21 January 1924. SOA Prague, RA Valdštejn, k 164 sig VI-52/17.

146. See Clary-Aldringen, *European*.

147. My general conclusions on noble marriage patterns derive from Vladimír Pouzar, ed., *Almanach českých šlechtických rodů* (Prague: Martin, 1996). Information on the genealogy of a much wider range of families can be found on a DOS disk in the electronic references section of the Czech National Library (Klementinum) in Prague.

148. Sternberg, *Journey*, 188.

4. Czech Nobles, Nationalism, and Catholic Conservatism, 1930–1939

1. Joseph Rothschild, *East Central Europe Between the Two World Wars* (Seattle: University of Washington Press, 1992), 116, 126. Note that these percentages include the Agrarian Party, which was a statewide (though primarily Czech) party. If one were to count the right's percentage of the Czech vote only, the increase from 1929 to 1935 would be more significant.

2. David Kelly, *The Czech Fascist Movement 1922–1942* (Boulder, Colo.: East European Monographs, 1995), 120.

3. For an overview of Czech conservatism in the interwar period, see Hans Lemberg, "Die tschechischen Konservativen 1918–1938," in *Mit unbestechlichem Blick . . .* (Munich: R. Oldenbourg Verlag, 1998), 185–206.

4. Karel Čapek, "Starý vlastenec," *Lidové noviny*, 25 March 1934, reprinted in *Ratolest a vavřín* (Prague: F. R. Borový, 1947), 100–101.

5. *Polední list,* 5 December 1937.

6. *Čechův kraj,* 30 January 1935. Quoted in Petr Placák, "Duch křest'anství a duch otroctví: Karel Schwarzenberg (1911–1986)," pt. 1, *Střední Evropa,* no. 85 (1998): 46.

7. Newspaper excerpts from *Národní politika* (3 October 1936), *Venkov* (4 October 1936), *Lidové listy* (4 October 1936), *České slovo* (3 October 1936), *Brněnský den* (4 October 1936), *Lidové noviny* (3 October 1936), *Národní republika* (9 and 16 October 1936), *Hospodářský rozhled* (8 October 1936), *Pošumavský kraj* (8 October 1936), *Písecký obzor* (10 October 1936), and others, reprinted in *Tradice,* no. 3–4 (July–December 1936): 322–325. *Národní republika* also claimed that the State's Rights Progressive Party had wanted to elect Bedřich Schwarzenberg king of Bohemia in 1918. The Catholic People's Party had also considered making Schwarzenberg their presidential candidate in 1935.

8. Zdeněk Kolowrat to Karl Podstatzky-Lichtenstein, 19 November 1934. SÚA SČV, k 190 ic 1604.

9. Jan Lobkowicz, speech to *Svaz* general assembly, 14 March 1932, text in SÚA SČV, ic 398 k 46.

10. *Samostatnost* article by A. Hajn and J. Špaček quoted in *Večerní České slovo,* 1 February 1935. Špaček had proposed using nobles for diplomacy as early as 1933. See "Výňatek z řeči nár. dem. poslance Špačka v pos. sněmovně," 30 November 1933. SÚA SČV, k 190 ic 1597.

11. *Večerní České slovo,* 1 February 1935.

12. *Polední list,* 8 February 1938.

13. Jan Lobkowicz to Eugen Czernin, 16 March 1935. SOA Jindřichův Hradec, RA Czernin, k 534.

14. KPR Záznam, 5 February 1934. AKPR T119/34.

15. Schwarzenberg's list can be found in AKPR T119/34.

16. KPR Záznam, 28 February 1935. AKPR T119/34.

17. Oswald Kostrba-Skalicky, "Die 'Burg' und der Adel," in *Die Burg,* ed. Karl Bosl (Vienna: R. Oldenbourg, 1974), 176.

18. There were a few exceptions to this rule. Max Lobkowicz was a diplomat and Zdeněk Bořek-Dohalský the editor of the newspaper *Lidové noviny. Montagsblatt,* 27 December 1937. But neither was a typical noble; they tended to distance themselves from the nobility, choosing bourgeois wives and sociability. See Kostrba-Skalicky, "Die 'Burg,' " 178–179.

19. See František Schwarzenberg, "Růst náboženské snášelivosti," in *Padesát let: sborník úvah a vzpomínek na masarykovu republiku,* ed. Ivan Herben and František Třešňák (Toronto: Naše hlasy, 1968), 195–198.

20. Placák, "Duch křest'anství," pt. 1, 49.

21. On publicity and nobility, see Heinz Reif, *Adel im 19. und 20. Jahrhundert, Enzyklopädie deutscher Geschichte; Bd. 55* (Munich: R. Oldenbourg, 1999), 25.

22. Milan Churaň et al., eds., *Kdo byl kdo v našich dějinách ve 20. století,* 3 vols., vol. 2 (Prague: Nakladatelství Libri, 1998), 57.

23. Valdštejn converted around 1606, when, returning from the Turkish wars, he found Catholicism more conducive to gaining access to the Habsburg

court. František Roubík, "Albrecht z Valdštejna, vévoda frýdlantský," in *Doba bělohorská a Albrecht z Valdštejna*, ed. Jaroslav Prokeš (Prague: Výbor výstavy "Albrecht z Valdštejna a doba bělohorská," 1934), 122.

24. Pekař describes the move as a "disgrace" for Valdštejn. Josef Pekař, "Valdštejn a česká otázka," *Český časopis historický* 40 (1934): 6. Geoffrey Parker describes him as "almost relieved" in *The Thirty Years' War* (New York: Routledge, 1987), 112.

25. Pekař, "Valdštejn," 3.

26. Ibid., 10.

27. Kruh pro studium českých dějin vojenských to Zdeněk Kolowrat (Přípravný výbor), 23 October 1933. RA Kolowrat, Rychnov nad Kněžnou, k 37 ic 928.

28. Kolowrat to Prokeš, 21 October 1933. RA Kolowrat, Rychnov nad Kněžnou, k 37 ic 928.

29. Karl Buquoy to Zdeněk Kolowrat, 5 August 1933. RA Kolowrat, Rychnov nad Kněžnou, k 37 ic 928.

30. Zdeněk Kolowrat to Karl Buquoy, 14 August 1933. RA Kolowrat, Rychnov nad Kněžnou, k 37 ic 928.

31. On the Pekař-Masaryk debate, see Miloš Havelka, preface to *Spor o smysl Českých dějin 1895–1938*, ed. Miloš Havelka (Prague: Torst, 1995), 7–43.

32. Jaroslav Durych, "Hlavní úkol," *Rozmach*, 5 September 1925. Quoted in Jan Rataj, *O autoritativní národní stát: Ideologické proměny české politiky v Druhé Republice 1938–1939* (Prague: Karolinum, 1997), 76.

33. Rothschild, *East Central Europe*, 102.

34. See Miloš Trapl, *Political Catholicism and the Czechoslovak People's Party in Czechoslovakia, 1918–1938* (Boulder, Colo.: Social Science Monographs, 1995), 78–92.

35. Durych quote from *Lidové listy*, 10 May 1923, quoted in Cynthia Paces, "Religious Images and National Symbols in the Creation of Czech Identity, 1890–1938" (Ph.D. diss., Columbia University, 1998), 217. See also Paces, 208–249 and Trapl, *Political Catholicism*, 82–83.

36. Jaroslav Durych, "Bílá hora," *Řád* 4 (1937): 322.

37. Trapl, *Political Catholicism*, 85. Scheinost had actually joined a Czech fascist party before returning to the Populists in the early 1930s.

38. Pope Pius XI, *Quadragesimo Anno*, encyclical on reconstruction of the social order (1931), 83, 136. Vatican Encyclicals, *www.vatican.va/holy_father/pius_xi/encyclicals/index.htm* (accessed 13 September 2004).

39. From *České slovo* article quoted in "Habsburská šlechta a fašističti vůdcové v čele katolického sjezdu," *Rudé pravo*, 26 June 1935.

40. Středa, which in Czech suggests "center," was a strange pen name for the right-wing Schwarzenberg. I have not seen a convincing explanation for this choice.

41. Placák, "Duch Křest'anství," pt. 1, 43–45.

42. Karel Schwarzenberg, *Obrana svobod* (Prague: Československý spisovatel, 1991), 32. Original article appeared as "Kato čili o svobodě plněním zákonů," *Řád* 2 (1935): 551–559.

43. Jindřich Středa (Karel Schwarzenberg), "Svoboda a totalita," *Řád* 4 (1937): 363. See also Schwarzenberg, *Obrana*, 27–37.

44. Karel Schwarzenberg, *Obrana*, 62–65. Original article appeared as "Konce křesťanské společnosti," *Řád* 3 (1936): 234–241.

45. Středa, "Svoboda a totalita," 357. See also Schwarzenberg, *Obrana*, 27–37.

46. Středa, "Svoboda a totalita," 362–363.

47. The quote is a summary of Adorno's position by David Harvey in *The Condition of Postmodernity* (Cambridge, Mass.: Blackwell, 1997), 13–14. For a particularly chilling application of Adorno's critique, see Detlev Peukert, "The Genesis of the 'Final Solution' from the Spirit of Science," in *Reevaluating the Third Reich*, ed. Thomas Childers and Jane Caplan (New York: Holmes and Meier, 1993), 234–252. For a consideration of the relationship of the French Terror to ideas of direct democracy, see the writings of Francois Furet, summarized in David Bien, "Francois Furet, the Terror, and 1789," and Donald Sutherland, "An Assessment of the Writings of Francois Furet," *French Historical Studies* 16, no. 4 (Fall 1990): 777–791.

48. Karel Schwarzenberg, "Mezinárodní bezpráví," *Obrana*, 78–79.

49. Schwarzenberg, *Obrana*, 66–67.

50. On Schwarzenberg and *Vlajka*'s corporatism, see Milan Nakonecný, *Vlajka: K historii a ideologii českého nacionalismu* (Prague: Chvojkovo nakladatelství, 2001), 80.

51. Schwarzenberg, "Kato," in *Obrana*, 32–35.

52. Rudolf Voříšek, "Kapitalismus, socialismus a stavovství," *Řád* 3 (1936): 28–41.

53. Schwarzenberg, "Kato," in *Obrana*, 35.

54. Jindřich Středa, "Dohoda s našimi menšinami," *Řád* 4 (1937): 52–56.

55. Placák, "Duch Křesťanství," pt. 3, 118–119.

56. Schwarzenberg's family archive contains a membership card bearing his name for the *Vlajka* political section in 1934, though he appears to have been a member at least until 1937. See SOA Třeboň RA Schwarzenberg, k 393 ic 1763 and sig. IV-5.

57. Kelly, *The Czech Fascist Movement*, 136. It is important to note that *Vlajka* moved closer to Nazi Germany after 1936. It appears that Schwarzenberg cut his ties with the group before its collaboration with the German occupiers began in 1939. For an undated statement of the *Vlajka* program, see Rataj, *O autoritativní*, 37–38. Schwarzenberg is listed on the program as a contributor to the organization's journal *Nové Československo*.

58. See clippings from right-wing and fascist press in SOA Třeboň RA Schwarzenberg Secundogeniture, ic 1773–9, k 394–396. Karel Schwarzenberg published a number of articles in the fascist paper *Národní vyzva* under the pseudonym "Bojna." See Petr Němec, "Česká a moravská šlechta v letech nacistické okupace," *Dějiny a současnost* 15, no. 1 (1993): 27.

59. Schwarzenberg's fellow Populist and writer for *Řád*, Jan Scheinost, was also a member of the National Community of Fascists *(Národní obec fašistická)*. Jan Rataj notes that many local fascist meetings took place in Catholic forums. See Rataj, *O autoritativní*, 130.

60. Rataj, *O autoritativní*, 71–72. See also Výbor Národního shromaždění to Presidium Zemského úřadu, 4 April 1939. SUA 207–767–15/210.

61. Tomáš Pasák, *Český fašismus 1922–1945* (Prague: Práh, 1999), 117. Jindřich Thun-Hohenstein was also in the leadership of the Czech fascist organization *Vlajka*. See Němec, "Česká a moravská šlechta," 27. On noble financing of fascist organizations, see also police report of 6 December 1938. SUA 225–1286–2/182.

62. KPR Záznam, 5 February 1934. AKPR T119/34.

63. "Jak žije v Československu bývalá šlechta," *Polední list*, 5 December 1937.

64. Placák, "Duch Křest'anství," pt. 1, 50. Karel Schwarzenberg gave 250,000 crowns and his wealthier relative Jan Schwarzenberg reportedly donated 1 million crowns.

65. Declaration of members of the historic nobility, delivered 17 September 1938 to President Edvard Beneš. Copy in AKPR, D3038/40. The declaration was signed by Karel Schwarzenberg, Jan Lobkowicz, Zdeněk Radislav Kinský, František Kinský, Zdeněk Kolowrat, Rudolf Czernin, Leopold Sternberg, W. Colloredo-Mannsfeld, Karel Parish, Jindřich Dobrzensky, Hugo Strachwitz, and Karel Belcredi. The full text appears in translation in the appendix. Though only twelve nobles signed the declaration, many more supported its content (see František Schwarzenberg, letter to the editor, *Svědectví*, 20, no. 79 [1986]: 707). A more complete tally of Czech noble loyalists can be drawn from the second noble declaration in 1939. See chapter 6, "War and Revolution: The End of the Old Regime, 1939–1948," for more details and the appendix for a list of 1939 signatories.

66. Here the adjective "český" can be translated as either "Czech" or "Bohemian." In most contexts, the distinction is clear, though here it more likely carries both meanings. Elsewhere Schwarzenberg made clear that he considered the Bohemian Kingdom a historically Czech state, even if it also had a German component.

67. Kostrba-Skalicky makes this point in "Die 'Burg,' " 176–177.

68. For a similar interpretation of the risks involved with the declaration, see Zdeněk Kárník, *České země v éře První republiky, díl třetí, O přežití a o život (1936–1938)* (Prague: Nakladatelství Libri, 2003), 585.

69. On the Second Republic, see Rataj, *O autoritativní;* Theodore Prochazka, "The Second Republic, 1938–1939," in *A History of the Czechoslovak Republic 1918–1948*, ed. Victor Mamatey and Radomír Luža (Princeton, N.J.: Princeton University Press, 1973), 255–270; and Kelly, *The Czech Fascist Movement*, 142–143.

70. Rataj, *O autoritativní*, 14.

71. Rataj calls this "little Czech nationalism." See ibid., 93–119. "Jewish scum" comes from a November 1938 *Vlajka* poster reproduced on p. 108.

72. For an example of Thun's anti-Semitic speeches, see police report from Pilsen, 3 February 1939. SUA 225–1286–2/187.

73. J. Zahradníček, *Národní obnova*, vol. 2, no. 41 (15 October 1938), quoted in Rataj, *O autoritativní*, 66.

74. Rataj, *O autoritativní*, 66.

75. Quote from J. Scheinost, *Stěžen*, 8 November 1928. Corporatist program in Ladislav Švejcar, "Nástin stavovské ústavy demokratické," *Tak*, 28 February 1939. Both quoted in Rataj, *O autoritativní*, 73–75.

76. Rataj, *O autoritativní*, 26.

77. Ibid., 31.

78. Ibid., 35

79. Záznam KPR, 25 October 1938. AKPR T119/34.

80. The remaining participants were Zdeněk Radoslav Kinský, Karel Parish, Rudolf Czernin, Leopold Sternberg, Hugo Strachwitz, Jiří Sternberg, Jan Pálffy, and Jindřich Dobrzenský. ČTK press release, 24 January 1939. AKPR D3038/40.

81. Text of Kinský speech provided to KPR in advance by Jan Lobkowicz on 22 January 1939. AKPR D3038/40.

82. ČTK press release, 24 January 1939. The ČTK release appeared the next day in a variety of Czech and German newspapers, including *Národní politika*, *Lidové noviny*, and *Prager Tagblatt*.

83. "Popud, který lid jistě uvítá sympaticky: Stará česká rodová jména budou obnovena?" *Lidové listy*, 2 February 1939. Note that a similar appeal appeared in *Národní Obnova* on 12 November 1938. Quoted in *Tradice*, nos. 5–6 (1938): 166.

84. "Obnovení šlechty?" *Národní práce*, 3 February 1939.

85. "K obnově starých rodových jmen českých," *Lidové listy*, 8 February 1939.

86. Ladislav Karel Feierabend, *Politické vzpomínky*, vol. 1 (Prague: Atlantis, 1994), 109.

87. For an example of this argument, see Eugen Durych to Minister without Portfolio Jiří Havelka, January 1939. AKPR D3038/40.

88. František Schwarzenberg, letter to the editor, *Svědectví*, 20, no. 79 (1986): 706.

89. In a well-documented example, working-class voters in Germany moved between the Social Democrats and National Socialists with remarkable ease during the early 1930s. See Peter Fritzsche, "Did Weimar Fail?" *The Journal of Modern History* 68 (1996): 640–642. Fritzsche and others refer to this meta-materialistic trend as the "primacy of politics."

5. German Internationalism and National Socialism: German Nobles in the 1930s

1. My focus is on fascism as an ideology and belief system, not fascism in practice. Like most ideologies, fascism in practice differed substantially from its rhetoric. On the distinction between fascist rhetoric and fascist practice, see Robert Paxton, "The Five Stages of Fascism," *The Journal of Modern History* 70 (March 1998): 1–23.

2. On the distinction between National Socialism and other varieties of fascism, see Mark Mazower, *Dark Continent: Europe's Twentieth Century* (New York: Alfred A. Knopf, 1999), 31–32.

3. On the use of the term "Austrofascism" to describe the Dollfuss re-

gime, see Barbara Jelavich, *Modern Austria: Empire and Republic, 1815–1986* (New York: Cambridge University Press, 1987), 204.

4. See Elizabeth Wiskemann, *Czechs and Germans* (London: Oxford University Press, 1938), 165–173.

5. Henlein's organization went by the name *Sudetendeutsche Heimatfront* (SHF) until just before the 1935 elections, when the Czech government insisted that its name change to *Sudetendeutsche Partei* (SdP). See Joseph Rothschild, *East Central Europe Between the Two World Wars* (Seattle: University of Washington Press, 1992), 128.

6. Wiskemann, *Czechs*, 204–205.

7. John Haag, " 'Knights of the Spirit': The Kameradschaftsbund," *Journal of Contemporary History* 8, no. 3 (July 1973): 134. See also the useful history of the SdP by Michael Walsh Campbell, "A Crisis of Democracy: Czechoslovakia and the Rise of Sudeten German Nationalism, 1918–1938" (Ph.D. diss., University of Washington, 2003).

8. Spann's views summarized by Haag, " 'Knights of the Spirit,' " 135.

9. Ibid., 136–138, 140.

10. See Ronald Smelser, *The Sudeten Problem 1933–1938: Volkstumpolitik and the Formulation of Nazi Foreign Policy* (Middletown, Conn.: Wesleyan University Press, 1975), chapter 6. See also Haag, " 'Knights of the Spirit,' " 147–150.

11. Karl Anton Rohan, "Führertum," *Europäischer Revue*, vol. 6, pt. 1 (January–June, 1930), 233–240.

12. Karl Anton Rohan, "Europäische Revolution," *Europäischer Revue*, vol. 9, pt. 2 (July–December 1933), 523.

13. Ibid., 527. On the origins of the idea of a "conservative revolution," see chapter 3, "Nationalization of the Nobility: Noble Lobbying Strategies in the 1920s." For more on the connection between a "third way" and "conservative revolution," see George Mosse, in *Germans and Jews: The Right, the Left, and the Search for a 'Third Force' in Pre-Nazi Germany* (New York: Howard Fertig, 1970).

14. Karl Anton Rohan, "Adel," *Europäische Revue*, vol. 4, no. 1 (1928): 13–20. See chapter 3 "Nationalization of the Nobility," for a description of this article.

15. Karl Anton Rohan, "Adel," *Europäischer Revue*, vol. 9, pt. 2 (July–December 1933), 567.

16. Ibid., 570. In the previous month's issue of the *Revue*, Edgar Jung also wrote of the potential of the blood nobility for joining the National Socialist elite. See Jung, "Adel oder Elite?," *Europäischer Revue*, vol. 9 pt. 2 (July–December 1933), 533–535.

17. Documented members also included Karl Rohan's brother Alain, Friedrich Kinský, Max Egon (Prince) Hohenlohe (1897–1968), and Waldemar Thienen-Adlerflycht.

18. See, for example, Karl Rohan, "Rundschreiben an die Grusbacher Herren" (6 January 1927) and other *Grusbacher* communications in the Ledebur family archive. SOA Litoměřice (Děčín) RA Ledebur, k 24 ic 193. It is unclear whether Ledebur took part in the group.

19. The most likely reason for the choice of Grusbach was its central location (a short trip from Brno and Vienna) and its proximity to Karl Rohan's estate in Melk in Lower Austria.

20. For example, he was awarded the "Silberne Militärverdienstmedaille" in October of 1917. SZA Brno RA Althann/Khuen-Lützow (G 145), k 55 ic 381.

21. Zora Ouřadová, "Sudetoněmečtí velkostatkáři a jejich styky s chamberlainovskou Anglií 1934–1938," (Diploma thesis, Charles University, Prague, 1974), 25–26. Ironically, Nora's uncle Franz Lützow (1849–1916), was a Czech patriot and wrote a pro-Czech history of Bohemia in English in the early 1900s. Petr Mašek, *Modrá krev* (Prague: Mladá fronta, 1999), 198.

22. Karl Anton Rohan, "Denkschrift für den Zusammenschluss des Adels in Oesterreich" [1926]. SOA Litoměřice (Děčín), RA Ledebur, k 24 ic 193.

23. Diary of Adolf Dubsky, 19 February 1933, quoted in Ouřadová, "Sudetoněmečtí," 55.

24. Dubsky diary, 27 March 1933, in ibid., 56.

25. Adolf Dubsky to Hermann Keyserling, 18 April 1932. ZA Opava (Janovice) RA Dubský (velkostatek Žadlovice), k 19.

26. See Mašek, *Modrá krev*, 74–75, and Robert Luft, "Die Mittelpartei des Mährischen Grossgrundbesitzes 1879–1918," in *Die Chance der Verständigung: Absichten und Ansätze zu übernationaler Zusammenarbeit in den böhmischen Ländern 1848–1918*, ed. Ferdinand Seibt (Munich: R. Oldenbourg, 1987), 239.

27. Dubsky began in London as a Legationsekretär, first category, and was promoted to Legationsrat, second category, in September 1918. ZA Opava (Janovice) RA Dubský, k 18.

28. Dubsky to Keyserling, 18 April 1932.

29. Adolf Dubsky, "Anlässlich der Denkmals-Enthüllung für gefallene Theresianums," 26 June 1927. ZA Opava (Janovice) RA Dubský, k 19.

30. Dubsky to Schmitz, 2 March 1927. ZA Opava (Janovice) RA Dubský, k 19.

31. Dubsky to editor of the *Prager Tagblatt*, 18 February 1934. ZA Opava (Janovice) RA Dubský, k 23.

32. Peter Stirk, ed., *Mitteleuropa* (Edinburgh: Edinburgh University Press, 1994), 13–15. See also David Blackbourn, *The Fontana History of Germany, 1780–1918* (London: Fontana Press, 1997), 482.

33. Karl Anton Rohan, "Deutsche Einheit," *Europäische Revue*, vol. 12, pt. 1 (January–June 1936): 307.

34. Karl Anton Rohan, *Schicksalsstunde Europas* (Graz, Austria: Leykam Verlag, 1937), 377.

35. Wilhelm Medinger, "Die zehn handelspolitischen Aufbaupläne Mitteleuropas: Eine sudetendeutsche Betrachtung," *Deutsche Rundschau* 234 (January–March 1933): 86.

36. Stirk, *Mitteleuropa*, 17.

37. Rohan, *Schicksalsstunde*, 348–352.

38. Ibid., 366.

39. Ibid., 374.

40. Haag, " 'Knights of the Spirit,' " 134–135.

41. Rohan, *Schicksalsstunde*, 367–368.

42. Zorka (Zora) Ouřadová and Josef Polišenský also point out that Karl Khuen and other Grusbachers moved from "Catholic monarchism and a 'greater Austrian' attachment to a 'greater German' one and after 1933 to Nazism." See "Hrušovanská skupina sudetoněmeckých velkostatkářů a A. J. Toynbee," *Jižní Morava* 12 (1976): 70.

43. The leadership in 1936 included Alfons Clary-Aldringen (vice president), Wilhelm Medinger Jr., and Friedrich Westphalen. RA Clary, k 446. Members in 1937 included Eugen Ledebur, Karl Waldstein, Baron Liebig, Adolf Schwarzenberg, Alain Rohan, Kinskys, Karl Buquoy, R. von Geymüller, Max Fürstenberg, Franz Thun-Hohenstein, Thurn-Taxis, and K. Zedtwitz. RA Clary, k 447. Many of these nobles had ties to the *Grusbacher* group.

44. Smelser, *Sudeten Problem*, 297. Rutha was arrested on charges of homosexuality in 1937 and committed suicide in his jail cell before he went to trial. See Mark Cornwall, "Heinrich Rutha and the Unraveling of a Homosexual Scandal in 1930s Czechoslovakia," *Gay and Lesbian Quarterly* 8, no. 3 (2002): 319–347.

45. On Sebekowsky, see Jaroslav César and Bohumil Černý, *Politika německých buržoazních stran v Československu v letech 1918–38*, vol. 2 (Prague: Československé akademie věd, 1962), 2, 562. On Vogt's title, see Smelser, *Sudeten Problem*, 296.

46. On Clary and the *Völkerbundliga*, see RA Clary, k 448. See chapter 3, "Nationalization of Nobility," for background on Clary.

47. Brand quoted in Smelser, *Sudeten Problem*, 196.

48. Smelser, *Sudeten Problem*, 146–148. Christie helped to arrange Henlein lectures at the Chatham House and Arnold Toynbee's Royal Institute of International Affairs. See Laurence Thompson, *The Greatest Treason: The Untold Story of Munich* (New York: W. Morrow, 1968), 22.

49. Grahame Christie to R. W. Seton-Watson, 12 December 1935. In Thomas Marzik, Jan Rychlík, and Miroslav Bielik, eds., *R. W. Seton-Watson and His Relations with Czechs and Slovaks* (Prague: Ústav T. G. Masaryka and Matica Slovenská, 1995), 471.

50. Paul Vyšný, *The Runciman Mission to Czechoslovakia, 1938: Prelude to Munich* (Houndmills, Basingstoke, Hampshire: Palgrave Macmillan, 2003), 8.

51. On the Anglo-German Fellowship, see Ouřadová, "Sudetoněmečtí," 64–65, and Vyšný, *Runciman*, 92. Ouřadová claims that Walter Runciman himself was a member of the Fellowship, but Vyšný reports no conclusive evidence of his membership. For a flavor of Dubsky's lobbying and the "un-state" quote, see his letter to Doctor Grosse, 10 April 1939. ZA Opava (Janovice) RA Dubský, k 19. Dubsky's lobbying picked up in intensity in 1938. See Ouřadová, "Sudetoněmečtí," 90.

52. See, for example, "Ein Beitrag zur Geschichte der jüngsten deutschen Entwicklung," *Deutsch-englische Hefte* 3 (June 1939): 82–87. My copy is from ZA Opava (Janovice) RA Dubský, k 2.

53. Ouřadová, "Sudetoněmečtí," 90–91.

54. Jan Masaryk to Kamil Krofta, 22 July 1938. Quoted in *Mnichov v dok-*

umentech, pt. 1 (Prague: Státní Nakladatelství Politické Literatury, 1958), 75.

55. Ouřadová, "Sudetoněmečtí," 91.

56. Smelser, *Sudeten German Problem*, 149.

57. The Grusbach guest book is located in ZA Brno RA Althann/Khuen-Lützow, k 58 ic 458. Toynbee's visit is recorded as taking place on 22 May 1937. For an analysis of the Khuen guest book and Toynbee's visit, see Ouřadová and Polišenský, "Hrušovanská skupina," 69–74.

58. Arnold Toynbee, "Czechoslovakia's German Problem," *Economist*, 10 July 1937, 71–74.

59. See Ouřadová and Polišenský, "Hrušovanská skupina," 72.

60. Wiskemann, *Czechs*, 283.

61. See, for example, Rutha's report to the SdP leadership on his activity in England in 1936. "Bericht über die Durchführung der Londoner Aktion," June 1936. In Václav Král, ed., *Die Deutschen in der Tschechoslowakei 1933–1947* (Prague: Nakladatelství československé akademie věd, 1964), 97–101.

62. Smelser, *Sudeten Problem*, 149.

63. Vaughan Burdin Baker, "Selective Inattention: The Runciman Mission to Czechoslovakia in 1938," *East European Quarterly* 24, no. 4 (1990): 425, 441.

64. César and Černý, *Politika*, 478. See also Vyšný, *Runciman*, 150.

65. Mašek, *Modrá krev*, 106–110.

66. See secret report of Ashton-Gwatkin to the Foreign Office, 15 August 1938. PRO London, FO 800/304#252–4.

67. Undated reports from "eine Arbeiterin" on Runciman and Kinsky trips on 14 and 15 August 1938. PRO FO 800/307 #29–32. After Ulrich Kinsky's untimely death later in 1938, Karl Khuen mourned the loss of his "best friend," who was so well-liked in Vienna and England. "Lord Runciman's favorable report," he added, "is undoubtedly much indebted to him." Karl Khuen to Chief of the German General Staff, 15 December 1938. ZA Brno RA Khuen-Lützow, k 55 ic 381. For a published account of Runciman's visit to Kinsky's estate, see Vyšný, *Runciman*, 170.

68. Ashton-Gwatkin to the Foreign Office, 15 August 1938. PRO London, FO 800/304#252–4.

69. Herr Schmitt of Volksdeutsche Mittelstelle to Auswärtige Amt, Berlin, 23 August 1938. From a report by Konrad Henlein. In Král, *Die Deutschen*, 273–276.

70. Notes from 23 August 1938. PRO FO 800/304 #237. A Czech Interior Ministry report from 1946 suggests that Schwarzenberg was hesitant to host Runciman, only agreeing to do so in a nonpolitical capacity. Národní bezpecnost report, Český Krumlov, 12 August 1946 (p. 82). AMV 305–38–6.

71. Policejní ředitelství v Praze to Presidium zemského úřadu, 22 August 1938. SUA 207–810–55/1–2.

72. See Hilda Runciman's letter thanking Clary for the invitation, 25 August 1938. SOA Litoměřice (Děčín) RA Clary-Aldringen, k 448.

73. Hilda Runciman's diary entry of 27 August 1938, reproduced in German translation in Rudolf Czernin, *Ein Boehmisches Maerchen* (Graz, Austria: Leopold Stocker Verlag, 2003), 76–77.

74. Basil Newton to Eugen Czernin, 8 September 1938, SOA Jindřichův

Hradec RA Czernin, k. 539. Newton and other English dignitaries had visited Czernin's estate before for tennis, hunting, and conversation about politics. See Czernin's diary entry for 20 August 1938. SOA Jindřichův Hradec RA Czernin, k. 544. Also reproduced in Czernin, *Maerchen*, 74.

75. Vyšný, *Runciman*, 275–276. Vyšný mistakenly reports that the weekend was spent with Count Edmund Czernin, who was actually a member of the pro-Czech Vinoř branch of the family. Contrary to Vyšný's assertion (p. 332), Eugen Czernin of Petersburg, Runciman's host, was not associated with the Czech noble declaration of loyalty in September 1938. Nor was Adolf Schwarzenberg, another of Runciman's hosts. For genealogical material on the Czernins, see Vladimír Pouzar, ed., *Almanach českých šlechtických rodů* (Prague: Martin, 2003), 109–129.

76. Reported in KPR Záznam, 25 October 1938. AKPR T119/34. Czernin's politics are unclear in this report. It appears from the Záznam that Czernin may have personally arranged for the SdP demonstration, though he later claimed loyalty to Czechoslovakia.

77. AMV 551–16–2 (Eugen Czernin), report from 25 October 1956.

78. Eugen Czernin, diary entries of 9 and 11 September 1938. SOA Jindřichův Hradec RA Czernin, k. 544.

79. Vasil Škrach (Archivist of the T. G. Masaryk Library) to R. W. Seton-Watson, 1 July 1938. In Marzik et al., *Seton-Watson*, 506.

80. Dr. Mayer (*Svaz* secretary) to unnamed recipient, 30 July 1938. SÚA SČV k 191 ic 1609.

81. Ibid.

82. Baker, "Selective Inattention," 439.

83. Lord Walter Runciman to Edvard Beneš, 21 September 1938. ANM Vojtěch Mastný, k 8 ic 1268.

84. Count Westphalen, "Land Reform and Its Effects upon the Sudeten German Nationality Group," August 1938. In documentation of grievances presented to the Runciman Mission. PRO FO 800/305 #164–171. I found in the Runciman Mission collection no corresponding brief on land reform from the Czech side.

85. Vyšný, *Runciman*, 324–325.

86. Walter Runciman to Edvard Beneš, 21 September 1938. ANM Vojtěch Mastný, k 8 ic 1268.

87. Baker, "Selective Inattention," 441.

88. Copy of Kinsky telegram to Ashton-Gwatkin, 29 September 1938. SÚA SdP dodatek, k 1. Kinsky reminded Ashton-Gwatkin of his "charming visit with Lord Runciman to my Balzhütte."

89. Obituary for Czechoslovakia, 1 October 1938. SOA Litoměřice (Děčín) RA Clary-Aldringen, k 434.

90. Karl Buquoy to "Kreisleitung in Gratzen," 16 October 1938. SOA Třeboň RA Buquoy, k 275 ic 1351.

91. Karl Waldstein-Wartenberg, speech to Deutscher Forstverein, December 1938. Transcript in SOA Prague RA Valdštejn, k 198 sig VI-86.

92. *Verband* der deutschen Grossgrundbesitzern, Rundschreiben, 11 October 1938. Copy in SOA Prague RA Valdštejn, k 198 sig VI-86.

93. Hilda Runciman's diary entry from 9–12 September 1938 in Czernin, *Maerchen*, 83.

94. Eugen Czernin, diary entry from 21 September 1938, in Czernin, *Maerchen*, 94.

95. Alfons Clary-Aldringen, letter to the editor of the *Times* of London, 6 October 1938 (not printed). Copy in SOA Litoměřice (Děčín) RA Clary-Aldringen, k 445.

96. Alfons Clary-Aldringen, "Kameraden und Kameradinnen der Gefolg-schaft der Turner Brauerei!" n.d. (October 1938). Text of speech located in SOA Litoměřice (Děčín), RA Clary-Aldringen, k 445.

97. In a different context, Robert Paxton notes "Fascist 'revolutionaries' believe in change in the sense used by Tancredi, scion of the decaying noble Sicilian family in Giuseppe di Lampedusa's great novel *The Leopard*: 'If we want things to stay as they are, things will have to change.' " Robert Paxton, "The Five Stages of Fascism," *The Journal of Modern History* 70 (March 1998): 8.

98. Richard Coudenhove-Kalergi, *Crusade for Pan-Europe* (New York: G. P. Putnam's Sons, 1943), 223. Adolf Schwarzenberg would take refuge uptown, where he studied the history of politics at Columbia University.

99. Alfons Clary-Aldringen, *Geschichten eines alten Österreichers* (Berlin: Ull-stein, 1977), 267.

6. War and Revolution: The End of the Old Regime, 1939–1948

1. See Vojtech Mastny, *The Czechs under Nazi Rule: The Failure of National Resistance, 1939–1942* (New York: Columbia University Press, 1971).

2. See for example "Naše půda bude vyrvána z cizáckých rukou [Our soil will be snatched out of foreign hands]," *Rudé právo*, 7 June 1945, 1.

3. Tomáš Pasák, *Pod ochranou Říše* (Prague: Práh, 1998), 38–40.

4. Walter Jacobi (head of the Prague office of the Sicherheitdienst [SD]), "Politické poměry v protektorátu v létech 1939 až 1945" [1945?], 5. AMV 325–166–3.

5. Gotthold Rhode, "The Protectorate of Bohemia and Moravia 1939–1945," in *A History of the Czechoslovak Republic, 1918–1948*, ed. Victor Mamatey and Radomir Luza (Princeton, N.J.: Princeton University Press, 1973), 302.

6. Petr Němec, "Česká a moravská šlechta v letech nacistické okupace," *Dějiny a současnost* 15, no. 1 (1993): 27. See also Jacobi, "Politické poměry," 13.

7. Ladislav Karel Feierabend, *Politické vzpomínky*, vol. 1 (Prague: Atlantis, 1994), 190.

8. Information on committee assignments from NS Zápisy of 1939 in SUA 48–10/34 and 225–1496–1/147. On Schwarzenberg's youth leadership, see Jacobi, "Politické poměry," 16.

9. František Schwarzenberg speeches, 18 June 1939 and 11 November 1939. SOA Třeboň RA Schwarzenberg, k 414 ic 1832.

10. The real power on land issues rested with the revived Land Office, which the SS took over in 1939. Mastny, *The Czechs*, 88. Bubna-Litic was arrested in 1945 on suspicion of collaboration. Released fourteen months later

without a trial, he escaped to Austria after the Communist putsch in 1948. Vladimir Votypka, *Příběhy české šlechty* (Prague: Mladá fronta, 1995), 152, 158.

11. At least one noble would have a prominent role in the London-based Czechoslovak government in exile. Edvard Beneš and Jan Masaryk, exile president and foreign minister respectively, chose the career diplomat Max Lobkowicz (1888–1967) to be the ambassador to Britain. They reportedly preferred Lobkowicz because of his noble origins, Irish wife, and perfect English. See Ladislav Karel Feierabend, *Politické vzpomínky*, vol. 2 (Prague: Atlantis, 1994), 156.

12. Jacobi, "Politické poměry," 62. See also Mastny, *The Czechs*, 138.

13. Jacobi, "Politické Poměry," 64.

14. Ibid., 67.

15. Ibid., 69.

16. See Bruno Helbig-Neupauer to Karl Count Waldstein, 1 February 1939. SOA Prague RA Valdštejn, k 192 ic 4265.

17. Helbig could report only that the *Verband* was still working on restitution more than a year later. Bruno Helbig-Neupauer to Karl Waldstein, 21 September 1940. SOA Prague RA Valdštejn, k 192 ic 4265.

18. See Jan Rychlík, "Pozemková reforma z let 1919–1935 a změny v pozemkové držbě za druhé světové války," *Československý časopis historický* 87 (1989): 197–199. See also Volker Zimmermann, *Sudetští Němci v nacistickém státě*, trans. Petr Dvořáček (Prague: Prostor, 2001). Zimmermann reports that by October 1943, a total of 65,000 ha from the land reform had been reconfiscated by German authorities (p. 267). Little, if any, of this land went to its original owners.

19. Ralf Gebel, *"Heim ins Reich!" Konrad Henlein und der Reichsgau Sudetenland (1938–1945)* (Munich: R. Oldenbourg Verlag, 1999), 293–295. See also Zimmermann, *Sudetští*, 264–269.

20. Ladislav Karel Feierabend, *Ve vládě Protektorátu* (New York: Universum, 1962), 47.

21. Oswald Kostrba-Skalicky, "Die 'Burg' und der Adel," in *Die Burg*, ed. Karl Bosl (Vienna: R. Oldenbourg, 1974), 177–178.

22. See Verband der deutschen Grossgrundbesitzer Geschäftsstelle Prag to Leopold (Count) Thun Hohenstein, 25 March 1941. SOA Zámrsk. RA Thun-Choltice, k 106 ic 1362.

23. President Emil Hácha to Reichsprotektor Konstantin von Neurath, 25 August 1939. AKPR D3038/40.

24. Němec, "Česká a moravská šlechta," 29.

25. Documents on Salm-Reifferscheidt from July and August 1939. AKPR D3038/40. Note that President Hácha wrote to von Neurath on Salm's behalf, but to no avail.

26. See the petition from residents of the town of Rájce to the Chancellery of the President, January 1946. AKPR D10429/47.

27. "Prohlášení příslušníků; historické šlechty, předané v září 1939 prezidentu dr. Emilu Háchovi." AKPR D3038/40. A full translation and a list of the sixty-nine signatories appears in the appendix.

28. Ibid. For a translation of Renan's 1882 speech "Qu'est-ce qu'une nation?" see Geoff Eley and Ronald Grigor Suny, eds., *Becoming National* (New York: Oxford University Press, 1996), 42–55.

29. "Prohlášení."

30. The Nazi concept at work was actually "national" statehood. Nazis were well aware that "race" was largely meaningless in mongrel Bohemia.

31. Jiří Doležal, "Úvahy o české šlechtě v čase První republiky," *Svědectví* 20, no. 77 (1986): 57.

32. Výbor Národního souručenství to President Emil Hácha, 12 October 1939. AKPR D3038/40.

33. Zimmermann, *Sudetští*, 201.

34. Rhode, "Protectorate," 311–313.

35. SÚA SČV, k 191 ic 1614. The only previous sequestration of noble property had been that of Adolf Schwarzenberg, whose estates had been sequestered by the Gestapo for "police reasons" in August 1940. Regarding the Schwarzenberg estates, see Jiří Záloha, "Zabavení majetku hlubocké větve Schwarzenberků Gestapem v roce 1940," *Československý časopis historický* 89, no. 1 (1991): 65–77.

36. Němec, "Česká a moravská šlechta," 29.

37. See, for example, *Svaz* memo to President Hácha, July 1942. SÚA SČV, k 101 ic 854. The *Svaz* reported that 71,573 ha of noble land had fallen under sequestration as of July 1942. Owners included Karel Belcredi, Rudolf Czernin, František Kinský, Christof Kolowrat (nephew of the deceased Zdeněk), Jan Lobkowicz, Karel Parish, Leopold Sternberg, Hugo Strachwitz, Karel Schwarzenberg, Colloredo-Mansfelds, Zdeněk Radoslav Kinský, Josef Hrubý-Gelenj, Alfons Mensdorff-Pouilly, and Františka Lobkowiczová.

38. Mastny, *Czechs*, 88–89.

39. Heydrich quote from report to Martin Bormann, 16 May 1942, in Miroslav Kárný, ed., *Deutsche Politik im "Protektorat Boehmen und Maehren" unter Reinhard Heydrich 1941–1942* (Berlin: Metropol, 1997), 261.

40. On Šlik's ties to the ČSSN, see SOA Zámrsk RA Šlik, k 80 ic 586.

41. Okresní národní vybor Jičín, report of 28 February 1947. AMV 315–130–147/1–4.

42. Summary of speech by Jan Mertl [1940?]. AKPR A2493/43.

43. On the ČSSN's activities, see AKPR A2493/43.

44. For a short account of the Union's liquidation, see "Interní záznam kanceláře státního presidenta o likvidaci Českého svazu pro spolupráci s Němci," February 1943. AKPR 2493/43.

45. Sicherheitsdienst Leitabschnitt Prag to Karl Hermann Frank, 10 March 1941 and 4 April 1941. SUA 109–7–66/3.

46. See Karel Belcredi's account of his participation in the Union in his Protokol, 15 May 1945, and a letter to the Státní bezpečnostní oddělení (state security division) Brno, 18 May 1945. AMV 315–50–65.

47. For the definition of fascist organizations, see "Směrnice ministerstva vnitra," 16 January 1946. Reprinted in Mečislav Borák, *Spravedlnost podle dekretu* (Ostrava, Czech Republic:-Tilia, 1998), 327–331.

48. On Nazi Party membership for SdP members, see Zimmermann, *Sudetští*, 116–119.

49. Alfons Clary-Aldringen to Kanzlei des Führers und Reichskanzlers, 16 November 1939. SUA 123-165-4/70–71.

50. Abschrift of Auswartiges Amt re: Clary, 4 April 1941. SUA 123-67-4/16. NSDAP Gauleitung Sudetenland re: Clary, 11 September 1941. SUA 123-165-4/88.

51. Chief of the General Staff to Karl Khuen, 15 December 1938 and Karl Khuen to "Herr Oberstleutnant" [December 1938]. ZA Brno RA Khuen-Lützow, k 55 ic 381.

52. Petr Mašek, *Modrá krev* (Prague: Mladá fronta, 1999), 75.

53. SOA Plzeň (Klatovy) RA Schönborn, k 23 ic 133.

54. Mašek, *Modrá krev*, 42. On Hieronymus's Iron Cross, see the congratulatory letter from Konrad Henlein to Hieronymus Clary-Aldringen, 30 July 1940. SOA Litoměřice (Děčín) RA Clary-Aldringen, k 477.

55. Alfons Clary-Aldringen to Karl Clary-Aldringen, 14 October 1944. SOA Litoměřice (Děčín) RA Clary-Aldringen, k 485.

56. Mašek, *Modrá krev*, 310–311.

57. Jesenská died in the Ravensbruck concentration camp on 17 May 1944, only a few days after receiving a care package from Zedtwitz. George Bibian, "Germans, Czechs, and One Brave Man: Transcending Nationalism," *The New Leader*, 3 June 1996, 11–12. My thanks to Benjamin Frommer for providing me with this article.

58. Ibid.

59. Pasák, *Pod ochranou*, 350–383, 417. For more on Zdeněk Bořek-Dohalský's underground activities, see Mastny, *Czechs*, 161–164.

60. Mašek, *Modrá krev*, 72.

61. Prohlášení of Národní výbor in Čimelice, 18 July 1945. SOA Třeboň RA Schwarzenberg Secundogeniture, ic 1781/82, k 397.

62. SOA Třeboň RA Schwarzenberg Secundogeniture, k 393 ic 1793.

63. František Schwarzenberg, *Česky šlechtic František Schwarzenberg* (Prague: Rozmluvy, 1990), 157–158.

64. Ibid., 170–175.

65. Svaz osvobozených věnů v Kostelci n Orl. to Poverenictvo priemislu a obchodu v Bratislavě, 4 April 1946. SOA Zámrsk RA Kinský-Kostelec, k 3 ic 57.

66. Mašek, *Modrá krev*, 141.

67. See Leopold Deym's correspondence with Chancellery of the President, 2 January 1947. AKPR D10429/47.

68. Schválení osvědčení o národní spolehlivosti for Alois Podstatzký-Lichtenstein [1945]. Copy in AKPR D10429/47. See also Radomír Luza and Christina Vella, *The Hitler Kiss: A Memoir of the Czech Resistance* (Baton Rouge: Louisiana State University Press, 2002), 63, 85, 234. Luza reports that Podstatzký-Lichtenstein gave over 2 million Czech crowns to the resistance effort. Note that Podstatzký-Lichtenstein was unrelated to the better-known Liechtenstein family, whose name is also spelled Lichtenstein in Czech.

69. Kinský was arrested in 1943 for listening to English radio broadcasts. He spent over two years in Protectorate prisons. Kinský was released on 30 June 1944 and later joined a partisan group called Velký Josef (Big Joseph). See SUA 110–4–88/11 and SOA Zámrsk RA Kinský-Kostelec, k 3 ic 57. Rudolf Czernin and Charles Viktor Rohan were also arrested for listening to foreign radio broadcasts with Kinský in late 1943, though both were released in early 1944. Der Oberstaatsanwalt beim deutschen Landgericht an das Sondergericht in Prag, 1 March 1944. SUA 109–4–398/11.

70. The main parties in the National Front were the Communists, Social Democrats, Czech National Socialists (unrelated to the Nazis), Catholic Populists, and Slovak Democrats. Victor Mamatey and Radomir Luza, eds., *A History of the Czechoslovak Republic, 1918–1948* (Princeton, N.J.: Princeton University Press, 1973), 404.

71. *Košický vládní program* (Prague: Svoboda, 1974), 23–24. In overwhelmingly German areas, centrally appointed administrative commissions played the same role as the national committees did elsewhere.

72. "Směrnice pro Národní výbory o nejnutnějších opatřeních v zemědělství," 10 May 1945. SÚA MZ-S 195, k 372.

73. Vladimír Verner, *Státní občanství podle dekretu presidenta republiky ze dne 2. srpna 1945 Č. 33 Sb.* (Prague: Právnické knihkupectví a nakladatelství V. Linhart, 1945), 11, 14.

74. Decree 12/45 Sb. Josef Šebestík and Zdeněk Lukeš, *Přehled předpisů o Němcích* (Prague: Ministerstvo vnitra, 1946), 23. Note that this decree preceded Decree 33/45. Decree 12 defined as German all those who declared German nationality on any census after 1929. Nationality was considered independent of state citizenship, so an ethnically German citizen of Switzerland would lose his or her land in Czechoslovakia.

75. Ibid., 23–27.

76. "Naše půda bude vyrvána z cizáckých rukou," *Rudé právo,* 7 June 1945, 1.

77. Zdeněk Fierlinger, 1 July 1945, in *Odčiňujeme Bílou Horu* (Prague: Jednotný svaz českých zemědělců, 1945), 12. Note that the actual anniversary of the battle was on 8 November.

78. Technically, the Transylvanian (Hungarian) forces of Gabor Bethlen were allied with the Protestant Bohemian rebels in 1620, though Bethlen had agreed to a truce with the Habsburgs not long before White Mountain. Geoffrey Parker, *The Thirty Years' War* (New York: Routledge, 1987 [1984]), 58–59.

79. *Odčiňujeme,* 16.

80. Ibid., 22.

81. Expulsion and flight figures are from Theodor Schieder, ed., *Documents on the Expulsion of the Germans from Eastern-Central-Europe,* vol. 4 (Bonn: Federal Ministry for Expellees, Refugees, and War Victims, 1960), 127. Czech and German sources have long disagreed on the number of deaths. German historians, many of them Sudeten expellees, have claimed upwards of 200,000 deaths during the expulsions from Czechoslovakia. See, for example, Friedrich Prinz, *Geschichte Böhmens 1848–1948* (Berlin: Ullstein, 1991), 468. A recent joint report of the Czech-German historians' commission has settled on the range of 17,000

to 30,000 dead, a more reasonable figure. See *Konfliktní společenstvi, katastrofa, uvolněni: Náčrt výkladu německo-českých dějin od 19. stoleti* (Prague: Ústav mezinárodních vztahů, 1996), 29–30.

82. Mašek, *Modrá krev*, 156.

83. These card files are located in SOkA Děčín. My thanks to Jan Němec of Děčín for providing me with a copy of Thun's expulsion card.

84. Though the court did not dispute Waldstein's denial of formal activity for the NSFK, it appears that he was more involved with the group than he admitted. A letter from the Teplitz division of the NSFK to Waldstein on 28 May 1940 thanks Waldstein for providing the local group with timber. The note concludes: "May I also tell you, Count Waldstein, that the many demonstrations of your extra-ordinary willingness, and if I may say so, fatherly cooperation (Entgegenkommen) with the NS-Fliegerkorps in the Sudeten Gau will certainly find recognition and a corresponding appreciation." SOA Prague RA Valdštejn, k 197 ic 4289.

85. Rozsudek 436/46 of Mimořádný lidový soud in Česká Lípa, Karel Waldstein, 30 April 1946. SOA Litoměřice (Děčín). An Interior Ministry directive clarifying the retribution decree of 19 June 1945 categorized the NSFK as a criminal organization; membership alone was enough for conviction. In the NSDAP, however, only "functionaries and leading members" were subject to prosecution. See Směrnice Ministerstva vnitra 16 January 1946, reprinted in Borák, *Spravedlnost*, 327–331.

86. Karel Albrecht Waldstein-Wartenberg, *Tisíc let Valdštejnů v Čechách* (Bratislava, Slovakia: IRIS, 1998), 78.

87. Borák, *Spravedlnost*, 198–199. In her memoires, Cecilia Sternberg recalls that Larisch's son Hansi stopped by the Sternbergs' apartment in Prague during the Prague uprising of May 1945. Driving a car with German plates, Larisch put his hosts at great risk by staying with them. Asked why he was driving around with German plates and German papers, Larisch answered that "Father thought they'd win the war." The Sternbergs secured false Czech papers for Hansi, and he successfully escaped to Vienna. Cecilia Sternberg, *The Journey* (London: Collins, 1977), 188, 193.

88. Benjamin Frommer, "Retribution against Nazi Collaborators in Postwar Czechoslovakia" (Ph.D. diss., Harvard University, 1999), 270–274. Many Germans convicted of membership in the NSDAP or SdP during the flurry of trials in 1945 ended up being released for expulsion the following year.

89. Confiscation was based on Decree 5 of 19 May 1945, which allowed the appointment of national administrators for the property of "Germans, Magyars, traitors and collaborators." Reprinted in Karel Kaplan and Karel Jech, eds., *Dekrety prezidenta republiky 1940–1945*, vol. 1 (Brno, Czech Republic: Ústav pro soudobé dějiny, 1995), 216–222.

90. Oblastní úřadovna státní bezpečnosti, Brno to Ministerstvo vnitra, 3 December 1946. AMV 305–182–2/57–58. Salm still had over 11,000 ha of land in 1930, according to the State Land Office. See Jan Voženílek, *Předběžné výsledky československé pozemkové reformy* (Prague: Státní pozemkový úřad, 1930). See also the account of Salm's daughter Marie in Boris Dočekal, *Osudy českých šlechticů* (Jihlava, Czech Republic: Nakladatelství Listen, 2002), 124–130.

91. Sbor národní bezpečnosti, okres Kaplice, to Ministry of Interior, 3 July 1946. AMV 2M:13411.

92. "Zámky—majetek cizáckých šlechticů bude sloužit lidu," *Osidlování* vol. 1, no. 13 (25 November 1946): 283–284.

93. Ministerstvo zemědělství, "Výměr o zavedení národní správy a jmenování národního správce," 26 June 1945. AKPR D10429/47.

94. "Příloha k notě z 30.8.1945." AKPR D10429/47.

95. See Zemská komise pro agrární operace v Brně to KPR, 20 December 1945 and Leopold Deym to KPR, 22 August 1945. AKPR D10429/47. Leopold Deym also proposed fancifully that he be compensated for the loss of his mother's property with land in Germany. In 1947, Deym tried unsuccessfully to transfer property from his mother-in-law (a German) to his daughter Světlana. See Deym to KPR, 2 January 1947. AKPR D10429/47.

96. Jiří Kot'átko, *Land Reform in Czechoslovakia* (Prague: Orbis, 1948), 13.

97. Jiří Kot'átko, Zpráva o postupu prací při konfiskaci a rozdělování půdy Němců a zrádců, n.d. [probably May or June 1945]. SUA A UV KSC 100/1, sv 157 c 1019.

98. Jiří Kot'átko, *Pozemková reforma v Československu* (Prague: Ministerstvo informací, 1949), 24–25.

99. Kot'átko, *Land Reform*, 18–19, 23; around 100,000 ha went to public entities, for military and other public uses.

100. Ibid., 27.

101. This range comes from my database on land holdings and nationality. Figures on extent of estates in 1945 are prorated from 1930 totals. Though only a rough estimate, it gives a sense of the magnitude of noble holdings in 1945.

102. For an informative account of agricultural resettlement, see Lubomír Slezák, *Zemědělské osídlování pohraničí českých zemí po druhé světové válce* (Brno, Czechoslovakia: Blok, 1978).

103. Decree 5/1945 Sb. in Jech and Kaplan, eds., *Dekrety*, vol. 1, 216.

104. Drahomíra Kopejková, "K úloze národních správ a nucených nájmů jako nástroje změn v pozemkovém vlastnictví v Československu na konci 40. a na počátku 50. let," *Slovanský přehled* 77, no. 5 (1991): 397.

105. Ibid., 397.

106. Kot'átko, *Land Reform*, 29.

107. Vlastislav Lacina, "Pozemková reforma v lidově demokratické československé republice," in *Zápas o pozemkovou reformu v ČSR*, by Milan Otáhal (Prague: Československé akademie věd, 1963), 216. See also Slezák, who points out that 80 percent of the resettled border regions gave the Communists a majority of votes (in a third of the districts, the Communist vote exceeded 60 percent). Slezák, *Zemědělské osídlování*, 109–112.

108. See Jiří Sláma and Karel Kaplan, *Die Parlamentswahlen in der Tschechoslowakei 1935–1946–1948* (Munich: R. Oldenbourg, 1986), 58–59.

109. Kot'átko, *Land Reform*, 33.

110. Smejkal, 66. schůze Ústavodárného Národního shromáždění, 10 July 1947. Elektronická knihovna—Český parlament: dokumenty českého parlamentu *www.psp.cz/cgi-bin/win/eknih/* (accessed 13 September 2004).

111. In the interwar period, the term "large estate" (velkostatek, Grossgrund-

besitz) generally referred to holdings of 200 ha or more. See Wilhelm Medinger, *Grossgrundbesitz, Fideikommiss und Agrarreform* (Vienna: Carl Gerold's Sohn, 1919), 14.

112. "Zákon o revisi první pozemkové reformy" (142/1947 Sb.) (Prague: Brázda, 1947).

113. Jana Burešová, "Návrat k první československé pozemkové reformě po druhé světové válce v mezinárodních souvislostech," (Uherské Hradiště, Czech Republic: Slovacké muzeum, 1994), 132.

114. Kot'átko, *Pozemková reforma*, 30.

115. Ibid., 28.

116. Lacina, "Pozemková reforma," 229.

117. Usnesení Ústavodarného Národního shromáždění, 10 July 47. Copy in AKPR D10429/47.

118. Schwarzenberg's thesis on his relative Prince Felix Schwarzenberg became the book *Prince Felix zu Schwarzenberg, Prime Minister of Austria 1848–1852* (New York: Columbia University Press, 1946). The book fondly remembers Felix Schwarzenberg's pursuit of a Central European empire that was dynastic rather than national.

119. Schwarzenberg claimed that an employee filled out his 1930 census form and listed German nationality without consulting him. Moreover, he had listed Czech nationality in his forms for membership of the Czechoslovak reserve officer corps from 1932–1939. Further complicating matters, Schwarzenberg was a citizen of Switzerland, Austria, Hungary, and Bavaria, as well as Czechoslovakia. Ministry of Interior to Ministry of Foreign Affairs, 19 September 1947. AKPR D10429/47.

120. On the Schwarzenberg case and the so-called Lex Schwarzenberg of 1947, see Jiří Záloha, "Likvidace nědejšího schwarzenberského majetku v Čechách," *Jihočeský sborník historický* 62 (1966): 1–9; Jiří Záloha, "Lex Schwarzenberg: O slávě a rozpadu jednoho majetku v Čechách," *Dějiny a součastnost* 16, no. 2 (1994): 46–50; and Jiří Záloha, "Zabavení majetku," 65–77. See also the debate in the National Assembly, 65th meeting, 10 July 1947, pp. 9–18.

121. For more on the transition to collectivization, see the useful document collection, *Vznik JZD, kolektivizace zemědělství 1948–1949* (Prague: Státní ústřední archiv, 1995).

122. Kot'átko, "Vláda národní fronty dělá pořádek na české půdě," *Tvorba* 14, no. 2 (2 August 1945): 18–19.

123. Joseph Rothschild, *Return to Diversity* (New York: Oxford University Press, 1989), 96.

124. František Schwarzenberg, letter to the editor, *Svědectví*, vol. 20, no. 79 (1986): 707.

125. Votypka, *Příběhy*, 113, 117.

126. Ibid., 222.

127. Ibid., 141.

128. Ibid., 186–187

129. See Sternberg, *The Journey*.

130. Oblastní úřadovna státní bezpečnosti v Brně to Státní zastupitelství v Brně, 7 September 1948. AMV 305–182–6.

131. Mašek, *Modrá krev*, 111.

132. See regional intelligence reports from 19 July 1945 and 16 November 1945 in SUA 316–166/4/51+.

133. Alfons Clary-Aldringen, *A European Past*, trans. Ewald Osers (London: Weidenfeld and Nicolson, 1978), 224, 240. Special thanks to Elizabeth and Robert Lown for introducing me to Villa I Tatti.

134. Ferdinand Thun to Jan Němec, 20 April 1995. My thanks to Jan Němec for providing me with a copy of this letter.

135. Jan Gross, "War as Revolution," in *The Establishment of Communist Regimes in Eastern Europe*, ed. Norman Naimark and Leonid Gibianskii (Boulder, Colo.: Westview Press, 1997), 17–40.

136. See Tomáš Staněk, *Persekuce* (Prague: Institut pro středoevropskou kulturu a politiku, 1996). There were few cases of actual German terrorist activity.

137. See Bradley Abrams, "Morality, Wisdom and Revision: The Czech Opposition of the 1970s and the Expulsion of the Sudeten Germans," *East European Politics and Societies* 9, no. 2 (1995): 234–255.

138. There was, however, no shortage of Nazi rhetoric coming from Czechs in 1945. See in particular the speeches of President Beneš after liberation. *Edvard Beneš, Odsun Němců z Československa*, ed. Karel Novotný (Prague: Dita, 1996).

Conclusion

1. Radmila Slabáková, ed., *O exilu, šlechtě, Jihoslovanech a jiných otázkách dějin moderní doby* (Olomouc: Univerzita Palackého v Olomouci, 2004), 106.

2. Schwarzenberg's internationalism and cosmopolitanism are manifest in the scores of interviews he has done for Czech newspapers and magazines. See, among others, "Zeman s Klausem jsou moji soupeři," *Zemské noviny*, 21 May 1999, 1; and "Česká aristokracie," *Lidové noviny, Nedělní LN*, insert, 26 July 1999, 25–27.

3. Hilary Appel, "Justice and the Reformulation of Property Rights in the Czech Republic," *East European Politics and Societies* 9, no. 1 (Winter 1995): 30.

4. In spite of the 1948 cutoff, at least seventy-five noble families have filed for restitution of property taken under the Beneš Decrees in 1945. Jan Kubita, "Největší část ukradeného majetku náleží šlechtickým rodům," *Lidové noviny*, 17 March 1998, 3.

5. Slabáková, *O exilu*, 106.

6. "Prostě jsem byl k mání: Rozhovor s Williamem Lokowiczem o návratu ke kořenům," *Respekt* 30 (21–27 July 1997): 12.

7. Christine Temin, "William Lobkowicz Tackles the Ultimate Fixer-Upper: 250 Rms., Nds. Wk.," *Harvard Magazine* (November–December 1995): 52–54.

8. To be eligible for Czechoslovak citizenship in 1992, foreigners had to be fluent in Czech and have lived at least five years in Czechoslovakia at some time in their lives. Carl Albrecht Waldstein met neither of these criteria. See Jan Kubita, "Původní dělicí čáru soudy občas posunou," *Lidové noviny*, 17 March 1998, 3.

9. Kubita, "Největší část."

10. Rozsudek 436/46 of Mimořádný lidový soud in Česká Lípa, Karel Waldstein, 30 April 1946. SOA Litoměřice (Děčín). See chapter 6, "War and Revolution: The End of the Old Regime, 1939–1948," for more on the Waldstein case.

11. Karel Albrecht Waldstein-Wartenberg, *Tisíc let Valdštejnů v Čechách* (Bratislava: IRIS, 1998), 75–78.

12. "Poslanci ČSSD upozorňují na několik případů neoprávněných restitučních nároků šlechty," *Slovo*, 2 May 1996.

13. Inge Rohan, *Sychrov Castle: Monument of the Rohan Family* (Turnov, Czech Republic: Friends of Sychrov Castle, 1996), 1.

14. Tour of Sychrov by the author in May 1998.

Index